# CORELDRAW 3.0

A USER'S GUIDE

*About the Author*

ALAN BALFE originally trained as a programmer on mainframe computers and then went on to work in industry for a number of years. Later he worked for a small software company when IBM launched the PC. He went on to teach in Further Education for some time, becoming a journalist with one of the UK's leading computer magazines. Today he is a full-time author and freelance journalist, as well as being Technical Director of CDR, the Official Independent Organization for CorelDRAW Users, and of the PageMaker User Group. His time is mainly spent in writing books, providing technical support in beta testing hardware and software for major manufacturers. He has had a number of books published on a range of software and hardware topics and has been one of the judges of the CorelDRAW World Design Contest.

■

*Colour plate section:* reproduced by kind permission of Corel Corporation. It shows the winners of the 1992 CorelDRAW World Design Contest and demonstrates what can be achieved using CorelDRAW.

■

*Front cover:* The graphic depicted on the front cover is reproduced by kind permission of Corel Corporation. It is called 'Rex' by Bill Frymire of Showmaker Production and is the winner of the 'Best of the Show' award in the 1992 third annual CorelDRAW World Design Contest.

*Entry details can be obtained from :*

**Corel Corporation,**

1600 Carling Avenue, Ottawa, Ontario, Canada, K1Z 8RT.

# COREL DRAW! 3.0

## A USER'S GUIDE

ALAN BALFE

PRENTICE HALL
New York · London · Toronto · Sydney · Tokyo · Singapore

First published 1992 by
Prentice Hall International (UK) Ltd
Campus 400, Maylands Avenue
Hemel Hempstead
Hertfordshire, HP2 7EZ
A division of Simon & Schuster International Group

Typeset in Palatino 10pt by GLM Ltd.,
Mountsorrel, Loughborough, England

Printed and bound in Great Britain by
Dotesios Ltd., Trowbridge

Library of Congress Cataloging-in-Publication Data

*Available from the publishers*

British Library Cataloguing in Publication Data

*A catalogue record for this book is available from the British Library*

ISBN 0-13-014581-5 (pbk)

1 2 3 4 5 96 95 94 93 92

# Dedication

Every program is the result of a vast amount of hard work, late nights, hair-pulling and effort by a team of dedicated people who, because they work in the back room, are largely unnoticed. CorelDRAW 3.0 is no exception and by way of recognition of all their hard work this book is dedicated to them.

So to Bill Cullen, Tim Benner, Kim Connerty, Dave Dawkins, Krista Martens, Allan McInnis, Russell Miller, Gary Paquette and Diana Real
thank you all for a superb program.

# TRADEMARKS

# CONTENTS

# FOREWORD

In three short years CorelDRAW has become the world's leading illustration and graphics package. Its power, ease of use and intuitive interface have captured the hearts of over 350,000 users worldwide and won more than 60 international awards. Following the release of CorelDRAW 2.0, the program firmly established itself as the market leader. Many users probably wondered "What will they think of next?"

On May 15th. 1992, Corel Corporation answered that question with the announcement of CorelDRAW 3.0. With this new release, CorelDRAW has become more than just an illustration program, it is now *the* complete graphics solution. The complete package now includes six powerful modules; CorelDRAW, CorelCHART, CorelSHOW, CorelPHOTO-PAINT, CorelTRACE and CorelMOSAIC.

CorelDRAW itself contains over 200 enhancements and improvements including full colour, live blends, true 3-D manipulation, unlimited layering, roll-up menus and much more.

CorelCHART is a full featured, stand alone charting program which allows users to import data directly from other industry standard programs and/or create their own data within the package.

CorelSHOW allows you to create professional, full-featured slideshow presentations including animation and sound.

CorelPHOTO-PAINT adds superb bitmap editing and retouching capabilities to the graphics toolkit.

CorelTRACE has been accelerated and improved to give even better and more powerful bitmap to vector format conversion.

Finally, CorelMOSAIC has become a full feature graphics file manager with the capability to read and display all of the world's most popular graphics file formats.

In keeping with Corel's international strategy, CorelDRAW 3.0 is being translated into 20 different languages and the program is being ported to Unix, OS/2 and Mac platforms.

As Alan Balfe's book will illustrate, CorelDRAW has become the only graphics software package that anyone will ever need. After reading Alan's book, users will have mastered the intuitive yet powerful features included in CorelDRAW 3.0. Graphics add emphasis to any presentation and with CorelDRAW the solution for all your needs can be found in one box. As Dr. Michael Cowpland, Corel Corporations CEO has said,

> *"CorelDRAW has inspired personal computer users around the world to create great graphics and enjoy working with their computers. Our belief has always been that the easiest way to transpose an idea into reality via the computer is to do it intuitively."*

With the tools provided by CorelDRAW, anyone can use the package to create anything from simple business graphics to fully fledged slideshow presentations. In the past CorelDRAW has been used to create candy moulds, holograms, and stained glass windows; design clothing patterns, VISA cards and currency; illustrate comic books, greetings cards and to produce bible illustrations; and for numerous different applications of sign cutting involving everything from wood to granite.

Each year the International Design Contest attracts entries from around the world, from Taiwan to the USA, from Finland to Autralia. The competition is open to all registered users of CorelDRAW. The winners of this year's contest will be found on the colour plates in this book and the cover shows the winning entry. Next year's competition details are not yet finalised but the total value will be in excess of $1,000,000! Watch the press for details.

At this point I would like to thank you for purchasing CorelDRAW and I know you will enjoy using it. No doubt you will enjoy reading this book, and remember the most important aspect of working with CorelDRAW is to "Have Fun!"

Yours Truly,
Debra Gassewitz,
International Sales and Marketing Manager

# .CDR - THE LOGICAL EXTENSION TO CORELDRAW!

.CDR is the official independent organisation for CorelDRAW users, established to provide a forum for the exchange of news, views and information and to help CorelDRAW users everywhere to make the most of their investment. It is such a fascinating program that when a support group was suggested, the idea was received with great enthusiasm, and so .CDR was born. It is supported by Corel Corporation, CorelDRAW's Canadian publishers, and the four distributors who represent the company in Britain.

.CDR offers you some very specific advantages:

1. A quarterly magazine with tips and information, reviews of complementary hardware, software and peripherals, regular columns by well-known writers on both computing and design issues, case studies, and a gallery of CorelDRAW artwork. In the intervening months a newsletter is sent to members containing up to the minute news and information on matters of interest. Members use the magazine and newsletter as a way of contacting each other either through editorial or advertisement.

2. Regular meetings are held in various parts of the country. These give members the opportunity to swap ideas and assist each other with problems as well as hearing specialist speakers on creative and technical topics at venues convenient to them.

3. Special offers are made on software, hardware and peripherals, for example high quality papers. Special discounts are arranged for members with various suppliers of goods and services. Following the success of the Corel Blockbuster the user group markets its own CD-ROM Multimedia package and upgrades.

4. Training workshops. At least two per year are being planned and they cover a range of specific subjects. Professional designers and computing experts will be on hand for guidance.

5. .CDR has its own Technical support line, which complements the support services provided by Corel's distributors, and is backed up by Corel Corporation.

The support line deals not only with CorelDRAW but also with associated programs such as Windows and Pagemaker; it is often used by members who are experiencing difficulties with hardware, for example printers.

6. .CDR provides a Bulletin Board. You will find this a rich source of information and files, and the opportunity to exchange news with CorelDRAW users throughout the world via the Fido electronic mail network.

7. A direct Line to Corel. Because in the U.K. Corel Corporation has no base specifically for users, .CDR provides a contact point. We can raise issues with Corel Corporation on your behalf and are a channel for the spreading of information from Corel in Canada.

We believe that .CDR has a great deal to offer to those who already use CorelDRAW, as well as those who are totally new to the program - whether you are a professional designer, or you simply need to manipulate existing graphic files, or if your needs are somewhere in between. However, we'll leave the last word to our tireless supporter at Corel, Debra Gassewitz, the International Sales Manager:

*".CDR is good news for CorelDRAW users. While the program's user interface remains extremely intuitive, its depth is now such that this type of forum will be of great help to users in exploiting CorelDRAW's power and potential."*

If you would like to know more about .CDR, then we'd be happy to hear from you. We would also be pleased to assist if you are interested in establishing a .CDR group in your own country. For information either way, please contact:

David Foster,
.CDR,
178 Loughborough Road,
Mountsorrel,
Loughborough,
Leics. LE12 7AX
England

Telephone: 0509-415101 or 0533-374948
International: +44509-415101 or +44533-374948
Facsimile: 0533-74949
International: +44533-374949

# PREFACE

DATELINE : MAY 15TH. 1992
LOCATION: NATIONAL GALLERY, OTTAWA, CANADA
EVENT: GRAND FINAL OF THE INTERNATIONAL DESIGN CONTEST 1992

The finalists have all been chosen, each has received their prize and Susan Wimmer takes the podium to make a special announcement. Within the next six weeks Corel Corporation will release CorelDRAW 3.0!

From my own point of view this means that I have to work damn hard to complete this book so that it will be released as close as possible to the actual release of the program. But what's so special about the new release?

CorelDRAW 3.0 has been dramatically enhanced and improved, over two hundred enhancements and additions have been made to the program. The entire suite now consists of seven programs:

**CorelDRAW** 3.0 itself. The world's best computer graphics program. With the new release there is absolutely no doubt about that. The program contains facilities and abilities that are just not possible in any other program. CorelDRAW 3.0 is the first program that is totally and completely Windows 3.1 compatible - not even Microsoft's own products can lay claim to that. Full colour editing, Blends, Extrude, Text Handling, you name it, it's got it. In fact there is so much new that it cannot really be itemised. Instead this book will concentrate on the program. The floppy version of the program includes 153 TrueType fonts, 4,600 symbol and clip-art images. If you use the CD-ROM version, which will be included in the box, you also have access to an additional 100 TrueType fonts, every font in Abode Type 1 format, over 14,000 Symbol and Clip-Art images and over 100 Autodesk animation files.

**CorelTRACE**, the program that allows you to convert from bitmapped images to vectored ones. The program is now faster, more accurate and capable of handling colour images. Full handling of GIF and TGA files is now included.

**Mosaic**, the graphics file handling utility par excellence. This has been dramatically enhanced, in fact it has been completely rewitten. It can now handle just about every graphics file format you care to mention. AI, BMP, CCH, CDR, DIB, EPS, GIF, PCC, PCX, SHW, SHB, TIF and TGA. All of them in full colour, if that's what they are, and at a speed I wouldn't have thought possible.

**CorelCHART** is new. It allows you to create dynamic graphical presentations from data. It includes its own built in spreadsheet and the range of graph types it can generate is enormous - all of them interactively.

**CorelPHOTO-PAINT** is also new. It has been licenced from Z-Soft, who sell it as PhotoFinish, and it allows you to do things with bitmapped images that are simply incredible.

**CorelSHOW** is a full blown, super enhanced presentation graphics program. Forget about doing simple slides, this will allow you to run complete animations and slides as a single presentation. You can include sound too.

**CorelCAPTURE** is a screen capture utility.

Notice that there is no WFNBoss any more. That's because CorelDRAW, and the associated programs, are now fully TrueType compatible. In fact all the fonts that accompany the program are sent to you in three different formats:

TrueType which is the one that is preferable.

Adobe Type 1 so that you can use Abode Type Manager if you prefer.

WFN format which is similar to, but not identical to, the original CorelDRAW format.

This book will concentrate mainly on CorelDRAW itself with only brief glimpses of the associated programs. (There will be an associated book that will concentrate on the other programs just as soon as I can write it.) The aim of this book is to show you every aspect of CorelDRAW in a structured and cohesive way and as such the book is holistic in its approach. You can dip into the book and refresh your memory on various aspects of the program but it is really intended to be used as a self-contained tutorial. Start at the beginning and work your way through to the end and you will learn to use every aspect of the program. Along the way you will create a number of graphics, some of which will build on previous ones, but the most important thing is to have FUN!

That's what CorelDRAW is all about - having fun in the course of doing something useful and constructive. CorelDRAW exemplifies everything that the interaction of a computer and software should be. Simple at the first level but more and more complex as you delve into its possibilities - but all the time it is a joy to use and it will allow you to do things you never thought possible.

I hope you will enjoy this book as much as I enjoyed writing it.

Before we go any further there are a number of people that must be thanked for their contributions to this book and I would like to thank them all publicly here.

Everyone at Corel Systems provided invaluable help and assistance. Special mention should be made of Dr. Michael Cowpland, Corel Corporations Founder and CEO, Bill Cullen, Debra Gassewitz. Special thanks to Diana Real for making sure I had the latest beta version. Without them this book simply would not have been possible. Thank you all.

David Foster, my partner in the CorelDRAW User Group, undertook a lot of extra work so that I could get on with writing the book. He also made valuable suggestions and comments that helped to make this book what it is.

Viki Williams, my editor at Prentice-Hall, was, as always, extremely helpful and she as much as anyone is responsible for making sure that this book came out on time.

Last but certainly not least, Patricia, my wife, proof-read the entire manuscript. Corrected my split infinitives, made me rewrite things that weren't as clear as they should have been and generally made sure that I didn't get carried away. Any mistakes that remain are purely my fault. Thank you.

Alan Balfe
June 1992

# CONVENTIONS

The following section details how keystrokes, commands and actions will be shown in this book.

### MAIN KEYS

The names of all keys will be shown, in Bold, exactly as they appear on the keyboard, e.g. **G**, **S**, **L**, **1**, etc.

### CURSOR KEYS

The major cursor keys are shown in Bold exactly as they appear, e.g. **PgUp**, **Home**, **Ins**, **Del**. The minor cursor keys, i.e. the arrow keys are denoted by their actions, e.g. **Left**, **Right**, **Up** and **Down**. You may use either the true cursor keys, that block of ten keys between the main keypad and the Numeric keypad, or the keys on the Numeric Keypad itself - provided you do not have the **Num Lock** turned on.

### ADDITIONAL KEYS

Those keys which have a specific function are also shown in Bold, again exactly as they appear on the keyboard, e.g. **Ctrl**, **Enter**, **Backspace**. Function keys are always shown as they appear, e.g. **F2**, **F8**, **F12**.

### KEY COMBINATIONS

Where it is necessary for you to press two or more keys together these will be shown joined by a hyphen. For example, **Ctrl-F12** means that you press and hold the **Ctrl** key and then press **F12**, **Ctrl-Alt-Del** means that you press all three keys together.

Where the keys are meant to be pressed sequentially they will be shown in Bold but without the hyphen. Thus **Ctrl F12** means that you press and release **Ctrl** before pressing and releasing **F12**. **Shift-F10 F** means that you press and hold **Shift** and then press **F10**, before releasing both and then pressing **F**.

### ENTERING COMMANDS

Throughout this book anything that you have to type verbatim will appear in Bold. For example, the phrase enter **SETUP** means that you have to type SETUP and then press the **Enter** key.

MS-DOS and Windows commands will also appear in Bold, for example **COPY A:*.*** or **ATTRIB C:\DOS*.EXE**. Where you are required to supply a word, phrase or filename it will appear enclosed in square brackets. For example, **MD C:\WINDOWS\[directory]** means that you enter **MD C:\WINDOWS** followed by a directory name of your choice, but excluding the brackets.

### USING THE MOUSE

Where you are required to press a mouse button the text will say, for example, click on **File** and then on **Open**. This means that you move the mouse pointer to the File menu and then click once so that the menu pops-down. You then click on the word Open in that menu.

# ASSUMPTIONS

For various reasons it is necessary that I make a number of assumptions about your basic hardware, your disk drives and its directories and your familiarity with using text. Using a computer is a very personal thing and your system is liable to be different to mine and it will contain different software. Therefore, before we go any further here is a list of the assumptions that this book makes and what they imply. Likewise the following section provides definitions of various commands and actions for those who are unfamiliar with using computers.

### FAMILIARITY WITH WINDOWS

This book assumes that you are reasonably familiar with the Windows operating environment and what it does. However, it also assumes that you are not totally conversant with every aspect of Windows and the exercises that this book contains reflect this. The exercises start with very simple steps, including, for example, full details of how to open menus and select a command, but as you progress through the book the exercises become more generic, until by the final set of exercises the detailed step by step approach will no longer be used.

### FAMILIARITY WITH MS-DOS

This book assumes that you are using MS-DOS as your main operating system and that you are reasonably familiar with the major commands that the operating system contains.

### HARD DISK IS DRIVE-C

Throughout this book it is assumed that you are using a hard disk and that this is Drive-C. The reason for doing so is that every hard disk based computer that runs under MS-DOS must have Drive-C in order to boot. Except in special circumstances this book will not prompt you to supply a drive designator: if you wish to use an alternative disk at any point you should include the drive letter before any filename. For example, if you wanted to save a file to Drive-D instead of Drive-C you would include the full path to the target by including **D:\[directory]** before the filename.

## TEXT KNOWLEDGE

This book assumes that you know the difference between upper and lower case letters, i.e. A, B, C are upper case while a,b,c are lower case.

## USING A MOUSE

The final assumption is that you know how to use a mouse and that you have one connected to your machine. In order to use CorelDRAW properly you must have a mouse. Trying to use the program without one is so nonsensical as to be totally impractical.

Because the majority of people are right handed this book must reflect that and it therefore presupposes that you are right handed. If you are left handed you can either use the mouse in your left hand, which is possible although awkward, or you can change the mouse buttons in the Windows Control Panel so that they act the other way round. Therefore please bear in mind that when you see the words 'click once' it refers to the right hand button - but if you have reversed these then it means the left hand one.

# TERMINOLOGY

The following section gives brief definitions of phrases, terms and specific words that will appear in this book.

### ALT DEFINITION

The **Alt** key is that one which is normally found just to the left of the space bar on the majority of AT keyboards. The key allows you to generate alternative characters using the numeric keypad. In addition the key is used by Windows to activate menus and commands.

### BEZIER CURVE

A Bezier Curve is a special type of line on which you can change various aspects very easily. The line is shown, in certain resolutions, with two or more small square 'handles' appended to it. By moving one of these handles it is possible to change the aspect of the line.

### BIT MAP

A bit map refers specifically to a graphic file format. Any file that is bit mapped contains a list of all the pixels that the file contains, along with their attributes. Bit map files therefore tend to be fairly large.

### CLICKING

This refers to a mouse action and it simply means moving the mouse pointer, usually shown on screen as a white arrowhead, to the object you want and then clicking the left hand mouse button once.

### CTRL DEFINITION

The **Ctrl** key is the one normally found at the extreme left hand edge of the keyboard, on the same line as the spacebar. The key produces a signal that allows specific action to be generated by the software.

### CUT

Within Windows applications it is possible to select an object, or group of objects, e.g. lines of text, and then transfer this to the Clipboard before deleting it from the original document. This copy and delete action is called cutting. You can use **Shift-Del** as a shortcut.

### DIALOGUE BOXES

A Dialogue Box is a pop up box within Windows that allows you to set preferences from a predetermined list of options. Once you have made your selection you click on **OK** or press **Enter** to accept your choice and action it.

### DOUBLE CLICK

This simply means pressing the right hand mouse button twice, in rapid succession. If you don't click fast enough then nothing happens. You can change the speed of the double click using the Control Panel of Windows.

### DRAGGING

This is a mouse action. It means clicking on an object and then, while still holding down the mouse button, you move the mouse and so drag the object around the screen.

### EXPORT

To export a file means to save that file in a format different from that in which it was loaded. For example, in CorelDRAW you can open a CDR file (Corel Draw's own format) and then save that graphic, or selected parts of it, as a PCX file.

### FLOPPY DISK

A floppy disk is a small disk of Mylar, coated with a magnetisable resin, that is used for storing small amounts of data. Floppy disks are prone to damage and thus should be handled carefully.

### HARD DISK

A hard disk is a self-contained unit that contains a number of aluminium disks, called platters, coated with a magnetisable material. The unit also contains a Read/Write head assembly that floats just above the platters. Hard disks are extremely susceptible to damage caused by jolting and banging and thus you should always take care to park the heads before moving any computer fitted with a hard disk. This action moves the Read/Write heads to a safe position and then locks them in place so that they cannot impact the platters.

Please note: You cannot use CorelDRAW without a hard disk, though you can run it directly off the CD-ROM. The program is so large and the files it can create so complex that you must have a hard disk to run the program. Also the speed of your hard disk will affect how the program runs. CorelDRAW is the most disk-intensive program that I know of and a slow disk will slow it down considerably. Equally you should ensure that you have at least 2 Mb of free space on your disk before you create any graphics with CorelDRAW - you don't actually need that much space but it is better to have too much than too little.

### Import

This means to load a file into an existing document so as to combine a number of files together. For example, in CorelDRAW you can create a picture then insert a piece of clip art from another CorelDRAW image, and then combine the two to make a single graphic. Importing files is especially important with graphic programs because it allows you to build complex graphics from simpler elements. CorelDRAW will allow you to import a large range of different graphic file formats.

### List Boxes

A list box is a pop down box that contains a list of items from which you can choose any one item. For example all Windows menus are list boxes from which you select a single command that you wish to action.

### Mouse

A mouse is a complementary input device that is used in conjunction with, or occasionally, instead of the keyboard. Within the Windows environment you can use the keyboard and the mouse in conjunction to do things much faster than using either device by itself.

Please note: To use CorelDRAW properly you must have a mouse and this book assumes that you do so.

### Object Orientated Graphic

An object orientated graphic is one where the program keeps track of what objects are where by reasoning. For example, a filled square may be recorded as 'there is a black bordered square, having sides x units long, positioned at x,y which is filled with yellow'. Because the information is recorded in this fashion object orientated files can be much smaller than bitmapped ones. However, because object orientated files tend to be much more complex than bitmapped ones the files tend to be much larger. CorelDRAW normally uses only object orientated files.

### OPEN

To load a file into an application.

### PASTE

Within Windows this means to insert the contents of the Clipboard at the current cursor position. You can use the shortcut Shift-Ins in all Windows programs.

### PIXEL

A pixel, also called picture element, is the smallest area of the screen that can be independently illuminated. The number of pixels on your monitor depends on the quality of the monitor and its type, e.g. VGA monitors generally have more pixels than CGA ones.

### POINT SIZES

All type is traditionally measured in Points, a single point being one Seventy Second of an inch, and this refers to the height of the characters. Until recently and the advent of laser printers all type in computer applications was measured, normally, in Pitch - the number of characters that could be squeezed into a one inch horizontal space.

### POSTSCRIPT

PostScript is a form of computer language used by printers. It was invented by Adobe and it allows whole pages to be printed at high speed because it is not concerned with individual characters. All PostScript printers must therefore have a large amount of on-board RAM to handle the calculations necessary for describing and printing the page. This is especially true when using CorelDRAW - any printer must have at least 2 Mb of on-board RAM if you want to print graphics larger than A5.

### SAVE

The action of writing a file from the current application to a disk for permanent or temporary storage using the default filename and extension. The keyboard shortcut is usually **Ctrl-S**.

### SAVE AS

The action of saving a file from the current application to the disk using an alternative filename and/or extension.

### UNDO

To cancel the last operation. Many applications have an undo facility and how they work varies from program to program but all of them will at least allow you to annul the last act, whether it is an operation or a action, that you performed, e.g. because of an error. The keyboard shortcut is always **Alt-Backspace**.

### WINDOWS

The operating system front end developed by Microsoft to enhance MS-DOS. The Windows environment is bright, colourful, intuitive and a joy to use. The most fundamentally important software development since the development of the original IBM PC and the creation of MS-DOS.

### WYSIWYG

The acronym for What You See Is What You Get which is normally used to refer to word processors, though it also applies to graphic programs - especially to CorelDRAW. Basically the acronym means that any changes you make to the document will cause the display to reflect that change. The level of WYSIWYG depends on the program concerned and the quality of the monitor display and its controller. To get the best from CorelDRAW you will need, at the very least, a 16-bit VGA colour monitor.

# EQUIPMENT USED

Whenever I write a book I always try to use machines that are readily available to everyone. For the purposes of this book I used the following:

a. My own personal computer. This is an AT clone made by MCA who are based in Luton. However, because I need a super powerful machine it has been greatly enhanced. The machine is basically an 80486 running at 33 Mhz but it has 16 Mb of RAM, which will shortly be upgraded to 32 Mb, and a 660 Mb SCSI hard disk, partitioned into five 128 Mb logical drives. It also has a Sound Blaster Pro board and CD-ROM drive fitted. The machine runs MS-DOS 5.0 and Windows 3.1 and has been specially configured to run both at optimum levels. Windows reports 34,159 Kb of Free Memory and 86% Free Resources. To be frank, it goes like a bat out of hell!

b. A now ancient VTEC Laser 80386 fitted with 2 Mb of RAM - it really needs more. The hard disk is a 64 Mb RLL drive with Stacker running on it to increase the capacity. The computer runs under MS-DOS 5.0 and Windows 3.1. By default this machine runs in Enhanced mode. Windows reports, via the About command in the Help menu, that this machine has 2720 Kb of memory and 86% of the system resources are free. I used this machine simply to show that it is possible to run CorelDRAW 3 on a system with extremely limited resources - but I wouldn't recommend it.

c. A Mitac portable. This is an 80386 running at 20 Mhz. Unfortunately it only has 1 Mb of RAM - I only use it when I'm training as a kind of giant floppy disk - and as such is woefully inadequate for running CorelDRAW 3.0. The machine does run Windows 3.1 without any problems.

d. My own printer, a Star Micronics LaserPrinter 4 StarPage, fitted with 3 Mb of RAM. This is a PostScript clone and has been fitted with new EPROMS which allows it to accept downloaded Abode Type 1 fonts. It has served me well for the last fifteen months, during which time it has had over 17,000 pieces of paper through it. It has no problems printing anything from CorelDRAW.

# 1 - INSTALLATION

## BEFORE WE BEGIN

In order to have this book finished at roughly the same time that the software is being released it means that there are certain aspects of the timing that have to be taken into account. Firstly, I am using the beta test version of the CorelDRAW Graphics Package for writing this book. The version I am using should be the penultimate version, i.e. one step back from the actual release version. This means that the basic layout of the program, its commands, screen handling, etc. should not change at all between the version I am using and the one you are upgrading to.

However, there may be slight changes in some aspects of the program - not least of which may be in the installation. For this reason what follows may change slightly, albeit not very much, in the release version. Thereafter the actual operation of the program will not change at all.

CorelDRAW 3.0 is being released on both CD-ROM and floppy disks in the same box. Unfortunately, I don't yet have the CD version, as it is not yet available, so what follows is based on using the floppy disks. Based on past experience, with the CorelDRAW Blockbuster, using the CD-ROM will allow you to install the software in about one fifth of the time that the floppies will take. However, the basic installation will remain the same.

When you open the box you should find a number of floppy disks, possibly as many as twelve, a manual, a CD-ROM disc and other bits and pieces. One of the most important is the Registration Card. Before you do anything else, fill it in and then make sure you post it. In the past there has been a lot of confusion about the registration card because people assumed that the address was incorrect. This is not the case. The card does have to go back to Canada.

The reason for filling the card in is simple - you will get advance notice of new releases of CorelDRAW before anyone else does. It also allows you to use the Corel Technical Support line, also based in Canada, and it allows you to enter the Annual Design Contest which is only open to registered users. Since the prizes are worth up to $1,000,000 (Yes, I do mean One Million Dollars!) it is well worth entering the contest. At the time of writing this, June 1991, the full details of next year's contest have not been finalised but you will be informed of them if you are registered user and/or if you are a member of .CDR, the CorelDRAW Users Group.

Anyway, back to the installation. The first thing you must do is ensure that your hard disk has been compressed using PC Tools Compress or Norton Speed Disk. You are going to need lots of contiguous disk space for the installation. (Contiguous simply means that all the files on your disk are in adjacent sectors so that they load faster.) Having your disk properly compressed can mean that Windows, and thus CorelDRAW, works up to about 30% faster - depending on circumstances - than it would if your disk was not compressed.

One thing that must be made clear before we go any further. CorelDRAW works in Windows which is an operation system shell that works on top of MS-DOS. Because of that it means that you have to have your machine properly configured to run each layer properly. A single error in configuring MS-DOS, for example, can have major repercussions for the way that Windows works and that in turn will affect CorelDRAW or any other Windows program for that matter. Chaotic theory in action! By way of example, here is the CONFIG.SYS for my 486 machine.

```
FILES=30
BUFFERS=10
DEVICE=C:\DOS\HIMEM.SYS
DOS=HIGH,UMB
DEVICE=C:\DOS\EMM386.EXE NOEMS
DEVICEHIGH=C:\DOS\RAMDRIVE.SYS 4096/E
DEVICEHIGH=C:\DOS\SETVER.EXE
DEVICEHIGH=C:\DOS\SBPCD.SYS /D:MSCD001 /P:220
COUNTRY=044,,C:\DOS\COUNTRY.SYS
LASTDRIVE=I
STACKS=9,256
```

Before we go any further let's examine this in detail. The first line sets the number of files that MS-DOS can have open at any one time. You can omit the line completely, in which case the operating system will use its default values that are based on the chip type, disk size, memory, etc. but it is much better to set the number of files yourself. How many you need depends on what applications you are using. If you are using a database for example which requires a lot of files to be open at once then you need a higher value that if you are just using a word processor. Setting the value to 30 is a good compromise. I use a database, a spreadsheet, a word processor, CorelDRAW of course and PageMaker plus some other bits and pieces and a value of 30 is perfect for these.

Setting the buffers to 10 is all you need to run Windows because SmartDrive handles all the necessary buffering for you. You certainly don't need any more than that.

The next line, the one that contains HIMEM.SYS, is vital as is its position in the CONFIG.SYS. Himem allows you to access the upper memory levels and it is this that makes Windows work correctly. Without Himem you will have problems. It must be the first device that is loaded in the file and it cannot be loaded high - because it is this file that creates the pathway to the high memory area.

The next line loads the operating system into high memory and activates the upper memory blocks. You don't need to know what these are - you simply use them. Without the UMB parameter you cannot use the next line.

The next line, containing EMM386, is also important and it must follow the previous line. In my case I have it set so that there is no expanded memory. That's what the NOEMS parameter means. This in turn means that all the computer memory is available as extended memory which is what Windows uses.

The next line should not be used on any computer that has 8 Mb or less of memory. I can get away with it because I have 16 Mb of RAM on my machine. A ramdrive is an electronic disk that operates very fast and so it speeds things up. The 4096/E sets the size of the disk, in kilobytes, and ensures it uses extended memory. In fact it is a bit on the small side but I compromise between speed and Windows resources. Note that the driver which creates the ramdrive is loaded into high memory.

SETVER is necessary to operate the CD-ROM drive. Again it can be loaded into high memory. If you don't have a CD-ROM you don't really need it but it does depend on which software you are using. SETVER itself is simply a list of programs followed by the version of MS-DOS that the program works best with. You can view its contents from the system prompt or add things to it if you need to. If you enter **SETVER/?** from the system prompt you'll get full details.

The next line is needed for the Sound Blaster card and its CD-ROM drive.

Country is vital if you want your keyboard to operate correctly.

The Lastdrive line is only necessary if you have more than five logical drives on your system. MS-DOS automatically handles up to five drives, i.e. A to E, so if you have this number or less you don't need this line. I actually have nine logical drives: A and B are floppies, C to G are partitions of the hard disk, H is the ramdrive and I is the CD-ROM drive. Don't use more drive letters that you actually need because each additional letter uses memory.

The Stacks line was set by Windows 3.1 when it was installed. On the whole it doesn't seem to make a great deal of difference so I just leave it alone.

On the whole my CONFIG.SYS is fairly standard. I don't use anything special, other than the Sound Blaster, and so you could use it as a basis for configuring your own machine. However, each machine is slightly different and the contents of the file will depend on what resources your machine has available.

As well as the CONFIG.SYS you need an AUTOEXEC.BAT file, which in many places will complement the former file. Mine looks like this:

```
@ECHO OFF
PATH C:\;C:\DOS;C:\WINDOWS;C:\UTIL;C:\EXCEL;C:\WORD;C:\ALDUS;
MSCDEX /V /D:MSCD001 /M:15
SET BLASTER=A220 I7 D1 T4
LH C:\DOS\SMARTDRV.EXE H-
PROMPT $P$G
LH \KEYB UK,,C:\DOS\KEYBOARD.SYS
MD H:\TEMP
SET TEMP=H:\TEMP
SET SOUND=C:\SBPRO
SBP-SET /M:12 /VOC:12 /CD:12 /FM:12
DS NE/S
MIRROR/1
CLS
PATH
DIR/W
```

Again, most of this is fairly standard (I like to keep things simple) with only minor additions for special drivers. The path statement is purposely kept short, for example I install the PageMaker files into the Aldus directory instead of a directory of their own. I also keep directory names short.

The third line loads the MS-DOS extensions that I need to use the CD-ROM. Unfortunately these cannot be loaded into high memory which is a nuisance because they do take a lot of the available RAM.

The next line sets certain of the parameters for the Sound Blaster card. SmartDrive is loaded next. It can be placed into the high memory area so it's preceded by LH, short for Load High. Notice that it contains a parameter **H-** which means that the cache does not apply to the ramdrive.

The prompt is standard, $P$G means it shows the current directory. The keyboard driver is loaded next, again into high memory.

The next two lines apply to the ramdrive. The first creates a directory called TEMP and the next points to it. I create a directory in the ramdrive because some software is awkward and insists on using a directory called TEMP rather than the root of a drive. The next two lines concern the Sound Blaster again.

The final lines are simply house keeping. DS is Norton's Directory Sort so that my files are always in alphabetical order. Mirror is a utility, which comes with MS-DOS 5.0, that keeps track of where files are so that they can be unerased if I accidentally delete something I want. The last three lines simply clear the screen, display the path and then give a wide listing of the directories and files on Drive-C.

The one thing that I do religiously every day is compress my hard disk - all of it. I use PC Tools Compress because it is faster than Norton Speed Disk. At the end of every working day I run Compress so that my hard disk and its partitions are fully contiguous for the next day's labours. In fact it only takes about five minutes to do all 660 Mb and in terms of the benefits this brings to running Windows it is time well spent.

There is something else I do which often startles people. About every three months of so I clean out my hard disk completely, i.e. I delete everything from it, and then reinstall things. In particular I reinstall Windows. The reason is that I do a lot of testing of various software and this affects Windows and occasionally the AUTOEXEC.BAT. The advantage of reinstalling everything is that it returns everything to its proper speed. As you add bits and pieces here and there things, of necessity, can get a bit cumbersome. I'm not for a moment suggesting that you do the same thing with the same frequency but it certainly is worth doing a major housekeeping operation on your hard disk at least once a year.

# MAKE A BACKUP

Right, having got all that out of the way, let's get on with installing CorelDRAW 3.0. You should make backup copies of the floppy disks before you do this. You will need a number of floppy disks, equal to how ever many there are the box, and they must be the same size and format as those in the box - preferably use new disks. The disks you will copy on to do not have to be pre-formatted. The simplest way to make disk copies is to use Windows - it's faster than using MS-DOS. If you are going to use the CD-ROM you obviously don't need to do this.

a. Run Windows as normal and then activate the File Manager. Take the first of the CorelDRAW installation disks and place it into the relevant floppy drive. Open the **Disk** menu and click on **Copy Disk**. A dialogue box appears:

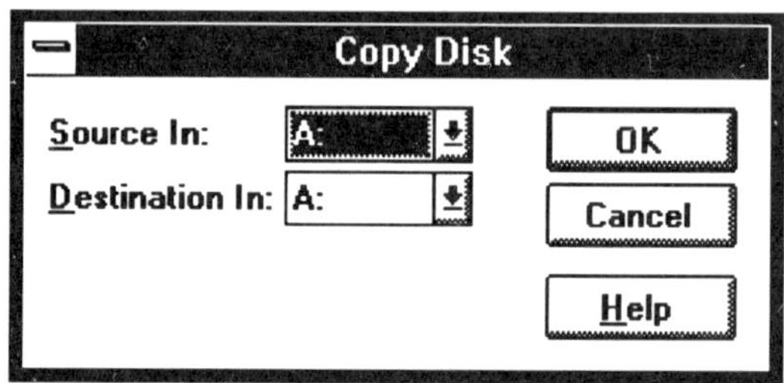


**1.01 Copy Disk dialogue box**

b. Change the drive letters in the dialogue box if necessary, it always defaults to Drive-A, and then click on **OK**. A message box appears telling you to insert the source disk. As you have already done so just press **Enter** or click on **OK** and the process begins. As the copying continues you get another message box telling you how complete the operation is.

c. After a while you will get another message box asking you to insert the destination disk, i.e. the disk you want to make the copy on to. Swap the disks over and press **Enter** again. The process dialogue box continues to give an indication of how far the process has to go as the disk is copied.

**1.02 Destination message box**

d. Once the disk is copied the dialogue box vanishes. You don't get the option of copying another disk as you would using the MS-DOS DISKCOPY. But at least you know the disk is copied.

e. Repeat the process for each of the CorelDRAW floppy disks.

That's all there is to it. Label each of the copies appropriately and then put the master disks away somewhere safe. You should only use the copies you have made for any installation from here on in. Never use the master disks directly. If one of the copies becomes corrupted for any reason, make another copy of the relevant master disk and use that but don't use the master itself.

# INSTALLATION

Having made the copies of the floppy disks and compressed your hard disk you are now ready to begin the installation of CorelDRAW 3.0. One major, and possibly devastating, point that you do need to bear in mind - you need an absolute minimum of 30 Mb of disk space to install all of it! In keeping with the current trend for making software better and more powerful, and therefore larger, CorelDRAW is huge - one reason why you need to compress your hard disk first. Assuming you have the necessary space you can install it. Oh, one other thing, the installation from the floppy disks takes at least 20 minutes depending on what you do!

a. Run Windows (CorelDRAW 3.0 must be installed from within Windows) preferably version 3.1. You can run CorelDRAW 3.0 from Windows 3.0 but it works much better from 3.1. Place the first floppy disk into the drive and then press **Alt-F R**, or open the **File** menu and click on **Run**. In the dialogue box that appears enter **[drive:]SETUP** where [drive] is the floppy drive that contains the disk. Don't forget the colon. Press **Enter** again or click on **OK**.

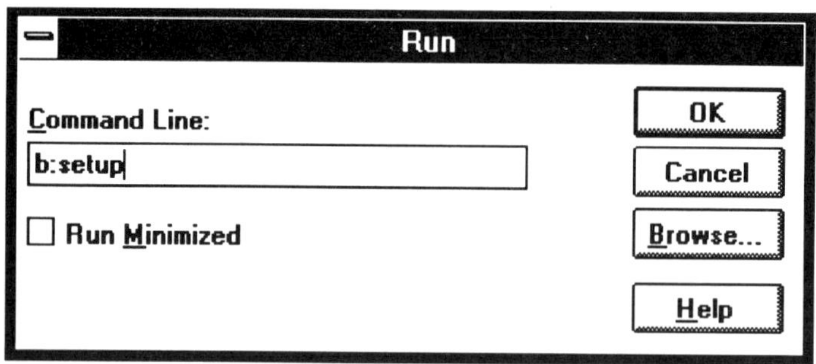


**1.03 Run dialogue box**

b. A message box appears telling you that setup is being initialised and asking you to be patient. What's happening is that the setup program is checking the available resources and what have you to make sure the program will run. Just wait a while. How long you have to wait depends on your machine. Eventually the installation dialogue box proper will appear.

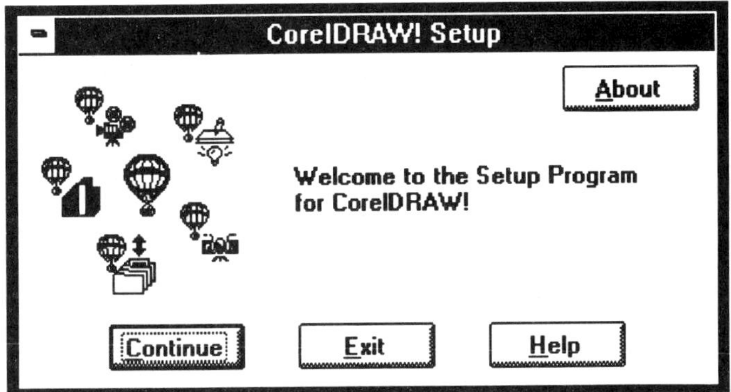


**1.04 Installation begins**

c. Press **Enter** or click on **Continue**. A new message box appears:

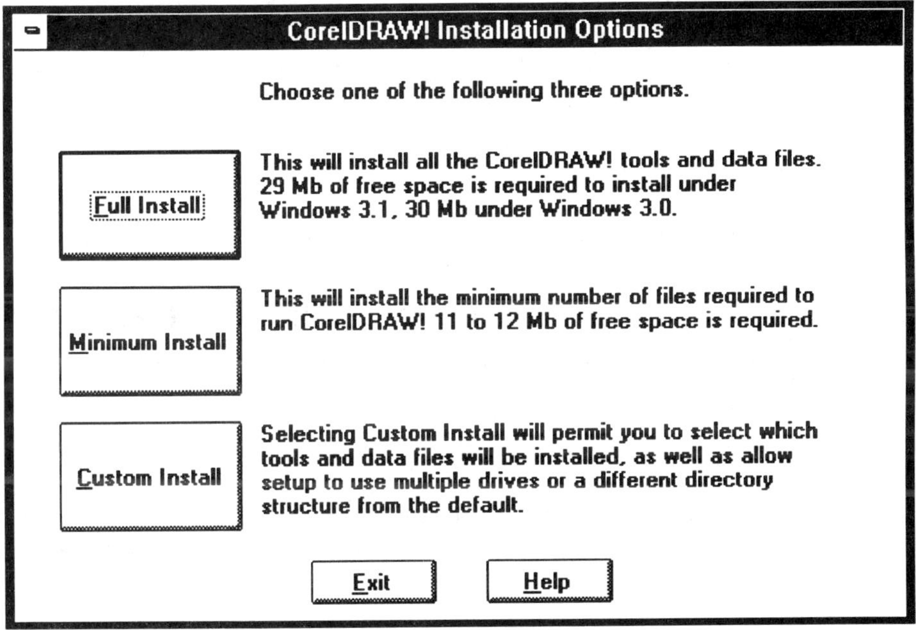


**1.05 Installation options**

d. The simplest method is to select **Full Install**. This just gets on and does it and you don't have to make any real decisions, other than to select a directory name if you want to. This is the option that is highlighted by default so just press **Enter** to select it.

e. Alternatively you may elect to have just CorelDRAW and its major associated programs installed - the **Minimum Installation**. The third option is **Custom Installation**. This gives you much greater control over where things are put and which options are installed. Click on the button to use it. What follows is based on the custom installation.

f. Regardless of which option you choose the next dialogue box to appear asks you to select a destination directory for the program. By default this is **C:\CORELDRW**. Note that this is no longer sub-tended off the Windows directory as it was in CorelDRAW 2.0. If the directory is okay with you just press **Enter**. If not you may change the directory to anything you wish.

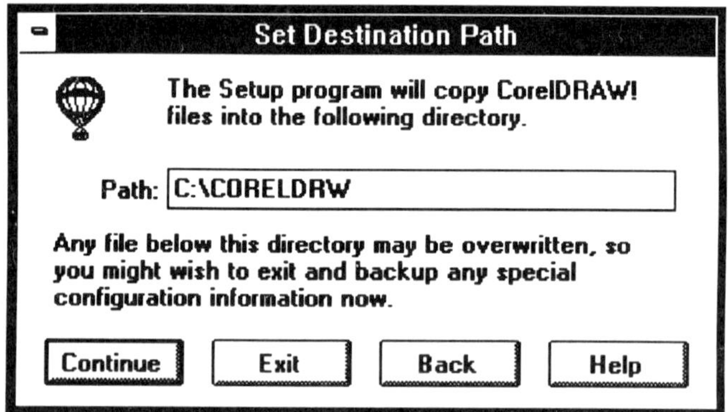


**1.06 Destination directory dialogue box**

g. What happens next is that the installation program checks the amount of disk space available and various drivers. Again just be patient. Eventually the main dialogue box appears.

**CorelDRAW! Custom Installation**

Choose which tools to install:

| | All: | Some: | None: | | Disk Usage: |
|---|---|---|---|---|---|
| CorelDRAW!: | ◉ | ○ | ○ | C:\CORELDRW\DRAW\ | 7936 K |
| CorelCHART!: | ◉ | ○ | ○ | C:\CORELDRW\CHART\ | 7480 K |
| CorelSHOW!: | ◉ | ○ | ○ | C:\CORELDRW\SHOW\ | 2288 K |
| CorelPHOTO-PAINT!: | ◉ | ○ | ○ | C:\CORELDRW\PHOTOPNT\ | 1520 K |
| CorelTRACE!: | ◉ | ○ | ○ | C:\CORELDRW\DRAW\ | 272 K |
| CorelMOSAIC!: | ◉ | ○ | ○ | C:\CORELDRW\DRAW\ | 1192 K |
| Fonts & Symbols: | ○ | ◉ | ○ | C:\CORELDRW\FONTS\ | 6064 K |
| Root Directory: | | | | C:\CORELDRW | 1480 K |

Drive: C:
Space Required: 28232 K
Space Available: 39432 K

Continue | Exit | Back | Help

**1.07 Custom Install main dialogue box**

h. Now you get a glimpse of what CorelDRAW 3.0 contains. The dialogue box lists all the programs in the package. CorelDRAW itself is first and it requires just over 7.75 Mb of space. CorelCHART, the program that allows you to create dynamic presentations, is next and it requires just under 7.5 Mb of space. CorelSHOW, the slide presentation program, needs just under 2.25 Mb. CorelPHOTO-PAINT needs nearly 1.5 Mb, CorelTRACE uses the least amount of disk space - a mere 272 Kb. CorelMOSAIC, the graphics file manager, requires just under 1.25 Mb. The fonts and symbols need nearly 6 Mb and the other ancillary files need another 1.5 Mb. Add all that up and it comes to just over 27.5 Mb. But you also need additional space for files to be temporarily copied to.

i. If you want to be selective about what is installed, click on the button in the **Some** column. This will bring down another dialogue box that allows you to select various options.

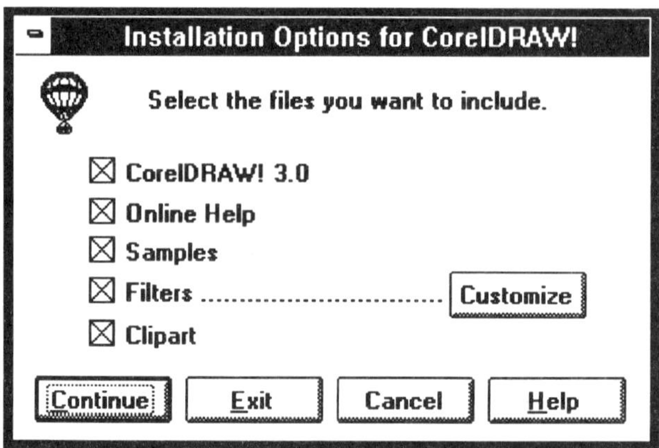


**1.08 CorelDRAW options dialogue box**

j. At any point in the preceding you can click on the button labelled **Back** to go back one step. As you select options for each of the programs the values noting the amount of space required will change accordingly. Once you have made all your selections click on **Continue** to begin the actual installation.

k. Another dialogue box appears asking you to name the Program Manager group title that will be used for the CorelDRAW 3.0 files. By default it is set to be **Corel Graphics** but you can make the name whatever you wish. The default name seems fine to me so I just click on **Continue** again.

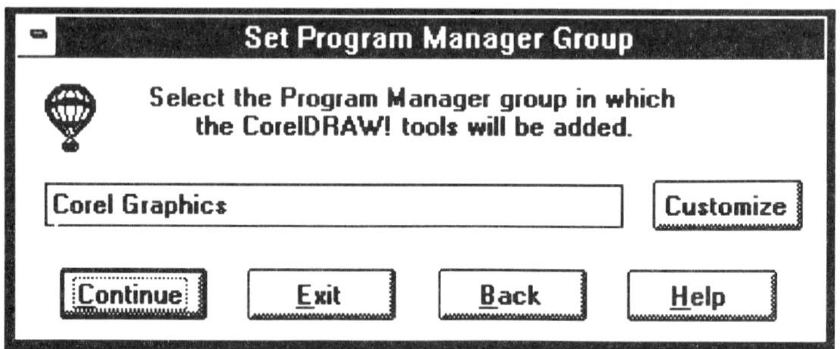


**1.09 Group Name dialogue box**

l. Finally, you get another message telling you that the installation is ready to begin! Just press **Enter** or click on **Install** to continue.

CorelDRAW! Setup Disk 1

Source File:
B:\ZSOFT381.DRV
Destination File:
C:\CORELDRW\PHOTOPNT\ZSOFT381.DRV

0%

Cancel

**1.10 Installation in progress**

m. Now you basically have to just sit and wait, swapping the disks when prompted to do so. As the installation proceeds you are shown various images and told how far the process has got. One thing that you should notice is that CorelDRAW is installing TrueType fonts. The program now uses TrueType and Adobe Type 1 fonts rather than its own WFN format. To the best of my knowledge Corel is the first company to supply and make use of TrueType fonts, other than the few that are supplied with Windows 3.1.

**1.11 Installation in progress**

n. Eventually you will get a message telling you that the installation is complete:

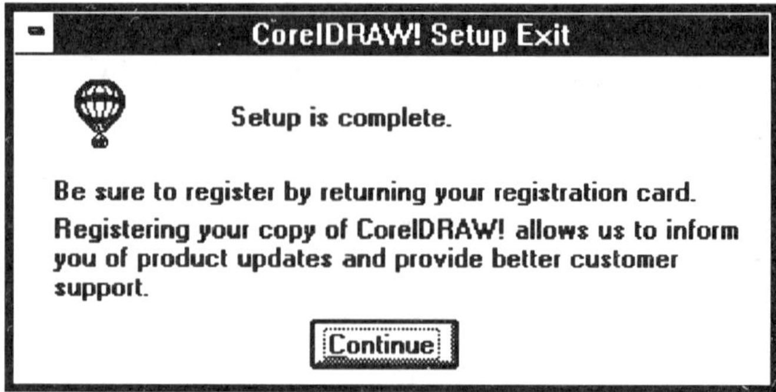


**1.12 Installation complete**

o. Clicking on **Continue** to close the dialogue box will take you back to the Program Manager where you will find a new program group, called whatever you called it, containing the CorelDRAW Graphics Toolkit.

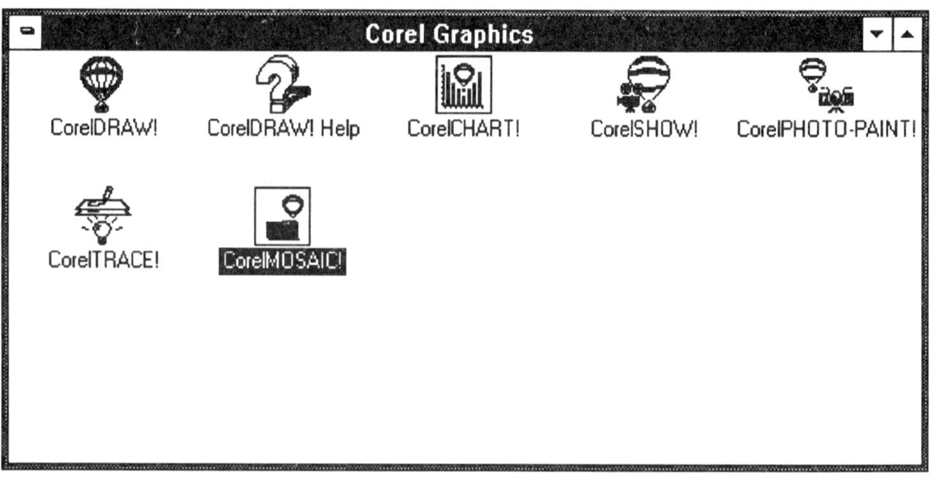


**1.13 CorelDRAW Graphics group**

That's the installation complete. Along the way more that 150 TrueType fonts will have been added to your system and they are all now operable. The CorelDRAW setup automatically adds them to your system ready for use. You don't have to reboot Windows to use them - they are available now. However, if you want to use the fonts in any other application, e.g. a word processor, you must run that application and click on **Printer Setup** in each case. Once the dialogue box appears click on **OK** to close it and the fonts are available for use by that program.

The CD-ROM version contains an addition 100 fonts plus over 14,000 (That is not a misprint!) Clip-Art images plus over 100 Autodesk Animations for use with CorelSHOW. Plus the entire set of fonts, all 253 of them, in Adobe Type 1 format.

All in all you have to say CorelDRAW is 3-Mendous!

# 2 - Screen Layout

## Main elements

When you run CorelDRAW 3.0 the first thing you notice is that the program looks identical to CorelDRAW 2.0. This is intentional on Corel's part. They didn't want people to have to go through another learning curve in order to use the new version so the basic layout remains the same.

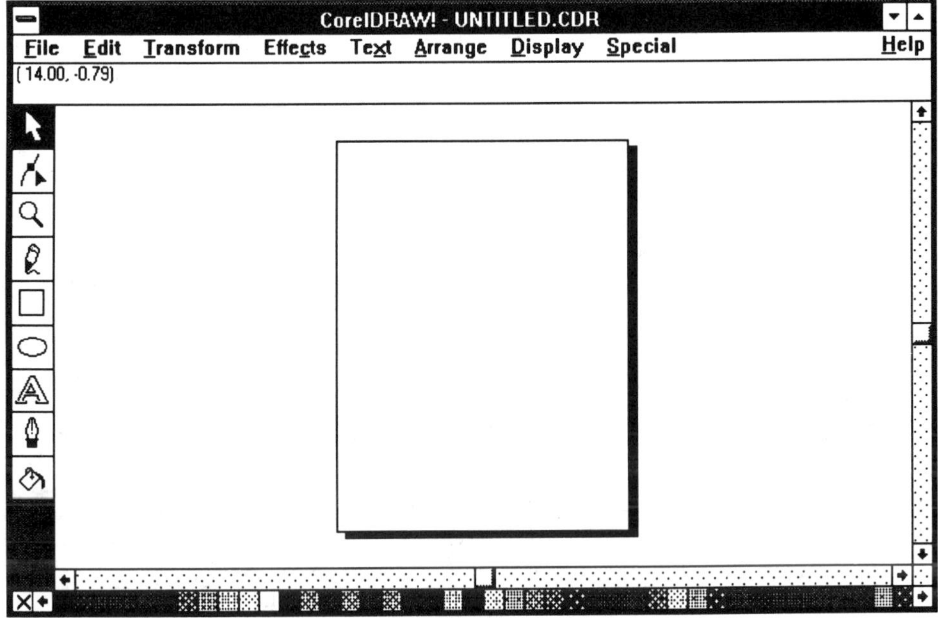


**2.01 Opening screen**

Along the top of the screen is the normal **Control Box**, not to be confused with the Control Panel which is a Windows application, in the top left hand corner. Following that is the **Title Bar**, which gives the program name, in this case CorelDRAW, followed by the name of the current file. As we have yet to open or save a file the file name is given as UNTITLED.CDR. At the top right hand corner of the screen are two buttons, each bearing arrowheads. The first of these, which has an arrow pointing downwards, is the **Minimise** button. Clicking on this will reduce the window to an icon. The second button, with the upward pointing arrowhead, is the **Maximise** button. Clicking on this will expand the window so that it fills the entire screen area. Thereafter the button will change to the **Restore** button, i.e. it will contain a double arrowhead. When you click on it in that state the window will be restored to its previous size and position on the screen.

Immediately below the title bar is the **Menu Bar**. This contains the list of menu names. Clicking on any menu name will pop-down the associated menu.

The third line on the screen is the **Status Bar**. At present this bears just some numbers, e.g. (13.32, 1.95), which gives the co-ordinates for the current mouse position. Be aware that the co-ordinates cannot be outside the CorelDRAW window, if you move the mouse outside the CorelDRAW window then the Status Bar will be blank.

Down the left hand side of the screen is the **Toolbox** which contains some of the tools that you have available for use in CorelDRAW.

The top one is the **Pointer**, used to select items, which is active by default. From most of the other tools, but not the text tool, you can always go back to the pointer tool by pressing the **Spacebar**.

The next tool is the **Node Edit tool**. You use this to manipulate the Bezier control points of lines and curves. It can also be used to perform certain effects with text. You can switch to the Node Edit tool at any time by pressing **F10**.

The third tool is the **Magnification tool**. This allows you to magnify any part of the screen, the exact level of magnification depends on how large an area you select. There is no single keystroke to activate the magnifier per se because the tool has a number of sub-options. Clicking on the tool will pop-out the available choices:

**2.02 Magnifier options**

The first sub-tool is the actual **Magnifier**. This allows you to enlarge a selected area of the screen. The keyboard shortcut for this aspect of the tool is **F2**. To use it you simply drag a bounding box around the area you want to enlarge. (A bounding box simply means that you click at one corner of the area then, still holding down the mouse button, you drag the mouse to the diagonally opposite corner of the area you want. When you release the button the bounding box is activated. In this case the selected area will be enlarged to fill the screen.)

The second sub-tool is the **De-magnifier**. This has the opposite effect the previous one but it does so in a single step. The keyboard shortcut is **F3**. When you use the tool, either by pressing a key or by opening the toolbox, the magnified area will be returned to the previous level of magnification. In this way you can step back one level of magnification if you need to.

The third sub-tool is labelled **1:1**. This will display the image at the size that it will appear when printed. There is no keyboard shortcut for this sub-tool.

The fourth sub-tool is **Fit in Window** and the keyboard shortcut is **F4**. When you click on this or press the key all the images currently on screen will be magnified, or shrunk, so that you can see the whole lot in the CorelDRAW window. However, you may have objects too far apart for them to be seen together in which case you will get an error message telling you so.

The final magnification tool is **Show Page** and the keyboard shortcut is **Shift-F4**. What it does is magnify, or shrink, the entire page so that it fills the entire CorelDRAW window.

The third major tool is the **Line drawing tool**. CorelDRAW gives you the option of drawing Freehand or with Bezier curves. If you click on the tool and hold down the mouse button you will get a pop-out showing the two tool types. Any lines you draw will be drawn in the currently selected line width and colour. The keyboard shortcut to select the freehand drawing tool is **F5**.

The next major tool is the **Rectangle drawing tool** and its keyboard shortcut is **F6**. When you select this tool the mouse cursor becomes an open cross. You draw rectangles by clicking on where you want one corner of the rectangle to be and then, holding down the mouse button, dragging the cursor to the diagonally opposite corner. If you want to draw squares, rather than rectangles, hold down **Ctrl** as you drag the mouse. (CorelDRAW uses the **Ctrl** key as a constraint for many operations. In other words you hold down the key to make using a tool perform definite actions rather than the standard ones.) Any square or rectangle will be drawn in the currently selected line width and colour and it will be filled with current foreground colour.

The next tool is the **Ellipse tool**, the keyboard shortcut for which is **F7**. You use this in the same way as you would the rectangle drawing tool. Ellipses are drawn within imaginary rectangular boxes. So you click on one corner of its rectangle and then drag the cursor to the diagonally opposite corner. When you release the mouse button the ellipse appears. In fact as you move the mouse you can see a representation of how the ellipse will appear. Again you can constrain the ellipse tool to draw pure circles by holding down **Ctrl** as you move the mouse.

The next tool is the **Text tool**, the keyboard shortcut for which is **F8**. If you click on the text tool icon and hold down the mouse button for a couple of seconds a pop-out will appear. This bears the standard text tool, i.e. an upper case A, and the **Symbol Library tool**, which appears as a star shape. In previous versions of CorelDRAW you had to select the text tool and then hold down **Shift** as you clicked the tool on the page in order to get at the symbol libraries but with version 3 you no longer need to do that - although you still can if you want to.

The penultimate tool is the **Outline Pen tool**. There isn't a keyboard shortcut as such for this tool, instead there are shortcuts for some aspects of it. If you click on the tool you will get a pop-out like this:

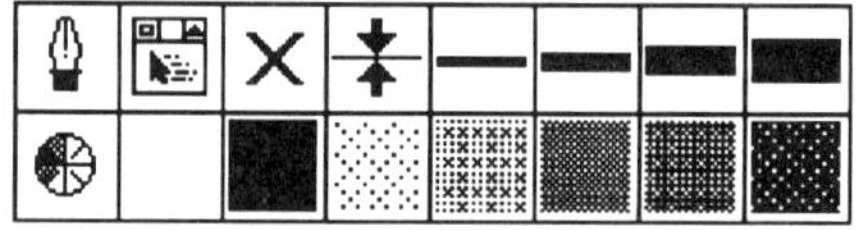

**2.03 Outline Pen tool pop-out**

The pop-out consists of two lines of preset options, the top row is basically concerned with the line thickness. On the top line the first sub-tool activates a dialogue box which we'll come back to in a minute.

The second icon activates the line width **Roll-up**. Roll-ups are a completely new, and novel, feature developed by Corel. Many of the options within CorelDRAW can now be used with roll-ups. We'll come back to this one in a minute also.

The third icon, which bears an **X**, means no line. Clicking on this will turn off any line width, either for future objects or for selected items.

The fourth icon, the one bearing a line between two arrows, is the thinnest default line width that CorelDRAW produces. (You can make it thinner using the dialogue box.) It produces a line that is 0.003 inches thick, that's 0.1 millimetres or 0.2 points.

The remaining icons on the top line also produce line thicknesses, ranging from 0.028 inches (0.7 millimetres or 2 points) to 0.111 inches (2.8 millimetres, 8 points) to 0.222 inches (5.6 millimetres, 16 points) to the final 0.333 inches (8.5 millimetres or 24 points).

The icons along the bottom row of the pop-out have to do with the line colour. The first icon, which looks like a pie chart, activates a complete dialogue box and we'll come back to it later.

The next two icons are solid colours. The first is White and the second Black. The remaining icons gives shades of grey ranging from 10% black through 30% black, followed by 50% and then 70% black. The final preset is for 90% black.

The final tool is the **Fill tool**, in other words the colour or pattern that will be used to fill the selected object. Clicking on the tool will bring up a pop-out divided into two lines. The top line is mainly for patterns and the second for shades of grey.

The first icon on the top row brings up a dialogue box.

The second icon is the Fill roll-up.

The third icon, the one bearing an **X**, means no fill.

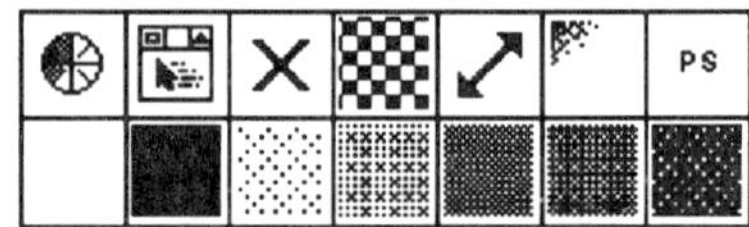


**2.04 Fill tool options**

The fourth, bearing a checker board pattern, is for what used to be called Bitmap fills. In CorelDRAW 3.0 they are called **Two-colour Fills**. You can create bitmapped fills from vectored images if you want to but they will always be in two colour only. The icon activates a dialogue box.

The fifth icon, the one with the diagonal arrow, is for vector fills - now called **Full-colour Fills**. Again it activates a dialogue box.

The penultimate icon, the one with the shaded pattern, is for **Fountain Fills**.

The final fill tool is labelled PS for **PostScript Pattern Fill**. You cannot see PostScript fills on screen, largely because they are dependent on a PostScript interpreter and computers don't have internal interpreters. Besides which the fills can be extremely complex and beyond the capabilities of even the best monitor.

On the bottom line you have a choice of White, Black, 10%, 30%, 50% 70% or 90% black. Just select an object and click on one of these to fill the object with the shade.

Along the bottom of the screen is the **Colour Palette** which can display the standard Process or Spot colour fills. If you select an object and click on a palette colour with the left hand mouse button then the object will be filled with the chosen colour. Click with the right hand mouse button to apply the selected colour to the object's outline. At the extreme left hand side of this is a small square bearing an X. Click on this with the left mouse button to have no fill in the selected object, clicking with the right hand mouse button gives a no colour outline. You can scroll the palette by clicking on the arrows at either end of it.

Immediately above the palette is the **Horizontal Scroll Bar** which allows you to scroll the page, and the objects it contains, horizontally. On the right hand side of the screen in the **Vertical Scroll Bar** which allows you to move the page up and down.

# E1 - FIRST STEPS

Okay, having got the basic screen layout out of the way, let's do some playing about and actually create something. Something simple and easy to do. The trouble with CorelDRAW is that there so much you can do, so simply, that it's hard to know where to begin. Try a rendition of the New York skyline. Normally you would set up all the program defaults first but it's not necessary for this exercise.

a. Switch to the **Rectangle** tool either by clicking on it or by pressing **F6**. Move the cursor, which is now an open cross shape, anywhere on the page. Click the left mouse button and then, while holding down the button, drag the cursor diagonally away from where you clicked. It doesn't matter whether you go up or down. As you move the cursor a rectangle appears.

b. When you have a pleasing shape release the mouse button and the rectangle will be 'frozen' onto the page.

c. Move the cursor down to the Colour palette at the bottom of the screen and click the left mouse button on any colour. The rectangle is instantly filled with the selected colour. If you don't like the colour click on another one.

This is the first major new thing to notice about CorelDRAW 3.0 - you are drawing, editing and manipulating things in full colour.

d. Draw some more rectangles and fill each one with a different colour.

e. Add some squares. Hold down **Ctrl** as you drag the mouse once you have placed the first corner of the object.

You want about a dozen squares and rectangles and you can put them wherever you want on the page - because the next thing to do is align them.

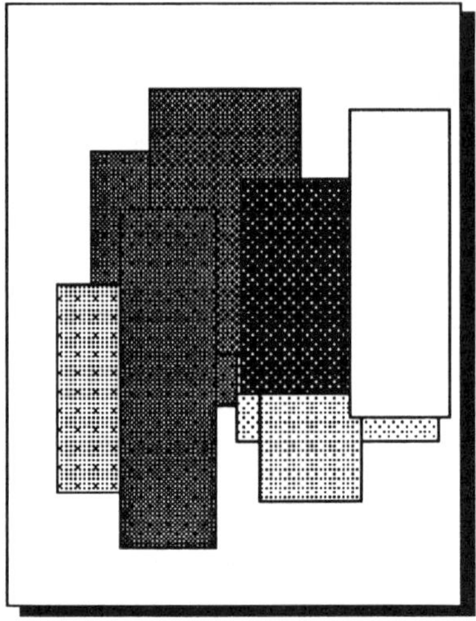

**2.05 Lots of rectangles**

f. Switch back to the Pointer tool by pressing the **Spacebar**. Then click the left mouse button anywhere on screen where there isn't an object, e.g. to the left of the page.

g. Move the pointer to roughly the top left hand corner of the page. Click and hold the left mouse button and then drag the cursor to the bottom right hand corner of the page. As you do so a rectangle appears the outline of which is a dotted line. This is a **Selection Box**. No, it has nothing to do with Christmas chocolates. It is used to select a number of objects all at the same time.

h. Release the mouse button and you will find that the Status Bar says "**x Objects selected on Layer 1**". (We'll come back to layers later.) You should have all your rectangles enclosed within the selection box. If you haven't just do it again. You can drag the box up or down, left or right. Notice that nine black squares have appeared around all the rectangles. These are the **Object Handles**.

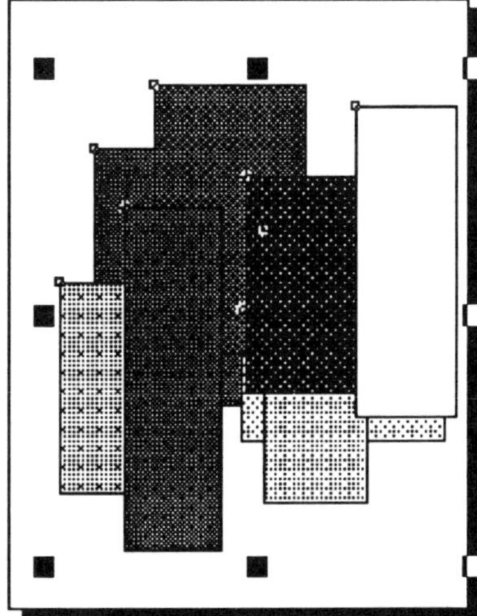

**2.06 Rectangles and Handles**

i. To go off at a tangent for a minute, handles allow you to change the shape and size of objects. Move the pointer on to any one of the corner handles. Click the left mouse button and drag it diagonally away from its current position. The objects within the selection box will grow as you do so. Release the mouse button and the rectangles are resized.

j. But suppose that's not what you want. Simply **Undo** it. Open the **Edit** menu and click on **Undo**. Alternatively press **Alt-Backspace** to activate the command directly. The rectangles return to their former sizes and shapes.

You can always undo you last action if you need to. You can even undo an undo. But it only applies to the last thing you do - CorelDRAW does not have multiple levels of undo unfortunately.

k. Right, back to the exercise. We want all the rectangles aligned along the bottom so that they all share the same baseline. Press **Ctrl-A** which activates the **Align** dialogue box. (You can also activate the dialogue box by opening the **Arrange** menu and then clicking on **Align** but that's more long winded. One of the really nice things about CorelDRAW is the number of keyboard shortcuts that exist for the main things you are likely to want to do.)

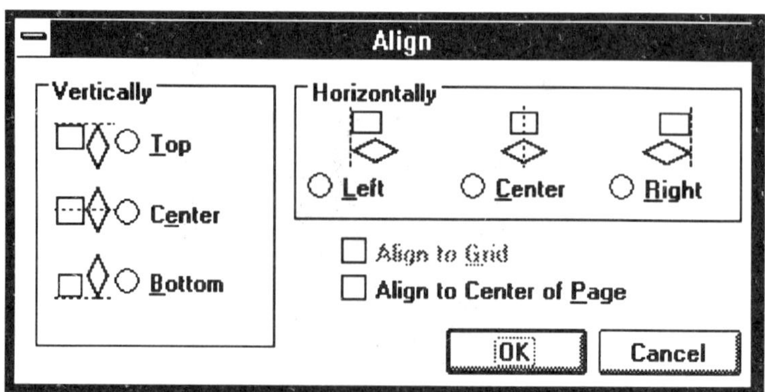


**2.07 Align dialogue box**

1. The dialogue box allows you to align objects vertically, horizontally or both. It also allows you to place an object, or objects, in the centre of the page. Just to see what I mean, click on **Align to Centre of Page** and then on **OK**. All the rectangles are now placed in the centre of the page, one on top of the other in a stack. The first one you drew is at the bottom of the stack and the last one is at the top.

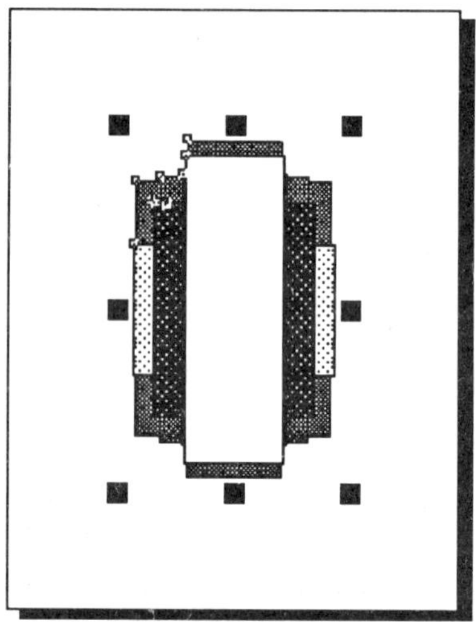

**2.08 Stacked rectangles**

m. That's definitely not what we want so press **Alt-Backspace** to undo it. Notice that all the rectangles are still selected. Press **Ctrl-A** again to bring up the Align dialogue box a second time.

n. This time click on **Bottom** in the Vertical section of the dialogue box. Then click on **OK**. All your rectangles now share a common baseline. In fact they all share a baseline common to the last object you drew.

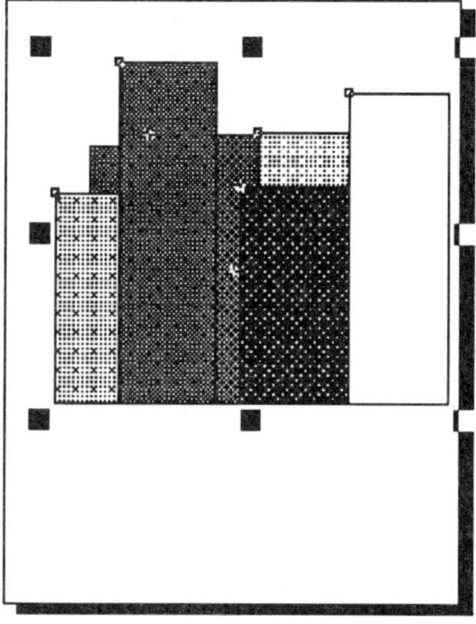

**2.09 Aligned rectangles**

o. All the rectangles are still selected en masse so you can move them as a unit. Move the pointer tool on to any rectangle. Click the left mouse button and then drag it any way you wish but remain within the CorelDRAW window. All the rectangles move with you.

p. Here's another new feature of CorelDRAW 3.0. Click on a rectangle and then drag the mouse way to the right - off the screen. The window will change as you do so. CorelDRAW 3.0 now has active and dynamic scrolling. Drag the pointer way to the left, the window scrolls back. The same happens if you drag up or down.

q. Release the mouse button, it doesn't matter where the rectangles currently are. Press **Alt-A** again. This time click on **Bottom** in the vertical section and on **Align to Centre of Page**. You will have to turn off **Centre** in the Horizontal section of the dialogue box - otherwise you just get the stack of rectangles again. Click on **OK** and the rectangles reappear on the page.

r. It's all well and good being able to see and work with the full colour screen but I bet there are some rectangles behind the visible ones. Ones that are too small to be visible. Just to check, switch to the **Wire Frame Screen** - which is the one you are used to in CorelDRAW 2.01. Press **Shift-F9** to do so. Now you just get the outline of the shapes and no colour.

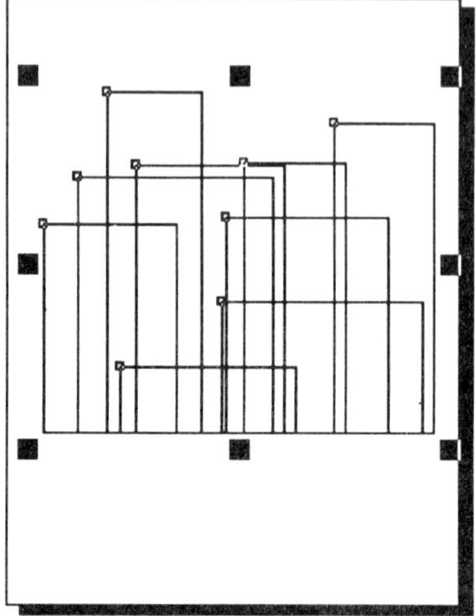

**2.10 Wire Frame Screen rectangles**

s. Sure enough in the illustration above there is a rectangle that is not visible in full colour. As it happens it's the littlest one. Move it to the front of all the others. Click off the page to deselect all the rectangles. Now move the cursor to that rectangle. Because you're on the wire frame screen you have to place the tip of the pointer tool on the outline of the rectangle. Click once to select just that rectangle.

t. Put it on the top of all the others. Press **Shift-PgUp** and its relative position moves to the top of the stack. If you want to do it the long way, open the **Arrange** menu and then click on **To Front**.

u. Switch back to the full colour screen by pressing **Shift-F9** again and there's the rectangle at the front. If you like you can resize just that rectangle by moving its own handles.

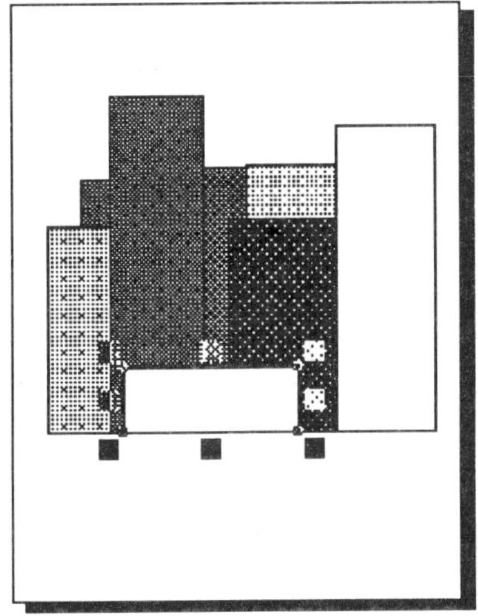

**2.11 Rectangle at front**

v. Play with features of the Align dialogue box yourself. Because it gives you a total of nine possible alignments (three vertical multiplied by three horizontal) compounded with the Align to Centre of Page, it is actually very powerful but at the same time it is simple in execution. The essence of a good feature.

w. You can also use the Align dialogue box either with individual shapes or with pairs. Try selecting two rectangles only - click on one and then hold down **Shift** and click on another - and playing with the alignment features with just those two.

x. Equally play with the stack movement options. Select any individual rectangle. If you press **PgUp** it will be moved forward one place relative to the other rectangles. Pressing **PgDn** will move it back one place. **Shift-PgUp** moves the selected shape right to the front, **Shift-PgDn** moves it right to the back.

# E2 - SECOND STEPS

Drawing the rectangles is probably the simplest thing you can do with CorelDRAW. It's certainly the fastest way to create a quick image that actually looks like something vaguely familiar, hence its use as the first exercise. You can have lots of fun with ellipses and circles too.

a. Select all the rectangles and then press **Delete**. They all vanish. That is the only way to erase images in CorelDRAW by the way. Because CorelDRAW uses vector graphics you cannot rub out a line or a shape you can only delete it in its entirety.

b. Press **F7** to select the **Ellipse** tool. The cursor becomes the same shape as for the rectangle tool. You draw ellipses and circles in exactly the same way as you did rectangles and squares. Just drag the cursor to draw ellipses, hold down **Ctrl** as you drag and you get circles.

c. Now to create some instant Pop Art. Draw some circles and ellipses. Each one should have no fill - click with the left mouse button on the **X** at the extreme left hand side of the colour palette. Draw big circles and little ones, some overlapping, some completely inside others and so on. Something like Figure 2.12, it doesn't matter if they go over the edge of the page.

d. Drag a selection box around the whole lot. The Status Bar will say "**x objects selected on Layer 1**". Now press **Ctrl-C**. This is the **Combine** command - which we'll cover in more detail later. You can also activate it by opening the **Arrange** menu and then clicking on **Combine**. The Status Bar now says "**Curve on Layer 1 Number of nodes: xx**". What you have done is take all the circles and ellipses and combined them into a single object.

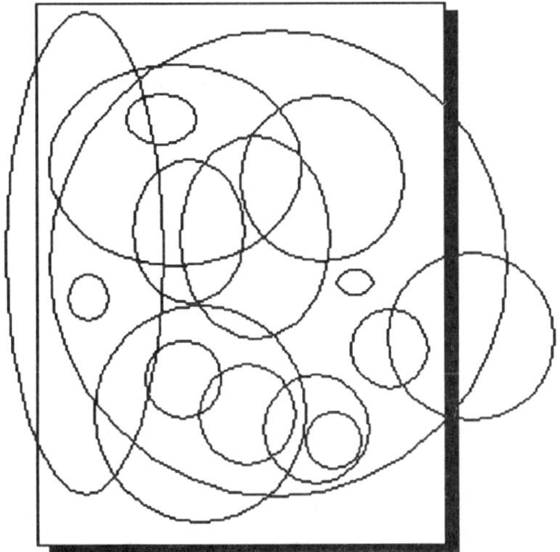

**2.12 Circles**

CorelDRAW regards all objects, other than rectangles, ellipses and text, as curves. Even then rectangles and ellipses are merely special varieties of curves. Text is a special case which we'll come to later but even that can become curves.

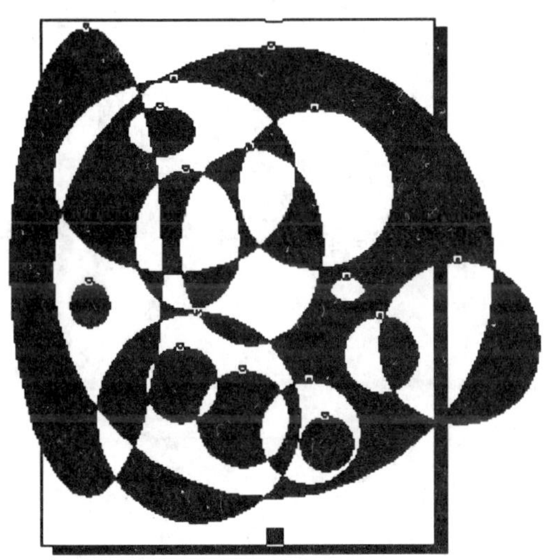

**2.13 Pop Art**

e. Now move the pointer down to the colour palette along the bottom of the screen and click the left mouse button on the full Black - it's the first colour in the palette. You should get something like Figure 2.13 on the previous page.

f. The non-coloured areas are not white - they are holes in the image. Draw a square that is roughly the same size as the page. Fill it with blue and then send it to the back of the image by pressing **Pg-Dn**. You can see the blue fill through the holes in the combined ellipse. Can you work out why a hole appears in a particular place? Rather than tell you I'll show you.

g. Delete the blue square and the combined ellipse. Draw a vertical ellipse that covers most of the page. Then draw a horizontal ellipse that overlaps it but which extends either side of it. Now draw a circle in the middle of the two. Finally draw a third ellipse that overlays the central circle and extends only over the vertical circle. You should have something like Figure 2.14 - it's easier to show than to describe.

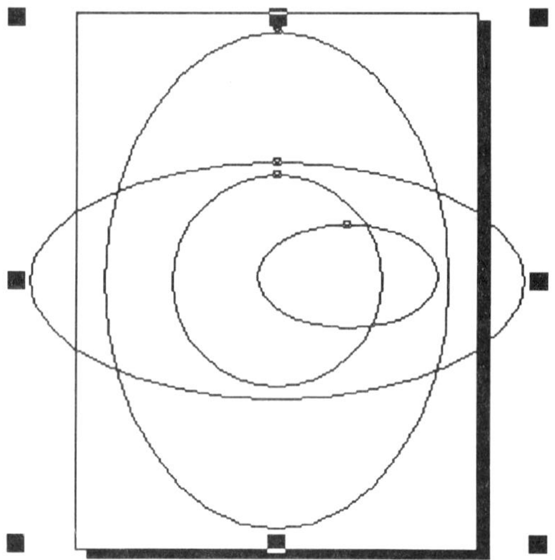

**2.14 Ellipse and circle**

h. Now select the four objects by dragging a bounding box around them and then press **Ctrl-C** to combine them into a single curve. Fill this with black. You'll end up with something like Figure 2.15.

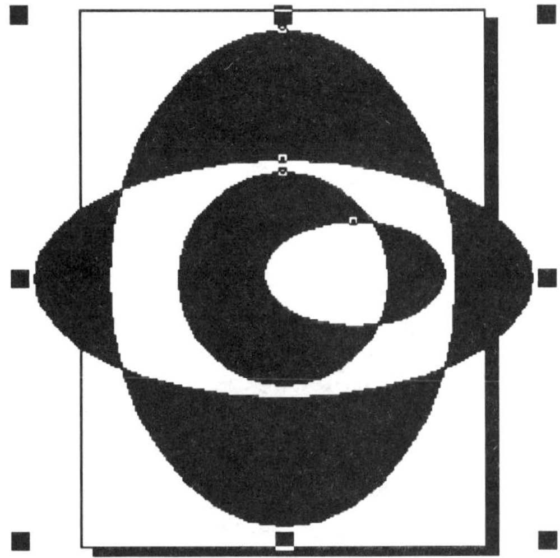

**2.15 Filled curve**

The black areas are filled and the white areas are the actual holes. The trick to working out what is where is in the number of objects that are stacked on top of each other.

Consider the first two ellipses. Where these overlap there is a hole but the parts outside the overlap are filled as normal. Where the circle overlaps the hole, things get filled in again but where the final ellipse overlaps, it is filled in. That's the clue. Anywhere where a multiple of two objects overlap will be a hole, i.e. when the number of objects is an even number. Where one, three or five objects overlap they will be filled, i.e. when the number of objects is an odd number.

By the way, if you combine two or more objects that contain colour the filled areas will automatically become the colour of the last object selected. In the case of selecting objects with a selection box this means that last object within the selection that you drew.

i. If you want to separate the objects back to individual items press **Ctrl-K** or open the **Arrange** menu and click on **Break Apart**. (Be warned, once you break the objects apart you no longer have ellipses and circles. Instead you have individual curves.)

j. Delete the objects and draw a single rectangle, about half the size of the page. Fill it with any colour you like and then switch back to the Pointer tool. The object has its handles around it.

k. Click on the object a second time, or double click on it if the handles aren't present. The handles now appear differently. On each side they are double headed arrows, at the corners they are curved arrows and in the middle there is a circle with a dot in it. These are the **Rotation Handles**. You can go back to the normal handles at any time by clicking on an object a second time.

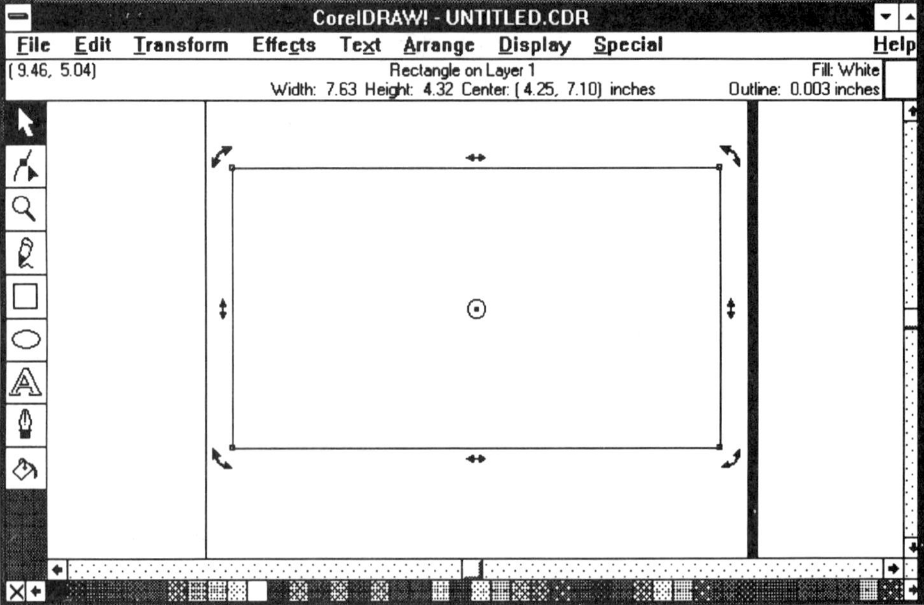


**2.16 Rotation handles**

l. Take things a bit at a time. Click on the top left hand handle. Now move the mouse down to the bottom left, while holding down the mouse button. The rectangle will rotate. As it does so the Status Bar tells you what the rotation angle is, e.g. Angle 42.3 degrees. The rectangle is rotating around the central circle. Release the mouse button and the rectangle is moved to the new position.

m. Press **Alt-Backspace** to undo the rotation and the shape returns to its original position. Move the pointer on to the central circle - it will become a cross shape. Drag this down to the lower left hand corner of the rectangle so that the centre of the circle roughly overlays the corner of the shape. For the minute exact accuracy is not too important. Release the mouse button.

n. Now move the pointer back to the top left hand handle and drag it down again. This time the rectangle rotates around the bottom left hand corner of itself. It's as if that corner is fixed in place. Try moving the centre of rotation, i.e. the circle, to a different corner and then rotating the rectangle again.

o. Open the **Transform** menu and click on **Clear Transformations**. The rectangle will be placed back into its original position and the rotation handles vanish to be replaced by the ordinary ones. Click on the rectangle again to bring the rotational handles back.

p. The handles at the edges of the rectangle control the skewing of the shape. Move the pointer to the one at the top of the shape. Again it will become a cross. Drag this to the right, you can only move the handle horizontally, and watch what happens to the shape. It becomes a rhombus. Clear the transformation again, either by pressing **Alt-Backspace** or by using the command in the **Transform** menu.

q. Now move the pointer to the handle at the right hand edge of the rectangle. You can drag this vertically. Notice that when you move any of the skewing handles the side opposite the handle you are moving remains fixed in place. Try skewing the shape horizontally and then vertically. Then rotate it. The combinations of possible shapes are almost infinite.

r. You can also constrain the rotation or the skewing by using the **Ctrl** key. Get the original rectangle back again and its rotational handles. Move the pointer to the top left hand corner handle. Hold down **Ctrl** and then drag the handle. Watch the Status Bar as you do so. The rectangle now moves only in increments of 15 degrees. (You can change the constraining angle as you'll see later.) The constrain also affects skewing.

You can rotate and skew circles and ellipses, and text for that matter, in exactly the same way.

# E3 - LINES AND FILLS

Let's take a look at the new roll-ups. A roll-up is an interactive dialogue box that exists on the screen all the time - but only if you want it to. Corel's major innovation though has been to make the dialogue box act as window blinds. You can have the roll-ups open where they occupy screen space of course but you can also cause them to roll up out of the way so that only the title bar of each dialogue box is visible. Then when you want to use the dialogue box you simply roll it down again. This exercise only uses two of the roll-ups - we'll come to the rest later.

a. Select the rectangle drawing tool and draw a large square that almost fills the page. Now press the **Spacebar** to reselect the Pointer tool. The handles will appear around the square. Now click once on the **Outline** tool to open it out. Click on the roll-up icon - the second from the left on the top row.

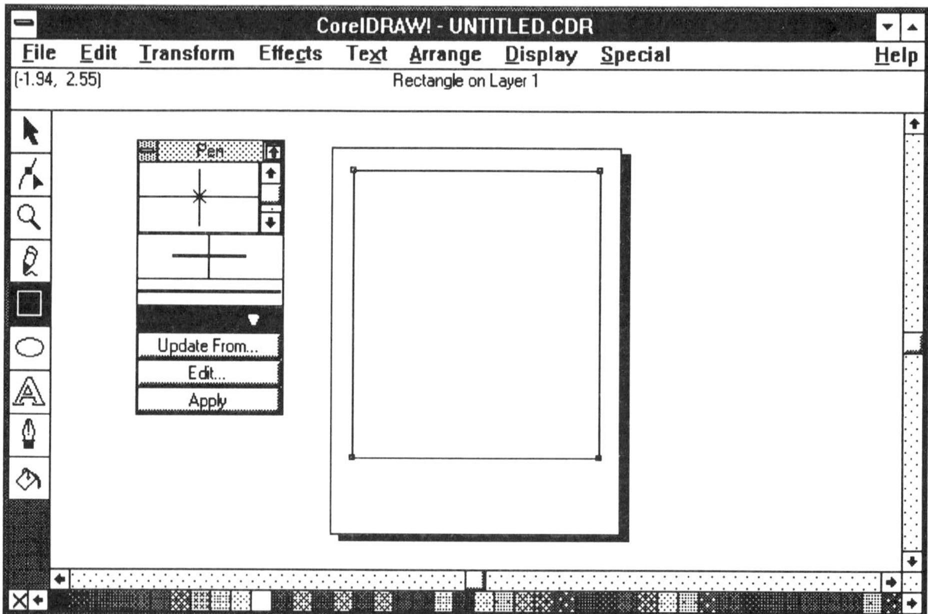


**2.17 First square and roll up**

The roll-up is divided into a number of sections. The top section, which currently shows a line between two arrows, is the **Line Thickness**.

Immediately below this are two sections side by side. These affect the **Arrows** that can be applied to any line. The left hand one is always the start of the line, the right hand one is the end of the line.

Below that is another line that runs the width of the roll-up box. This is the **Dashed Line** selector. CorelDRAW allows you to use dotted lines - you can even create your own.

Beneath this is the **Line Colour**, by default it will always be whatever colour you last used.

Finally there is a set of three buttons. The first is labelled **Update From** and what it does is update the outline pen roll-up with the information from a selected object. The second button is labelled **Edit** and that activates the full dialogue box for the Pen Outline. The final button is labelled **Apply** which simply means apply the settings to the selected object.

b. As you have the square selected you can use the roll-up immediately. Go through the options in the roll-up one by one. Firstly, click on the arrowheads to the right of the Line Thickness. If you click on the down arrow you get a large cross, meaning no line. If you click on the up arrow the line becomes thicker.

   Unfortunately you cannot tell from the roll-up just how thick the line is. You have to click on **Apply** so that the Status Bar tells you the thickness of the line you have selected. As it happens, each click on the arrow head makes the line 0.01 of an inch, or roughly 0.75 points, thicker. The maximum line thickness that you can apply from the roll-up by the way is half an inch or 36 points.

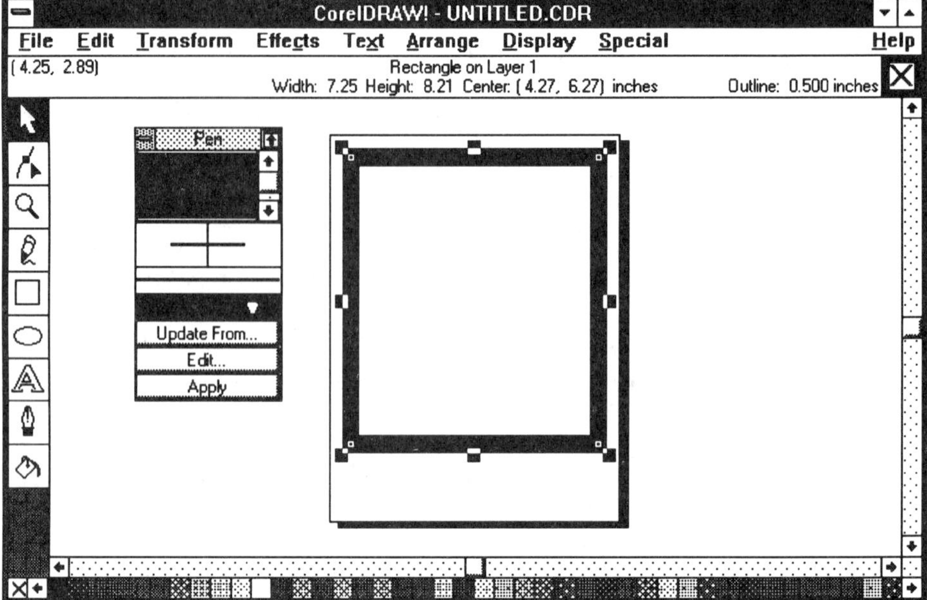


**2.18 Line thickness applied**

c. You can't apply arrowheads to a square so skip that one for a minute. Click on the **Dashed Line** button instead. When you do so another selection box pops-out from the roll-up. This is actually an independent dialogue box.

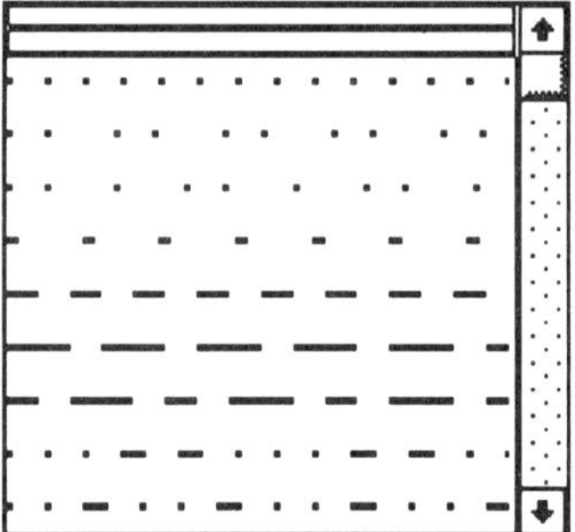

**2.19 Dashed line selector**

d. You can select any of the dashed lines that are available, and there are sixteen pre-defined ones for you to choose from. Just click on the one you want to select it, the dialogue box vanishes and the line is shown in the roll-up. Now click on **Apply** to use it with the square. Be warned, you can get some very odd effects when you use dashed lines with large line thicknesses.

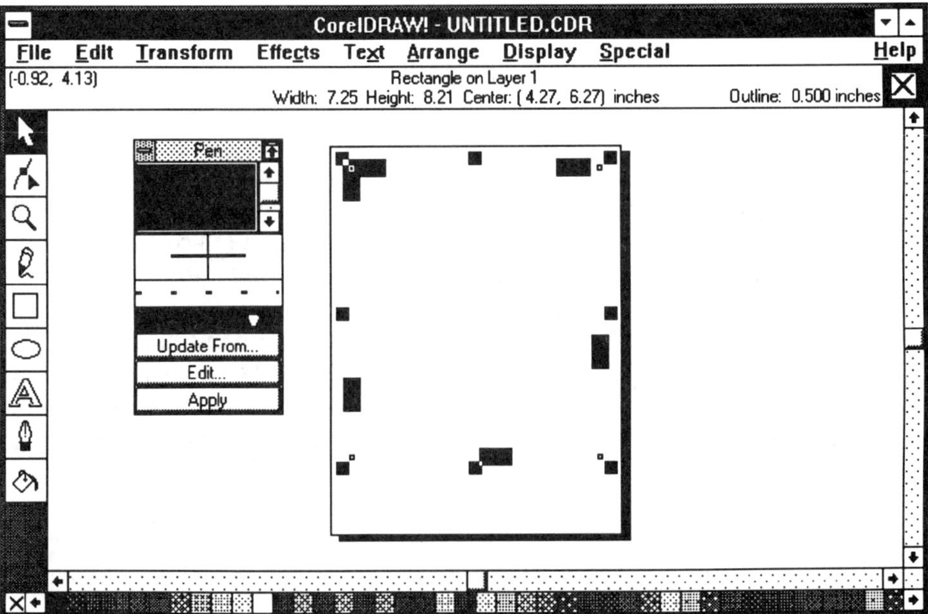


**2.20 Dashed line applied**

e. To remove a dashed line simply click on the selector button again and then on the first line in the dialogue box. This will give you back the solid line.

f. To change the line colour, click on the solid colour button, the one just above the button labelled **Update From**. When you do so a little mini-palette will appear from which you can select any of the available colours. When you click on the colour the roll-up is updated, in both the colour button and the line thickness area, and you then have to click on **Apply** to apply it to the selected object.

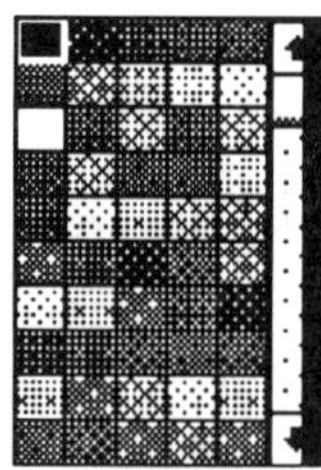

**2.21 Mini-palette**

g. You can apply colour to a selected object in another way too. Move your cursor down to the palette along the bottom of the screen. Clicking on a colour with the left mouse button will apply the selected colour as a Fill colour. Clicking with the right mouse button will apply the colour as an Outline colour.

h. Having applied your changes you don't need the roll-up until the next time. You could close it completely and reactivate it the next time you want it but it is better if you just roll it up. Click on the top right hand corner of the roll-up and the main area of it vanishes. You are left with just the title bar of the roll-up.

i. However, it is now overlaying some part of the screen area. Open its own Control Box, i.e. click on the left hand corner of it. This contains a number of commands.

**Roll down** does just that. It is only active when the dialogue box is rolled up.

**Roll up** closes the box. Again, only active when the box is rolled down.

**Arrange** will move the roll-up to the top left hand corner of the screen area, because this is currently the only roll-up on screen.

**Arrange All** has the same affect as the previous command but it will apply to all roll-ups that are on screen.

**Help** activates the on-screen help.

**Close** terminates the roll-up.

j. Click on **Arrange** to place the roll-up out of the way.

k. With the square still selected, click on the **Fill** tool and then on the **Fill Roll-up**, the second icon on the top line that appears.

**2.22 Fill Roll-up**

l. This roll-up contains a wealth of available options. The main part of the roll-up contains the mini-palette but down the left hand side of this are four buttons that control other types of fill. We'll cover them one by one. The first button is already depressed. This controls the normal colour fill.

m. To fill the square with a colour simply click on the colour you want to use - there is no need to click on **Apply**. The colour will be applied almost instantly, though this depends on the machine you use. For example, on the Laser which has very limited resources the hour-glass barely has time to appear as the colour is applied. On the 486 the process is literally instantaneous. You can scroll through the colours in the palette by clicking on the scroll bar to the right of it.

n. A minor nuisance. There is no way to apply no fill from the roll-up. You have to click on the **X** at the extreme left of the palette along the bottom of the screen to do that.

o. Click on the second button on the left - the one that contains a graduated colour. This is the **Fountain Fill**. When you do so the appearance of the roll-up changes.

**2.23 Fountain fill roll-up**

p. The main part of the dialogue box shows a grey graduation with white at the top and black at the bottom and a series of greys in between. Beneath this there is a black button and a white button - clicking on either one brings up the mini-palette of colours. Under these are two further buttons, the one on the left, which is depressed, is for **Linear Fountain Fill** and the one on the right is for **Radial Fountain Fill**. If you click on the radial button the roll-up changes again so that white appears in the centre. Then click on **Apply** to fill the square.

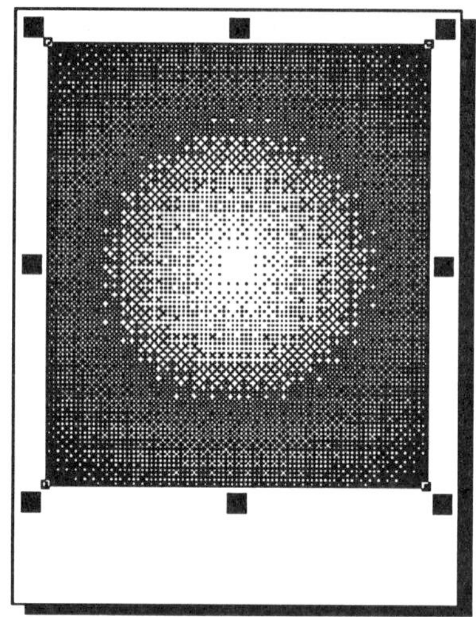

**2.24 Radial filled square**

q. But life is now much more interesting than that. The fountain fill roll-up is now interactive! Move the cursor into the fountain in the roll-up. Click and hold the left mouse button. Two lines will appear. Where they cross is the centre of the fountain fill. Move the mouse around, e.g. to the bottom right hand corner, and then release the button. The fill changes so that white is in that corner.

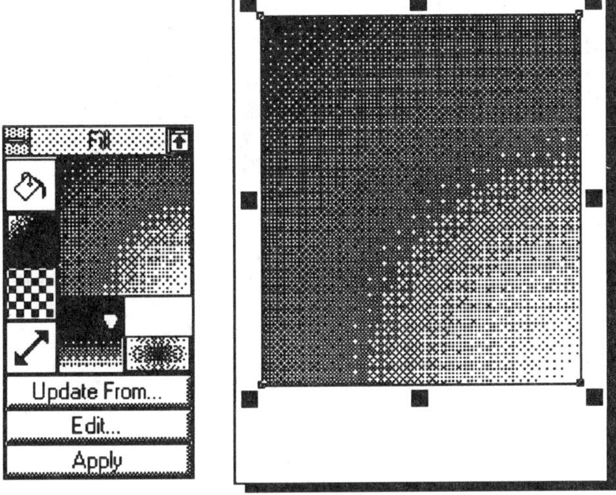


**2.25 Fountain fill changed**

r. If you're careful you can even move the lines right outside the roll-up fill area and have the fountain shunted beyond the edge of the roll-up. That sounds odd but I can't think of another way to describe it. Play with it and you'll see what I mean.

s. To get back to the original standard fill hold down **Ctrl** and click in the roll-up. Be careful you don't move the mouse as you do so, the cursor needs to be somewhere near the centre of the fill area. It won't work if you have the cursor in the left hand corner for example.

t. Click on the **Linear** fill button again. You can manipulate this in the same way as you did the Radial fill. Move the cursor into the fill area, click and hold the mouse button. This time you get a single line that radiates from the centre of the fill. You can rotate this around the area until you get an angle you like. Then click on **Apply** to fill the object with it.

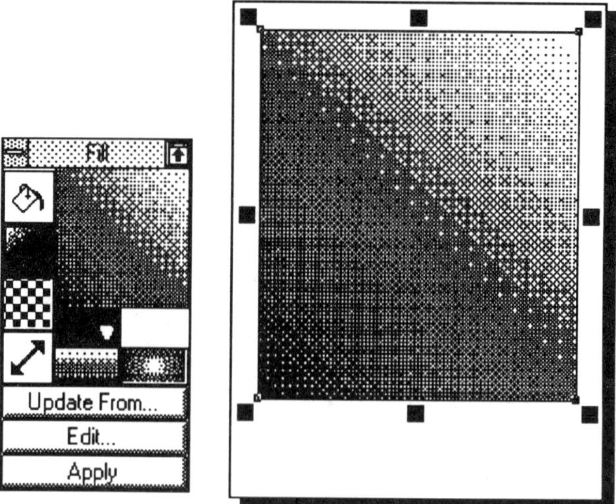


**2.26 Linear fill rotated**

u. If you want more control over the angle of the fountain fill, click on the button labelled **Edit**. This brings up a full dialogue box which gives you much greater control of the angle. Unfortunately clicking on the arrowheads beside the angle increases or decreases this in increments of five. If you want other angles you have to overwrite the angle manually. Notice that zero degrees means that the white is on the right which is a bit odd because when we opened the roll-up in the first place white was at the top, actually at 90 degrees.

v. You can also change the **Edge Pad** in the dialogue box. This refers to the amount of one colour that appears in the fill. Click on the arrowheads beside the command and watch what happens to the displayed fill. Again the increments are in fives.

w. Once you have made your selection click on **OK** to return to the roll-up. Then click on **Apply** to fill the selected object with the new settings.

x. If you hold down **Ctrl** while you move the indicator in the roll-up then the angle will be constrained to increments of fifteen degrees.

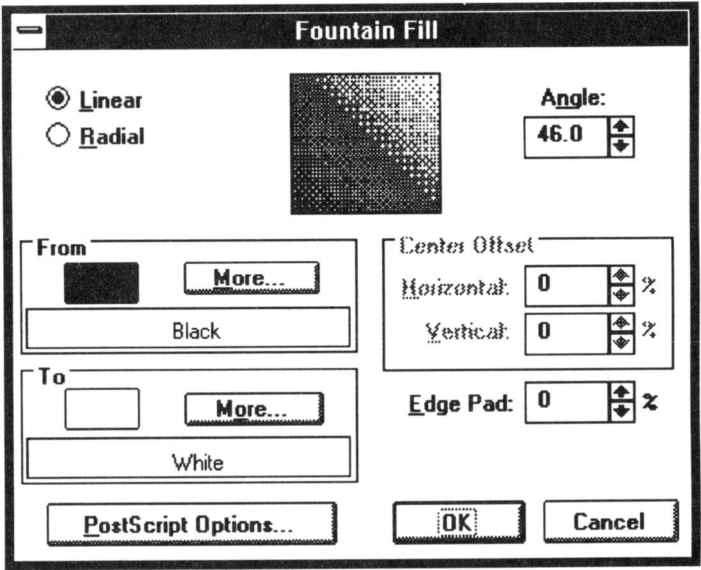


**2.27 Fountain Fill dialogue box**

The new interactive ways that you can use the fountain fills have removed a lot of the hassle that people used to experience with using these in earlier versions of CorelDRAW. The other fills are covered in the next exercise.

y. As with the Outline Pen roll-up you can close the Fill roll-up and arrange it on the screen. This time when you click on **Arrange** or **Arrange All** you will find that the Fill roll-up goes to the top left hand corner of the screen and the Outline roll-up is placed beneath it.

# E4 - ALTERNATIVE FILLS

CorelDRAW provides you with a total of five different kinds of fills. Pure colour and fountain fill are the first two and these were covered in the previous exercise. You can also use Two-Colour fills, previously called Bitmap fills, and Full-Colour fills, previously called Vector Fills. Finally there is an extensive range of PostScript patterns that you can use. The Fill roll-up allows you to set any of the first four fill options, the PostScript patterns are only available from the Fill tool itself - because they cannot be displayed on screen. In this exercise we're going to take a look at the pattern colour fills, still using the same square as before.

a. Make sure the square is still selected and then click on the top right hand corner of the fill roll-up to open it.

b. Click on the checker board pattern. This brings up the **Two-Colour fill** option. First of all just click on Apply to fill the square with the default pattern. In the illustration it looks as if the square is filled with squares - in fact it appears on my screen the same way - but it isn't. It is actually filled with little circles.

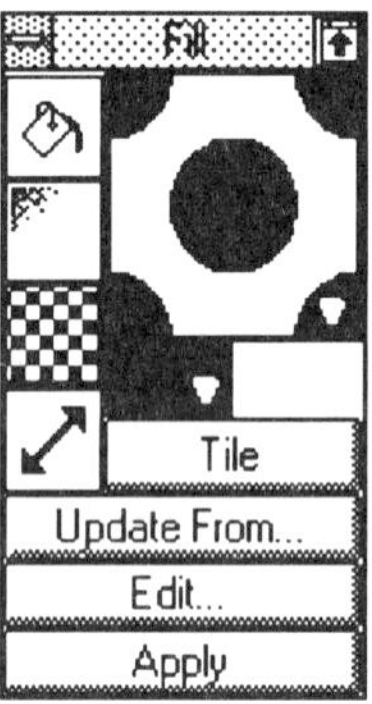


**2.28 Two-Colour fill roll-up**

c. Notice that the fill pattern in the roll-up has a little triangle in the bottom right hand corner. This shows that there are more patterns available. Click on the triangle or on the default pattern itself to expand the available patterns.

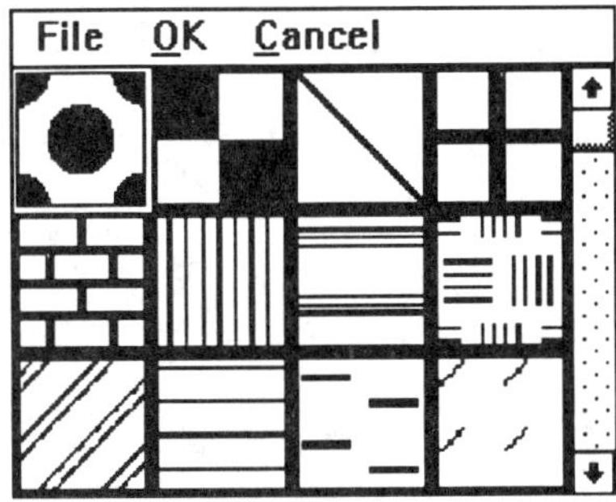


**2.29 Available patterns**

d. CorelDRAW 3.0 comes with 45 pre-defined patterns for you to use. To select one just double click on it. For argument's sake click on the Happy Face pattern - you'll have to scroll down through the patterns to find it. Then apply it to the square on the page.

e. Small, isn't it? Now for another new trick that CorelDRAW 3.0 includes. Click on the button labelled **Tile**. Two little tiles will appear on the square on the page. You can use these to reshape and resize the pattern interactively. If you look closely you'll see that there is a little square connecting the two tiles. Drag this down the square and the tiles expand as you do so. Drag it until the tiles just fit inside the square on the page.

f. You can move the tiles in other ways too. What you have done so far is simply enlarge the tile pattern. Let's actually reshape it. Click and hold the mouse button in the right hand tile. Drag this downwards so that roughly half the tile is now below the original position.

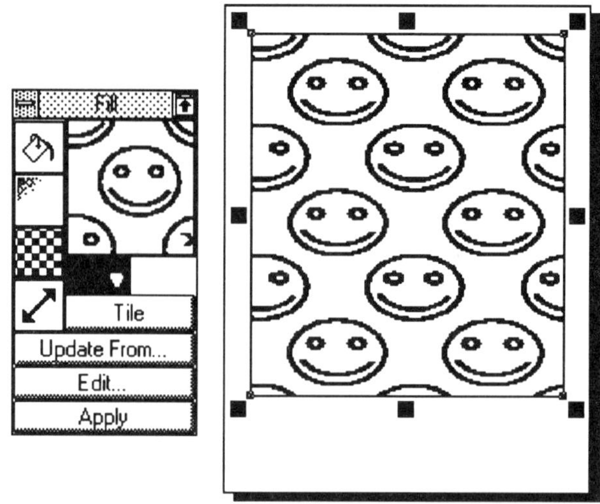


2.30 Pattern tiled simply

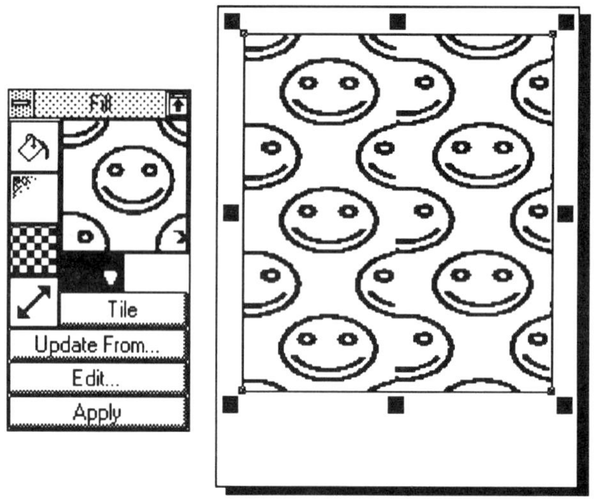


2.31 Tile dragged and applied

g. Now click on **Apply** in the roll-up and the new tiling is applied. (The tiling is not as interactive as it could be unfortunately - at least not on the beta version I'm using.) You should get something like Figure 2.31 opposite.

h. You can also use the tiles to fill an object completely with a single occurrence of a pattern. Put the right hand tile back where it came from and then drag the connecting square down and to the right so that the left hand tile fills the square on the page.

i. Now click on **Apply** again and the square is completely filled with the pattern.

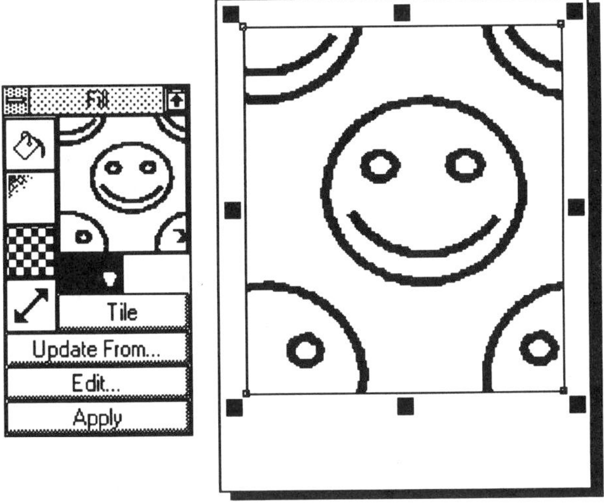


**2.32 Single pattern fill**

j. Try the **Full-Colour patterns**. These are stored on your hard disk as ordinary CorelDRAW files but they have an extension of .PAT. (Nice of them to name them after my wife, isn't it?) Click on the diagonal arrow button, the one below the checker board pattern. The fill area shows an empty space, actually it contains a diagonal line running from top left to bottom right which means the same thing.

k. Click on the fill pattern and it will expand, in the same way as the Two-Colour fill did, to show the available patterns.

**2.33 Full-Colour Patterns**

l. Excuse the illustration but trying to show full colour in monochrome is somewhat difficult. Double click on the CorelDRAW **Balloon** to select it as the pattern. The balloon appears in the fill pattern area. Click on **Apply** to fill the square on the page.

m. Notice that any previous tiling you applied with the Two-Colour fill is now lost and you have lots of little balloons. Retile the pattern to fill the square completely with just one balloon. Be warned, using full colour patterns on a machine with limited resources will make your computer really work. On the Laser it takes nearly seventeen seconds for the retiled image to appear. On the 486, admittedly with Dr. Watson, Word for Windows and CD-Audio running at the same time, it takes nearly nine seconds for the pattern to retile. Full-Colour patterns are very memory intensive.

n. If you open the pattern selector again and choose another pattern and then apply it you will find that the tile returns to the default. Again though this may be different in the actual release version of the program.

We'll cover creating Full-Colour patterns later. This is how you can create your own Two-Colour patterns.

o. Clear the pattern in the square by clicking on the **X** at the end of the palette along the bottom of the screen. Click on the checker board button again and then on the button labelled **Edit**. This will bring up a full dialogue box.

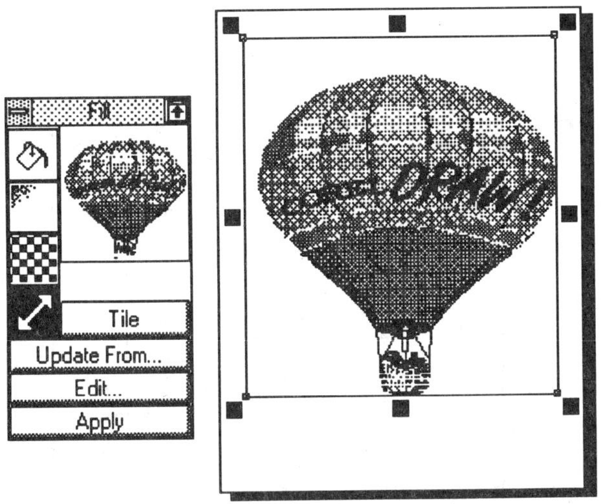


2.34 Single balloon pattern

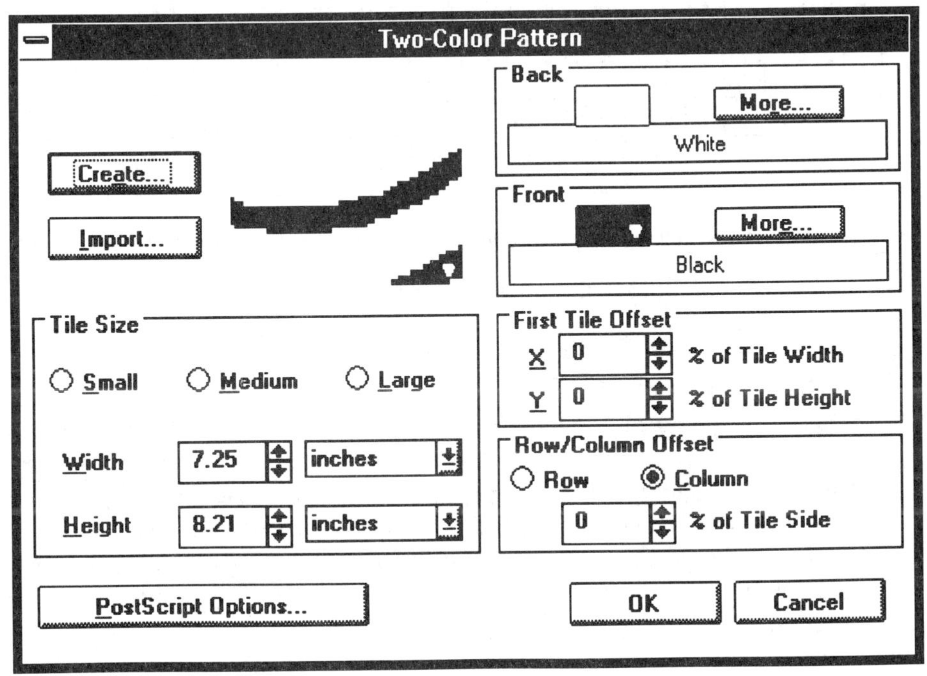


2.35 Two-Colour pattern edit dialogue box

p. Click on the button labelled **Create** and you get the Bitmap Pattern Editor dialogue box.

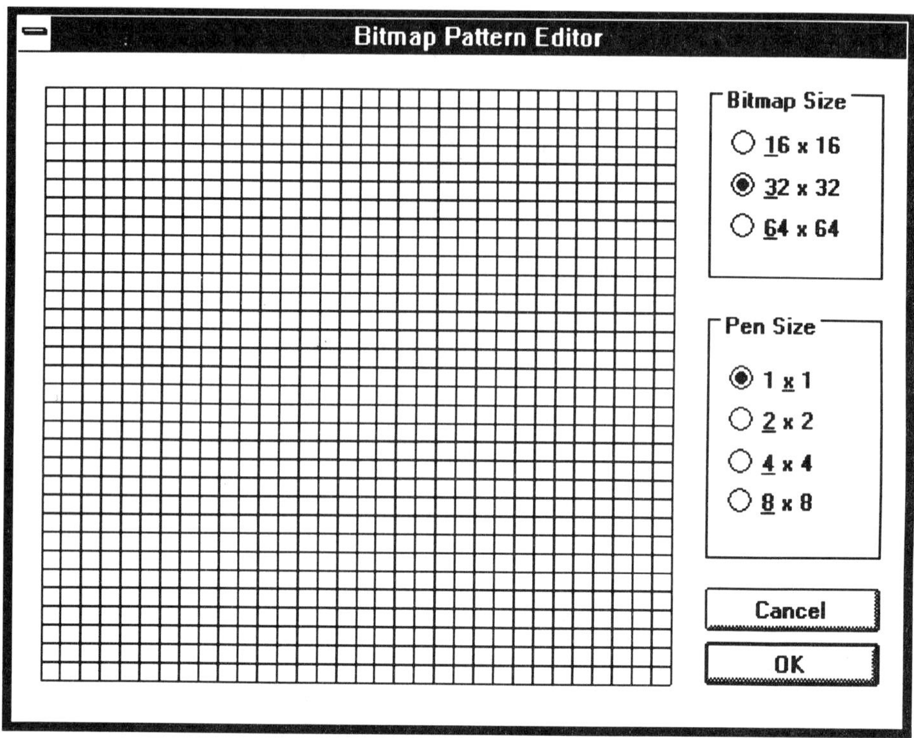


**2.36 Bitmap editor dialogue box**

q. You have a choice of three sizes of pattern. **16 x 16** should be used for simple patterns, **32 x 32** for intermediate patterns and **64 x 64** for complex ones, e.g. where you want curves to appear. The Pen size is simply the number of squares that will be changed at a time. To create a pattern, choose the size you want to use and the pen size. Move the cursor onto the grid and click. The grey squares of the grid become black. To remove a black square click the right mouse button. You build up the image as you would in any paint style program.

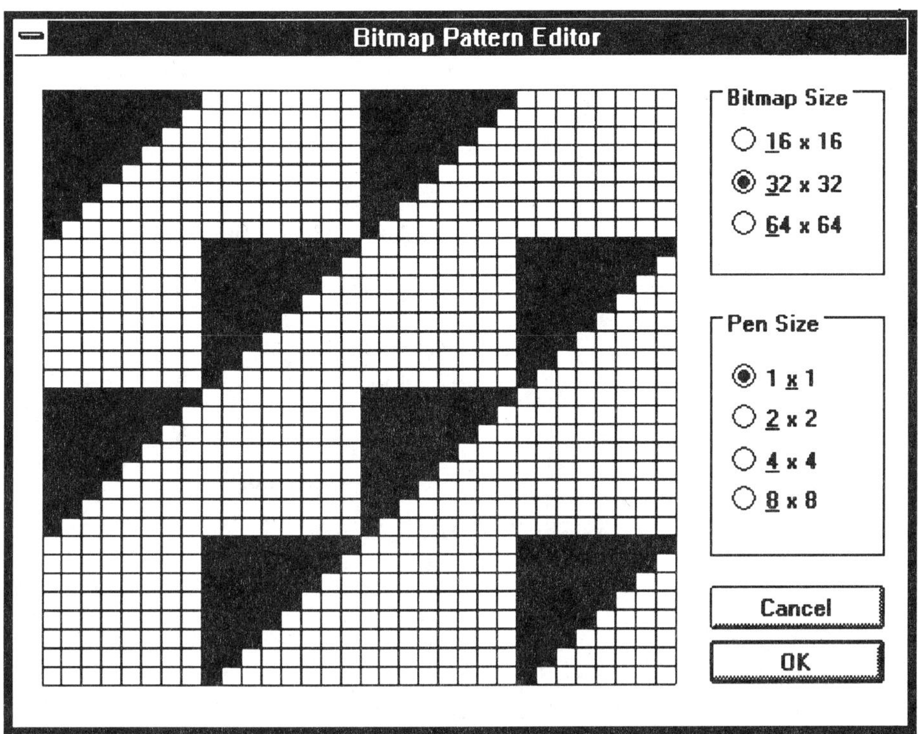


**2.37 New pattern created**

r. Once you have created your pattern click on **OK** to close the editor and go back to Two-Colour Pattern dialogue box. Click on Pattern area to select the new pattern you have just created. It will have been added to the end of the existing patterns. Click on **OK** again to close the dialogue box and go back to the roll-up. You can set the parameters for the new pattern in the dialogue box but using the roll-up allows you to do so dynamically.

s. You can now use the new pattern just as you would any of the others.

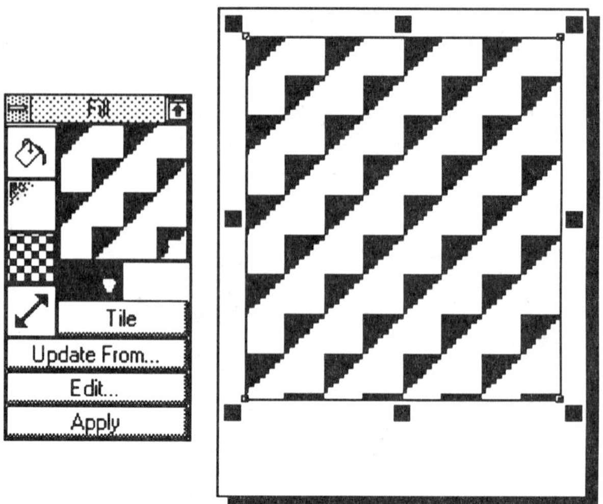


2.38 New pattern in use

t. As an alternative to creating patterns you can import any bitmap and use that as a pattern. Click on **Edit** again and this time when the dialogue box appears click on **Import** which brings up a second dialogue box.

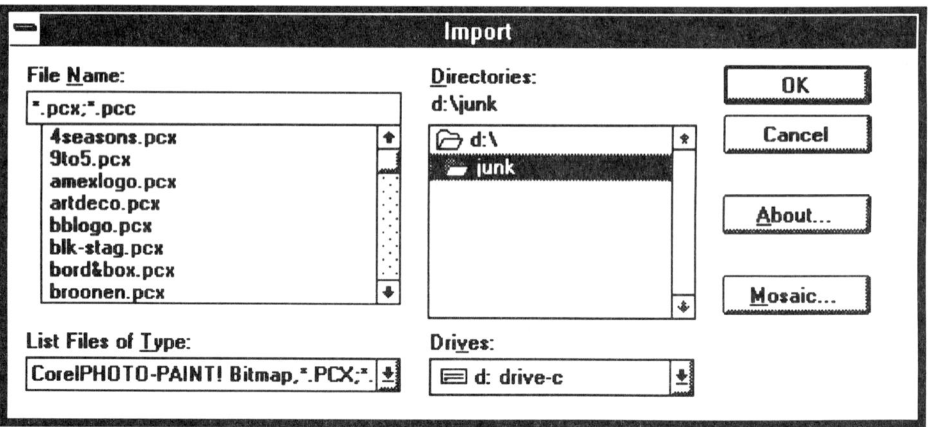


2.39 Import bitmap dialogue box

u. You can import any vector format graphic, e.g. a CDR file, and use it as a bitmap fill but why would you want to? The whole point of vector format files is that they tend to be full colour and easy to manipulate. Bitmaps on the other hand are two colour and fixed resolution. Therefore, I suggest that you only import bitmap format files for the Two-Colour fills, that means files with extensions of BMP, PCC, PCX, GIF, TGA and TIF.

v. Select the drive that contains the images you want to import, then select the **File Type** from the list of options. A list of files with the selected extension will appear in the dialogue box on the left. Double click on a filename and the file will be imported. As it is being imported a message box appears telling you far the process has got.

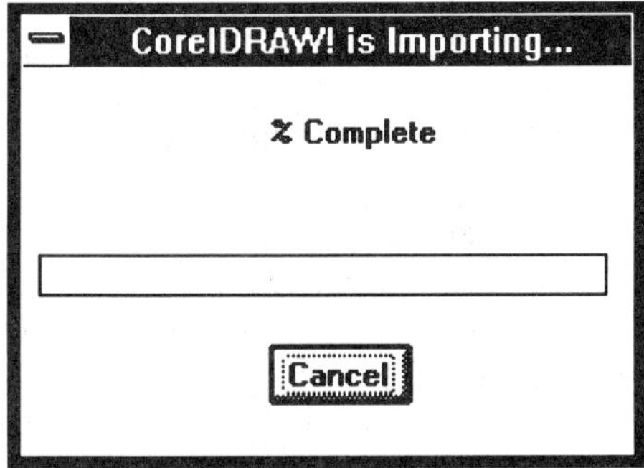


**2.40 Import message box**

w. As with creating an image, the imported file is appended to the end of the existing patterns. Click on **OK** to close the dialogue box and return to the roll-up. You can then apply the pattern, tile it and colour it as you wish. To change the colours click on the mini-palette buttons.

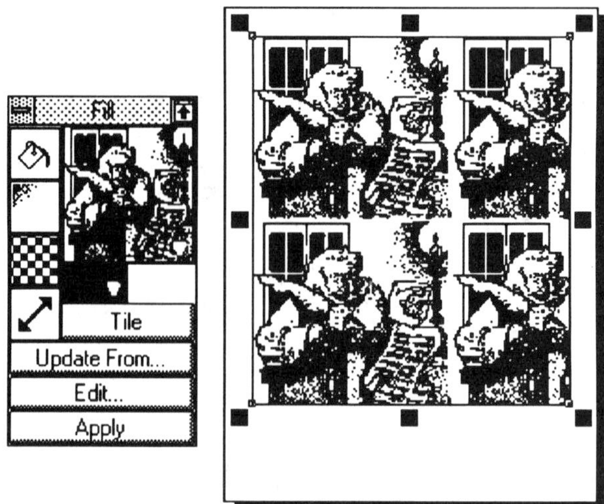


**2.41 Imported bitmap as fill**

You can import vector images to use as Full-Colour patterns in the same way. However, it has to be said that importing vector format files will place a heavy strain on your system resources. To import the Snowbarn file as a vector fill pattern, on the Laser, takes over twenty minutes! But then that particular image is very complex and it does contain fountain fills. On the whole you want to avoid images that have any fountain fills in them if you want to use the image as a Full-Colour fill.

Play with the facilities for creating bitmap fills and for importing simple images. But remember every pattern you create or import will increase the amount of disk space that CorelDRAW requires. If you are not careful you could very easily end up filling your hard disk.

By the way, if you find that the program crashes as you are importing a file it may be because you have run out of disk space for the temporary files that CorelDRAW will create in the process. CorelDRAW can create enormous temporary files, anything up to 6 Mb plus is not unusual, so make sure you have lots of free disk space before using the program. Equally it makes a lot of sense to ensure that your hard disk is compressed, using PC Tools Compress or Norton Speed Disk, before you use CorelDRAW.

# E5 - SAVING FILES

As a result of the previous couple of exercises you may want to save what you have done so far to work with it later. CorelDRAW allows you to save files very easily because it uses standard keyboard shortcuts.

a. Press **Ctrl-S**, the shortcut for **Save**, and a dialogue box will appear.

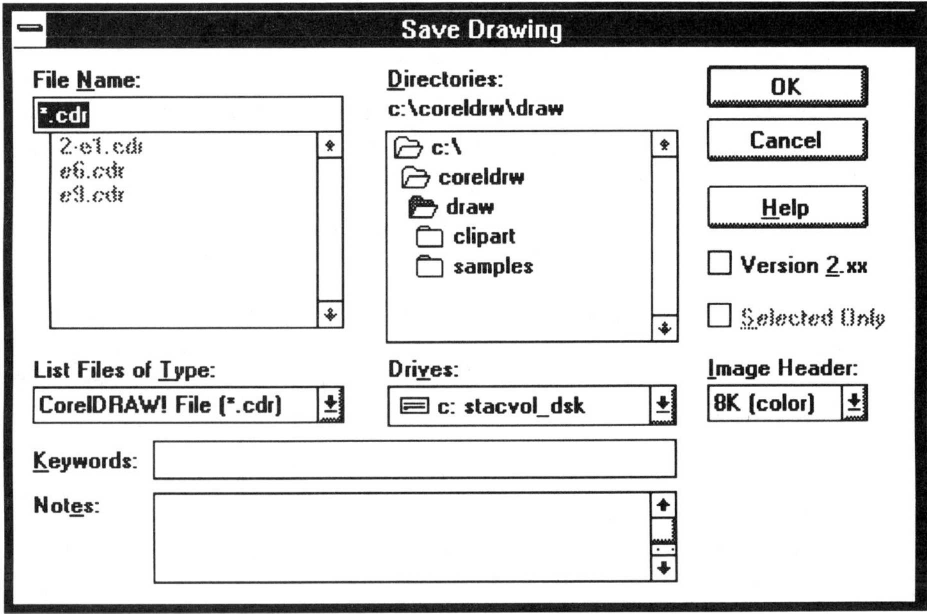


**2.42 Save dialogue box**

b. The dialogue box is sub-divided into a number of parts; all the major dialogue boxes that handle importing and exporting files in CorelDRAW look much the same. The thing that is immediately apparent is the filename because it is highlighted. You may name a file using any of the standard MS-DOS rules about filenames, e.g. up to eight characters. You don't need to add an extension because the program will do it for you. Anything you type will automatically overwrite the highlighted section.

c. The central area of the dialogue box allows you to log into any directory of the current drive. If you want change directory just click on the appropriate bit. For example, to go back to the root directory you click on **C:** at the top of the directory area and then you can navigate your way back down to another directory. You can do this with the keyboard but it's much faster to use the mouse.

d. Below the directory area is a single line labelled **Drives**. You have to use this to log onto a different drive - you cannot do it from the directory area. Clicking on the arrow at the end of the line will pop-down a list box containing all the available drives on your system.

e. Below the Filename area is a single line labelled **List Files of Type**. In this case you have a choice of either CorelDRAW file or CorelDRAW Pattern. Changing from one to the other will automatically update the file extension for you.

f. On the right hand side is a button labelled **Version 2.xx**. By clicking on this you can save the file in the format that was used for CorelDRAW 2.0 or 2.01. Version 3.0 uses a slightly different format to either of these and you cannot load a version 3 file into an earlier version of CorelDRAW although you can do the reverse. If you still have CorelDRAW 2.xx on your system you may want to use this format, otherwise I suggest you don't bother but use the CorelDRAW 3.0 format instead.

g. The button labelled **Selected Only** means that only those items that you have previously selected, e.g by dragging a selection box around them, will be written to disk rather than the entire file.

h. **Keywords** is a new feature. It actually doesn't have a lot to do with CorelDRAW per se, rather it is intended for use with Mosaic the graphics file management program that comes with CorelDRAW. In this program you can sort and/or find files on the basis of their keywords. You can use any words you like as they are intended to be used as a memory jogger for you - not the program. Keywords are optional, you don't have to use them.

i. **Notes** are just that. You can now add notes to your file. For example, in the case of saving the results of the previous exercise you could add "Produced in E4 of CorelDRAW 3 A User's Guide". Notes are optional.

j. Finally there is the **Image Header**. This allows you to specify the additional information that is saved about the file. In CorelDRAW 2.01 all files were saved with a monochrome image header and it is this that appears in the little window of the File Open dialogue box. CorelDRAW 3.0 allows you to specify the kind of header you want to use as follows:

 **None**, i.e. no header at all. Use this if you are getting short of disk space.

 **1 Kb Mono** is the simplest header of all and is similar to that used in CorelDRAW 2.0.

 **2 Kb Mono** is similar to that used in CorelDRAW 2.01.

 **4 Kb Colour** is worth using if you are using 16 colour only.

 **8 Kb Colour** is the default and it should be used if you are using 256 colours.

j. Once you have set the various parameters for the file, click on **OK** to save it.

When you save a file the following information is saved with it:

1. The page size and its orientation, e.g. A4 landscape, and its colour.
2. The grid frequency and starting point. This in turn affects the measurement system being used.
3. Whether or not Snap to Grid and Snap to Object are turned on.
4. Any guidelines that are in use.
5. Any bitmaps that are incorporated into the image. CorelDRAW does not change bitmaps to vector format when you save a file.

The first time you save a file it will be written to the disk as normal. The second time you save the file, the first file will be renamed to [filename].BAK and then new file is written to disk as [filename].CDR. Save the file a third time and the second is renamed to [filename].BAK and so on. You can turn this feature off if you wish. See the Appendix for details of the CORELDRW.INI file.

# E6 - LINES AGAIN

Okay, having played around with fills and lines around objects, let's go back to the actual lines themselves.

a. Start a new page by pressing **Alt-F N** or you can open the **File** menu and then click on **New**. If you haven't saved the previous file you will get a message box prompting you to do so. It is entirely up to whether or not you save the previous file.

b. Select the **Line Drawing tool** - the one that looks like a pencil. Move the cursor on to the page. Click once, this fixes the first end of the line in place. Move the cursor across the page - without holding down the mouse button - and you can see a line being generated. Click once wherever you want the line to end.

c. Press the **Spacebar** to switch back to the **Pointer** tool and the handles appear around the line.

d. Open the **Outline Pen tool** and select the **Outline roll-up**. (You have to do this because whenever you start a new file any previously existing roll-ups will vanish.)

e. Click on the **Start arrow** button. That's the one on the left immediately below the line thickness area. A new dialogue box appears that contains the available arrows.

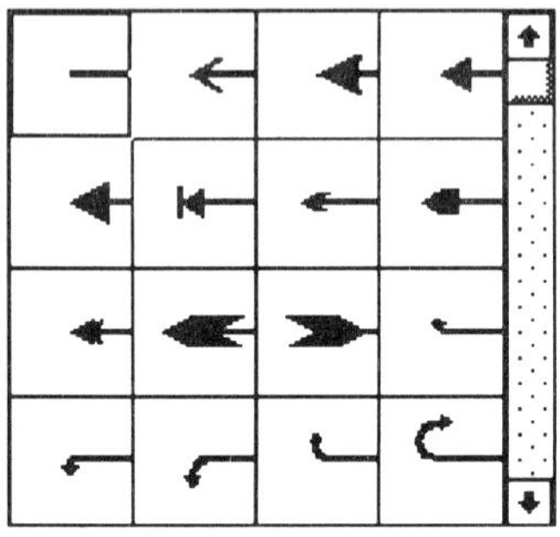

**2.43 Arrows**

f. There are actually 88 arrowheads you can add to a line. You want the very last one so scroll down through the list until you come to it. It looks like a mini-explosion. Once you find it, click on it once.

g. Now we want to apply another arrow to the other end of the line. Click on the **End arrow** button. In the dialogue box that appears find and select the airplane. In the roll-up click on **Apply** to add the arrows to the line.

h. You can see that there is something there but it's almost impossible to distinquish what it is. Press **F4** which is the shortcut for **Magnify All**. The line will expand to fill as much of the screen as possible. Even so the arrows are barely discernible.

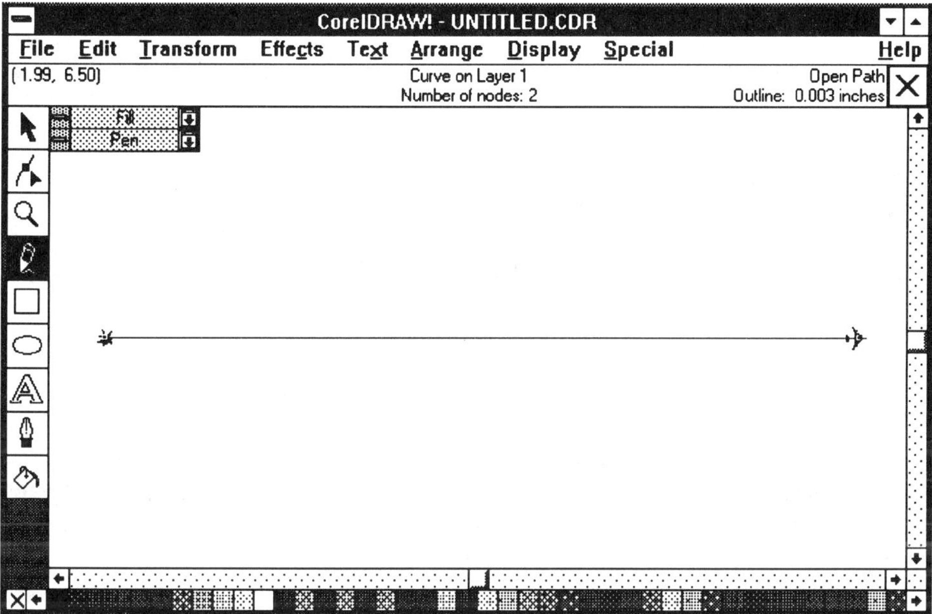


**2.44 Arrows applied to line**

The reason is that the size of the arrows is dependent on the line thickness. As we're currently using the default line thickness of 0.003 inches the arrow are very, very small. You can see them but...

i. Increase the line thickness and watch what happens. You may well find that you have to press **F4** again to get the ends of the line to come into the frame.

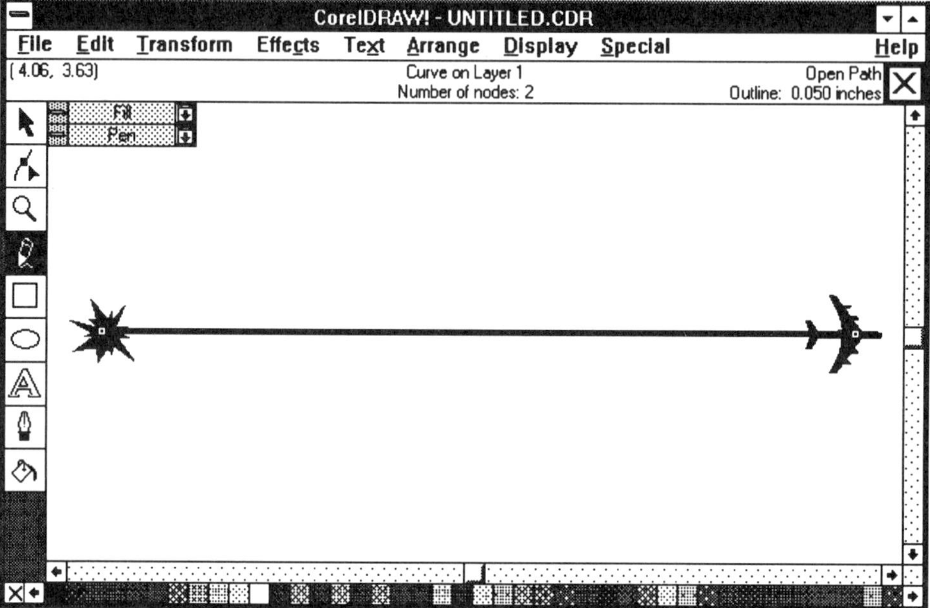


**2.45 Thicker line and visible arrows**

j. Notice that the tips of the arrows actually extend beyond the end of the line. The actual line, rather than the arrows, has the handles around it and these are overlaying the arrows. That is something to bear in mind for the future. Whenever you use arrows at the ends of lines the arrows will always extend beyond the end of the line itself.

k. Press **Shift-F4** to zoom out to the **Page View magnification**. Then either press **F10** or click on the **Node Edit tool** to select it. The cursor becomes a triangular shape. Move this to the line, so that the tip of the new cursor touches it, and then click once. The handles vanish and are replaced by two small squares, one at each end of the line, these are the **Nodes**. The **Status Bar** will say "**Curve: 2 nodes**".

l. You can drag either of these handles in any direction you please. Simply move the tip of the cursor to a node and then drag it wherever you want it. Notice as you do so that it is only the wire frame line that moves. It is not until you release the mouse button that the line, and its arrows, are redrawn. Move one end of the line up so you have a diagonal line.

m. Notice that there are two different node types. At one end of the line is the **First Node** and at the other is a **Line Cusp**. Click on each node in turn and watch the Status Bar. Knowing which is the first node of any shape will become important later. For now just be aware of it.

n. Click on the page to deselect the node you have been using. Move the cursor to the line itself and then double click. The **Node Edit** dialogue box appears.

**2.46 Node Edit dialogue box**

n. We'll come back to the main features of this dialogue box in the next exercise. For now just click on **toCurve**. Notice that the Status Bar still says exactly the same thing as before, i.e. **Curve: 2 nodes**.

o. Click on the node with the airplane attached to it. You should be able to see a thin dashed line extended from the node, at the other end of the line is a little solid square. This is the **Node Control Point**. This allows you to edit the line directly. If you drag the solid square downwards, left, right or in any other direction then the line will change shape.

p. Drag the node control point from the other node somewhere. Note that you can rotate the node control point all the way around the node that it is connected to. Equally you can move it further away or closer to the node itself. Any change you make in its relative position will have an effect on the actual line.

q. Double click on the first node. The dialogue box reappears. This time click on **Add**. This action will add a third node to the middle of the line. Again this has its own control points. Play around with them until you have a kind of staggered S-shaped line, something like Figure 2.47.

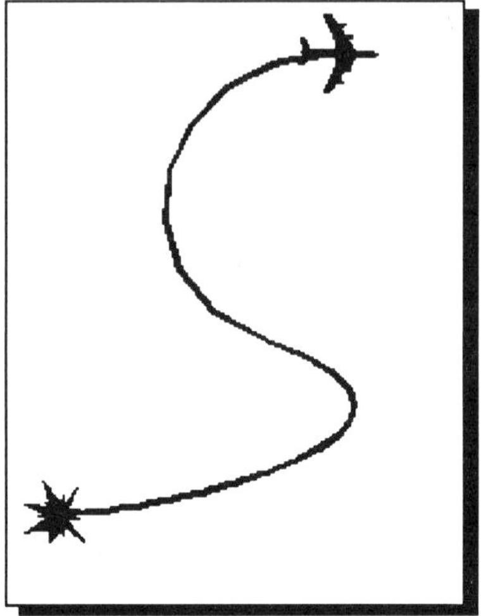

**2.47 Staggered line with arrows**

r. Press the **Spacebar** to go back to the **Pointer** tool. Play with the settings in the Pen roll-up. Notice that any changes you make to the colour will affect both the line and the arrows. You cannot have the line one colour and the arrows in another. But you can get some interesting effects with using dashed lines. Don't forget that making the line thicker will make the arrows larger, making the line thinner will reduce the size of the arrows. Try using different arrows.

s. A final silly thing to do. Select the line, press **+** on the numeric keypad. The screen will blip. What has happened is that you have duplicated the line by making a copy of it directly on top of the existing one. Click on the line again to get the rotational handles and then rotate it and you'll see what I mean. Duplicate and rotate lots of them and you end up with something like this:

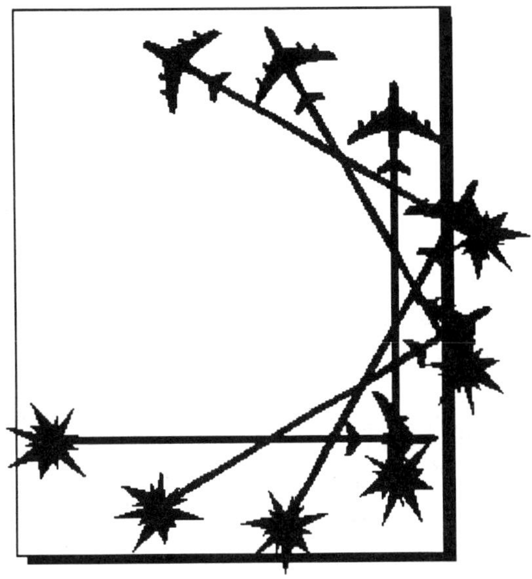

**2.48 Duplicated and rotated lines**

# E7 - NODES AND SHAPES

As well as using the Node Edit effects with lines, you can also use them with complete shapes. But here the effects are slightly different.

a. Start a new page using **Alt-F N**. By all means save the results of the previous exercise first although you won't want it again in this book. Later there will be exercises that you will need to save because you will need them again but not yet.

b. Draw a square and put it into the middle of the page, e.g. by using Align.

c. Switch to the Node Edit tool (**F10**), nodes appear at each corner of the square and the Status Bar will say **Rectangle: corner radius 0.00 inches (0.00, 0.00)**. In other words you have a rectangle; a square is simply a special instance of a rectangle, that has not been changed in any way.

d. Drag the node from the top left hand corner straight down the line. Notice that all the other nodes match your action as the square is deformed and the corners become rounded. Release the mouse button. You now appear to have eight nodes. Actually you don't, you still have four but each one is a pair. You will find that you cannot move a node other than along the lines of the square.

e. CorelDRAW will allow you to turn a square into a circle - well sort of. Drag any node as far you as you can along a line. The square becomes more and more distorted until you cannot go any further and you apparently have a circle. (It's not a real circle though - it's just a deformed square - see what's on the Status Bar.)

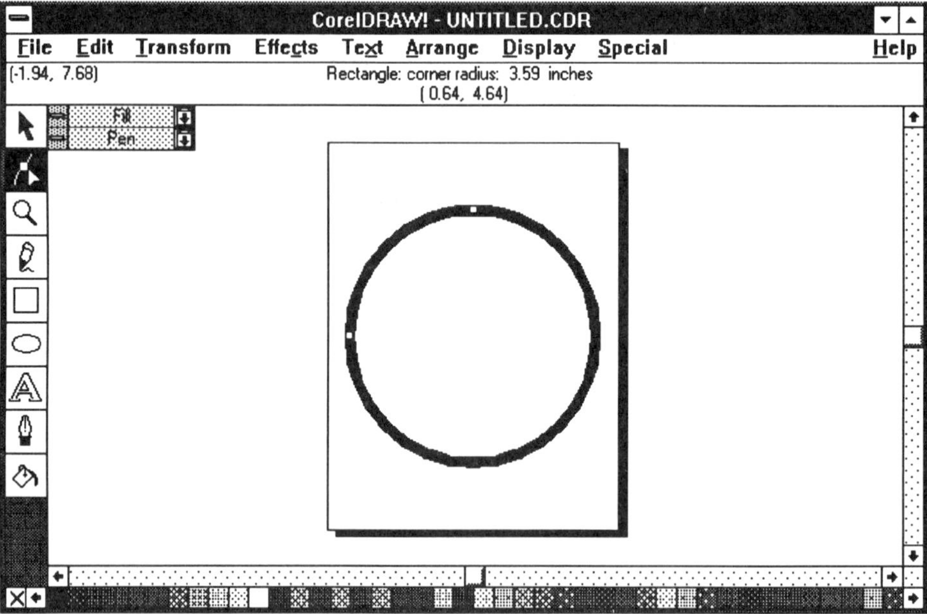


**2.49 Circular square**

f. Delete the square. Draw a circle and align it to the centre of the page.

g. Switch to the **Node Edit tool** again. Notice this time that you have only got a single node, though again it's actually a pairing.

h. Move the cursor so that it is inside the circumference of the circle and then drag the node around the circle. The cursor must be kept inside the circle. What you get is a pie with a piece missing from it.

i. Press **Alt-Backspace** to undo it. Now move the node with the cursor outside the circle. This time you get an arc instead of a pie.

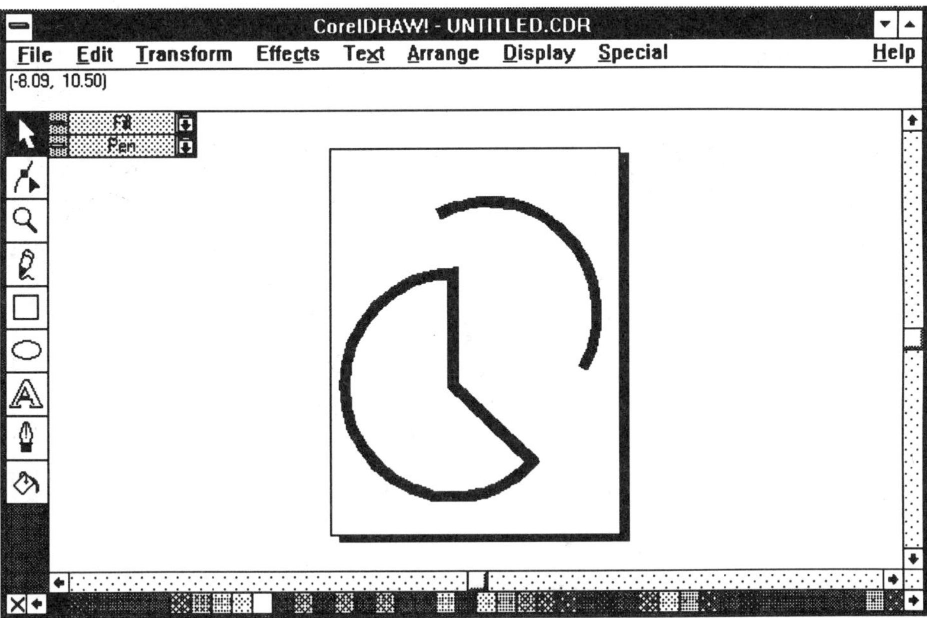


**2.50 Pie and arc from node edit**

That's the rule for node editing circles and ellipses. Move the node from inside the circle and you get a pie, move it from outside and you get an arc. If you hold down **Ctrl** as you move the node then it will move only in 15 degree increments and you have very precise control of the shape you generate. A pie can be filled with colour or a pattern, an arc cannot because it is open ended.

j. Delete the circle or what's left of it. I want you to create an isosceles triangle. (That's a triangle with two equal sides for those who have forgotten their school trig.) There is an easy way and a difficult way to do this.

k. The easy way is to draw a square. Press **Ctrl-V** to convert the square to curves. (We'll come back to this command later.) Switch to the **Node Edit tool**. Double click on the top right hand corner node. In the dialogue box click on **Add**. A fifth node will be added, equi-distant from the top two nodes. Click outside the shape to deselect the nodes. Click on either of the top corner nodes to select it and then press **Delete**. Then remove the other corner node. Voila, a triangle.

l. You can delete both nodes at once by the way. Click on one to select it. Hold down **Shift** and then click on the other. Both nodes are then selected at the same time. Press **Delete** to remove them.

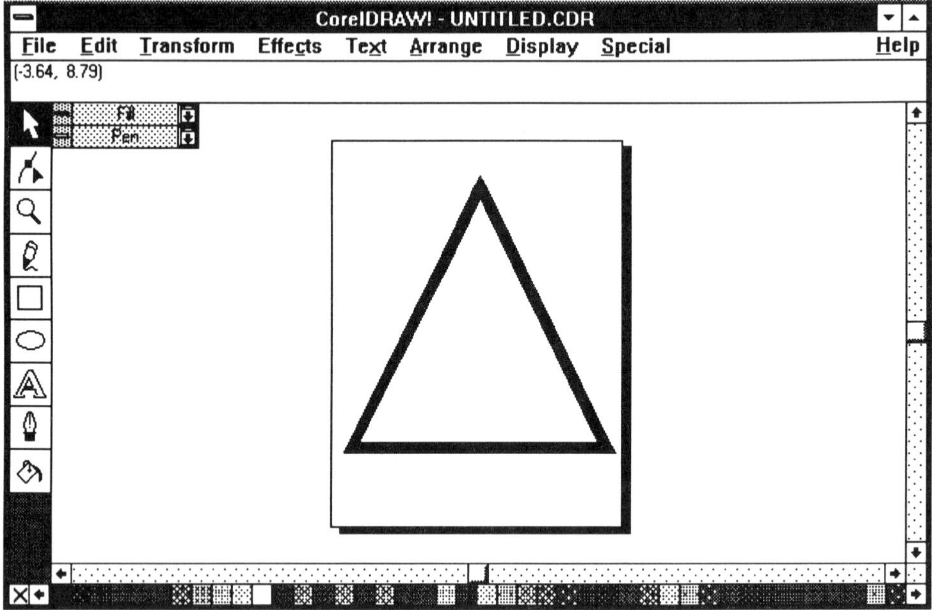


**2.51 Isosceles triangle**

m. The more complex way involves drawing individual lines. Select the **Drawing tool**. Draw a line, watching the Status Bar as you do so so you know the length of it, and hold down **Ctrl** at the same time so you get a straight line. In other words, click to anchor one end of the line, hold **Ctrl** and draw the line.

n. Now position the cursor exactly over one end of the line. Click once to anchor the end of the line. It will actually join to the existing line. Hold **Ctrl** again to constrain the angle of the line to fifteen degree increments and then draw the second line.

o. Position the cursor over the last end of the line. Click to anchor the line end and join it to the existing line again. Move the cursor to the free end of the original line and click. The line will now join to the first line. Viola, a triangle.

It is much harder to draw an isosceles triangle free hand then it is to do so using a square and then deleting the excess nodes. Because your triangles are contained shapes they can be filled with colours and patterns as normal. If they won't fill it means that the lines have not joined together properly. Try redrawing the triangle.

# E8 - FIRST TEXT

CorelDRAW will allows you to do things with text, in total, that you simply cannot do in any other programs. Granted there are other programs that you will you to do some of the things some of the time, but only CorelDRAW allows you to do all of the things all of the time. If you had to select one part of the program that is outstanding over and above everything else, then the text handling would probably be it. From my point of view, there is so much you can do with the text that it's hard to know where to begin. So we're going to start simply and work up to more complex things.

a. Clear the page, either start a new page or just delete everything that's on the current one.

b. Select the **Text tool**, either by clicking on it or by pressing **F8**. The cursor becomes a cross-head shape.

c. Move the cursor on to the page and click once. A vertical line appears on the page. This is one of the innovations of CorelDRAW 3.0. In previous versions you entered text via a dialogue box and it was only when you closed the box that the text appeared on the page. In CorelDRAW 3.0 you put text directly onto the page.

d. Type **Cogito, ergo perturbitas**. (It means "I think, therefore I am confused!" or as near as my dog Latin will allow.) The characters will appear as you type, the first one where you originally clicked and the other moving to the right - just as they would on a word processor or if you were using a pen. By default, the text will appear in whatever typeface is mentioned in the CORELDRW.INI - as it happens it is Avalon which is a variation on Avant Garde.

e. Switch back to the **Pointer tool**. In this case you cannot use the keyboard shortcut because that just produces a space - you have to click on the tool. When you do so handles will appear around the text and each letter will also have node points. The Status Bar will also tell you what text, effects and size are in use.

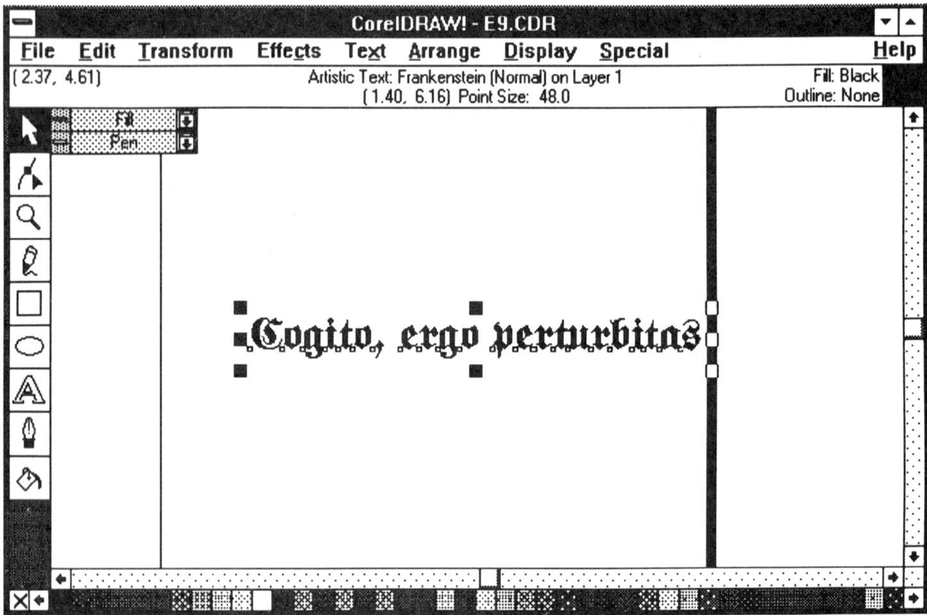


**2.52 Select text on page**

f. Press **F4** to make the text fill the available screen space so it's easy to work with. (You may need to press **F3** to step back a bit once you've done so.)

g. You can resize text directly. Move the cursor to the middle top handle, i.e. the one at twelve o'clock. Click and drag this upwards. As you do so the Status Bar will text you by how much you are stretching the text. Once you let go of the mouse button, the Status Bar tells you the new size.

A word of warning about text sizes on stretched text. The size refers only to the height of the characters. For example, 216 points means that the text is three inches high. But... When you create text of a given size the point size affects not just the height but also the width of the characters. When you stretch text this is not the case. All you have done is make the text taller but it remains the same width as when you typed it originally.

Mind you, it does have its uses. It's a great way to make ultra-stretched text. You know, the kind that you have to read by holding the paper almost horizontally in front of your eyes.

h. Press **Alt-Backspace** to undo what you've done. The text should return to normal. If you stretched the text from the top and then stretched it from the bottom, the undo will only cancel the last operation. To return the text to its original state you may need to press **Alt-T C** or open the **Transform menu** and click on **Clear Transformations**.

i. This time, click and drag one of the bottom corner handles. As you do so you should notice that no matter how far down the page you drag the cursor the text will only grow widthwise. In fact it's growing in both directions but the width of the text is the limiting factor. If you don't drag the cursor to one side nothing will happen.

j. You can change the colour of the text as you would anything else. Click on the palette with the left mouse button to change the fill, click with the right mouse button to change the outline. If you click on the **X** at the end of the palette with both buttons the text effectively vanishes - because it has no outline and no fill. It is actually still there, the handles remain for example, but it is invisible. Computerised invisible ink, perhaps?

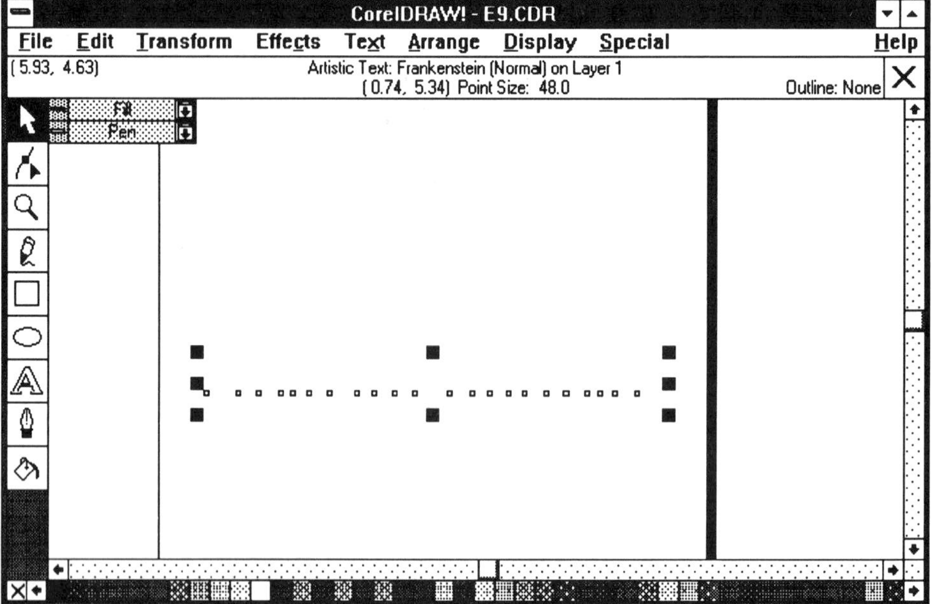


**2.53 Invisible text**

k. Even though the text is invisible it can still be stretched, changed and otherwise modified as if it was still there. Press **Ctrl-T** and you'll see why. What has happened is that the dialogue box, as it existed in CorelDRAW 2.01, appears - complete with the text string.

The dialogue box is essentially the same as in previous versions of the program. The main difference is 3-D buttons and the fact that you can now see more than just two characters in the chosen font.

The main part of the box, along the top, shows the text string. You can have up to 256 characters in this. This is for Artistic Text. When using Paragraph Text you can have up to 4,000 characters.

On the left hand side is the list of available **Fonts** - actually they are typefaces not fonts. CorelDRAW 3.0 comes complete with lots and lots of fonts. On the floppy disk version there are 153 TrueType fonts, on the CD-ROM there are an additional 100 TrueType fonts plus all the fonts in Adobe Type 1 format.

CorelDRAW no longer uses WFN fonts. (Well it will, but only if you modify the CORELDRW.INI file and force it to.) You can now use either TrueType, Adobe Type 1, WFN fonts or a combination of all three.

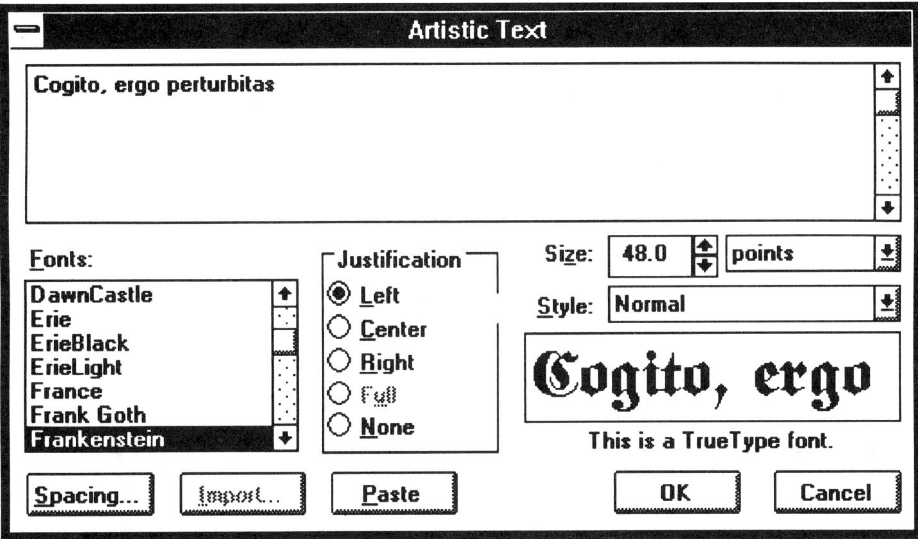


**2.54 Text dialogue box**

In the centre is the **Justification**. With Artistic Text you can use Left, Centre, Right or No justification. It is only with Paragraph text that you can have full justification.

On the right are a series of indicators. The first one is the **Size**, by default given in Points. (By the way, there are 72 points to an inch or roughly 2.8 to a millimetre.)

Below that is **Style**, e.g. Normal. To see the other available styles for the chosen typeface click on the arrowhead and the list drops down. Some typefaces are available in only one or two styles, e.g. Arabia (Similar to Arnold Bocklin) is only available in Normal, Zurich Calligraphic (Similar to Zapf Chancery) is Italics only.

Next is a little window that shows what the text will look like in the chosen typeface and style. The number of characters it shows depends on the typeface width but it should be roughly a dozen or so. It's still better than only the two characters shown in previous versions. Beneath the window is a line telling you the kind of font in use, e.g. This is a TrueType/WFN/ATM font.

Along the bottom of the dialogue box are a series of buttons. Click on the one labelled **Spacing...** and it will bring up a subsidiary dialogue box.

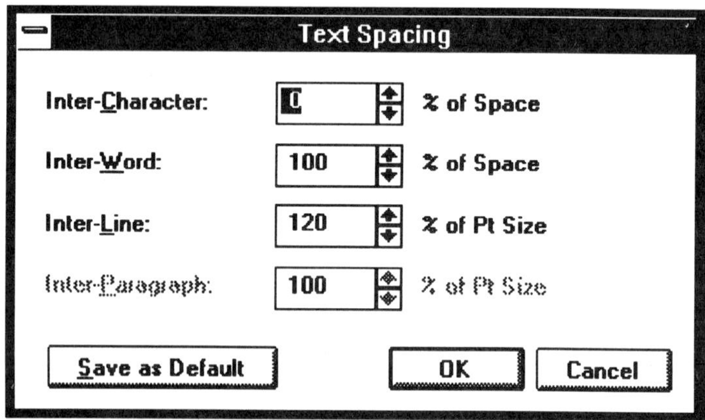


**2.55 Text spacing dialogue box**

The dialogue box allows you to set a variety of spacing attributes for the selected text, and/or set default values for all future text. **Inter-Character** is the amount of space, over and above the built-in amount, between the characters in the text string. By default it is set to zero. As each typeface has its own built-in spacing you shouldn't need to change this.

**Inter-Word** spacing is the amount of space between words, i.e. the amount of space assigned to a blank space. The default is 100% and again it doesn't really need to be changed.

**Inter-Line** spacing is just that, the space between lines. For artistic text the default of 100% should be okay because you are unlikely to use lines of text. However, if you are using a number of lines within a single string then the default spacing is inadequate. Personally, I always increase it to 120% and then modify it as necessary.

**Inter-Paragraph** spacing is greyed out because you're using artistic text and so you cannot, at this stage, modify it.

If you make any changes to the defaults values you can click on **Save as Default** to set your values as the new default. Then click on **OK** to close the dialogue box.

l. Change the typeface to **Frankenstein** and the point size to **48** - if you highlight the point size you can just overwrite it instead of having to use the arrowheads. Leave the style as **Normal** and then click on **OK**. The dialogue box closes and you're back at the page.

m. Make the text **Black** so you can see it, i.e. click on Black in the palette with the left mouse button.

n. Now for another new trick in CorelDRAW 3.0. Switch to the **Node Edit** tool by pressing **F10**.

o. Click on any individual node and then click on the colour palette with the left mouse button. The individual letter will change to the selected colour. To the best of my knowledge CorelDRAW is the only graphics package that will allow you to have individually coloured letters within a string of text.

p. Change the colours of every single letter so that no two colours appear side by side.

q. Now change them all back to Black. How? You could select them individually but that's long winded. Instead use the Node Edit tool to drag a selection box around all the nodes of the characters and then click on black. All the selected letters will be changed.

r. Now save the file because you will need it later. Press **Alt-F A** or open the **File** menu and click on **Save As**. Name the file **E8**, just type it as the filename is already highlighted, and then click on **OK**.

Play with the text yourself. Try the different typefaces and styles and using different colours. You can even use the Two-Colour and Full-Colour pattern fills from the Fill roll-up - though you will get some very odd effects with some of them.

# E9 - SYMBOL TEXT

CorelDRAW, as well as allowing you to use ordinary text, comes complete with a range of Symbol Fonts. These are not really fonts at all, they are miniature graphics but they can be used as fonts.

a. Start a new page by pressing **Alt-F N** or open the **File** menu and click on **New**. (Make sure you've saved the file from the last exercise first.)

b. Click on the Text tool and hold down the mouse button for a couple of seconds. A pop-out will appear with an A on the first button and a star on the second. (They might have changed this by the time they release the program.) Click on the star. It will replace the A in the toolbox.

c. Move the cursor on to the page and click once. The **Symbol Library** dialogue box appears.

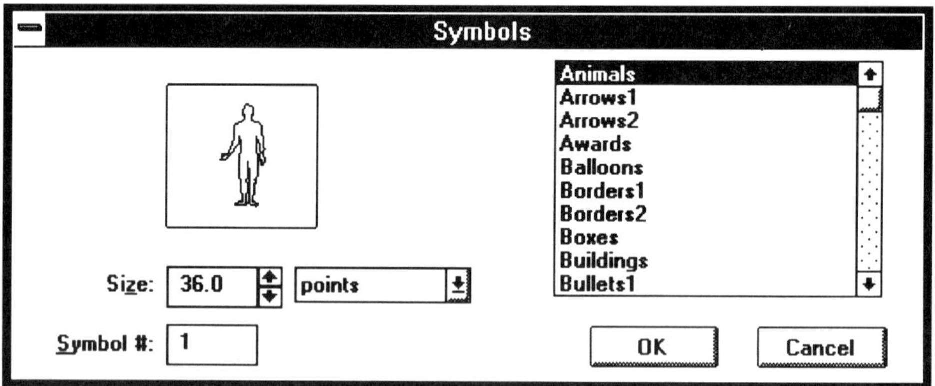


**2.56 Symbol Library dialogue box**

By default the dialogue box shows the Animals library and the symbol that appears is an outline of a human. The list of symbol libraries is given on the right, as you click on each in turn so the symbol on the left will change. There are hundreds of possible symbols.

On the left is a square box showing the human outline. In the lower right hand corner of this is a little triangle telling you that there are more symbols to be seen. Click on the triangle or the figure itself and a box similar to that in the fill roll-up appears. You can page through the selection box to find the character you want.

**2.57 Symbol selection box**

Below the symbol is a line labelled **Size**, which defaults to inches for some strange reason. Even if you change it to Points now it will return to inches the next time you open the dialogue box.

Beneath that is a line labelled **Symbol** which just tells you which symbol you are using. Different libraries have a different of symbols in them.

Finally there are two buttons labelled **OK** and **Cancel**. Guess what they do.

d. Just to keep things simple, we'll use the first symbol of the Animals library - the one shown in Figure 2.57 - the default one. Change the size to 144 points or two inches. Click on **OK** to select it. (You can only select a single symbol at a time.) The dialogue box closes and the symbol appears on the page.

e. You can treat the symbol as you would any other image within CorelDRAW - not as text - but as a drawing. It can be resized, rotated, filled, outlined and so on. Play with it and see what you can do.

f. To go back to using ordinary text you must click on the star in the toolbox, hold the mouse button down until the pop-out appears and then click on the **A**.

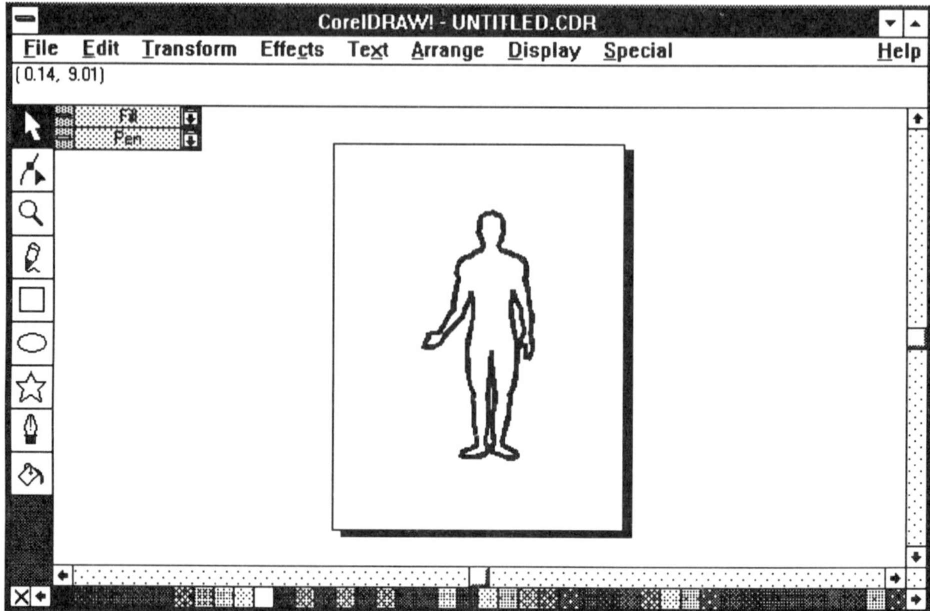


**2.58 Symbol on page**

# END QUIZ

That is effectively the end of this chapter. You can now move directly on to the next chapter or you can try your hand at this quiz. I've created a number of images, using only the tools and effects that we've covered in this chapter, and the idea is that you try to recreate them. The answers appear in Appendix C at the back of the book.

# Q1 - RECTANGLES AND CIRCLES

# Q2 - Diamond squares

## Q3 - SYMBOLIC

# Q4 - TRIGON

# 3 - PREFERENCES

Everything that you've done so far with CorelDRAW has been done using the programs own default settings. But before you go any further you need to set your own preferences for how the program behaves, how various controls work and other settings. Please note that you don't have to do any of this but if you do you will have a much better understanding of how CorelDRAW works and you will have far greater control over the program itself.

a. You must start with a completely clean program. Ideally this means that you run CorelDRAW afresh but if you already have the program open you can start a new page but you must close any roll-ups that you have on screen - not just roll them up - they must be removed.

b. The first thing to do is open the **File** menu and then click on **Print Setup**. (This should always be the first thing you do in any new program that you install on your system.) The act of opening the Printer setup forces the program to verify the contents of the WIN.INI file, assess the correct fonts and so on.

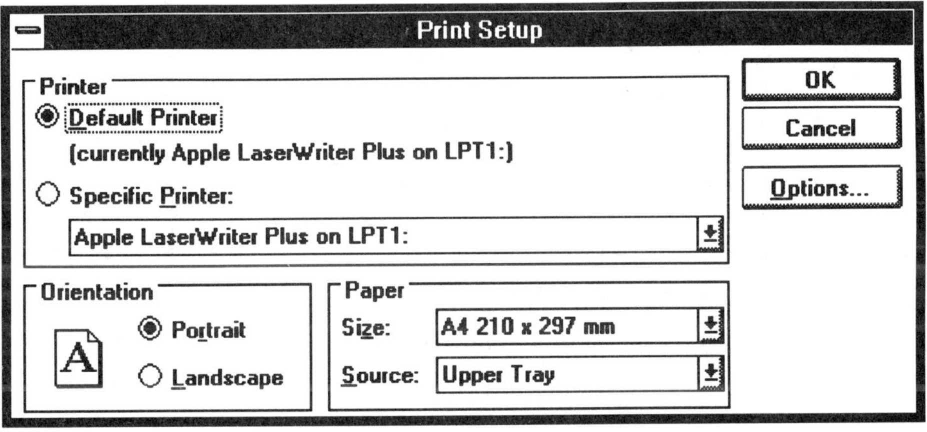


**3.01 Printer Setup dialogue box**

c. You don't actually have to do anything with the dialogue box. By default CorelDRAW will use whatever printer you have assigned as your system default in the Windows Control Panel. You can assign another printer if you have additional printers configured for your system. But don't forget that any changes you make here will affect the printer for the entire system not just for CorelDRAW itself. Because CorelDRAW will automatically change the paper orientation for you all you need worry about here is the paper size. However, you should have set all this up previously in Windows itself. Click on **OK** to close the dialogue box.

d. The next thing to do is set the page size within CorelDRAW. Open the **File** menu again and this time click on **Page Setup**.

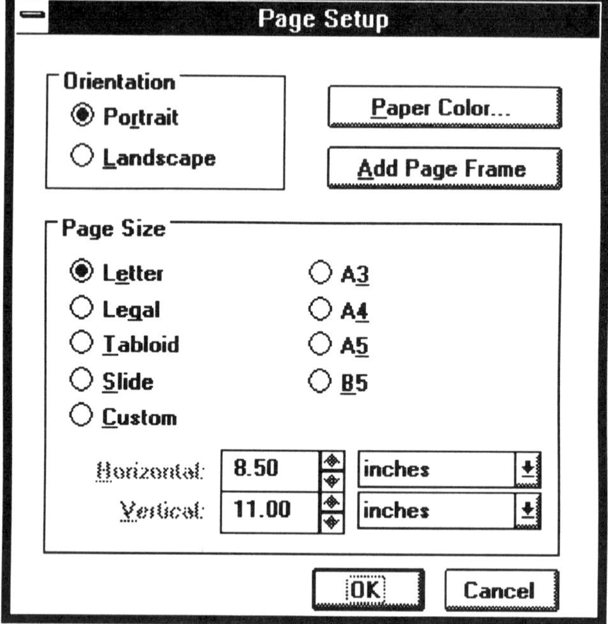


**3.02 Page Setup dialogue box**

e. The dialogue box allows you to make a number of changes to the on-screen page. Firstly, there is **Orientation**. Because CorelDRAW can turn the page around for me, I always use **Landscape** orientation, by default the program uses **Portrait**. Why use landscape? Because it effectively gives you an additional level of magnification on a standard 14" monitor. The page is roughly twice the size that it would be if you used portrait orientation. Yes, I know you can magnify any part of the page but it makes sense to have an additional level of magnification to start with. If you are using a larger monitor, e.g. 17" or 21", then you wouldn't need to bother though what I said above still applies.

f. Next is the **Paper Size**. By default, CorelDRAW uses American Letter size pages (and most of the clip-art that is supplied with the program is on that size) which is 11" by 8.5". In Europe we tend to use A4 instead but you can use any of the following:

| | | |
|---|---|---|
| **Letter** | 11.0" x 8.5" ............. | 279.4 by 215.9 mms |
| **Legal** | 14.0"x 8.5" ............. | 355.6 by 215.9 mms |
| **Tabloid** | 17.0" x 11.0" ............ | 431.8 by 279.4 mms |
| **Slide** | 11.0" x 7.33" ............ | 279.4 by 186.2 mms |
| **A3** | 16.54" x 11.69" .............. | 420 by 297 mms |
| **A4** | 11.69" x 8.27" ............... | 297 by 210 mms |
| **A5** | 8.27" x 5.83" ................ | 210 by 148 mms |
| **B5** | 10.12" x 7.17" ............... | 257 by 182 mms |

Plus **Custom** which can be any size up to 30" square (762 mms).

A little quirk of CorelDRAW. If you want to change the measurement system for the page you can only do so by clicking on Custom. Even though the word inches is not greyed out when you any other page size you cannot change it to millimetres until you click on Custom. Once you have changed it, it remains active. You actually have a choice of Inches, Millimetres, Picas and Points.

Set whatever page size and measurement you wish.

g. **Paper Colour** allows you to have coloured paper! Clicking on the button brings up the palette dialogue box (which we'll come back to in a minute) from which you can choose any colour you wish.

h. **Add Page Frame** is there to allow you to use a fill as paper colour. You add the frame and then close the dialogue box. Once on the page you can fill the frame with whatever you wish.

i. Once you have made your selections, click on **OK** to close the dialogue box.

j. Open the **Special** menu and click on **Preferences** or simply press **Ctrl-J**. A dialogue box appears.

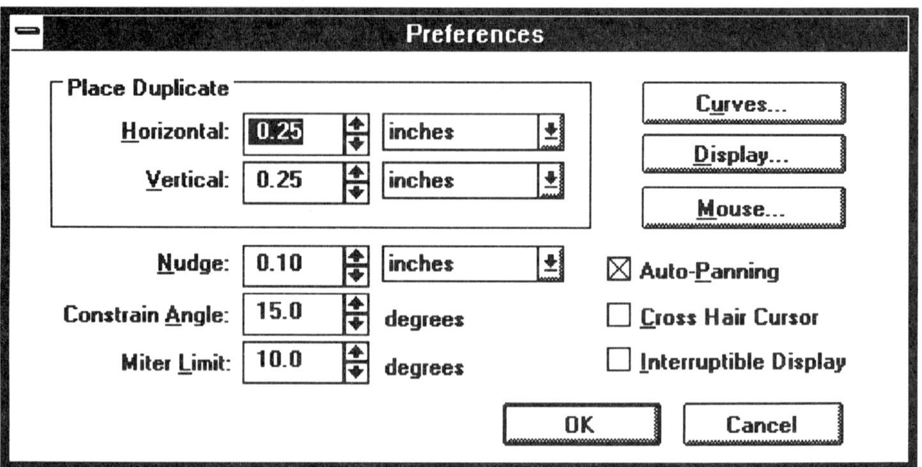


**3.03 Preferences dialogue box**

k. The first thing to notice is that everything is back to being in inches. It is one of the quirks of CorelDRAW that you can set an alternative measurement system, e.g. millimetres, in the page setup but then you also have to change it in every other dialogue box that uses measurements. In other words there is no way to set a global measurement system.

l. **Place Duplicate** applies to when you press **Ctrl-D**. This causes the selected object to be duplicated and then moved by the amount that you specify here. By default it is set to place the duplicate a quarter of an inch up and to the right. (Note that the normal starting point for the x,y axis in CorelDRAW is the bottom left hand corner of the page.) I usually change this to 5 mms for each axis but you can change it to whatever you wish.

m. **Nudge** allows you to move selected objects in small increments using the cursor keys. The increment is what you set here. I rarely use this but I set it to 2.5 mms. You can set a nudge value as low as 0.001 inches but the dialogue box apparently says 0.00. That is because the box cannot show values to three decimal places but it will still apply.

n. **Constrain Angle** is something that we used in the previous chapter. It is the angle that will be used whenever you hold down **Ctrl** while rotating an object or drawing lines. By default the angle is set to 15 degrees. I tend to leave it at that and only change it for specific images, for example when I'm drawing polygons and I want an exact angle.

o. **Miter Limit** really only applies visibly if you are using thickish lines. It actually applies to all lines but you can only see the results using thick lines. What it does is cause adjoining lines to be bevelled, i.e. the point where the lines join is flat rather than pointed, if the angle of the lines is *less* than the amount set here. Why? Because, especially with thick lines, you could end up with the point produced by the lines joining extending way beyond the node point where the lines join. I just leave it as the default.

p. **Auto-Panning** is a toggle, i.e. it's either on or off. With it turned on, which it is by default, if you move an object below the confines of the window then CorelDRAW automatically scrolls to keep the object in view. In other words the page itself moves in the opposite direction.

q. **Cross Hair Cursor** is also a toggle. By default it is turned off. What it does is cause the cursor to always be a cross hair instead of different shapes for different tools. Personally I like to be able to see at a glance which tool I'm using so I leave it turned off.

r. **Interruptible Display** is very useful, especially when you start producing complex images. Turn it on and then you can interrupt the redrawing process, e.g. to open a menu or move something, rather than having to wait for the redraw to finish.

s. Click on **Curves** and a new dialogue box appears. Notice that all the values apply to Pixels, i.e. screen elements. You should not need to change any of the value here but this is what they all mean.

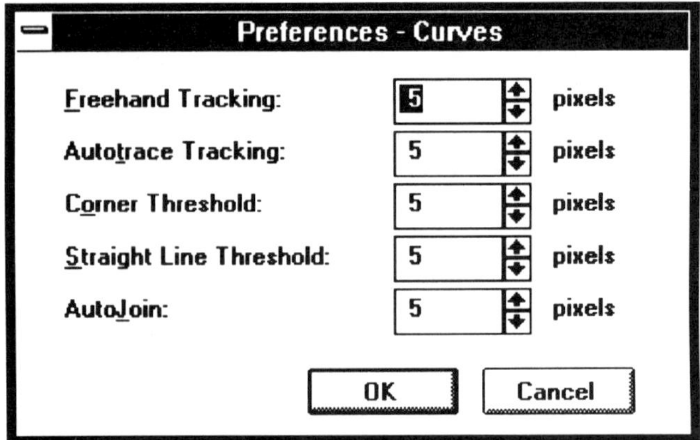


**3.04 Curves dialogue box**

**Freehand Tracking** is what makes CorelDRAW track your cursor when you are drawing. With the value set low, 1, 2 or 3, then you will end up with a precise track following and therefore lots of nodes. With the value set between 6 and 10 there will be less nodes but looser lines. By default the value is five which is good compromise.

**Autotrace Tracking** is similar to the above but it applies only when you are tracing a bitmap image. Again the default of five is fine.

**Corner Threshold** affects both freehand drawing and the autotrace. The value here changes whether CorelDRAW produces smooth or cusp nodes. The former give gentle rounding, while the latter give sharp corners. By default it is set to the compromise value of five again.

**Straight Line Threshold** also applies to autotracing and freehand drawing. With a low value, 1, 2 or 3, CorelDRAW will produce curves rather than linesr, with a higher value it produces lines instead of curves. The default is the middle course again.

**Auto Join** is the distance apart that two lines have to be before they will automatically join to become a single line. Lines can only join at the nodes at the end of the lines by the way.

With a low value you need to be very precise about how far the two lines are for them to join, a high value allows you to be less definite. However, if you set the value high you can end up with lines joining when you don't want them to.

Close the dialogue box by clicking on **OK** or by pressing **Enter**.

t. Click on **Display** to bring up that dialogue box.

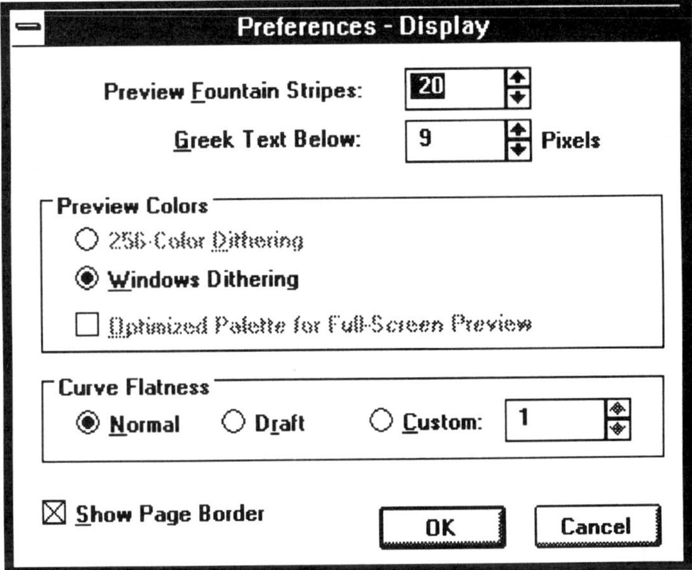


**3.05 Display dialogue box**

This dialogue box is much simpler than the one in previous versions of CorelDRAW. Everything has been refined to a few simple parameters.

**Preview Fountain Stripes** is the number of stripes used for the monitor and non-PostScript printers only. It does not effect printing on PostScript printers. With a low value, which can range from 2 to 256, you get fast drawing times but not much definition. With a high value redraw takes longer but you get few banding lines. The setting will also affect any file exported to SCODL. By default it is set to 20.

The value you use depends on your monitor and your system resources. On the 386 machine, which is very deficient in terms of resources, a value greater than the default slows things down enormously. On the 486 I can get away with using 256 stripes. Play with different values until you find one that is comfortable for you. I frequently use a low value for "sketching" and then increase it when I want to see the reality.

**Greek Text Below** is set to 9 pixels. This is a new setting for CorelDRAW 3.0 and it applies only to Paragraph text on screen - it makes no difference to the actual printing of text. What it does is cause paragraph text at small point sizes to be drawn as representations of characters instead of the actual characters themselves. This in turn means that the display is speeded up. The characters still appear as normal in the dialogue box. If you want to really speed up the display of paragraph text then set this value really high, like 500 or so. It will be illegible but the display speed will be very fast.

**Preview Colours** is dependent on your monitor and graphics card. You now have only two main choices, **256-Colour Dithering** or **Windows Dithering**. You can use the former automatically if your graphics card can support it, otherwise you use the latter.

**Optimised Palette for Full Screen Preview** changes the colours in use, only with 256 colours, so that you get 256 pure colours with no dithering. But - only if your system can do so and it will slow down your screen display.

**Curve Flatness** affects the amount of time that lines and curves take to redraw on screen or to print on non-PostScript printers. What it does is change the way curves are drawn. Consider a circle. With the curve flatness set to Normal, which is the default, you get a circle as you would expect. Set the flatness to Draft (which is the same as a Custom value of 10) and the circle will appear as a polygon. Custom allows you to set the value anywhere between 1, Normal, and 10, Draft. On most systems the default setting should be fine.

**Show Page Border** does just that. If you turn it off then you don't see the page on screen.

Make whatever changes you wish and then click on **OK** or press **Enter**.

u. Click on **Mouse** to being up that dialogue box which allows you to assign an action to the right mouse button. By default this feature is not turned on but you can have any of the following instead:

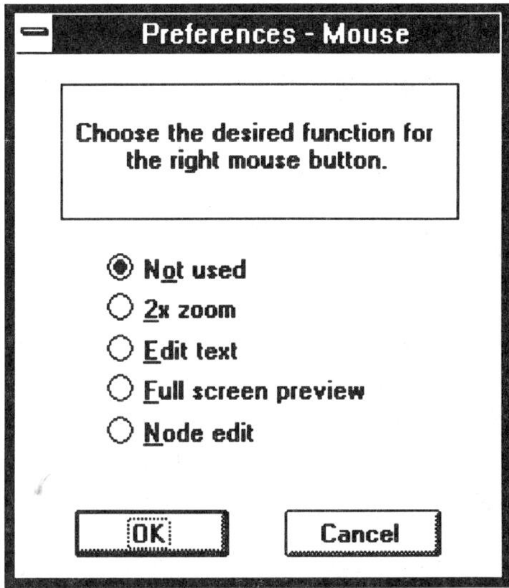


**3.06 Mouse dialogue box**

**2x Zoom** which gives you an instant way to magnify the image you are working with.

**Edit Text** brings up the text dialogue box, the equivalent of pressing **Ctrl-T**.

**Full Screen Preview** is the same as pressing **F9**. It displays your image without the surrounding window.

**Node Edit** is equivalent to pressing **F10** or activating the node edit tool.

I find that the 2x zoom is the most useful. Set it to whatever you want by clicking on the action you want to assign to the mouse button and then click on **OK** or press **Enter**.

v. Back at the main dialogue box click on **OK** to close it. You cannot just press **Enter** because the Mouse button is still selected and therefore pressing **Enter** will activate that again.

w. I've just discovered something that should not be possible. See if it works with the release version of the program. Press **Ctrl-S** to save the file. This shouldn't work because the file doesn't contain anything. If the dialogue box appears call the file **DEFAULT** and save it. If it doesn't work then draw a squiggle or something on the page and save it to the same filename. You're going to need this file in a minute.

# MORE DEFAULTS

What you have done so far is set the basic parameters for the program, the page size, screen display and so on. All the changes you have made are what you might term generic ones in that most of them will apply to everyone. The changes that you are going to make from here on are specific to you personally. There are no right or wrong settings. It now becomes purely a matter of personal taste.

a. Open the **Display** menu. Do you want the ruler to appear whenever you run CorelDRAW? Personally I find it useful so I turn it on - it's off by default. If you click on **Show Rulers** then the menu closes and the ruler appears below the Status Bar and down the left hand side of the window. One thing to note is that the ruler is in inches! As we're using ISO sized paper it would make more sense to have the rulers in millimetres.

b. Open the **Display** menu again and this time click on **Grid Setup**. It is this that defines the measurement system for the rulers. A dialogue box will appear.

c. Notice that is in inches. If you click on each occurrence of the word a list will appear and you can change each one to millimetres (or picas or points).

**Grid Origin** is just that, where is the 0,0 point for the grid definition. By default it is at the lower left hand corner of the page, which is a sensible place to have it. But you can place it wherever you wish by entering values in the top part of the box. Remember that the values are relative to the default position.

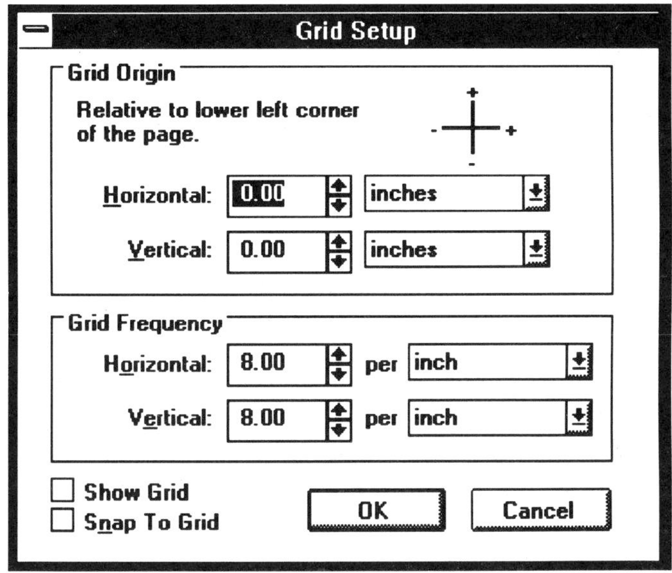


**3.07 Grid Setup dialogue box**

For example, if you wanted to place the grid origin at the top left hand corner of an A4 landscape page you would enter a value of 210 mms beside Vertical.

**Grid Frequency** is what actually changes the Rulers. By default it is set to 8 per inch and if you simply change the measurements to millimetres you will get an error message if you try to close the dialogue box because you cannot have 8 grid points per millimetre. You have to use a lower frequency.

What you are setting is the number of grid points per millimetre or inch or whatever. Note that it is *per* unit and not *to* a unit. This causes no end of problems because it is apparently backwards and I have more trouble explaining this that anything else. Suppose you want a grid containing centimetre squares. What grid frequency would you use?

Anyone who said 10 doesn't get any marks. If you said 0.1 then you get top marks. A setting of ten would mean that you were trying to set a grid containing tenth of a millimetre squares because there are 10 grid points *per* millimetre.

A value of 0.1 on the other hand means each millimetre is one tenth of the grid, thus giving 1 centimetre squares.

Similarly if you want a half centimetre grid you use a setting of 0.2 per millimetre not 2. If you want a 2.5 mm grid you use a value of 0.4 not 4. If you want a one millimetre grid then you use a value of 1 obviously.

I set the value to be 0.2 as a default and change it if necessary for a particular image. This gives a grid of five mms squares.

**Show Grid** causes the program to try and show the grid as a series of dotted lines on screen. Unfortunately the grid as shown rarely matches the actual grid frequency, you usually end up with a series of 2 cms grid squares. This is largely the fault of the monitor - it simply cannot show detail that fine. The net result is it's a waste of time turning the grid on.

**Snap to Grid** causes the cursor to move only to the grid points. It is a toggle that you can activate from within the program itself by pressing **Ctrl-Y**.

Make whatever settings you wish and then close the dialogue box by clicking on **OK**.

d. Open the **Display** menu again and this time click on **Show Colour Palette**. A pop-out appears to one side of the menu. What you set here controls the colour palette along the bottom of the screen. You have a choice of **No Palette**; **Process Colours.**, which is the default and which shows the CMYK colours; or **Spot Colours**, which are the Pantone ones. Select whichever you wish. I turn it off because it is so easy to select colours from the roll-up.

The next thing is to set the default characteristics for the pen and fill.

e. Click on the **Pen** tool and it opens out. Click on the **X**. A dialogue box appears as opposite.

   Because you have nothing selected, and at this point you shouldn't have any image on screen, the dialogue box appears. What you're going to do is set a default that means that all text will have no outline. Click on **Text Objects** and then on **OK**.

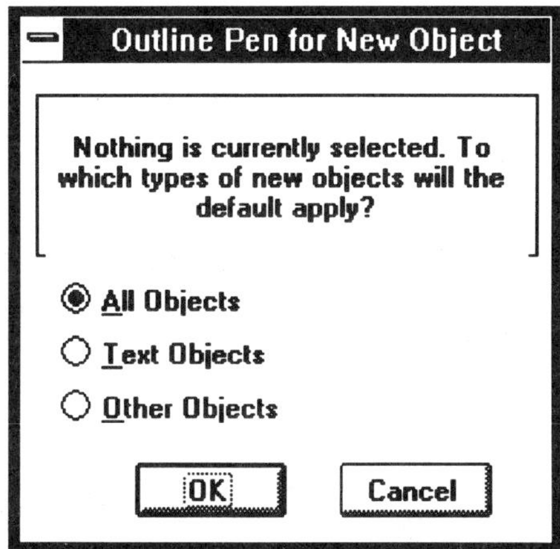


**3.08 Outline pen dialogue box**

Why do you want no outline for text? Essentially because all text is designed to be printed at the size and shape it is. By turning off the outline you get the pure text. This in fact gives you an advantage because if you want to make a normal typeface appear bold you can add an outline to it.

f. Click on the Pen tool again and this time click on the **Pen Nib**. When the dialogue box appears click on **Other Objects** and then on **OK**. A new dialogue box appears.

From here you can set a wide range of parameters that will apply to everything you draw from now on. In the top left hand corner you can set the **Colour** that the outline of the object will be. By default it is black and I tend to leave it as that.

**Arrows** cannot be assigned to a non-existent object so this option is greyed out.

**Width** is the line thickness. By default it is set to 0.003 inches. If you click on the word **inches** and change it to **points** you will find that it set to 0.2 points. I use that as the default line width.

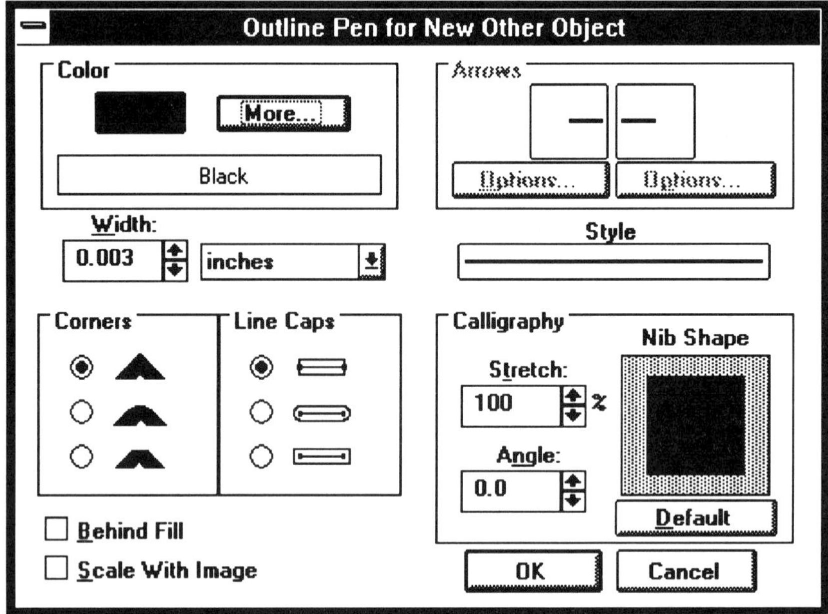


**3.09 New object outline pen dialogue box**

Why? Because that is the minimum line thickness that an ordinary laser printer can produce. With 300 dpi a thickness of 0.2 points is roughly 1 dot. There are seventy two points to an inch so you can calculate it as this: ((1 inch divided by 72 points) multiplied by 300 dpi) multiplied by 0.2 actually equals 0.83. In other words it is not worth making the line any thinner.

**Corners** is the shape that will be applied to the point where lines join. It also affects the nib shape. By default it is set to be a fine point, the top setting. The centre setting is for a round nibbed pen and gently rounded joins. The bottom one for a square nibbed pen and bevelled joins.

**Line Caps** are how the ends of individual lines appear. You have a choice of **Butt**, the top one, which means that lines are squared off at the end and do not project beyond the end point of the line. **Round**, the middle one, gives line with a gently rounded end. **Square**, the bottom one, means that the line continues beyond the end of it for half the line thickness before being squared off. By default the program is set for

Butt. You should note that any end cap will also apply to any dashed line you draw.

**Behind Fill** causes the outline to appear behind the fill! What more can I say.

**Scale With Image** means that when you change the size of an object, either increasing or decreasing it, the line will be resized accordingly. In other words if you draw a 10 cm square with a 2 point outline and then reduce the square to 5 cm the outline will become 1 point. Otherwise the outline would remain 2 points thick.

Scale with image also affects objects when they are rotated. If the parameter is turned off, as it is by default, then when you rotate the object the pen shape remains the same which can cause jagged lines. If you turn this parameter on then the nib shape is adjusted as the object is rotated so that the appearance of the outline remains unchanged.

For both these reasons I always turn this parameter on. Click on the box at the end of the phrase to do so.

**Style** is just another name for Dashed Line which you use in the last chapter. For the default outline I leave it set to a solid line.

**Calligraphy** refers to pen shape. By default the pen nib is a square but here you can change it to whatever you wish. For now I suggest that you leave it as it is and we'll come back to it later in some exercises. The button labelled **Default** by the way simply resets the nib shape to the normal default.

Make your selection and then click on **OK**.

g. Now to set the default fills. Open the **Fill** tool and click on **X**. A dialogue box similar to the one that appeared when you set the outline to nil appears. Click on **Other Objects** then on **OK**. Henceforth anything you draw will have no fill by default. This gives you much better control as you can fill things from the fill roll-up quickly and easily.

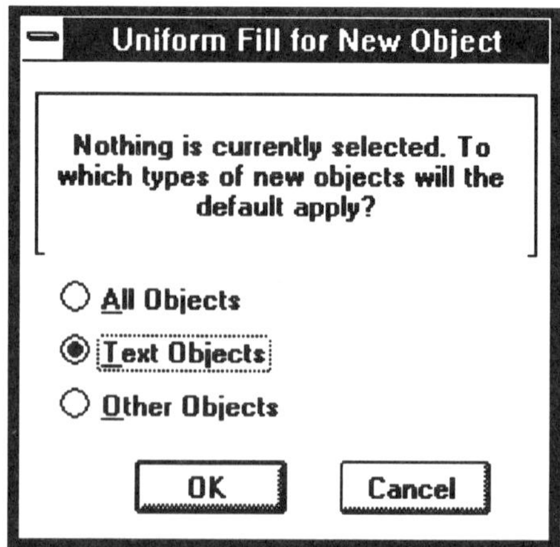


**3.10 Fill for new object selection box**

h. Click on the **Fill** tool again and this time on the first icon on the top line. The one that looks like a pie chart. When the new object fill dialogue box appears click on **Text Objects** then on **OK**. A new dialogue box appears.

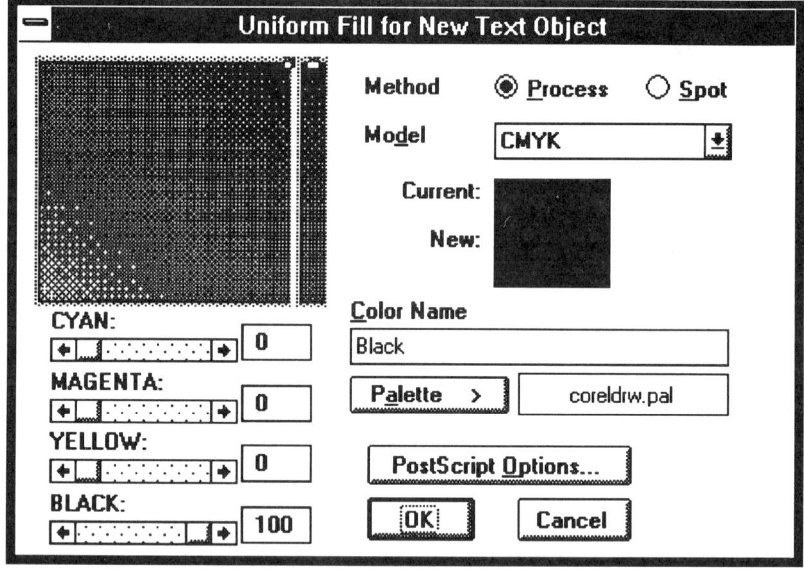


**3.11 New fill dialogue box**

This dialogue box allows you to set the default palette that will be used for the rest of the program, amongst other things. To start with you have two choices of fill method, **Process** and **Spot**. The former is generally the standard CMYK palette but it can be others. The latter is the Pantone colours. By the way if you want to save yourself grief, never mix Process and Spot colours in a single illustration - especially if you are going to have it printed by an outside bureau.

Sticking with Process Colours for a minute, you have a choice of **Model** types:

**CMYK** which stands for Cyan, Magenta, Yellow and Black and is the standard colour mixing palette used by litho-printers.

**RGB** stands for Red, Green and Blue and this is used on computers. It's often called the computer rainbow. The colours are actually the colours of the guns at the back of the monitor.
**HSB** stands for Hue, Saturation and Brightness and these are really an alternative for setting on-screen computer colours.

**Palette** gives you the palette of pre-defined colours whereas with the others you have to compose the colour. Because I'm lazy I use these and only switch to one of the other models when I need a blend of a specific colour that is not available on the palette.

The final option under Models is **Names**. This gives you a list of names in the current palette rather than images of the colours. For example, you don't see a pale blue but you get the name Baby Blue.

Back to Spot colours. If you select this then you have a choice of only two models, Palette and Names. In the case of spot colours the Names are probably easiest because you will assign colours from swatch cards not from the screen representation of them.

A word about colour before we go any further, well lots of words actually. There is a fundamental difference between the colours you see on a computer screen and the colours you see on a printed page. The former are Projected colours and the latter are Reflected colours. The difference has to do with the way that the colours are created and how the human brain interprets them.

Projected colours, i.e. the ones you see on your monitor or on a television screen, are created by three electron guns shooting charged particles at a phosphor coated screen. The guns are Red, Green and Blue. To create other colours the output from the guns is combined. For example, to get Yellow you combine Green and Blue, to get Magenta you combine Red and Blue and so on. The colours you see are very pure because they are made up of a finite number of originating colours but they are also very limited. That's why most monitors compose colours by using increments of colour saturation. For example, red can vary in intensity from 0 to 255 as can the others. This gives a total colour range of, theoretically, 16.4 million colours.

Unfortunately most monitors and television screens are not capable of displaying anywhere near that many. It takes a lot of electronics to even begin to approach that figure. Displaying lots of colours takes time and pushes the machine resources hard. To get a good compromise between speed of display and colour quantity, most video cards will not display more than 256 colours.

There is another factor to be borne in mind. The phosphor coating on the screen is made up of little dots. The density of these is referred to as Dot Pitch. On most monitors a dot pitch of around 0.28 mms is the average. The phosphor dots are placed in threes, in a triangular formation. The dot pitch is the distance between the dot at the apex of the triangle and the baseline - not the distance between the dots as you might imagine.

A single dot is the minimum that can be illuminated by a single beam from a colour gun. Thus the thinnest line that a monitor can display is limited by the dot pitch. That's why there is no apparent difference between a line of 0.1 points and 2 points on the average computer screen. It simply cannot show that level of definition.

Reflected colours are what you see everywhere else, on the printed page, in a forest, when you look through your window or even when you look at the window. Take a leaf as an example. Light comes from the sun in the full spectrum of colours, Red to Violet, and a few more besides but we'll ignore them. The leaf absorbs all the colours except the green. That is reflected back and that's why the leaf appears to be that colour. (If you want to see something really weird trying looking at leaves in pure red light!) In actuality it also reflects other parts of the spectrum but the green dominates.

The same thing applies to all other colours that you see. The paper you are reading is white because it reflects just about all the colours in the spectrum, the ink is black because that absorbs all the light, etc. A rainbow is caused by the drops of moisture in the air reflecting and refracting different colours.

The important point to realise is that the two types of colour are totally different and never the twain shall meet. It is not possible for them to do so. So any colour you see on the computer screen is only an approximation of the real colour and if you get it printed the colours will not match. They might be close but they will not be identical.

i. Where were we? The next thing that the dialogue box gives you is the **Colour Name**. Clicking on any colour in the palette will cause the name of that colour to appear here.

   Below that is a button labelled **Palette**. CorelDRAW comes with a range of palettes, collections of pre-defined colours, and by default the program uses one called CORELDRW.PAL. If you want to load another one click on this button. A list box will pop-out.

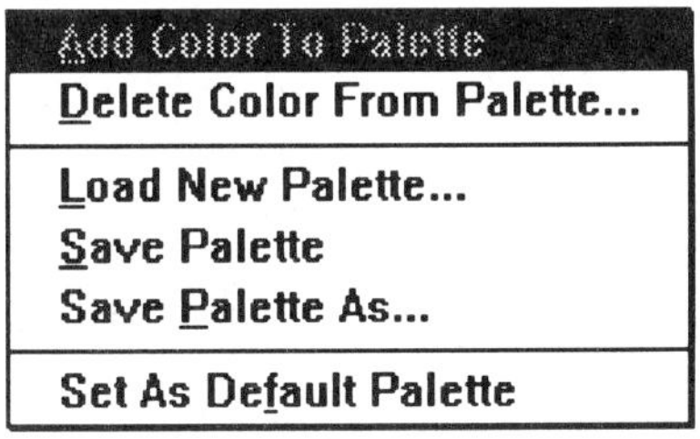

Add Color To Palette
Delete Color From Palette...
Load New Palette...
Save Palette
Save Palette As...
Set As Default Palette

**3.12 Palette list box**

   The list box allows you to do things with the palette. For now we're not going to do anything with most of these but click on **Load New Palette** and a dialogue box appears.

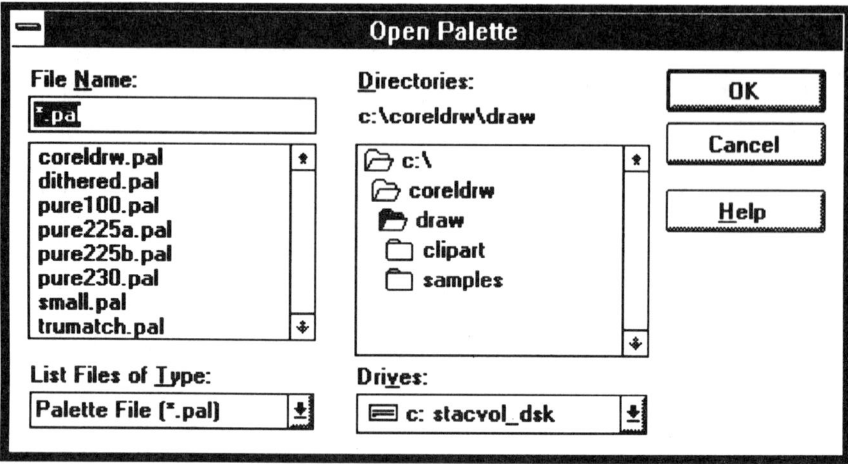


**3.13 Load palette dialogue box**

j. The dialogue box is the standard Windows load/save, import/export but this one is set to look for files with an extension of .PAL - the CorelDRAW palettes. You have a choice of eight possibles:

**CORELDRW.PAL** is the standard default.

**DITHERED.PAL** is an extensive one that works well on SVGA systems.

**PURE100.PAL** contains one hundred colours!

**PURE255A.PAL** and **PURE255B.PAL** each contain the same colours. The idea is that you can play around with one but always get it back.

**SMALL.PAL** contains just thirty colours, twenty of them greyscales.

**TRUMATCH.PAL** is new. It is a system similar to Pantone.

Select whichever palette you wish to use and then double click on it to close the dialogue box and go back to the original one. I use the Dithered one. Be warned, whatever palette you choose will be used for everything. You cannot have one palette for outlines and another one for fills.

k. **PostScript Options** can be ignored for now. It is concerned mainly with colour separations and we'll come to them much later.

l. After all that click on the colour that you want all text to appear in henceforth. For example, I use black because I've only got a monochrome printer. Click on **OK** to close the dialogue box.

m. Select the **Text** tool and then click on the page. Type the words "**My defaults**" and then switch to the **Pointer** tool again. Stretch the text so that it is legible by dragging the corner handles. You can even colour it if you wish. Notice that the text is in black with no outline - or whatever you have just set your new defaults to be.

n. Press **Ctrl-S** to save the file. Save it with the filename **DEFAULT**. That's it. You should now close down CorelDRAW just to make sure that the new defaults are properly written to the CORELDRW.INI file.

The reason for saving what you have just done as a file rather than just letting the CORELDRW.INI save things is twofold. Firstly, whenever you open any image, e.g. some of the clip-art, the settings that were saved with that image will overwrite your defaults. Being able to reload your default file gets them back quickly without having to mess about again. You then just start a new file using your own settings. The second reason for saving the file is to be sure that the defaults are written correctly. CorelDRAW should update various parts of the CORELDRW.INI every time you save a file. This makes sure of it.

# 4 - File Menu

CorelDRAW provides you with eight menus plus Help. The menus have been changed slightly since the previous release so that they are now more logical in terms of content. While the tools give you the basic implements to create images with, the menus give you major enhancements to those tools and to image manipulation. Rather than try to deal with all the menus in a single chapter, I've decided to have a seperate chapter per menu - after all there are 81 major commands and many of them include dialogue boxes and/or sub-commands. Along the way there will be various exercises to familiarise you with the main commands.

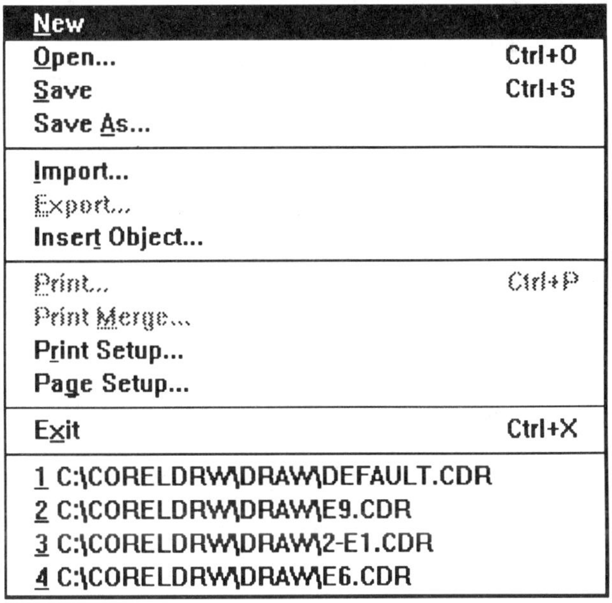

New
Open... Ctrl+O
Save Ctrl+S
Save As...
Import...
Export...
Insert Object...
Print... Ctrl+P
Print Merge...
Print Setup...
Page Setup...
Exit Ctrl+X
1 C:\CORELDRW\DRAW\DEFAULT.CDR
2 C:\CORELDRW\DRAW\E9.CDR
3 C:\CORELDRW\DRAW\2-E1.CDR
4 C:\CORELDRW\DRAW\E6.CDR

**4.01 File Menu**

The file menu is concerned with opening, saving, importing and exporting files. The commands it contains are:

### NEW

Starts a new file. Any current backup of the current file will be deleted when you issue this command. If you have not saved the current file since making changes to it you will be prompted about doing so before the new file is launched.

### OPEN

Allows you to open an existing CorelDRAW file, i.e. one with an extension of .CDR. You can use the command to load files from any previous version of CorelDRAW, including the original release. Activating the command, and you can use the keyboard shortcut **Ctrl-O**, brings up a dialogue box:

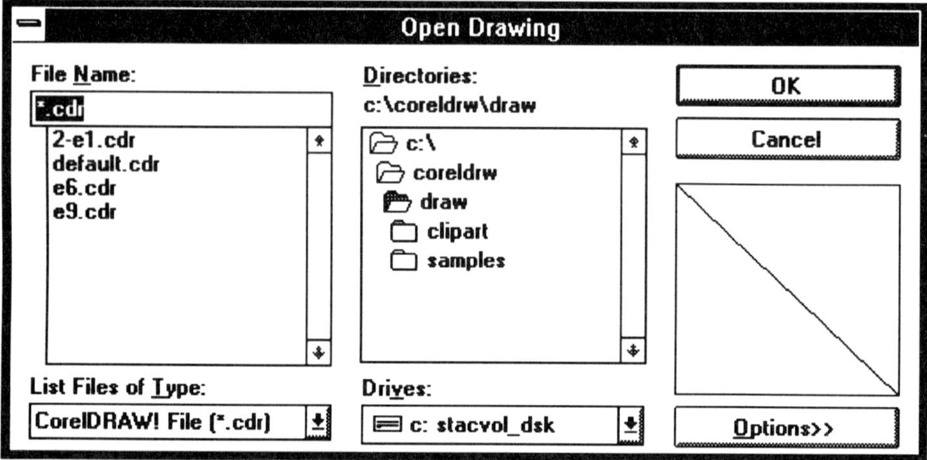


**4.02 Open dialogue box**

On the left hand side is the list of available files that have extensions which match that shown in **List of Files of Type** line. In this case there are four possible files. You can change the file type to .PAT - used for vector patterns.

In the centre is the list of your directory structure, part of it anyway. In this case you can tell that you are logged on to C:\CORELDRW\DRAW, both because that is the name specified and because that is the folder that is open in the window.

Beneath the main box is a line labelled **Drives**. This is a list box of the available logical drives on your computer. To log on to another drive, drop down the list box and double click on the drive you want to use.

On the right hand side are the usual **OK** and **Cancel** buttons. Beneath these is a large square, currently showing a diagonal line. If you click on a filename then the bitmapped header image of the file will appear here.

Click on the button labelled **Options** will expand the dialogue box:

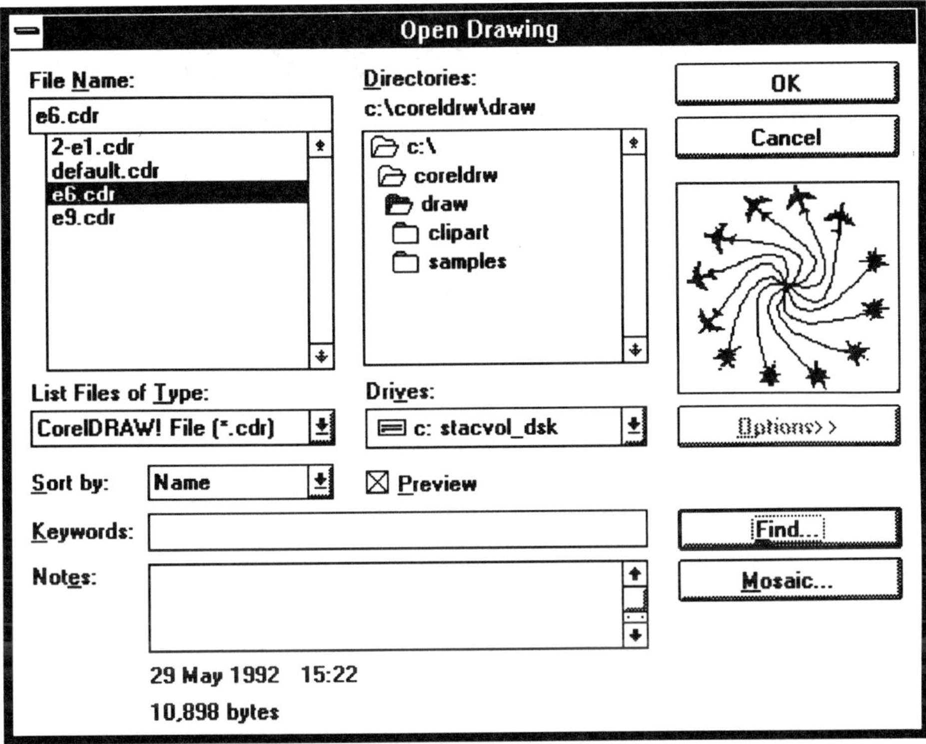


**4.03 Expanded open dialogue box**

**Sort by** changes the order of the displayed files. You can have the file listed in alphabetical or date order.

**Preview** turns the display of the header on or off. It is on by default.

**Keywords** will display whatever keywords you assigned to the file when you saved it. If there none then the line remains blank.

**Notes** appear if there are any.

**Find** brings up another dialogue box wherein you enter the keywords you want to search for. Be warned you must have the word exact. Only files with matching keywords will be displayed in the list box.

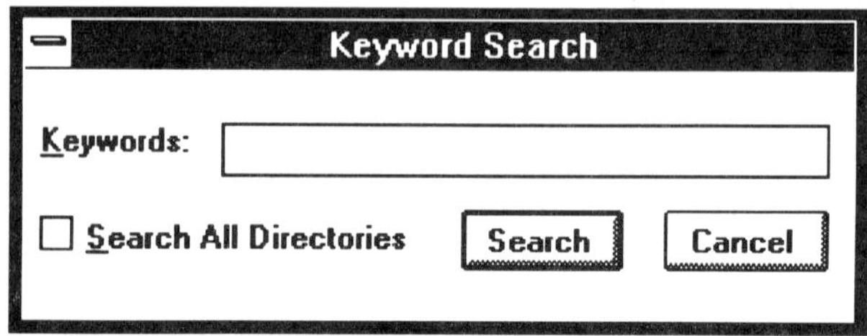


**4.04 Find dialogue box**

You can search the current directory, or by clicking on **Search all Directories** do just that. If no files match the keyword that you asked for then the list box of files will be blanked.

Clicking on **Mosaic** activates that program which can be used as an adjunct to CorelDRAW. Mosaic is covered elsewhere in this book so we'll ignore it here.

To load a file you simply double click on the filename once you've found it.

### SAVE

Writes the current file to disk using the name displayed on the Title Bar. If the file has not been named then issuing this command automatically calls the next one. The keyboard shortcut for this command is **Ctrl-S**.

### SAVE AS

Allows you to write a file to disk using a new name. It brings up a dialogue box:

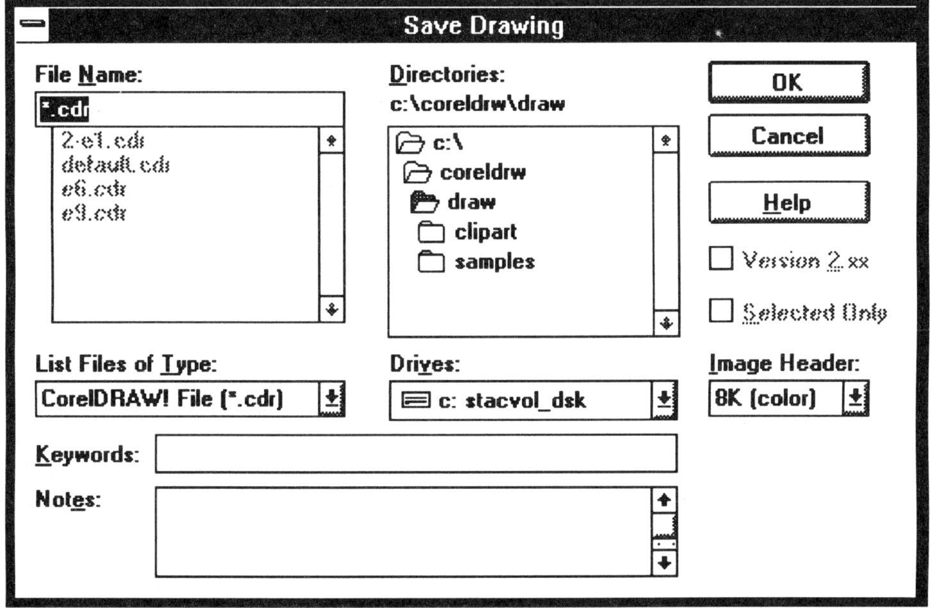


**4.05 Save As dialogue box**

This is essentially the same as the Open dialogue box but you use it in reverse, i.e. to save files rather than open them.

You can save a CorelDRAW file as either a standard .CDR file or as a full-colour fill pattern with an extension of .PAT.

**Image Header** refers to the size of the bitmap mini-picture that can be stored with each file. By default it is set to produce an 8 Kb full colour, i.e. 256 colours, header. However, you can change this to any of the following:

**None**, which means just that.

**1 Kb Mono** produces small headers that contain little information.

**2 Kb Mono** produces the kind of header used in CorelDRAW 2.0.

**4 Kb Colour** is identical to that used by CorelDRAW 2.01. Use this if you are using only 16 colours.

**8 Kb Colour** is the latest header size. It contains much more detail that the others. It is really only necessary if you are using 256 colours or more.

**Version 2.xx** is there so that you can save files in the old format if you wish. While you can load files from previous versions of CorelDRAW into Version 3.0 you cannot load a version 3 file in version 2.01 or earlier. By using this switch you can.

**Selected Only** allows you to save only those parts of the image that you have selected before issuing the command. If no objects are selected then the command is greyed out.

### IMPORT

Allows you to load an image from a vast range of other applications into CorelDRAW, both bitmap and vector formats. (A word of warning: A bitmap is a bitmap is a bitmap. Even if you import a BMP file and then save the whole as a CDR file the bitmap remains a bitmap. You cannot simply change things from one format to another by importing and saving them.) Issuing the command brings up a dialogue box:

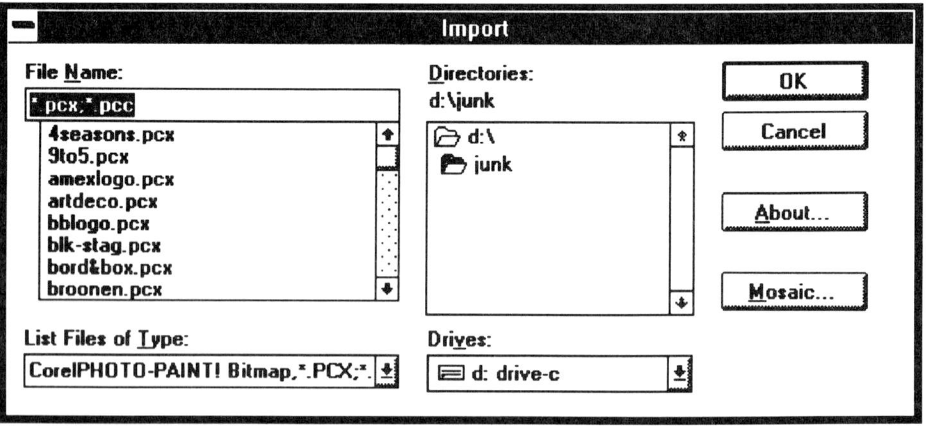


**4.06 Import dialogue box**

The dialogue box is similar to the load or save one in that it displays the list of available filename for a given format. CorelDRAW will now allow you to import any of the following file formats:

**AI** files from Adobe Illustrator.
**BMP** bitmap files from Windows Paintbrush.
**CDR** files created by CorelDRAW.
**CGM** files (Computer Graphics Metafile). An old, safe vector format. The only thing that lets it down is the fact that it cannot handle curves, it changes them to polygons instead. But it is fine if you want straight line stuff.
**DXF** files from AutoCAD.
**EPS** files from Adobe Illustrator or other standard EPS files.
**EPS** files from CorelTRACE. Note this is different to ordinary EPS!
**GEM** files.
**GIF** files using the CompuServe standard bitmap format.
**PCT** files from the Mac.
**PCX** bitmap files from Paintbrush or similar programs.
**PIC** files from Lotus.
**PIF** files.
**PLT** files from HP Plotter.
**TGA** Targa files.
**TIF** bitmap format.
**TXT** text files.
**WMF** which are Windows Meta Files.

Selecting a file type will cause only those files with a corresponding extension to be displayed in the list box. Once you double click on a file it is imported via the relevant filter.

A word of caution. There are at least three different versions of the EPS format. CorelDRAW can import two of them but it exports the third type. This means that if you export an EPS file from CorelDRAW you cannot re-import it.

### EXPORT

The opposite of the previous command. All you need do is set the filename and then select the type of file you want to create. CorelDRAW does the rest.

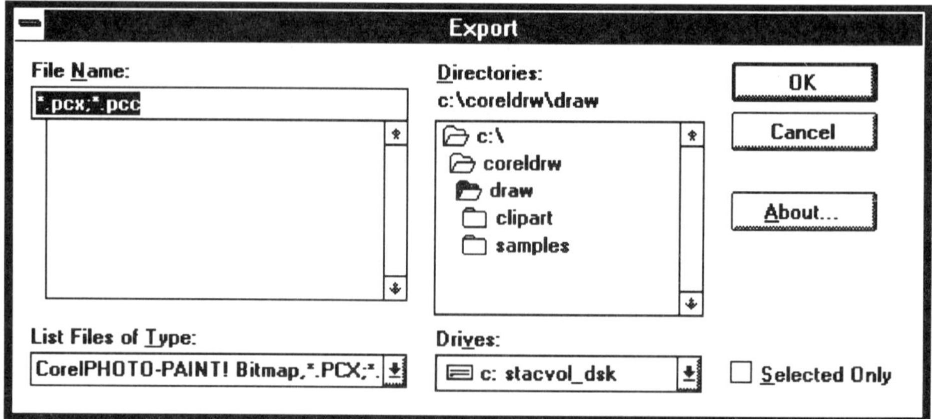


**4.07 Export dialogue box**

If you select to export a bitmap format then a new dialogue box appears:

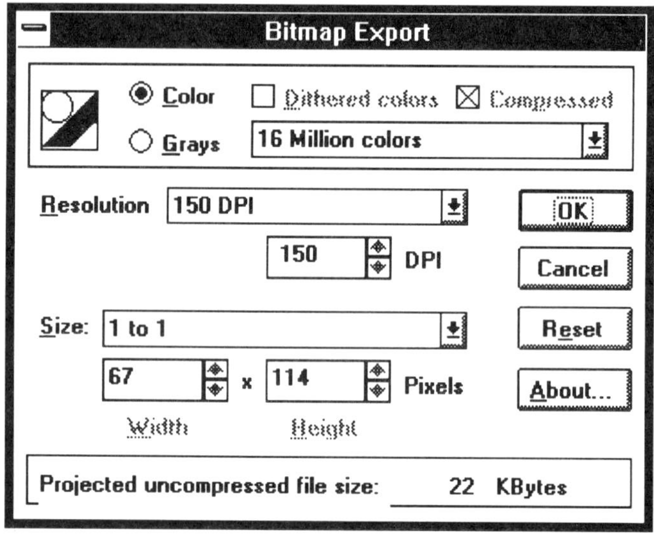


**4.08 Bitmap export**

You can specify whether to save the file in **Colour** or as **Greys**. With the former you can elect to use 16, 256 or 16 million colours. With the latter you can choose Black and White, 16 or 256 greyscales. All the bitmap filters, except the GIF one, allow up to 16 million colours. GIF only allows up to 256. You should also note that you cannot re-import a PCX file exported with 16 million colours.

The export features of CorelDRAW are device independent. That means that if you are working in monochrome you can still export colour images. Anyone else can then load these onto another system and have them display in colour.

The **Resolution** is important. You can now size an image as you wish, within limitations. However, the resolution is only available if you are using a 1:1 sizing. You have a choice of 300, 200, 150 or 75 dpi, plus two FAX settings of 200 x 100 and 100 x 100. There is also a Custom setting which allows you to specify up to 600 dpi. The higher the resolution the better the image but the size of the final file increases almost exponentially.

The **Size** can be any of the following:

**1:1**, i.e. the size it is in pixels.
**640 by 480**, which the VGA resolution.
**800 by 600**, the Super VGA resolution.
**1024 by 768**, the high resolution size.
**Custom**, which be anything from 32 to 2400 pixels in either direction.

Selecting a size other than 1:1 fixes the resolution.

Along the bottom of the dialogue box is a status line that tells you what the size of the saved file will be.

### INSERT OBJECT

Has to do with the Object Linking and Embedding features of Windows 3.1. As this is covered extensively elsewhere in this book, we'll ignore it here.

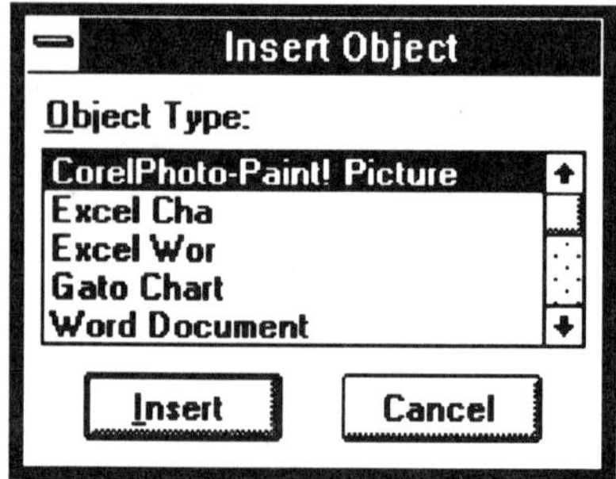


4.09 Inset Object dialogue box

## PRINT

Allows you to print your images. The keyboard shortcut is **Ctrl-P** and issuing it brings up a dialogue box.

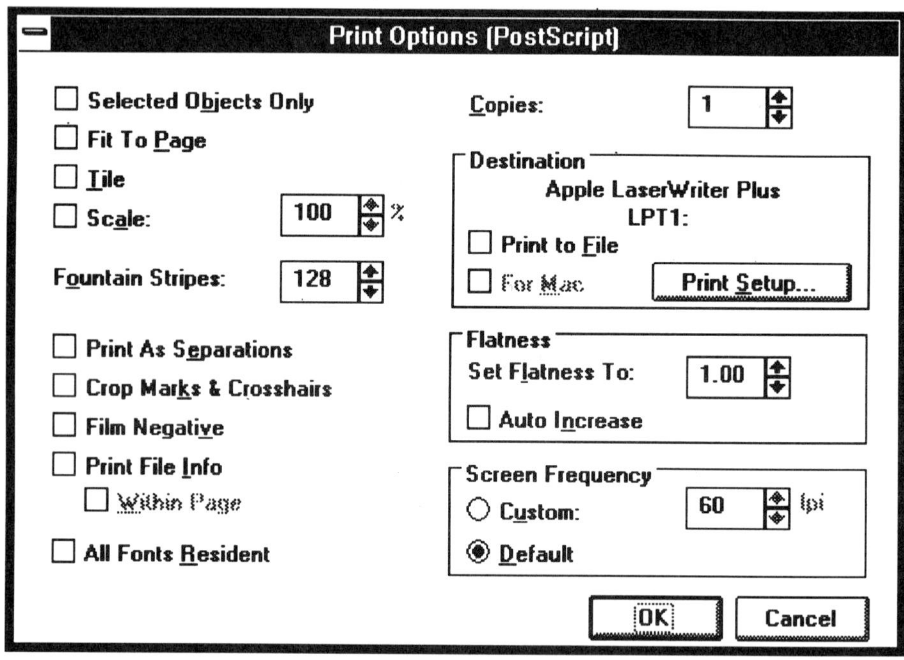


4.10 Print dialogue box

There is a complete chapter devoted to printing so we're only going to cover the dialogue box briefly here.

**Selected Objects Only** allows you to print only those object you have selected rather than the full file.

**Fit To Page** forces a change of magnification if necessary on the printed page. You can have a small image printed large or a large image printed small.

**Tile** is used if you are using a large page size within CorelDRAW but have a smaller page sized printer. The image will be 'cut up' and printed on separate pages for you rather than being scaled.

**Scale** allows you to set a scaling factor for the image. For example, to reduce an A4 image to A5 size you use a scaling factor of 72%.

**Fountain Stripes** only applies to PostScript printers. It allows you to define how many stripes are used for fountain fills.

**Print As Separations** prints the image in separate colour components. One page for Red, one for Blue and so on. See the printing chapter.

**Crop Marks & Crosshairs** will only work if you are using an on-screen page size that is smaller than your printer page size. What it does is produce alignment marks on the page.

**Film Negative** is only available if you are using a PostScript printer. What it does is create negative images, i.e. black becomes white and vice versa. Used for outputting to film negative rather than paper.

**Print File Info** allows you to add the information about the file to the printout. You have the option of including the data **Within Page** but only if the image leaves a large enough margin to include crop marks.

**All Fonts Resident** is also only available if you use a PostScript printer. (I've come to the conclusion that to use CorelDRAW properly you need a PostScript printer!) What it does is force the image to use the fonts that are resident in your printer rather than sending the CorelDRAW ones.

Don't try using this setting if you using something like Thor (the half uncial face) without having downloaded it first or all you will get is Courier.

A tip: Never use Courier for anything. All PostScript printers will default to Courier if they cannot find a particular font. If you never use it in your files then if it occurs you can quickly spot it and know that something is wrong.

**Destination** is the name of the current default printer and its port. You can change this by clicking on the button labelled **Print Setup** which brings up another dialogue box. From there you can select an alternative printer.

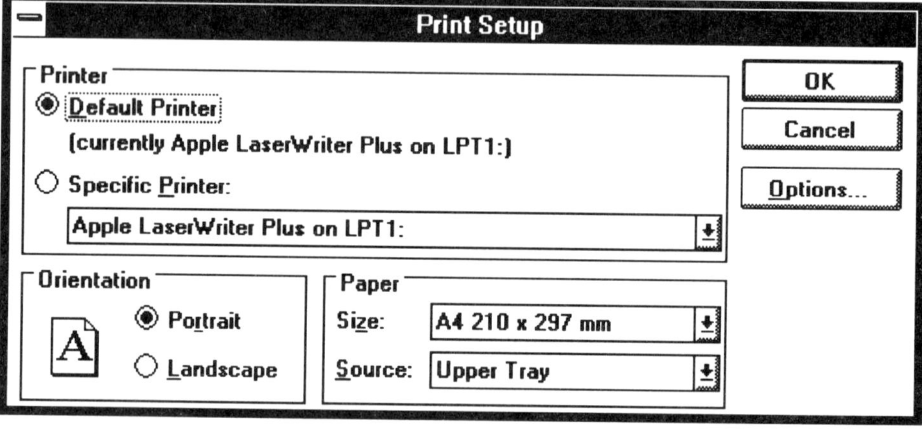


**4.11 Print Setup dialogue box**

**Print to File** allows you to generate a PRN file on disk rather than a printed page.

**Flatness** refers to how curves are treated. Only available on PostScript printers. Effectively the same as Curve Flatness in the Preferences menu.

**Auto Increase** is a new feature. By selecting it you force the printer to automatically change the curve flatness to try and print complex objects. It will keep on trying until it has increased the value to 10, the maximum, and if it still cannot print then it will omit the object completely. In this way you should always be able to print something though complex objects may be missing.

**Screen Frequency**, again only available for PostScript printers, is used for colour separations.

### PRINT MERGE

Allows you to do form letter printing. See the Printing Chapter for details.

### PAGE SETUP

We've already covered this in the previous chapter so we won't do so again.

### EXIT

Terminates CorelDRAW. The keyboard shortcuts are **Ctrl-X** or **Alt-F4**.

### DRAWINGS LIST

CorelDRAW now displays a list, of up to four files, showing the most recently opened .CDR files. To open any of these particular file just click on it or press **[Number]**.

# E10 - IMPORTING FILES

Run CorelDRAW as normal. It should have been shut down at the end of the last exercise. Once it appears on screen, you can maximise it if you wish by clicking on the **Maximise** button in the top right hand corner.

a. Open the **File** menu, either by pressing **Alt-F** or by clicking on the word.

b. In the drawings list at the bottom of the menu you should be able to see **DEFAULT.CDR**. To load the file just press the corresponding number.

c. If you have saved more than four files since you last saved this though then the file will not be listed and you will have to use the **Open** command. Press **O** and the load dialogue box appears.

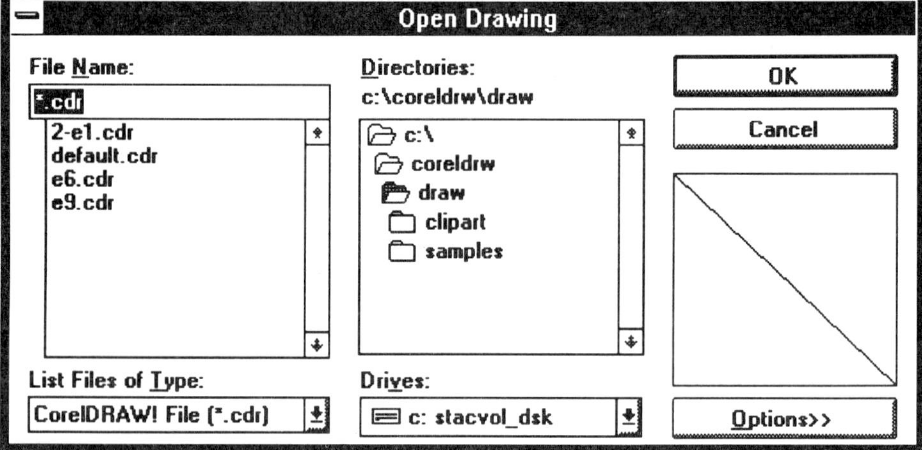


**4.13 Load dialogue box**

d. At this point you should be able to see the file in the list of filenames. But - it depends on where you last saved a file to. If you have been saving files to directories other than the one where you saved DEFAULT.CDR to, then you will have to navigate your way through the directory structure to get back to the CorelDRAW directory.

e. Once you are in the correct directory, double click on the filename and it will load, which means that CorelDRAW is now reset to your own personal defaults again.

f. Press **Alt-F N** or open the **File** menu and click on **New**. CorelDRAW retains the information from the last file, so your preferences remain in force.

g. Open the **File** menu again and click on **Import**.

h. Log on to the directory called **Samples**. It should be subtended off the main CorelDraw directory - unless you've put it somewhere else. You are looking for a file called **SHERMY.TIF**, so you have to change the filename type using the line at the bottom left of the dialogue box, to **TIFF 5.0 Bitmap. *.TIF**. The dialogue box will change to something like this:

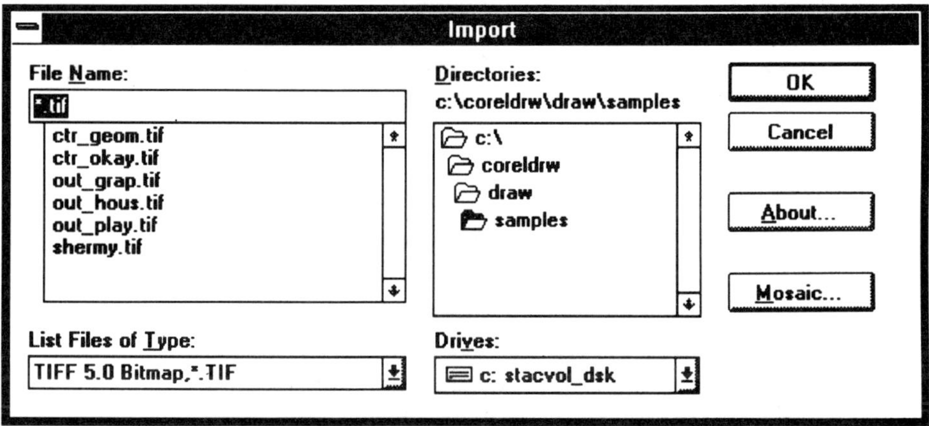


**4.14 Import all dialogue box**

i. Find the file and then double click on it. (This is a bitmap file, in the same format that might be generated by a scanner.) As the file is being imported you get a message appearing. The import is actually very fast and because Shermy is a small file the message box may flash on and off before you have a chance to read it. All it does is give you an indication of how far the importation has progressed.

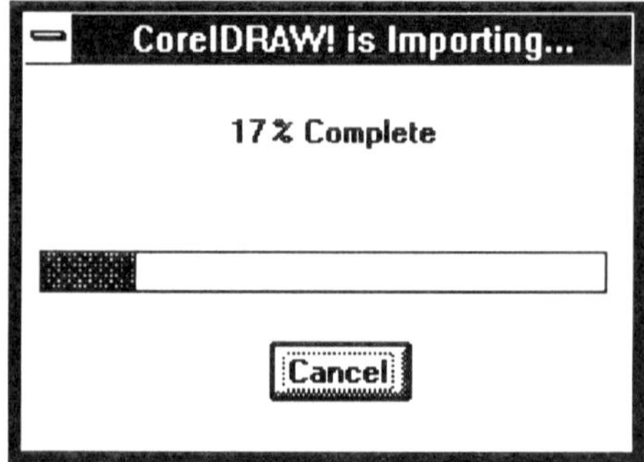


**4.15 Importing message box**

j. The file will be placed into the middle of the page as if you'd used Align to centre of page. Anything that is imported is placed in the middle of the page.

   Note: You have to change the file type when you are importing so that CorelDRAW knows which filter to use. If you tried to import a filename of a different type to that listed at the bottom of the dialogue box you will get an error message.

k. Because the file you've just imported is a bitmap it cannot be rescaled upwards without losing clarity. Drag the corner handles of the image to make it fill as much of the page as possible.

**4.16 Shermy resized**

On screen it looks fine but if you were to print it at this stage you would find that the edges are all jagged and uneven. With a bitmap, any change of scale or size will result in distortion of the image. A bitmap is literally a map of bits, the bits referring to pixels, and so when you resize an image the program does its best by adding pixels in some places when you enlarge the image or removing pixels in others when you reduce it, but you can never get the quality you expect from a bitmap unless you print it at its actual size.

l. If you zoom in at the edge of Shermy, try clicking the right hand mouse button a couple of times if you set it for 2x zoom, you will see that the image is all jagged. (I've blown the image right up to exaggerate the edges.)

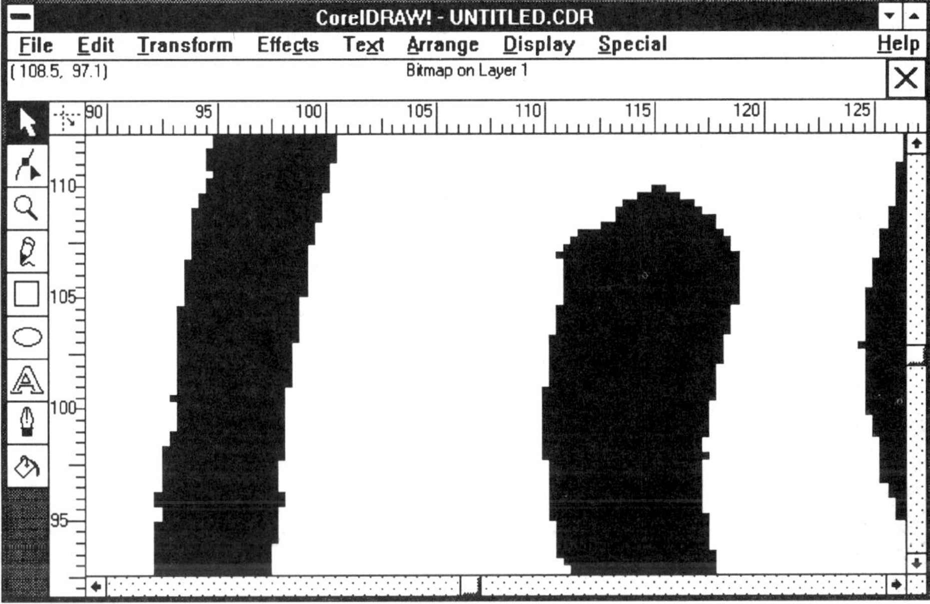


**4.17 Jagged edges**

m. Delete the current image and then re-import Shermy. You can never resize a bitmap down to its original size properly so it's easier to just delete it and then reload it.

n. Press **F4** to enlarge the image to fill the screen. This is not the same as resizing the actual image because all you're doing is changing the representation, not the image itself.

o. Click on the image a second time to bring up the Rotation Handles. Rotate the image 45 degrees to the left. In other words, hold down **Ctrl** and then drag the top left hand handle around to the left. Watch the Status Bar and when you get to 45 degrees stop. What you will end up with is a grey rectangle with one corner white.

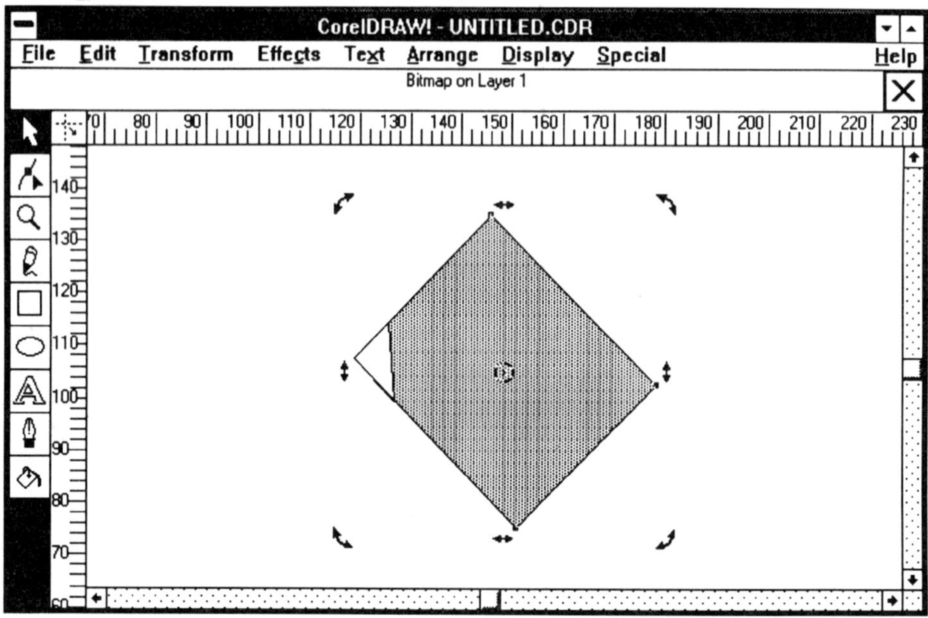


**4.18 Rotated bitmap**

The reason that you've got a grey square instead of an image is because redrawing the image at an angle is very complex and it's easier to show it as above. The image will print at that angle, and you get the image not a grey rectangle, but on screen it does not appear.

p. Rotate the image back and Shermy will reappear. You can only have a bitmap shown in the orientation it is imported in. The same grey rectangle will appear if you try to skew the image.

q. In most other respects you can treat the image normally. You can duplicate it, move it, colour it and so on.

r. Recreate the illustration below. The image in the middle is the original one. This was duplicated, by pressing the plus key on the numeric keypad, and then the duplicate moved to the top left hand corner of the page. That in turn was duplicated and then moved 40 mms to the right. That was duplicated and moved and so on. To go down the page, the corner image was duplicated and then moved 50 mms down. And so on.

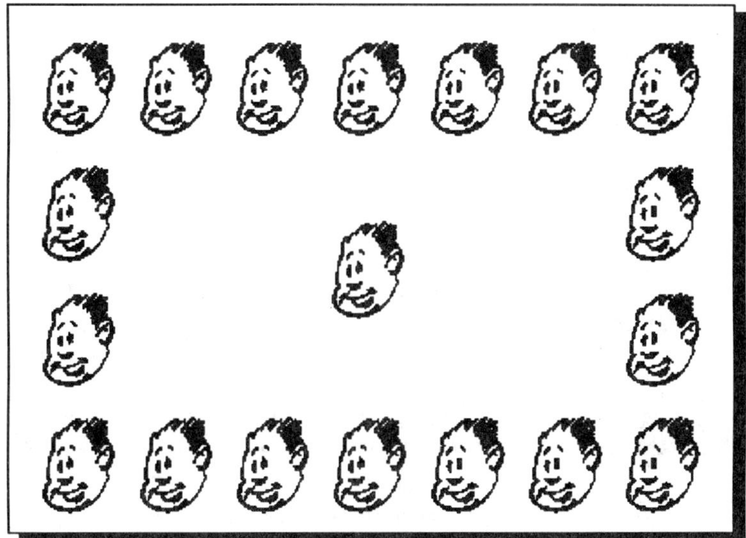

**4.19 Lots of Shermy's**

s. Save the file. Press **Ctrl-S** and the Save As dialogue box appears. Type **4-19** as the filename and then click on **OK** or press **Enter**. The file must be saved as a .CDR one.

t. Press **Alt-F N** or open the **File** menu and then click on **New**.

u. Open the **File** menu again and load the image you have just saved. (Just to prove that a bitmap remains a bitmap.) It will be number one in the drawings list so just press **1** when the menu opens.

v. If you click on any of the images the Status Bar will say "**Bitmap on Layer 1**". So, even though you saved the file as a CDR one, which is a vector format, the elements of the file remain bitmaps.

# E11 - CLIP-ART

The Clip-Art the comes with CorelDRAW is extensive - there are over 14,000 images on the CD-ROM. That's the entire current clip-art library that Corel possess! Of course if you don't have a CD drive then you are limited to the amount of Clip-Art available. The CD also contains an additional 100 fonts plus all the CorelDRAW fonts as Adobe Type 1 format in addition to various other things. It has got to the point where it is worth getting a CD drive just so you get the full benefit of CorelDRAW.

Anyway, some clip-art will be shipped on the floppy disks, albeit far far less than on the CD, so let's have a look at some of that.

a. To open any of the clip-art images, press **Alt-F O** or open the **File** menu and click on **Open**. In the dialogue box log on to the Clip-art directory, you will then find that there are a number of other sub-directories sub-tended off that.

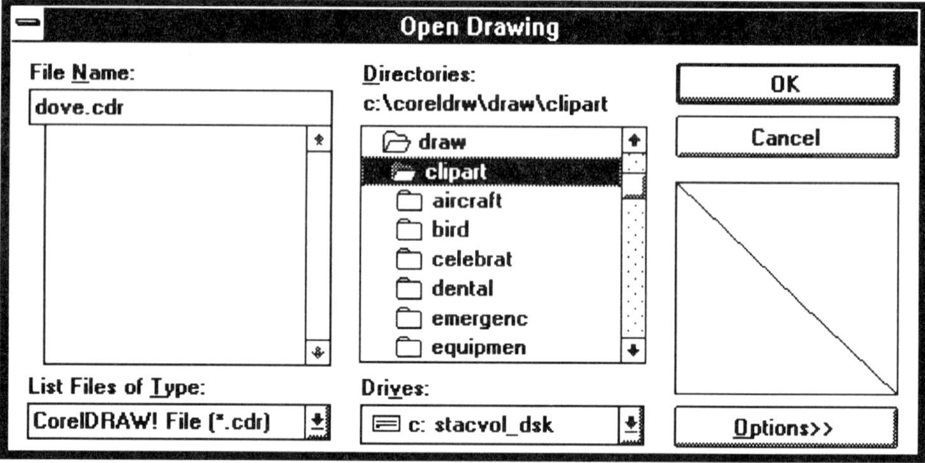


**4.20 Open dialogue box**

I don't know what clip-art is going to be shipped with the floppy disk version of CorelDRAW, but the principles of what follows remain.

b. Log on to the sub-directory that you want to look at. Based on the illustration above I'm logging into **BIRD** and then selecting **DOVE.CDR**. Double click on the filename to load it. Alternatively, click on a filename once and the header of the image appears in the view window. Find one you like and click on **OK**.

c. The page, rulers, grid etc. will change as the file is imported. The CorelDRAW hourglass will appear for large files as they are loaded. Sooner or later the image will appear - in full colour. (I loaded the dove because it is in Mono and so will make a reasonable illustration.)

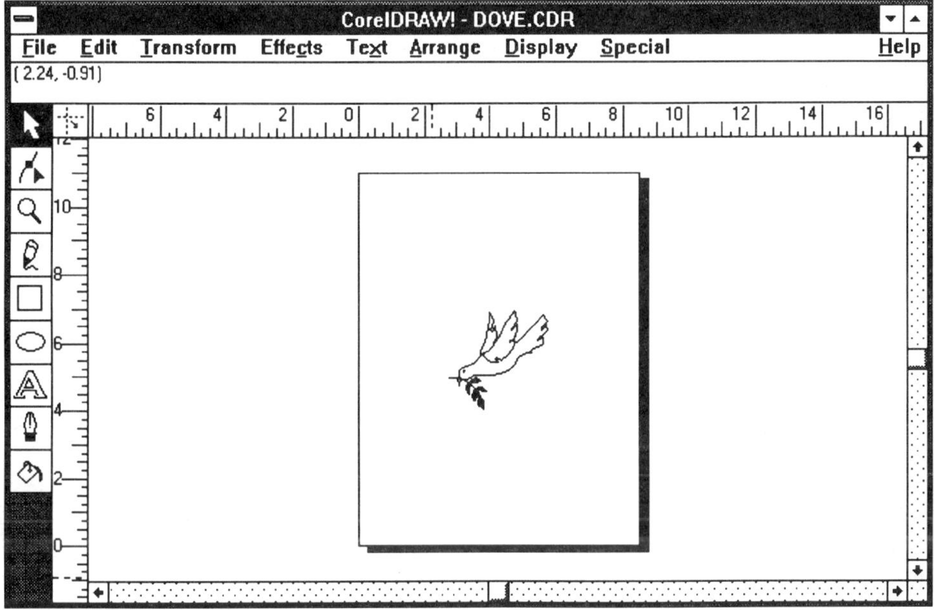


**4.21 Dove loaded**

d. Notice that the rulers have gone back to inches, the page size has returned to the original size (8.5" by 11") and the original orientation. However, you can now do whatever you want with the image.

e. There is another way that you can use the clip-art and that's to import the images. Load your default file again, it should be listed in the drawings list, and then press **Alt-F N** or open the **File** menu and click on **New**. You get all your own settings back.

f. Now, instead of opening the image you can **Import** it. Notice that the dialogue box 'remembers' where you last logged on to when you used it and what file type you imported. Change the file type to **CorelDRAW!, .CDR** and then log on to the Clip-Art sub-directory.

g. Find the file you want to import. This time, because you are using import, you do not see the header. Double click on the file and it will be imported.

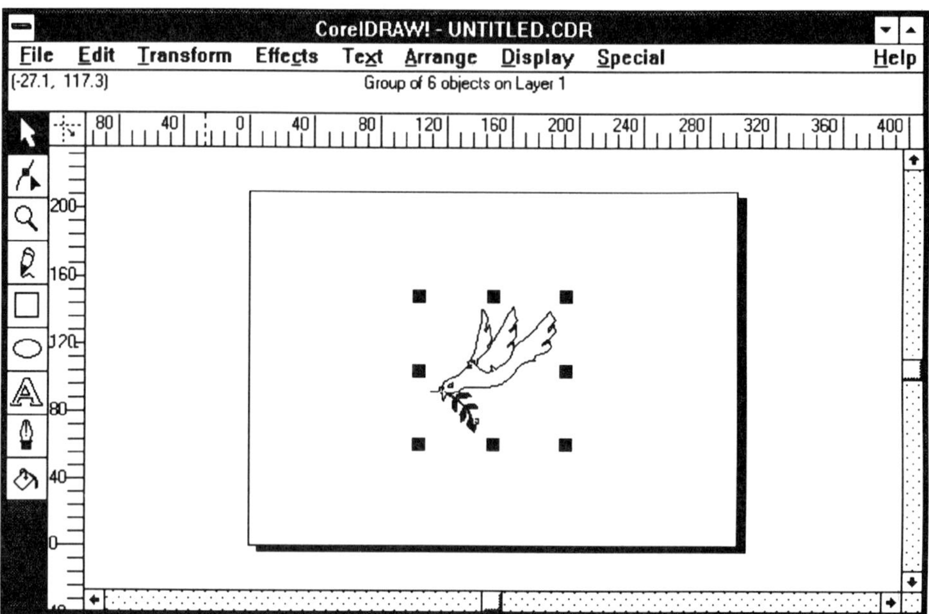


**4.22 Dove imported**

h. Notice that the Status Bar says "**Group of 6 objects on Layer 1**". Whenever you import a file, other than a bitmap, into CorelDRAW the file is imported as groups of objects. That just means that the image can be treated as a whole. (We'll come to groups and their use later in this chapter.)

i. You can now resize, rescale, rotate, colour and otherwise use the image as if you had created it yourself. By way of example, we're going to colour various parts of this image. Enlarge the image so that it fills most of the page using the handles. Before you can do so you need to ungroup it. Press **Ctrl-U**, with the image selected, and the Status Bar now says "**6 Objects on Layer 1**". In other words you now have separate elements for the image.

j. Click on the page, anywhere other than on the image, to deselect the image parts. Get the **Pen** and **Fill** roll-ups and in either one of them open the **Control Box** and click on **Arrange All**. The roll-ups will roll up and arrange themselves at the top left hand corner of the screen.

k. Open the **Fill** roll-up. Select the olive branch that the dove is holding. Click on a darkish green in the roll-up to colour it.

l. Open the **Pen** roll-up and select a light green. Apply this to the olive branch.

m. Zoom in to the bird's eye to make it easier to do things with. If you press **F2** you will get the magnifier. Drag a small bounding box around the eye and just that part of the image will be magnified. Fill the eye with Blue and then press **F3** to zoom back out.

n. You don't need to fill the wings or the body because they are already filled with white. Change the fill if you want to.

The six elements by the way are the two wings, the body, the eye, the beak and the olive branch.

o. Just by way of demonstration. Select all the elements by dragging a bounding box around them using the **Pointer** tool. Then group them again by pressing **Ctrl-G**.

p. What you're going to do is flip the image. You can do this using one of the menu commands but it is also possible to do it with the mouse. Click on the central handle on the left hand side of the image. Hold down **Ctrl** and drag the handle off to the right, straight across the image. Watch the Status Bar as you do so and when it says "**x scale: -100%**" let go of the mouse button. The image will flip and become a mirror image of the original.

q. You can flip an image vertically too. Hold down **Ctrl** and drag the central bottom handle straight up. You can also do it by dragging the corner handles but that flips the image horizontally and vertically at the same time.

s. Holding down **Ctrl** while you drag an image constrains the size change to increments of 100%. So if you drag the central left handle to the left the image will be stretched horizontally by 200%, drag it further and the image is stretched by 300%, then 400% and so on. Notice that the page on screen moves to accommodate the new size of the image. If you want to see the entire image on screen press **F4**.

t. If you hold down **Shift** while you are moving the handles something else happens. Dragging a corner handle causes all four corners to move, dragging a central handle causes opposite handles to move. In each case the paired handles move by equal amounts. You can also hold down **Shift-Ctrl** while moving the handles which combines the two effects.

u. You can also rotate the image as if it was a single object because it is grouped together. Or align the whole thing to the centre of the page by pressing **Ctrl-A** and then clicking on **Align to centre of page**.

Try importing a number of different images and creating a montage. Add some drawn objects of your own and you can create complex images very quickly. Remember that you can arrange things using **PgUp** and **PgDn**.

**4.23 Montage image**

# 5 - Edit Menu

The Edit menu contains the familiar commands that you would expect of any Windows application, i.e. those that handle the interfacing to the Clipboard. However, it also contains a range of commands that are specific to CorelDRAW.

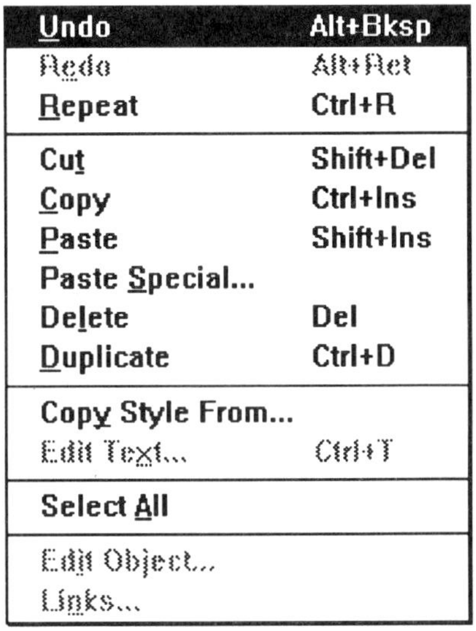

| | |
|---|---|
| Undo | Alt+Bksp |
| Redo | Alt+Ret |
| Repeat | Ctrl+R |
| Cut | Shift+Del |
| Copy | Ctrl+Ins |
| Paste | Shift+Ins |
| Paste Special... | |
| Delete | Del |
| Duplicate | Ctrl+D |
| Copy Style From... | |
| Edit Text... | Ctrl+T |
| Select All | |
| Edit Object... | |
| Links... | |

**5.01 Edit menu**

The commands available are:

**Undo** which cancels your previous action. You can only undo whatever action you carried out immediately prior to activating this command. For example, if you draw a line and then draw a circle you can undo the circle but not the line. The keyboard shortcut is **Alt-Backspace**.

**Redo** is the opposite of the above. It allows you to undo an undo command. In other words when you undo something you issue this command to cancel the undo. The keyboard shortcut is **Alt-Return**.

**Repeat** allows you to repeat an action! It's actually very useful because you can carry out a complex action, e.g. one involving a dialogue box command,

and then apply the same command structure to something else by using this command - without having to open the dialogue box again. The keyboard shortcut is **Ctrl-R**.

**Cut** is the standard Windows command to place something into the Clipboard and delete it from the page. The keyboard shortcut is **Shift-Del** and/or **Ctrl-X** - the latter only in Windows 3.1.

**Copy** is also a Windows command which simply copies selected objects to the Clipboard. The keyboard shortcut is **Ctrl-Ins** and/or **Ctrl-C** - again the latter is only available in Windows 3.1.

**Paste** is the complement of the previous two commands. It places the Clipboard contents into the current file. The keyboard shortcut is **Shift-Ins** and/or **Ctrl-V**, the latter with Windows 3.1 only.

**Paste Special** is to do with OLE. See Chapter 15.

**Delete** erases things! Select an object and press **Del**.

**Duplicate** is a CorelDRAW command. You can use this to make a duplicate of a selected object. The object will be placed at a position according to the setting in the Preferences dialogue box. The keyboard shortcut is **Ctrl-D**.

**Copy Style From** allows you to copy the fill, outline, colours and/or text attributes from one object and apply them to another one in a single action.

**Edit Text** does just that by bringing up the Text dialogue box. The keyboard shortcut is **Ctrl-T** once you have selected the text. If you don't select the text then you cannot issue this command.

**Select All** does what it says. All the objects in the current file will be selected as if you had dragged a selection box around the whole lot.

**Edit Object** is concerned with OLE. See Chapter 15.

**Links** is also concerned with OLE. See Chapter 15.

# E12 - CUTTING AND PASTING

The Windows Clipboard is actually a very powerful data sharing device and you can use it to copy and paste images from CorelDRAW to a wide range of other programs. The appearance of the objects you copy from CorelDRAW will depend, in part, on some of the settings in the CORELDRW.INI file. See the Appendix for full details. It is outside the scope of this book to cover copying images to other software so this exercise will concentrate on copying data in and out of CorelDRAW itself.

a. Start a new page then draw a circle, about 50 cms in diameter, in the centre of the page. Draw it and then align it is probably easier. If you press **Ctrl-Y** you will turn on the grid which will allow you to draw very precise measurements. The Status Bar will say "**Snap to Grid**" on the left.

b. Open the **Fill** roll-up and use it to fill the circle with blue. At this stage it must be a pure colour, nothing fancy.

c. Make sure the circle is selected and then press **Shift-Del**. This will copy the shape to the Clipboard and then erase it from the page.

d. Zoom in on the top left hand corner of the page, either using the right mouse button by pressing **F2** and then using the magnifier. It doesn't matter exactly how much you zoom but you don't want to be able to see the centre of the page.

e. Press **Shift-Ins** to copy the circle back from the Clipboard. Nothing happens. Zoom the page out by pressing **Shift-F4**. There's the circle back in the middle of the page.

That's the way that CorelDRAW always pastes things back. Any item copying or cut to the Clipboard will be pasted back in the same position that it came from. If you copy something from the top left hand corner of the page it will always be pasted back to that position. At times this can be a real nuisance but that's the way it works.

f. Delete the circle. Select the **Text** tool and write **CorelDRAW** on the page. Switch back to the **Pointer** tool by clicking on it. (You cannot switch from the text tool to another by pressing the spacebar for obvious reasons.) The text is selected. Press **Ctrl-T** to bring up the Text dialogue box.

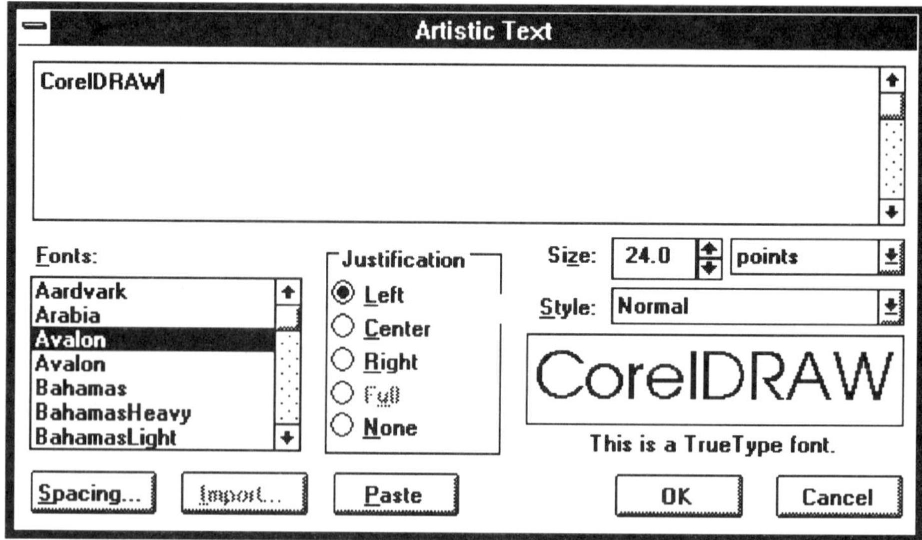


**5.02 Text dialogue box**

g. Change the typeface to **Bahamas Heavy** and the point size to **120**. Press **Enter** to close the dialogue box or click on **OK**. Then align the text to the centre of the page.

h. Fill the text with nothing, you'll have to use the Palette along the bottom of the screen because you cannot select no fill from the roll-up.

i. Open the **Pen** roll-up and click on **Edit**. The Outline Pen dialogue box appears. Change the settings in it to match the illustration above. The fastest way to change the Calligraphy effects is to overwrite the existing value by highlighting them and then typing the values you want. Click on **OK** to close the dialogue box and then click on **Apply** in the roll-up. Press **F4** to make the text fill the screen. You'll end up with some funny looking text.

Normally you would not use any outline with text because it causes the text to be fuzzy when you print it. Using text without an outline will give you crisp characters. However, there's method in my madness, so just bear with me for a minute. The calligraphic outline is one aspect of CorelDRAW that is rarely used, for some odd reason, but it can give you wonderful effects.

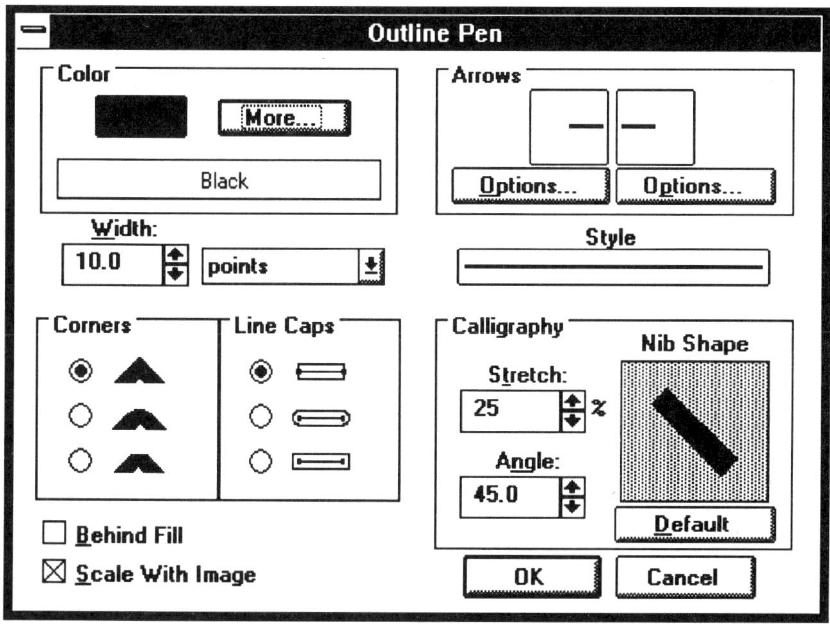


**5.03 Outline Pen dialogue box**

j. Open the **Edit** menu and click on **Copy**. A message box will appear telling you that CorelDRAW is copying. It may be on the screen for a measurable amount of time because calligraphic outlines take a long time to copy.

k. Press **Shift-F4** to go back to the full page view. Open the **Edit** menu again and click on **Paste**. The text is pasted back - right over the top of the existing text. You can pick this up and move it to reveal the original text. You can paste as many copies of the text as you wish because the image remains in the Clipboard until you copy something else to it.

l. Clear the page again. Draw a large rectangle, one that nearly fills the page, and fill it with a Radial Fountain Fill using just black and white. Copy this to the Clipboard as before. This time the message box will probably appear for much longer than last time.

m. If you want to see what the clipboard image looks like, reduce CorelDRAW to an icon. Open the Program Manager and find the Clipboard icon. Double click on that and it will appear, bearing the image you have just copied to it. Bring CorelDRAW back to full size by double clicking on it.

n. Change the fill in the rectangle to one of the bitmap fills then copy the rectangle to the Clipboard again. Look at this in the actual clipboard. It's all grey! But when you paste it back in it appears as normal. The Clipboard does have limitations when it comes to viewing things.

o. Finally, try a full colour fill in the rectangle. You'll probably have to tile this to make it a reasonable size. Copy the rectangle to the Clipboard again. Delete the original rectangle and paste it back again.

The object of trying all the different fills is two-fold. On the one hand it gives you practise using CorelDRAW and the Clipboard. But the second reason is far more important. It allows you to learn the limitations of your system. The length of time it takes to copy and paste image is very, very dependent on your system resources. On a machine with little memory, i.e. less than 4 Mb, or one with slow hard disks using the Clipboard can take a long time. If using the Clipboard does place a strain on your system then you should seriously consider upgrading it.

Experiment with the Clipboard commands until you are fully familiar with them. Try copying multiple images, with different fills in each one, or combinations of text and shapes.

# E13 - REPEAT AFTER ME

The Repeat command is one of the most useful that the program has because it allows you to effectively automate some commands. It really comes into its own once you start using dialogue box commands which we'll come to from the next chapter onwards. But for now, here's some simple things you can do with it.

a. Start with a clean page. Draw a 30 mms square. Move this down to the bottom left hand corner of the page.

b. Press **Ctrl-D**, the **Duplicate** shortcut. A second square appears slightly above and to the right of the original. (The actual distance between the two squares depends on the settings you made in the Preferences dialogue box originally.)

c. Press **Ctrl-R** and you get another square, again slightly to the right and above the second one. **Repeat** acts only on the last command you issued. However, you can use it with a number of objects at the same time.

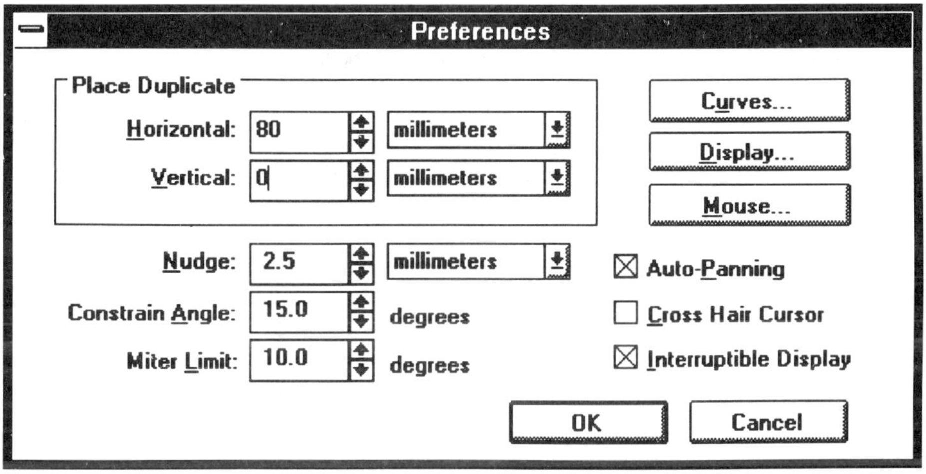

**5.04 Preferences dialogue box**

d. Press **Ctrl-J** to bring up the Preferences dialogue box. Change the values in the **Place Duplicate** section to read 50 mms Horizontal and 0 mms Vertical. (You cannot have a value greater than 50.8 mms or less than -50.8 mms - that's plus or minus two inches.) Click on **OK** to close the dialogue box.

e. Select all three squares by dragging a selection box around them. Then press **Ctrl-D** again. You will get the three squares being duplicated and placed 50 mms to the right of the originals.

f. You can use the Repeat command to do more than that though. Select the first set of squares. Rotate them 45 degrees. Then select the second set of squares and press **Ctrl-R**. These will rotate exactly the same amount.

g. Delete both sets of squares. Draw a circle about 75 mms in diameter. Give it a 1 point black outline and fill it with blue.

h. Draw a square, 75 mms to a side. It will have the default attributes you previously set, e.g. no fill and 0.2 point outline. Duplicate it using the plus key and place the duplicate away from the original so that it does not touch or overlap.

i. Open the **Edit** menu and click on **Copy Style From**. You must have one of the squares selected first or the command will be greyed out. A dialogue box appears:

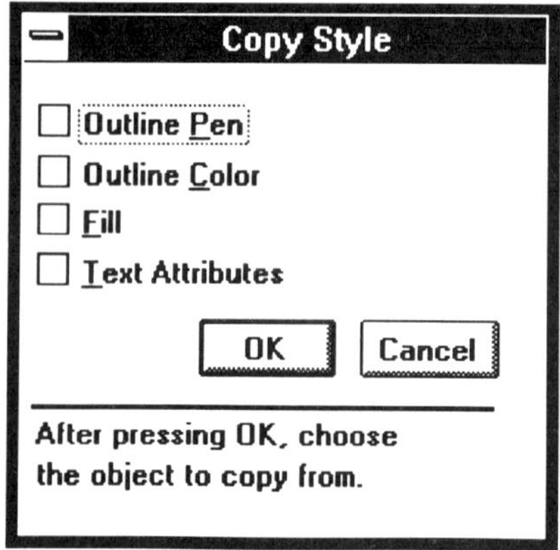


**5.05 Copy Style From dialogue box**

j. The dialogue box allows you to copy the Outline Pen, i.e. its size and attributes, the Outline Colour, the Fill and/or the Text Attributes from any object to the selected object. Click on **Outline Pen** and **Fill** and then on **OK**.

k. You get a thick black arrow with the word **From?** on it. Click on the circle and the selected square will instantly become filled with blue and have a 1 point outline.

l. Select the second square and then press **Ctrl-R**. That will be filled and outlined as if you had issued the Copy Style From command again but without you having to select an object to copy from.

Play with the command and explore its possibilities.

# 6 - Transform Menu

The Transform menu contains only four commands but their effects can be extremely powerful, interesting and useful - not necessarily in that order.

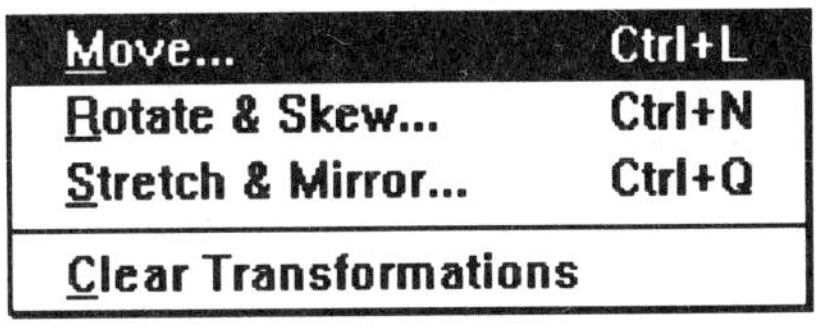

| Move... | Ctrl+L |
|---|---|
| Rotate & Skew... | Ctrl+N |
| Stretch & Mirror... | Ctrl+Q |
| Clear Transformations | |

**6.01 Transform Menu**

The commands, the first three of which activate dialogue boxes, available are:

**Move** which allows you to move selected objects around the page. Similar to just moving something by dragging it but you have total control of the positioning. The keyboard shortcut is **Ctrl-L**.

**Rotate & Skew** gives the same effects as using the rotational handles but it gives you much greater control. The keyboard shortcut is **Ctrl-N**.

**Stretch & Mirror** is used for making precise changes in the object. Use **Ctrl-Q** to open the dialogue box.

**Clear Transformations** does not just cancel the previous commands. It allows you to clear any changes you have made to an object and return it to its original state - subject to some minor limitations.

# E14 - MOVE OVER

a. Start a new page, using **Alt-F N**. Turn on the grid, using **Ctrl-Y**. It really wants to be set to half centimetre squares. Use a landscape A4 page.

b. One thing you can do in CorelDRAW is place **Guidelines** which allow you to accurately position things. You can use any tool to do this. Move the cursor on to the ruler on the left. Click and drag to the right. A dashed blue line appears. This is a guideline. Place it at 10 mms from the left hand side of the page.

c. Drag another guideline down from the top ruler and place it 10 mms from the top of the page. Guidelines can be moved at any time, unless they are locked which we'll come to later, and you can have lots of them on screen - up to 50 in fact - though you shouldn't have too many or they get in the way.

d. Draw a circle 25 mms in diameter and move it close to where the guidelines cross. You will find that suddenly the circle moves of its own accord and aligns itself with the guides. (Provided you have not turned off **Snap to Guidelines** in the Display menu when you were setting the defaults.)

e. Press **Ctrl-L** to bring up the Move dialogue box.

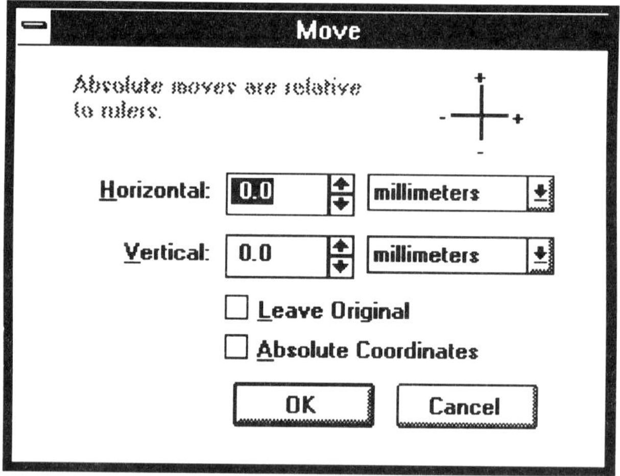


**6.02 Move dialogue box**

The coordinates are just like those in the Place Duplicate section of the Preferences dialogue box. You set a horizontal and a vertical shift amount. In this case set the Horizontal shift to 25 mms.

**Leave Original** is something that you will see in lots of dialogue boxes from now on. It means what it says, it effectively makes a duplicate and leaves the original behind. Click on it to turn it on.

**Absolute Coordinates** refer to actual positions on the page. If you turn this on now, when you close the dialogue box the circle would be placed 25 mms along the bottom of the page. Don't turn it on because we want to use Relative coordinates, the default.

f. Click on **OK** to close the dialogue box and you now have two circles. Press **Ctrl-R** and you get a third because the Repeat command uses the data from the dialogue box without having to activate it again. Press **Ctrl-R** another eight times until you have a line of circles across the top of the page. (That assumes you are using a landscape page.)

g. Press **Ctrl-L** to bring up the dialogue box again. Change the Horizontal shift to 0 and the Vertical shift to -25 mms. You must set it to a minus figure because we want to move the circle down the page. You have to click on **Leave Original** again by the way. Close the dialogue box and the circle moves.

h. Press **Ctrl-R** six times to get a line of circles down the right hand side of the page.

i. Drag a selection box around all the circles you have just created, i.e. not the one in the top right hand corner, on the right hand side of the page. Open the Move dialogue box again. Enter **-250 mms** in the Horizontal shift box and click on **Leave Original** before closing the box. You now have a line of circles down the left hand side of the page.

j. Use the dialogue box again to place a line of circles along the bottom of the page.

k. Select all the circles and combine them together into a single curve using **Ctrl-C**. (We come to combining objects later.) Save the file, call it **E14**.

# E15 - STRETCH & MIRROR

a. You now want to place a duplicate curve within the existing one. Select the current image and then press **Ctrl-Q** to bring up the **Stretch & Mirror** dialogue box.

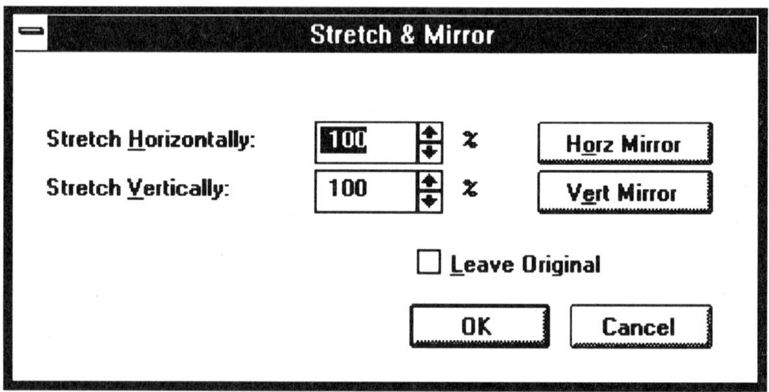


**6.03 Stretch & Mirror dialogue box**

b. This dialogue box is deceptively simple looking. You enter values, in percentage terms, for what you want to resize. We want the duplicated shape to be within the original but without touching it. Enter values of 75% and 50%. Click on **Leave Original** and then on **OK**.

c. Press **Ctrl-R** and you get a third set of circles. Save the file again, using the same filename. Press **Ctrl-S**. Notice that the circles within the two duplicates are now deformed. The more you stretch them the greater the deformation.

d. The Stretch & Mirror effects are much more visible with text. Start a new page, notice that the guidelines vanish as you do so. Guidelines are specific to the file they are applied to, when you open E14 later you'll find the guidelines are still there.

e. Type CorelDRAW on the page. Change the Typeface to **Arabia** and the size to **120 points**. Align it to the centre of the page. Open the Stretch & Mirror dialogue box again and this time click on **Horz Mirror** - short for Horizontally

Mirror. Don't click on Leave Original this time. The value in the Horizontal Stretch line will change to -100%. Click on **OK**.

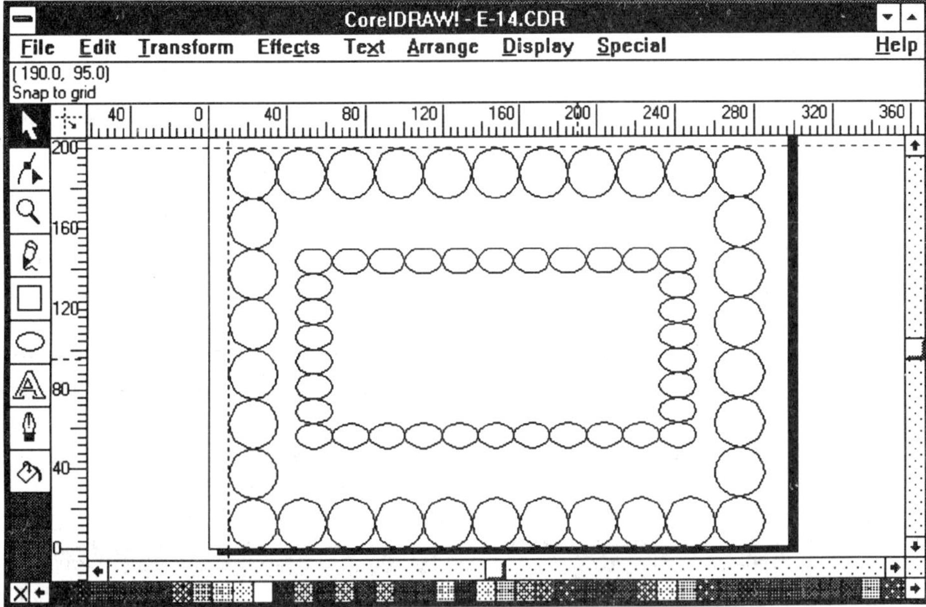


**6.04 Two sets of circles**

f. You now have a mirror image, correct in every detail, of the original text. Open the dialogue box again and time click on **Vert Mirror**. You now have text that is upside down and back to front. If you look at it standing on your head it's the right way up - don't fall off the desk!

g. Open the **Transform** menu and click on **Clear Transformations**. The text is returned to its original state.

Play with the dialogue box. Try some exception values, you can use anything in the range -3000% to +3000% for either axis - though if you do so you get some really weird effects.

# E16 - ROTATE & SKEW

The **Rotate & Skew** dialogue box allows you precise control of the these facilities, far finer than you can achieve quickly using the rotational handles.

a. Clear the page. Place two guides on the page so that they cross in the centre of the page.

b. Write the word **CorelDRAW**. Set the Typeface to **Avalon** and the size to **48 Points**. Place the word above the horizontal guide but 10 mms to the right of the vertical one.

c. Press **F4**, which will zoom in on the word, and then **F3** to step back fractionally. You should now be able to see the word and the intersection of the guidelines.

d. Bring up the rotational handles on the word. Drag the little circle from the middle so that it sits on top of the intersection of the guides.

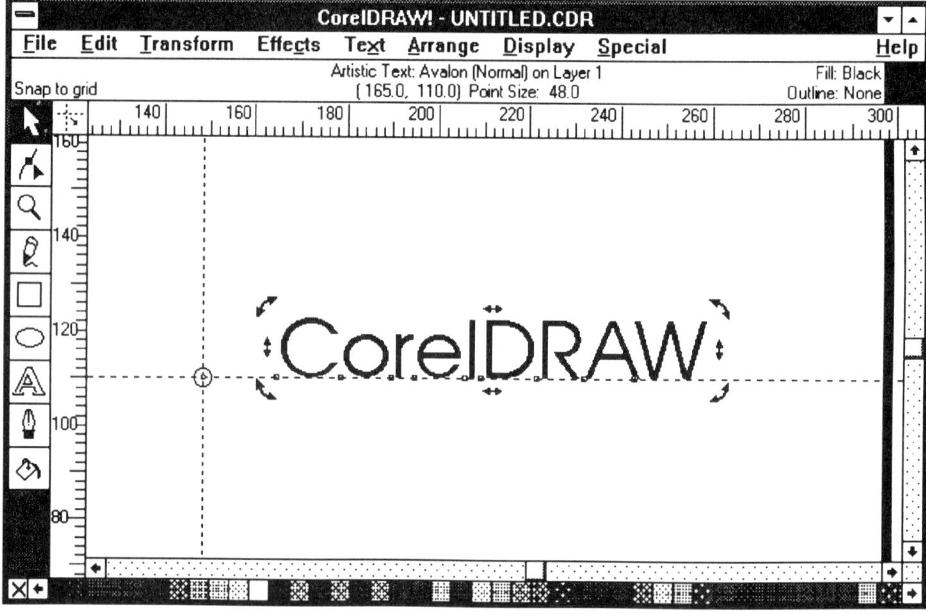


**6.05 Word and rotational centre**

e. Press **Ctrl-N** to bring up the dialogue box. Set the Rotational Angle to 24 degrees and click on **Leave Original**. Click on **OK**. The word is rotated, leaving the original behind, around the point where the guides intersect.

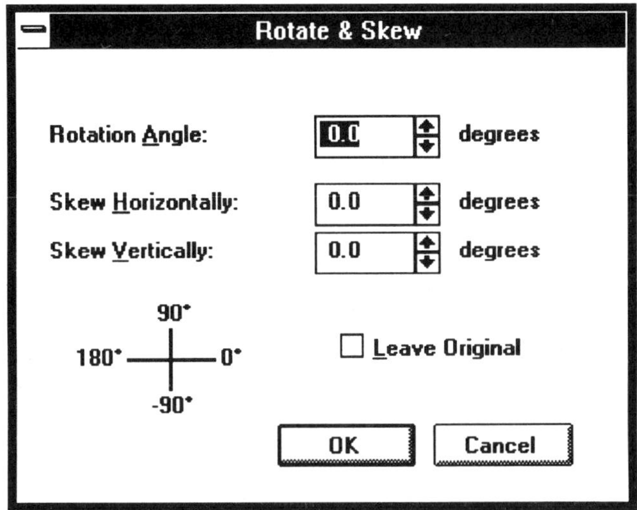


**6.06 Rotate & Skew dialogue box**

f. Press **Ctrl-R** repeatedly until you have a rosette of words. It actually produces an optical illusion if you look at it quickly.

That's using the rotational abilities of CorelDRAW at their simplest. The important point to realise is that objects rotate around the centre point which is now fully moveable. This gives you an enormous amount of effects you can generate. The more you play with the command the more you will discover. In particular, using the command in conjunction with Repeat can produce amazing effects quickly and easily.

# Q5 - Sphereville

This image was created using the Move and Rotate commands from their dialogue boxes. See if you can duplicate it. Be warned the angles are important and they are rather difficult to get right!

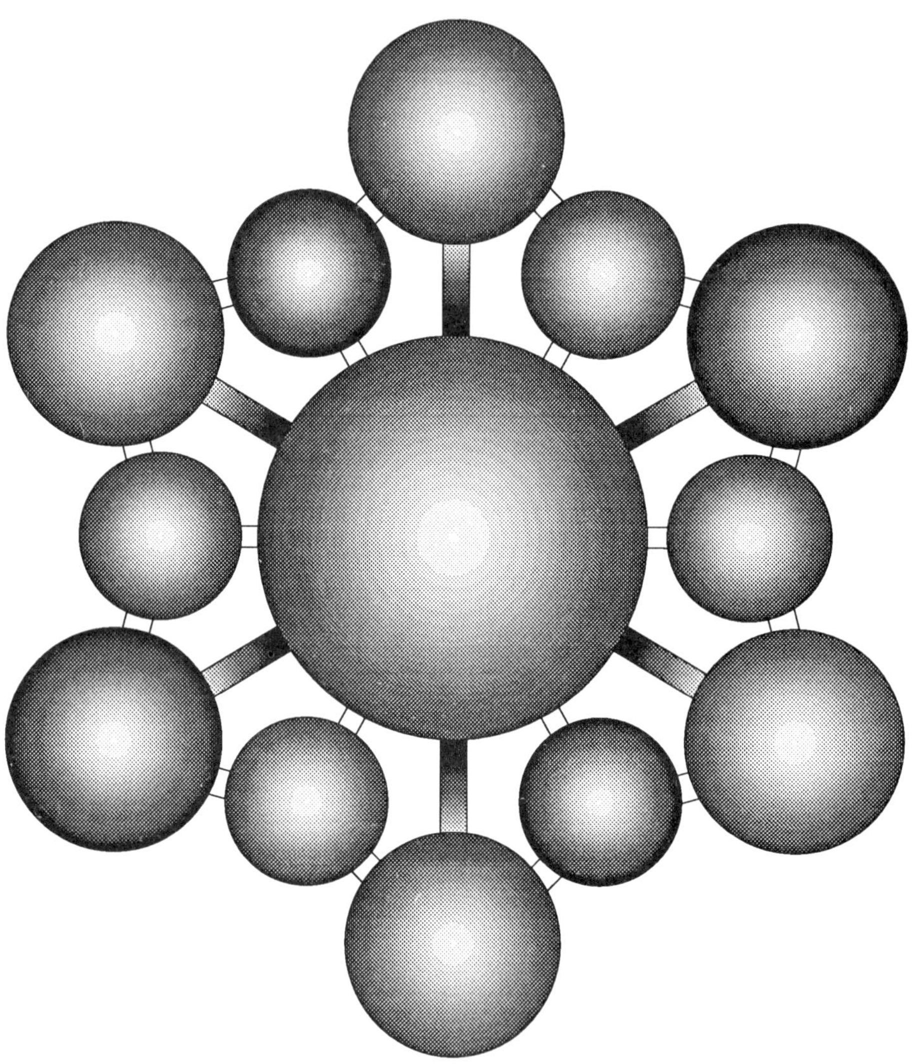

# 7 - EFFECTS MENU

The Effects menu creates effects! Essentially the menu contains commands that allow you to generate four basic effects, Envelope, Perspective, Blends and Extrusions.

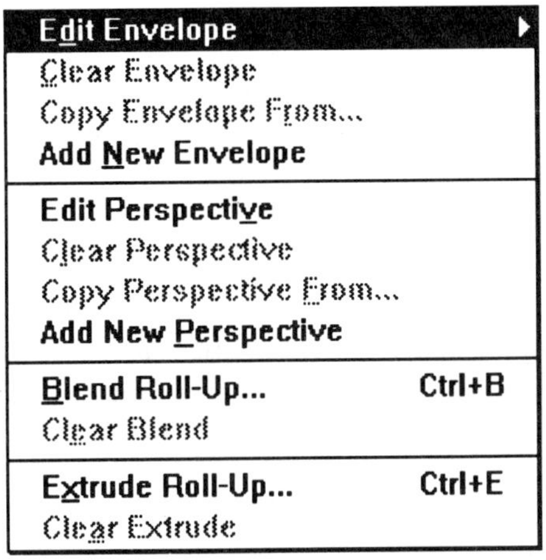

Edit Envelope
Clear Envelope
Copy Envelope From...
Add New Envelope

Edit Perspective
Clear Perspective
Copy Perspective From...
Add New Perspective

Blend Roll-Up... Ctrl+B
Clear Blend

Extrude Roll-Up... Ctrl+E
Clear Extrude

**7.01 Effects Menu**

**Edit Envelope** allows you to change the shape of the imaginary bounding box around an object to make dramatic changes to it. It is much easier to do than to describe so see E17 below. There are four possible ways to change the envelope of an object.

**Clear Envelope** restores an object to its original shape, in other words it cancels the previous command.

**Copy Envelope From** is rather like Copy Style From but it affects only the envelope of the object.

**Add New Envelope** allows you to define the distorted object's current shape as the new shape. A new envelope is added that then allows you to manipulate the object as that shape.

**Edit Perspective** allows you to change the perspective of an object. CorelDRAW is very good at doing this and any perspective will be mathematically perfect.

**Clear Perspective** cancels the previous command.

**Copy Perspective From** is self-explanatory.

**Add New Perspective** allows you to add a new bounding box to an altered image.

**Blend Roll-Up**, which can be activated by Ctrl-B, allows you to do all kinds of wonderful effects.

**Clear Blend** cancels a blend operation.

**Extrude Roll-Up**, for which the keyboard shortcut is Ctrl-E, does extrusions but with CorelDRAW 3.0 you can do amazing things with it.

**Clear Extrude** removes an extrusion.

# E17 - MAKE A BUBBLE

This is a nice simple exercise, albeit an old one, that shows the Edit Envelope facility to advantage.

a. You want six 50 mms diameter circles. The quickest way is to draw one and then duplicate it to get the others. Scatter them around the page so they are not touching each other.

b. Next you want the six letters B, U, B, B, L, E, each as a separate text string. Make the text Vogue, 120 Point Bold. Place one letter in each circle. They don't have to be exactly in the centre of the circles, in fact they will be better if each letter is slightly off centre. You should end up with something the Figure 7.02.

c. Save the file at this point, call it Bubble, because each step will add complexity and you don't want to have to redo it completely if anything goes wrong.

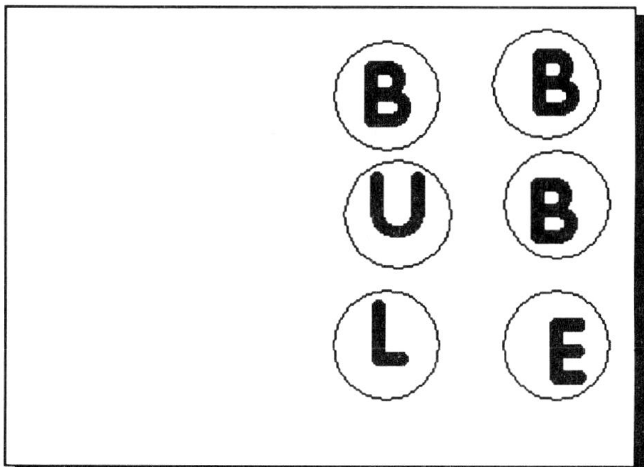


**7.02 Letters and Circles**

d. Zoom in to one of the circle and letter combinations. If you use **F2** you can magnify just the two elements that you want.

e. Select the letter and then open the **Effects menu**. Click on **Edit Envelope** and a subsidiary drop down menu appears bearing the envelope options.

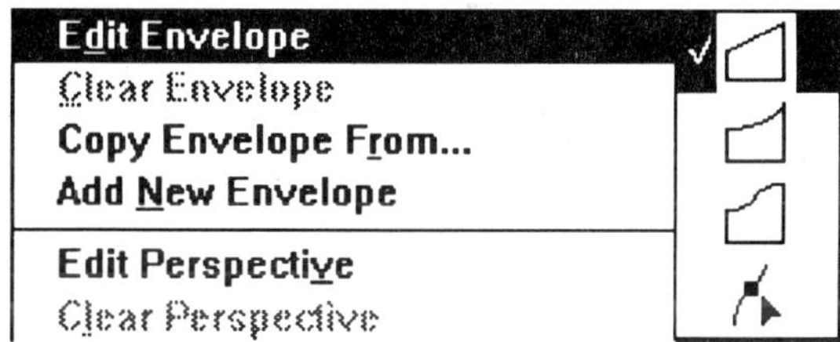


**7.03 Envelope options**

f. Select the bottom option, the one that looks like the Node Edit tool. This allows you to edit the envelope freely. Once selected the menu closes and you will have a triangular cursor. The letter is surrounded by eight small squares. These are the **Envelope Nodes**.

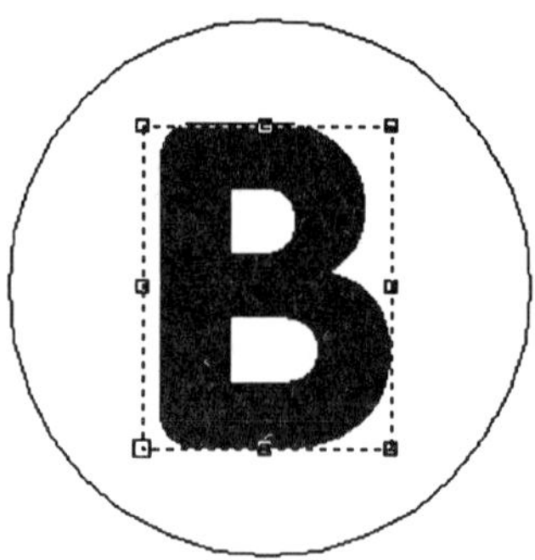


**7.04 Envelope nodes**

g. What you have to do is move these nodes. You have to do this in stages. Drag them to the edge of the circle, but still within it. As you do so you will notice the node handles appearing. Ignore them for a minute until you have all eight nodes moved.

**7.05 Nodes moved**

h. Once the nodes are in place you can then click on each one individually and manipulate the node handles to get a more pleasing shape, because at the moment the letter looks very angular. Do it gently and you should be able to make the envelope into a rough circular shape.

**7.06 Envelope into circle**

i. Once you've done one letter, do all the others in the same way. But don't make them all look the same, each letter should be distorted differently, but still basically making a round shape for each letter. Be warned you can fiddle around with this for ages.

**7.07 Distorted letters**

j. Save the file again. Now draw a large ellipse, so it nearly fills the page, and place it in the middle of the page, using Align to Centre if necessary. We want this to be behind everything else so, with it selected, press **Shift-PgDn**.

k. Save the file. (As you start doing more and more complex things with CorelDRAW it is vital that you save the file constantly.) Arrange the letters and circles so that they fit into the ellipse. They have to be in the right order to spell Bubble but they should not be in a straight line. To move a pair of shapes, drag a bounding box around the circle and letter and you can then move them together. They can even overlap slightly. If they are too small or too large you can resize them as necessary. You can even rotate each pair slightly to get a better effect.

**7.08 Word in ellipse**

l. Save the file. That's stage one complete. You now want to add some more circles, little ones, around the letters but still within the ellipse. Make them different sizes but not too big. Scatter the circles around: they are supposed to be bubbles rising and bubbling within the ellipse.

m. Save the file again. Now add colour. Because I need to make an illustration of this I'm limited to using greyscales but you should be able to use full colour. Each bubble wants to have a radial fountain fill. Use the roll-up and you can then move the centre of the radial to good effect. Make the letters prominent by using a different colour for each one.

**7.09 Bubbles in ellipse**

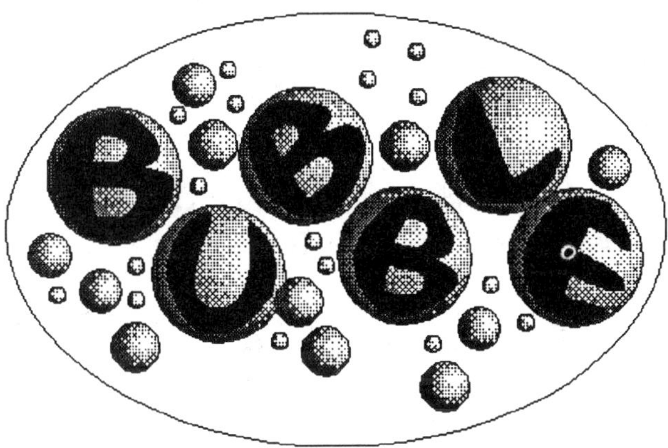


**7.10 Finished image**

n. Save the file. That's the basic thing finished. (The colour image looks much better than the illustration by the way.) To get to this point has taken me about an hour - but then I'm writing this and doing the exercise at the same time. You can now play around with it as you wish. Try different colours, change the angle of the radial fill and so on.

# E18 - MORE ENVELOPES

There are four possible envelope editing techniques. The Non-constrained one that you used in the last exercise is, arguably, the most useful but the others have their benefits as well. Here we're going to take a look at the other three. The effects are easiest to see with text so that's what we'll use.

a. Start a new page. Select the text tool and place the words "Exercise 18" in the centre of the page. Change the typeface to Homeward Bound and the size to 120 points. Place the text in the centre of the page using **Align to Centre of Page**.

b. Press **F4** and then **F3**. Open the **Effects menu** and click on **Edit Envelope**. This time select the first envelope option. This the **Straight Line Envelope** and it allows you to edit the envelope in straight lines only.

c. The words are surrounded by the eight envelope handles again. Click on the top left hand one. You will find that you can drag it up and down but not left or right. When you release the mouse button the envelope changes.

d. Cancel your changes, either by pressing **Alt-Backspace** or by opening the **Effects menu** and clicking on **Clear Transformations**.

e. Select the first edit envelope option again. Click on the middle handle on the top. Again you can only move it up or down. As you move it up, the envelope becomes a pentagonal shape - like a stylised house - and when you release the button the words change shape to fit.

f. Press **Alt-Backspace** again. You can use the Shift and Ctrl keys to affect how the envelope editing occurs, though not at the same time. Hold down **Shift** and drag the central right handle to the right. The left hand side of the envelope matches your movement.

g. Holding **Shift** again, drag either the top or bottom central handle away from its position. Again the other side of the envelope mirrors your actions.

h. Clear the effects again by opening the **Effects menu** and clicking on **Clear Envelope**. Then select the first envelope option again.

i. This time, hold down **Ctrl** while you drag the top central handle upwards. The bottom of the envelope will follow. Note that the envelope retains the same overall width. Hold down **Shift** and drag the lower left hand handle down.

j. If you click on the central top handle, without holding Shift or Ctrl, and drag it below the bottom handle you will get an odd effect. Try overlapping the other handles in the same way.

Even though the Straight Line envelope is the most basic of the options available to you, you can still create exciting and unusual shapes with it.

**7.11 Straight Line envelope**

k. Clear the envelope again. This time select the second Edit Envelope option. This is the **Single Arc** option. Whereas the previous tool allowed you to edit the envelope in straight lines only, this one allows you to use only curves.

l. Click on the top left hand handle and drag it upwards. The line along the top of the envelope becomes a gentle curve. As with the previous option, you can use **Shift** to affect opposing handles at the same time.

m. If you click on one of the central handles the envelope will become even more curved. You cannot affect the extent of the curve as such, i.e. the envelope nodes are not adjustable the way that ordinary nodes are, it is the amount of movement of the node which controls the curve.

n. Now for something odd. Hold down **Ctrl** and drag the central bottom handle down. What this should do is move the two opposing handles the same amount - but it doesn't. The top handle will move more than the bottom one. Don't ask me why, I don't know.

**7.12 Single Arc envelope**

o. Clear the envelope again. You might find that the word has moved slightly against the page background. Use **Ctrl-A** and realign it. Open the **Effects menu** and click on **Edit Envelope** again. This time select the third option. This is the **Double Arc** option.

p. It is similar to the previous one but it gives you two arcs at once. Hold down **Ctrl** and drag the upper left hand corner handle up until you almost touch the page margin. Hold **Ctrl** again and drag the lower right hand handle down towards the bottom page margin. You should end up with a ribbon shape.

q. Hold down **Shift** and drag the top central handle down beyond where the central bottom had been. You now have a twisted ribbon.

r. Unfortunately the points where the ribbon twists are rather close to the end. You cannot do anything to affect this directly because the envelope shape is dependent on how far you move the handles. Try make the right hand end of the ribbon larger by dragging one of the corner handles. Watch the envelope shape as you do so.

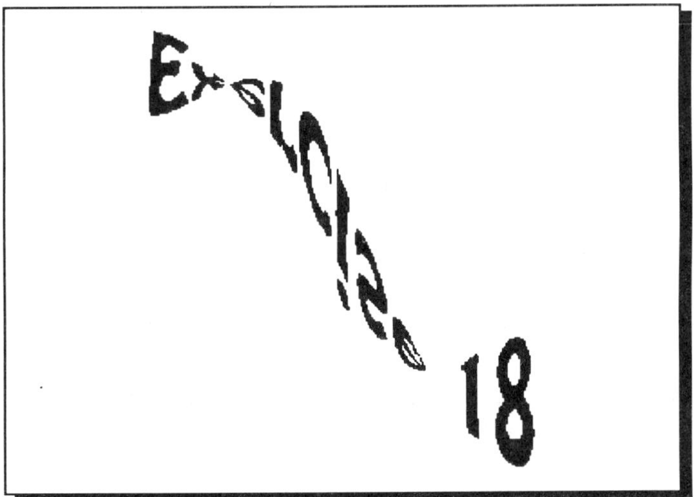

**7.13 Two Curve envelope**

The envelope options give you a wealth of control over the shape, far too much to be covered in depth here. Play with the different options and see what effects you can create, some will be simple but they are not to be despised for that, while others will be complex. It is very easy to end up making the envelopes too complex though so take care.

## Q6 - Valentine

See if you can recreate this. It makes extensive use of envelopes but it doesn't use any other techniques.

# E19 - PERSPECTIVE

Perspective is a mathematical function and as such you may find that using it on a machine with limited resources can be a nuisance.

a. Draw a series of 16 boxes, 25 mms squares, and make a larger box out of these. You should end up with a square grid. (Try using the **Duplicate** function.) You then have to combine them together using **Ctrl-C** or you cannot use the Perspective because it can only apply to one object at a time. Move the grid to the lower left hand corner of the page.

b. Open the **Effects menu** and click on **Edit Perspective**. You will find that there are now four little handles, looking like nodes, and a dashed line around your grid. The Status Bar tells you where the vanishing point is.

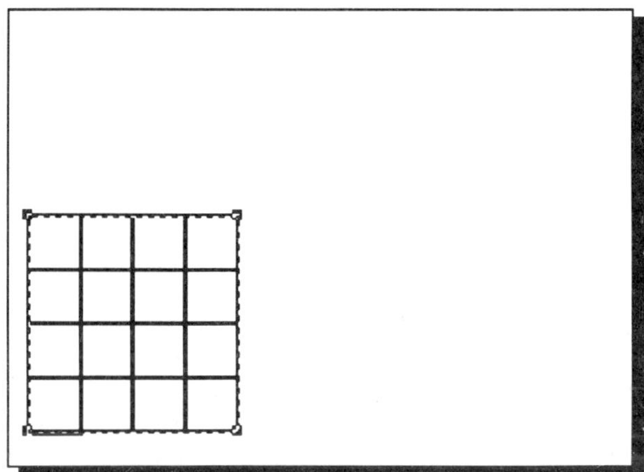

**7.14 Grid ready**

c. The vanishing point is where the imaginary perspective lines will meet. Before you can place it you need to make it visible. Move the cursor to the bottom right hand corner of the grid and move it up slightly. As soon as you see an **X** appearing let go of the button. The X is the vanishing point.

d. Move the cursor to the X. You can drag this around the page, or even the background, and as you do so the perspective will change. A dashed line, like a bounding box, appears and as you move the vanishing point so this box changes shape. Move it to the top right hand corner of the page.

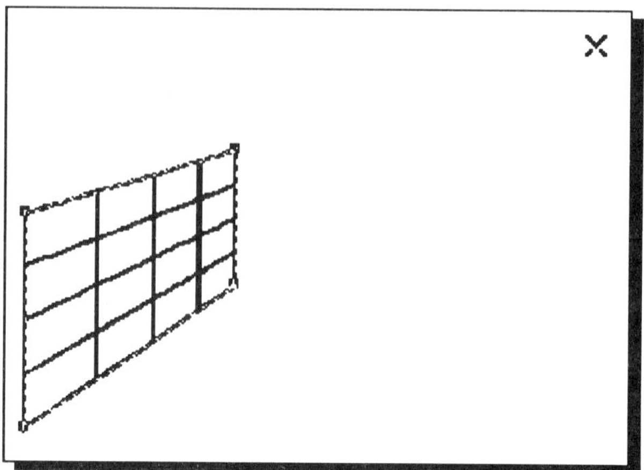

**7.15 Single point perspective**

e. CorelDRAW allows you to create two point perspectives as well as single point ones. Move the cursor to the node at the lower left hand corner of the grid. Drag this diagonally up and right to where the first grid lines cross. Release the mouse button and you have the finished grid.

f. There are actually two vanishing points for this shape. The first one which was near the top of the page has moved away as you dragged the corner node. The second vanishing point is for that movement. If you scroll the page up slightly you should be able to see it. (The first vanishing point is too far to reach.) As you drag this second point around the shape changes again.

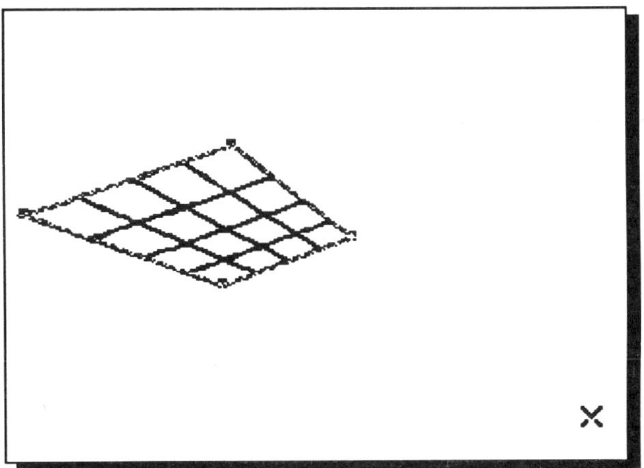

**7.16 Double point perspective**

Play with the perspective and find out just what you can do with it. At any time, if you click on **Clear Perspective** you will get the original grid back again. Try using the commands with filled figures - I bet you don't get what you expect, especially with bitmap fills.

# E20 - BLENDING

The blend capabilities of CorelDRAW have been enhanced and improved so dramatically that it is hard to realise how simple the feature was originally. The command is now controlled off a roll-up which makes life much simpler. Blending allows you to mix objects in strange ways and with CorelDRAW 3.0 you can even blend groups.

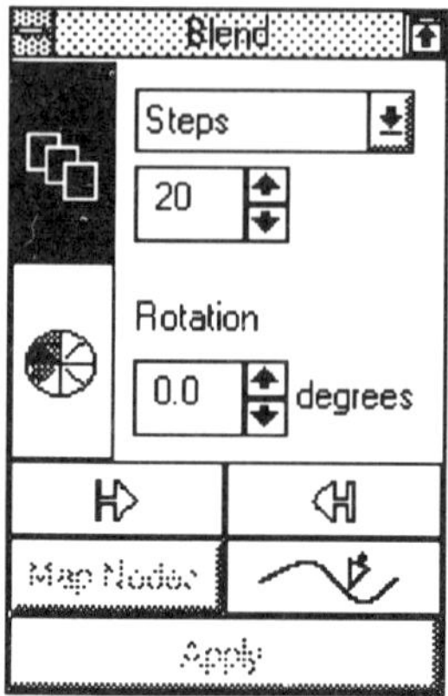


**7.17 Blend roll-up**

a. Start a new page. Draw a circle 40 mms in diameter in the upper left hand corner of the page. Draw a 40 mms square in the lower right hand corner of the page. Select both objects, either by dragging a selection box around both or by clicking on one, holding down **Shift** and then clicking on the other.

b. Press **Ctrl-B** to bring up the Blend roll-up. By default this is set to give you 20 steps, but for the time being change this to 5. Don't change anything else. Click on **Apply**.

c. What you now have is the original shapes plus an intervening five shapes that gradually turn from a circle to a square. Notice the nodes on the intervening shapes. On the original circle it is at 12 o'clock but by the time it reaches the square it is at the upper left hand corner. What you've just done is a straight line blend - the simplest there is.

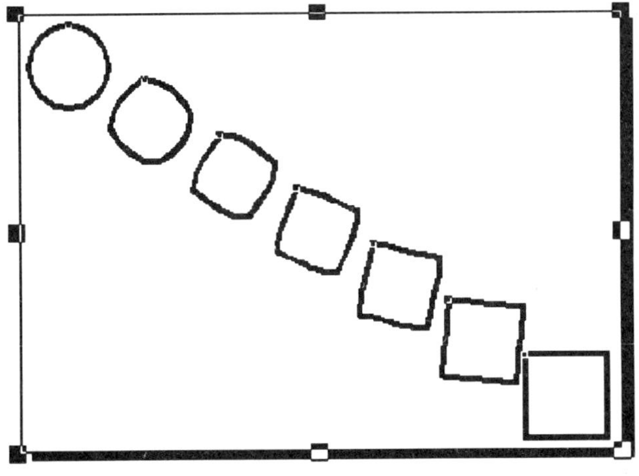

**7.18 Blend 1**

d. CorelDRAW 3.0 allows you to do things with even this though. Switch to the **Pointer** tool and select the circle. Enlarge it by 200%, i.e. hold down **Ctrl** and drag one of the corner handles. As soon as you release the mouse button the entire blend will change. Blending is now completely interactive. Shrink the circle back to its original size and the blend instantly changes back.

e. Change the colour of the circle or the square and the blend responds instantly with the colour flowing from one to the other.

f. Something that is new in CorelDRAW 3.0. You can use the same object more than once as the start or end of a blend. Draw a triangle in the bottom left hand corner of the page.

g. Select the circle and the triangle and blend them. Select the triangle and the square and blend those. You get some peculiar shapes but it does prove that you can blend repeatedly to the same objects.

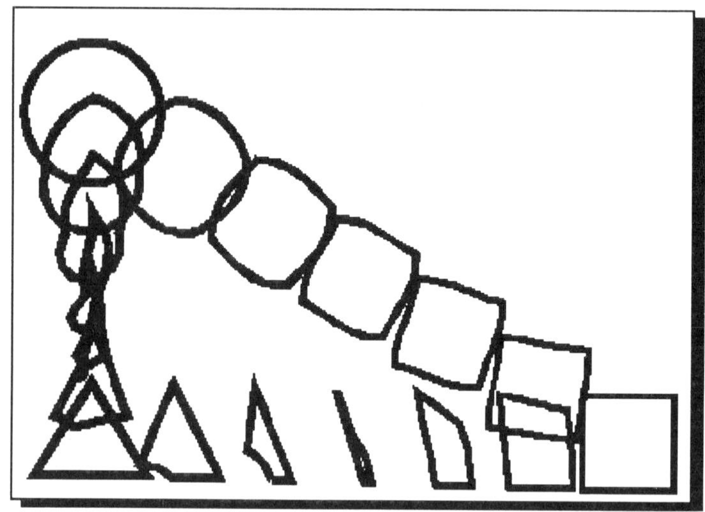

**7.19 Blend 2**

h. Select the shapes from the last blend. Delete them. The entire image vanishes. The reason is because of the interactive blend. The shapes are all linked together via the blending and so if you delete one you delete the whole lot. Press **Alt-Backspace** to undo the deletion.

i. Open the **Effects menu** and click on **Clear Blend**. That removes the blend shapes but leaves the three main objects on screen.

j. Try a curved blend. Select the circle and the square. Double click on either of them to bring up the rotational handles. Move the centre of rotation to the extreme right hand edge of the page.

k. Open the Blend roll-up again. Change the **Angle of Rotation** to 90 degrees and then click on **Apply**.

l. Play with different rotational angles and different positions for the centre of rotation. Then try using different angles independently. Don't forget that you can use negative values too.

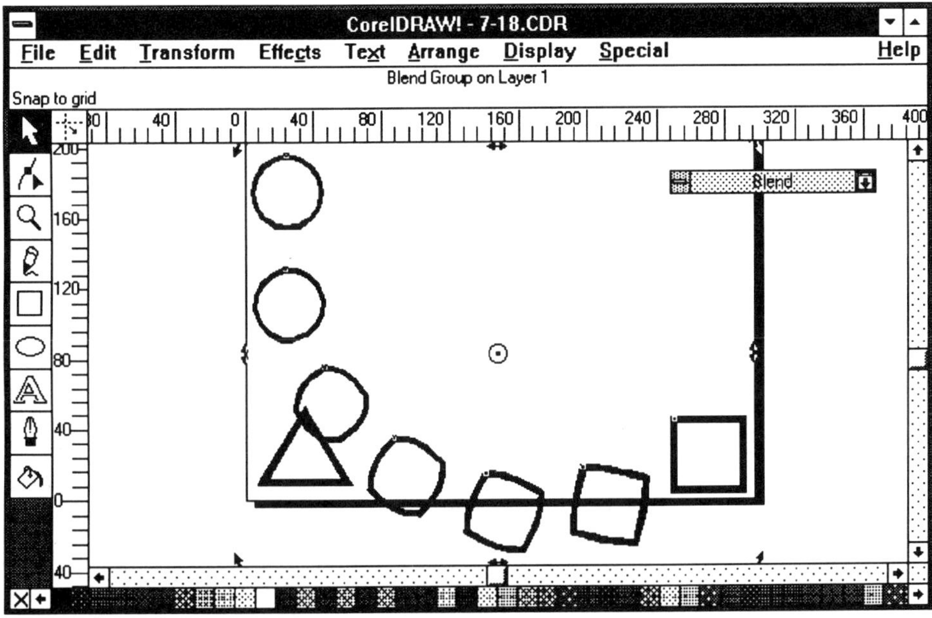


**7.20 Curved blend**

m. Blending can do more than just match outline shapes and colours. It will also blend fill colours. You cannot blend other fills though, for example bitmap or vector fills, not even if you use different colours for the same bitmap fill. Fill the circle with Blue and the square with Yellow. Blend them again. The intervening shapes will be shaded accordingly.

n. Try increasing the number of steps. By default the roll-up will show 20 steps. Try using that. Then do it again but use a value of 50, then 100 then 150. The maximum number of steps is 999 and the minimum is 1. (Mind you if you even need to use the former you could be waiting ages. I've just checked and on the 486 it takes 30 seconds, on the 386 it took nearly 3 minutes.)

o. Just out of interest. Try filling the circle with the first bitmap fill, the little circles, and the square with little squares. Blend them together. You should find that the all the intervening shapes are filled with whatever fill was in the second object selected.

# E21 - MORE BLENDING

What you've done with blend up to now was more or less what could have been done in CorelDRAW 2.01, with minor exceptions. But CorelDRAW 3.0 has lots more tricks up its sleeve.

a. Clear any blends to get back to the original circle, square and triangle. Empty these of any fills they contain.

b. Draw a line from the centre of the circle to the centre of the square.

c. Convert the line to a curve using Node Edit and then bend it so that it becomes a sort of S-shape.

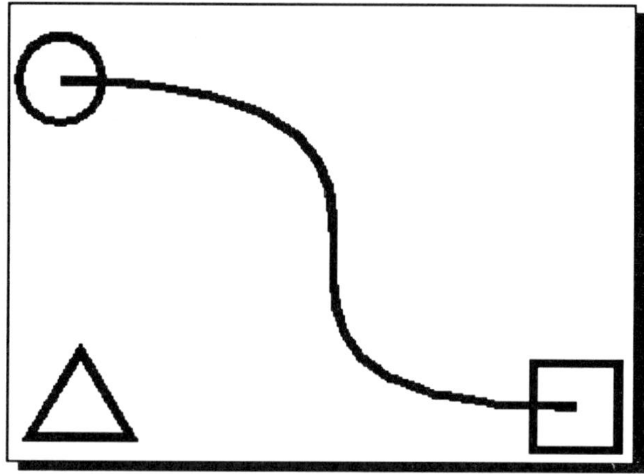

**7.21 Line added**

d. Select the circle and the square and open the Blend roll-up. Change the steps back to 5.

e. Click on the button beside the one that says Map Nodes - it has a line with an arrow pointing at it. This is the **Blend to Path command**. A little dialogue box appears bearing three commands: New Path, which is highlighted; Show Path and Detach from Path. Click on the first of these.

f. The cursor becomes a funny bend arrow shape. Move this to it touches the line and then click. Then click on Apply in the roll-up. This time the intervening shapes follow the line you drew.

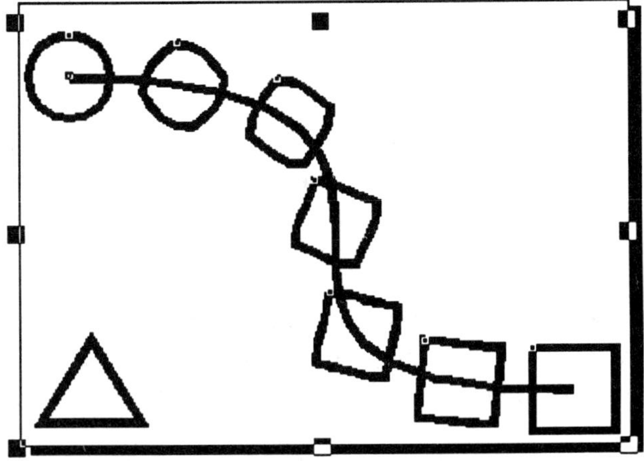

**7.22 Shapes on line**

g. Now select the **Node Edit tool** again. Click on the line to bring up the handles and their control points. Move either one of the latter to change the shape of the line. The intervening blend shapes instantly follow the new line once you release the mouse button.

h. Switch to the **Pointer tool**. Pick up the line and move it. The entire assemblage moves as well.

i. Click on the Blend to Path button again and click on **Detach from Path**. The shapes are taken off the path and the blend appears as it would have done if you had not used the path in the first place.

j. Press **Alt-Backspace** to get the blend back on the path. Click on **Map Nodes**. When you move the cursor back on to the page it has become an upwards pointing bend arrow and the nodes around the square become visible. Click on any node, e.g. the one in the bottom left hand corner.

k. The cursor then becomes a downwards pointing bent arrow and the nodes on the circle become visible. Click on one of these, e.g. the one at 12 o'clock. Now click on **Apply** in the roll-up. The blend shapes should change. Try doing it again using different nodes.

l. Select the Pointer tool and rotate the square 45 degrees. The blend changes yet again. Rotate it 90 degrees in the opposite direction. The blend changes again.

m. Try stretching the square or the circle. Then rotate these. Move the circle or square around the page. Change the shape of the line again. No matter what you do the blend remains an entity in its own right and any change to one part of it affects the whole.

n. Open the Effects menu and click on **Clear Blend** again. Delete the line. Fill the circle with Blue and the square with Yellow. (These colours are opposite in the colour spectrum.) Make sure you change the number of steps back to five.

o. Click on the button with what looks like a pie-chart on it. This is **Colour Blending control** and the roll-up changes to reflect this. Notice that the colours are displayed on a large wheel and there is a thin line running from one side to the other.

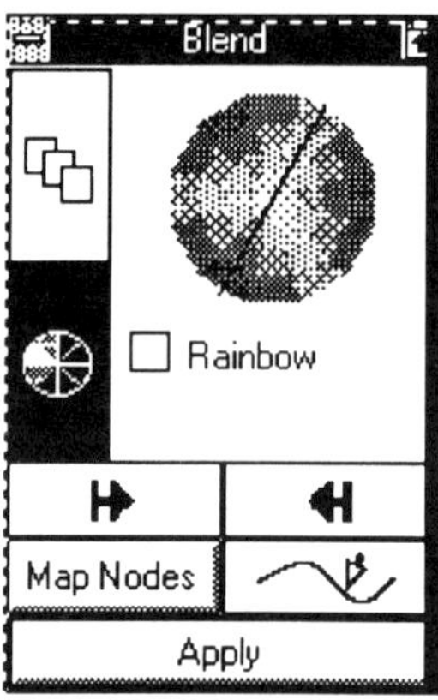


**7.23 Colour Blending**

p. If you click on **Apply** the two shapes will blend in colour along the line across the centre of the colour wheel as you've already seen. However, if you click on Rainbow, an arc will appear around the colour wheel and two additional buttons appear. The first goes anti-clockwise, this highlighted by default, and the second goes clockwise.

q. Now click on **Apply**. The intervening shapes this time will bear the colours from around the colour wheel rather than across it. Click on the clockwise button and then on **Apply** again. The colour changes as they go the other way. No other program will do this by the way, it is unique to CorelDRAW.

r. Try playing with different colours for the square or circle and then using the Rainbow effects. Increase the number of steps to about a dozen. You can create some very nice images just like that.

The final thing you can do with blending in CorelDRAW 3.0 is to blend groups of objects rather than just single ones. We haven't got to groups yet, they're in the next chapter, so just bear with me a minute.

s. Remove any blend you currently have to get back to the three base shapes. Select the circle and the triangle. Press **Ctrl-G** to group them.

t. Now select the square as well and click on **Apply** in the roll-up. You get a single blend group but it's in two lines, one running from the circle to the square and the other running from the triangle to the square.

u. Try changing the rotation angle in this case.

v. Clear the blend. Select the circle/triangle group and press **Ctrl-U** to ungroup them. Fill the circle with one colour and the triangle with another. Then group them again. Now fill the square with a third colour. Finally blend them all again.

w. Try the Rainbow effects.

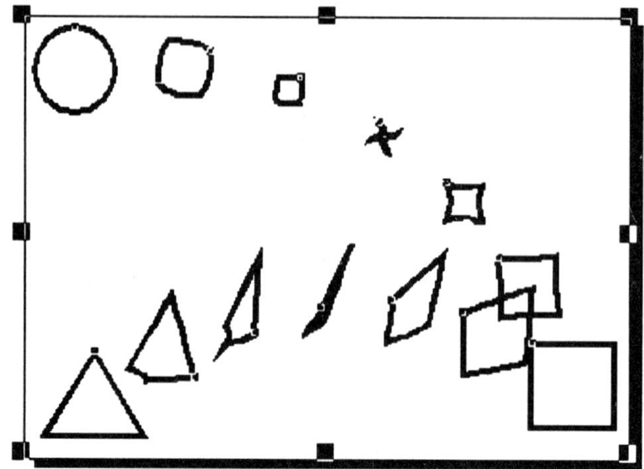

**7.24 Blended group**

You can spend ages just playing with the various blend possibilities. The important thing to realise is that the level of fun inherent in CorelDRAW has been enormously enhanced because of the improvements that have been made in the program.

# E22 - TEXT BLENDING

As well as being able to blend ordinary shapes, CorelDRAW will allow you to blend text. However, it has to be said that you can get some very odd effects if you're not careful, especially when it comes to blending mixed typefaces.

a. Start a new page. Select the **Text tool** and write your first name in the top left hand corner of the page.

b. Go back to the **Pointer tool** and then press **Ctrl-T**. Change the typeface to a fancy one, e.g. Frankenstein. Change the point size to 120 and the Justification to Centre. Click on **OK** or press **Enter**. The text will have moved slightly so reposition it so that it's on the page.

c. Back to the **Text tool** and put your surname in the lower right hand corner of the page. This will automatically be in whatever typeface you used for your forename. Select the **Pointer tool**, press **Ctrl-T** to bring up the text dialogue box again.

**7.25 Words blended**

d. Change the typeface to Renfrew and make the size about 100 points. (Renfrew is a larger typeface than Frankenstein.) Reposition the word as necessary.

e. Select both words, your forename first, and press **Ctrl-B** to open the Blend roll-up. Use 4 steps but don't change anything else. Click on **Apply**. You get a lovely mess with the intervening shapes being just blobs. They certainly won't be legible as text. Hardly surprising as they are not. They are shapes just as you got when you blended squares and triangles.

f. Select your forename, press **Ctrl-T** and change the typeface to something else, e.g. President which is a very fine typeface. The blend objects will change accordingly as soon as you close the dialogue box.

g. You can still use colours and fills as with ordinary shapes. Try filling the words with different colours. Equally you can use rotations with the blend.

h. When you blend objects, the first object selected is the Start and the second is the End. In the above you selected you forename first. Because you can now use the start and end objects for more than one blend you can create interesting effects by changing the order of things.

i. Clear the blend you have. Select your forename then your surname and blend these using a 90 degree rotation. The blend objects fall in an arc to the lower left.

j. Now select your surname and then your forename. Blend these using a -90 degree rotation. The new blend objects fall in an arc to the upper right.

k. Now to make another mess. Select your forename then your surname again. Blend these using 0 degree rotation, i.e. a straight line blend. The blend objects run diagonally between the words.

l. Try blending phrases. Change your forename to something like "The quick brown fox jumps over" and your surname to "the lazy dog". Don't forget to change the point size. Then blend the two together.

m. Move the top phrase right into the middle of the page and the bottom phrase left so it is beneath it. Then blend the two again using rotation.

n. Play with the text effects. Try mirrored text or large text at the top and tiny text at the bottom.

**7.26 Multiple blend**

Blending with text is not as straightforward as you would think. You have to allow for the typeface characteristics, difference typefaces have different amounts of white space around them, the various letters will be different sizes, the ascenders and descenders of the characters will be different and so on. All these things will have a bearing on how words or phrases blend together.

# Q7 - Sandglass

This image uses Blend, Stretch & Mirror and envelope editing. The text I used is Lithos Light which is not actually a CorelDRAW font but an Adobe one.

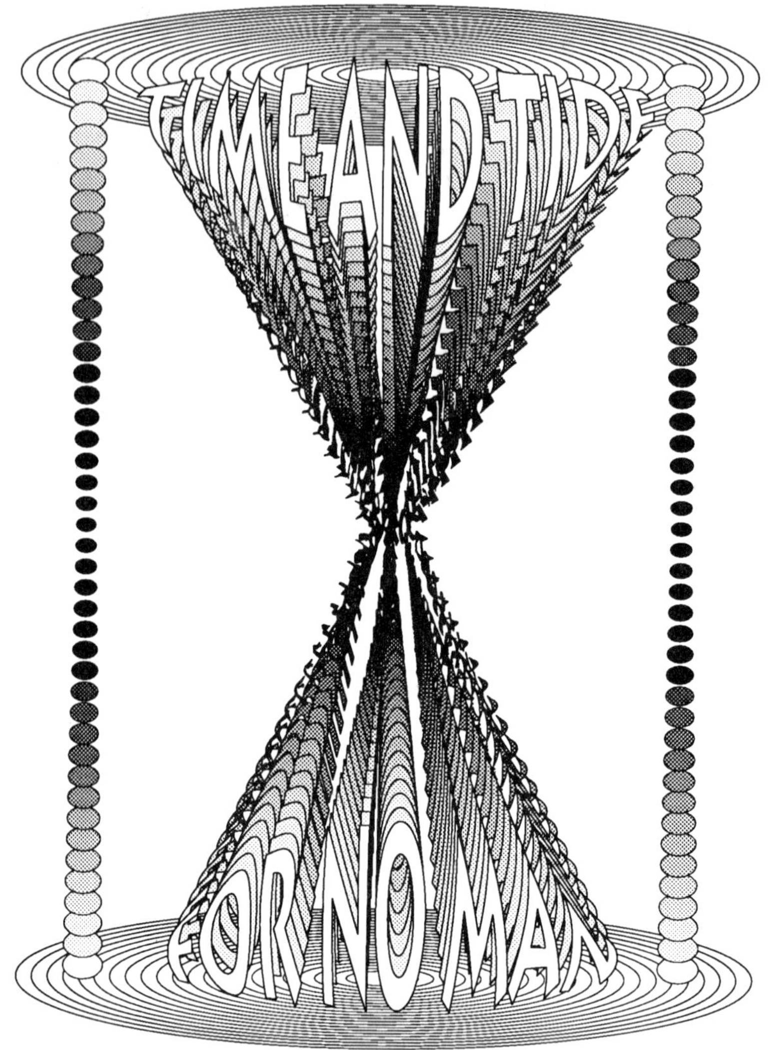

# E23 - EXTRUDE

The final command in the Effects menu is Extrude. This command originally appeared in CorelDRAW 2.0 and it was great for creating extrusion effects. However the command in CorelDRAW 3.0 has been changed dramatically. Whereas previously the command created images with the illusion of depth to them, in 3.0 the objects you create are genuine three dimensional objects with a life of their own. The command is now used via a roll-up and that makes it much simpler to use.

a. Start with a new file. Get the roll-up on screen first by pressing **Ctrl-E**.

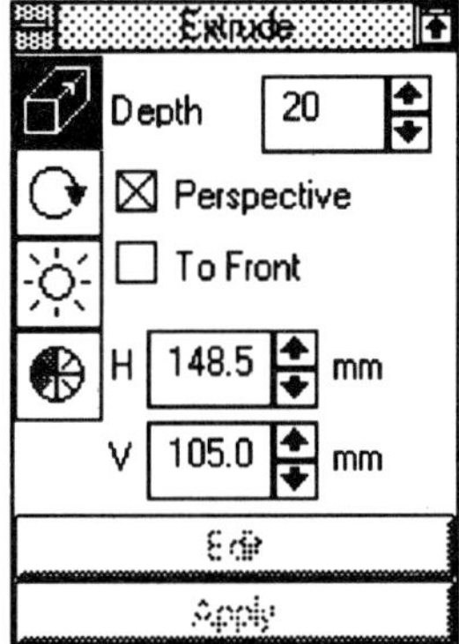


**7.27 Extrude roll-up**

Down the left hand side of the roll-up are four buttons. The top one is **Depth** and this controls the appearance of the extrusion. The second is **3-D Rotation** which allows you to rotate the entire extrusion as a single object. The third is the **Light Source** which is just that. The final button is **Colour fill** which works the same way as on other roll-ups.

One point that I want to make clear before we go any further, the illustrations in this section are not very good due to various limitations, not least of which is that they are confined to monochrome. Therefore they are intended to be a guide only but if you follow the steps in the exercises you will see the real thing on your screen.

b. Draw a square 75 mms to a side in the bottom left hand corner of the page. Open the roll-up and make sure **Depth** is selected. Click on **Apply**. What you get is an X appearing in the middle of the page and the square is replaced by a dashed wire frame image. The X is the vanishing point for the extrusion because you have Perspective turned on. (It is by default.)

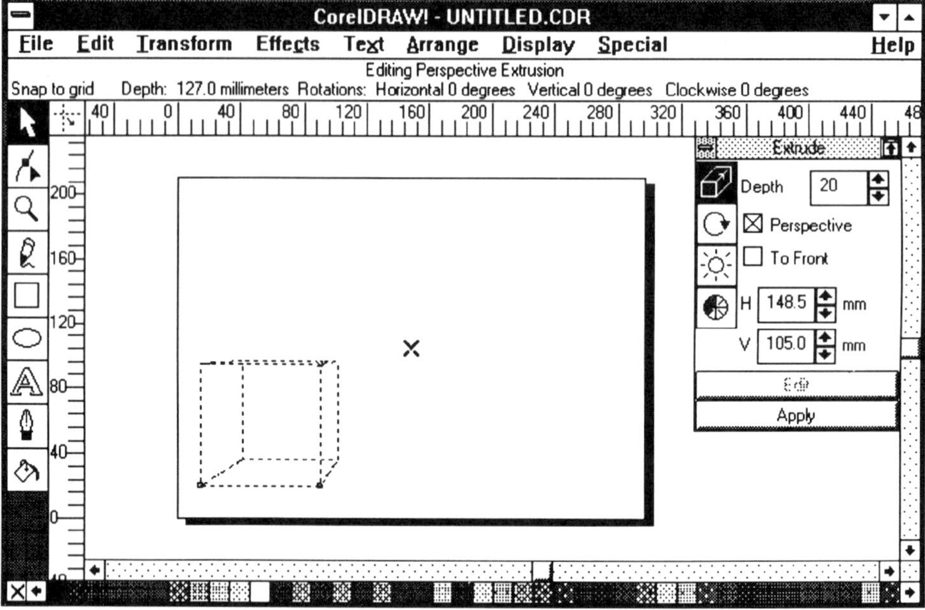


**7.28 Extrusion step 1**

c. Drag the X to the top right hand corner of the page. Notice that the wire frame changes as you do so. Click on **Apply** and the wire frame shape changes to give you a dice shape.

d. Turn off the Perspective and click on **Apply** again. You now have a tunnel.

e. Turn on the Perspective again. Change the value in the depth box from 20 to 75. The wire frame changes instantly. Click on **Apply** again. What you've done is set the percentage for the visible object. 100% means that the object reaches to the vanishing point, anything less than that is the ratio of the distance between the starting object and the vanishing point.

f. Click on the **Colour Fill** button. Change the fill to be **Shade** and click on **Apply** again. The image on screen changes so that it is light near the original square and darker as it goes towards the back. In fact it is a fountain fill but a rather special one.

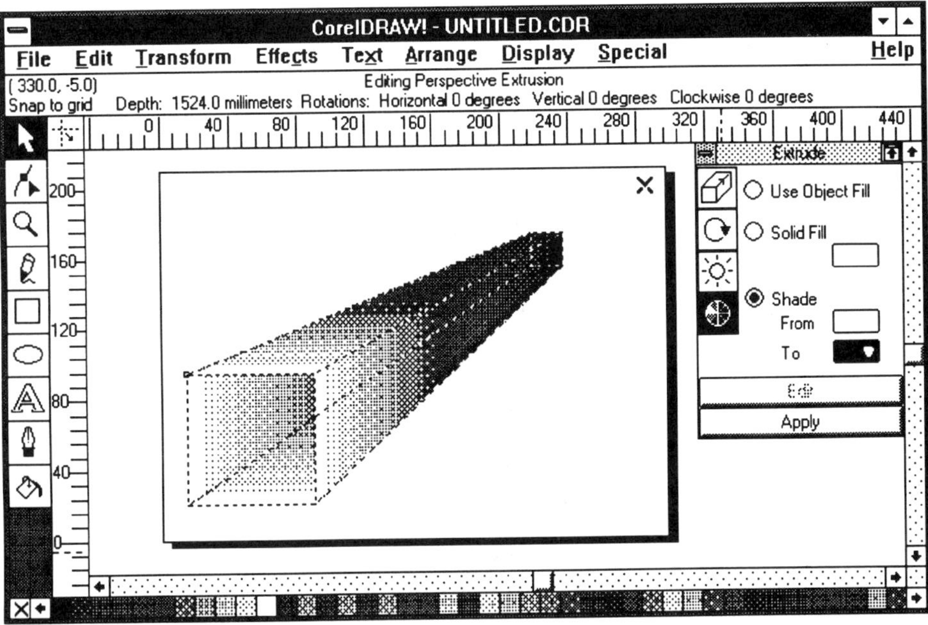


**7.29 Extrusion step 2**

g. Click on the **Light Source** button. By default this is turned off. Turn it on and a sphere appears in the set of boxes and an X appears at the top right hand corner of the boxes. The X in this case represents the light source. You can move it to any position where there are interconnecting lines.

h. Move the light source point to the middle of the front box. Your tunnel has gone black. That's because the light is at the front and CorelDRAW assumes that any object that is extruded is solid, therefore the light cannot go down the tunnel. (They might have fixed this is the actual release version but it certainly doesn't work in the current beta.)

i. Because it assumes that the original object is solid you might as well fill it. Select any colour you like from the palette at the bottom of the screen. It won't make any difference because the colour will be changed by the light source position. Remember you now have a dynamic object - not the one you started with.

j. Go back to **Depth** and change the value to 30%. Click on the **3-D Rotation** button. The roll-up changes again.

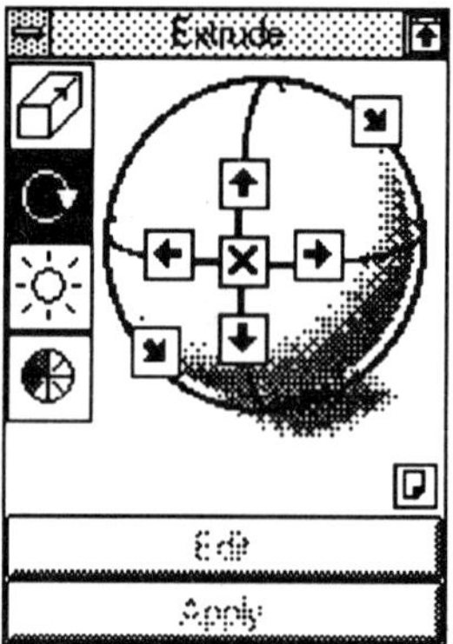


**7.30 3-D rotation roll-up**

k. This you have to play with for yourself. The central X will return the shape to where it is at present. All the other arrows cause the entire extrusion to rotate, relative to the original square that the extrusion is based on. Therefore if you click, and hold, on the upwards pointing arrow the square will rotate up and over, if you click on the left pointing arrow then the extrusion rotates anti-clockwise.

   Click on the right pointing arrow and it rotates clockwise, click on the down arrow and it rotates down and under. In each case the effect applies to the entire extrusion not just the original square. The arrows around the circumference of the sphere cause the extrusion to rotate side to side.

l. Each click on an arrow cause a incremental rotation of 5 degrees. Watch the Status Bar as you do it. You can also see the effects of the rotation because it appears as the dashed wire frame. To fix it in place click on **Apply**.

m. To cancel any rotation, in whatever direction or even all of them, click on the **X** in the middle of the sphere.

n. As you rotate the object the colours will be changed accordingly depending on where the light source is set.

o. If you need to rotate the object in increments of other than 5 you can click on little button in the bottom right hand corner of the roll-up, just below the sphere. Here you can enter any rotational angle, in any of the three possible dimension directly. Click on **Apply** to have the object do what you want.

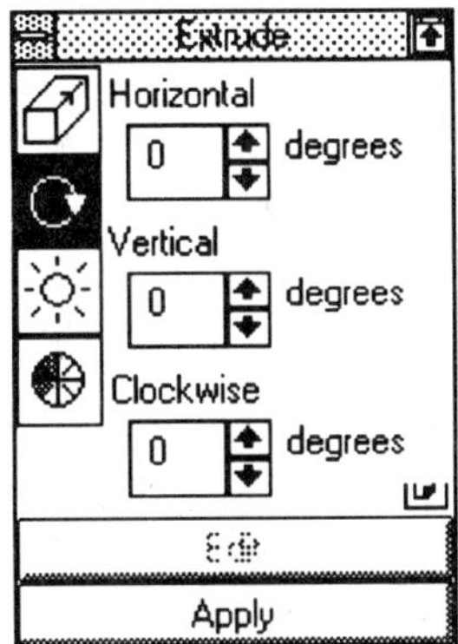


**7.31 Non-incremental rotation**

To get a full understanding of what you can do with the Extrude roll-up you have to play with it. On the surface everything seems nice and simple, but the ramifications and combinations you can produce are incredible.

To get back to your original shape open the Effects menu and click on **Clear Extrude**. The extrusion will be deleted and you'll go back to your original shape.

By now we are half way through the possibilities that the program provides and you should have got a feel for the program. At this point I want to introduce you to the Balfe's Rules of Computing. They apply particularly to using CorelDRAW, especially the first one. The rules are:

1. **Computers bend and distort the space/time continuum out of all recognition.**

   This simply means that time in front of a computer bears no relationship to time anywhere else. What seems like minutes to you, seems like hours to someone else. Or, what seems like hours to you seems like minutes to a non-computer user.

2. **If it ain't fun, it ain't worth doing.**

   Any program that limits the amount of fun you get out of life is a bad program. If you don't enjoy what you're doing then you won't do it well and it just becomes a chore. Chores are for robots!

3. **Playing is the most constructive thing you can do.**

   Children learn by playing with things. They learn that balls bounce because they play with them not because someone tells them they do. Adults think that playing is for children because they've forgotten what playing is about. Playing is about discovering things in an exciting and inventive way. Learn to play again the way that children do and you'll learn more than you ever thought possible.

# 8 - Text Menu

CorelDRAW is rightfully known for its ability to handle and manipulate text. If you can do it with a square or circle, you can do it with text. CorelDRAW was the first Windows program to allow free rotation, blending, fitting to path and a host of other features. All these have been retained in this release and most of them have been dramatically enhanced.

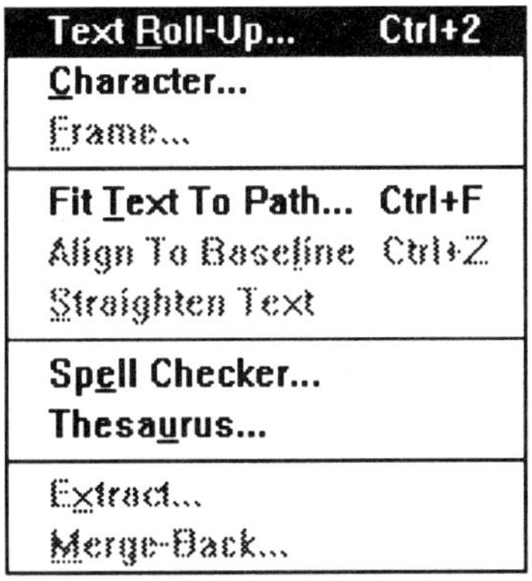

Text Roll-Up... Ctrl+2
Character...
Frame...
Fit Text To Path... Ctrl+F
Align To Baseline Ctrl+Z
Straighten Text
Spell Checker...
Thesaurus...
Extract...
Merge-Back...

**8.01 Text menu**

**Text Roll-up** brings up the roll-up. What a surprise! We'll come back to that in a minute.

**Character** allows you to define character attributes. This used to be accessible by double clicking on a character with the Node Edit tool but it's now a command in its own right.

**Frame** applies to Paragraph Text and defines the parameters for that.

**Fit Text to Path** is a lovely command that allows you to make text run along any path. It actually brings up a roll-up even though it doesn't say so.

**Align to Baseline** causes all characters in a text string to align themselves to the baseline of that string. It is a quick way of cancelling any individual vertical movement of characters, it does not affect any rotation.

**Straighten Text** is similar to the above but it cancels any changes made to individual text attributes.

**Spell Checker** is new and it uses the Houghton Mifflin Dictionary which contains roughly 116,000 words. (Who counted them?) It does what it says.

**Thesaurus** is also new. It gives synonyms for selected words.

**Extract** saves text strings as ASCII characters. It is used primarily for doing CorelDRAW version of mail-merge.

**Merge-Back** is the compliment to the above.

# E24 - Text and Nodes

You have already discovered that you can use the Node Edit tool with text to apply different colours to every character. However, you can do much more than that.

a. Load the file that you saved in Exercise 9. Open the **File menu** and click on **Open** or simply press **Ctrl-O** and the Open Drawing dialogue box will appear.

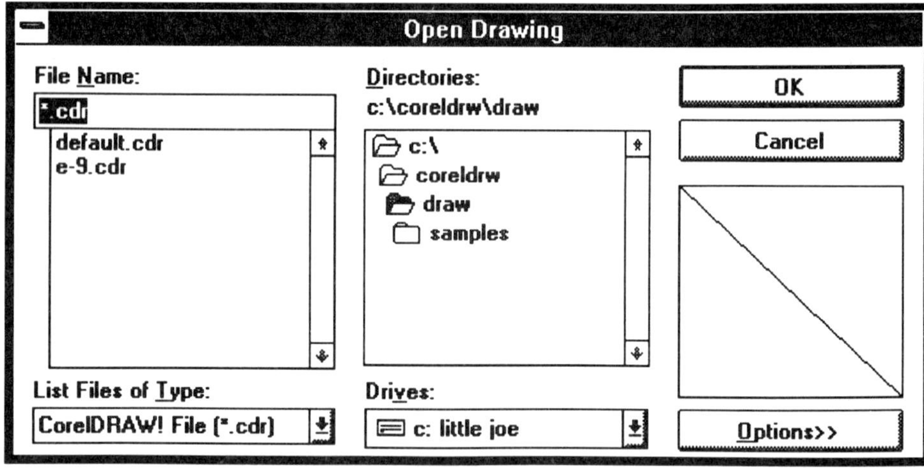


**8.02 Open drawing dialogue box**

b. In the filename box on the left hand side there is a list of all the .CDR files that are stored in the designated directory of your hard disk. The dialogue box automatically logs on to the CorelDRAW directory or whatever directory you last used to load files from. Find the file called **E-9** and double click on it. The file loads, closing the dialogue box in the process, and the **Title Bar** now bears the name of the file.

c. Select the text. (Whenever you load a file the tool automatically resets to the Pointer tool.) Press **Ctrl-T** to bring up the text dialogue box. Move the text cursor within the main area of the dialogue box to just before the word "ergo". Press **Backspace** once, to remove the space, and then **Enter** to make the phrase fit on two lines. Change the size to 100 points. Then click on **OK**. Press **Ctrl-S** to save the file.

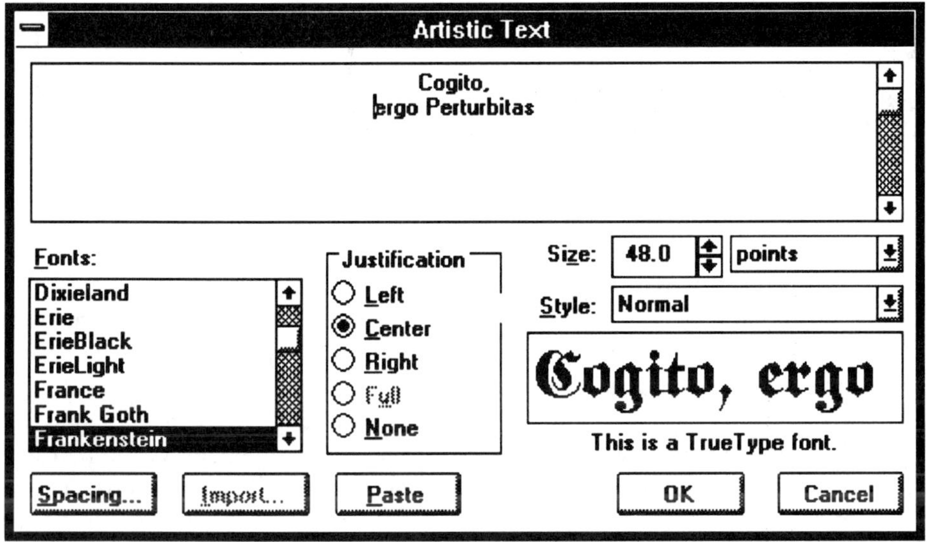


**8.03 Text dialogue box**

d. The text should be in the centre of the page. Just to make sure press **Ctrl-A** and click on **Align to Centre of Page**. Select the **Node Edit tool** either by clicking on it or by pressing **F10**.

**8.04 Text nodes**

e. Notice that you now have nodes on each letter but you also have two funny shaped handles. They look like arrows and one points down which the other points right. These are the **Kerning Handles** and they allow you to change the spacing between characters, words and lines.

f. Drag the one pointing down towards the bottom of the page. As you do so, a dashed right-angled line appears. Originally it shows you where the descenders of the text lie. It will move with you as you move the mouse. Release the button and the spacing between the lines is increased. You have increased the kerning between the lines.

g. Drag the right pointing one to the right and the dashed line appears again. As you move the handle to the right so the text will open up. You are increasing the kerning between the letters. If you drag the handle to the left the kerning is decreased.

h. Play with the two handles. What is the smallest space that you can get all the characters into? What is the largest space you can get visible characters into? (The key word here is visible. If you stretch text too far it becomes an amorphous jumble.)

i. The quickest and simplest way to get the text back to normal is to switch back to the **Pointer tool** and then press **Ctrl-T** again. Then click on **Spacing** and reset the values back to normal. (The illustration below gives the normal values.) Click on **OK** and then on **OK** again and the text returns to normal.

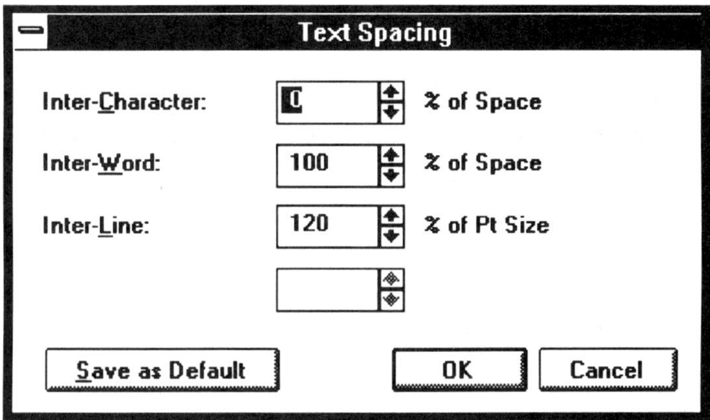


**8.05 Normal Spacing values**

j. Press **F4** to zoom in to the words so they fill the available screen area. Select the **Node Edit** tool again and then double click on any character, e.g. the initial C. The Character Attributes dialogue box appears.

k. From here you can change the typeface, character weight, point size and what-have-you. For now just change the typeface and, if you wish, the weight. For example, change the typeface to **Aardvark**. This has only one weight, called Style, so just accept that by clicking on **OK**.

l. Change every letter in the phrase in the same way.

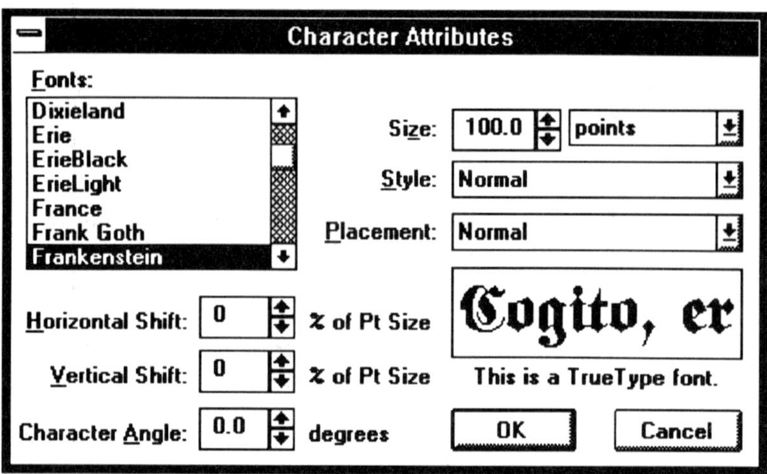


**8.06 Character Attributes**

m. How to change them all back again? The answer is that there is no shortcut way of doing so. You have to change them all back manually by reversing what you have just done. The reason is that using Character Attributes takes precedence over everything else. You can't use **Clear Transformations**, because you haven't transformed them, merely changed them. You can't use **Undo** because that applies only to the last change. And you can't use **Ctrl-T** because the character attributes over-ride that option.

n. The quickest way is simply to reload the file again. That's why you should save often when using CorelDRAW. When you do so a message box appears:

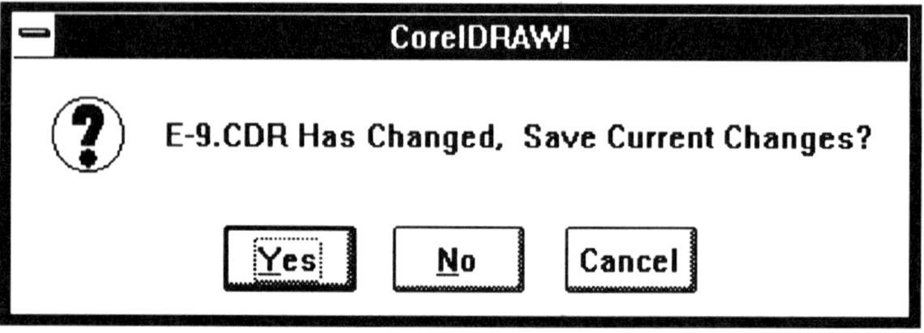


**8.07 Open message box**

o. In this case you don't want to save the file so click on **No**. You can then reload E-9 as it was before you changed all the characters.

p. Select the text and change the typeface, for the whole thing, to **Avalon** using **Ctrl-T**.

q. Back to the **Node Edit tool** again. There is one other thing you can do with this tool and text. You can move individual characters around. Click on any character node once then drag the character around the screen.

r. If you double click on a node you can also change the rotation of individual letters. In the Character Attributes dialogue box you can set a **Character Angle**, using positive or negative numbers, by which the letter will rotate.

s. To move multiple characters, or to apply a change to multiple letters, click on one, then hold down **Shift** and click on another, just as if you were selecting multiple objects. Then double click on any of the highlighted nodes to bring up the Characters Attributes dialogue box. Any change you make will apply to all the selected letters or characters.

# Q8 - KEYBOARD

You can only do this exercise if you have the CD-ROM version of CorelDRAW 3.0. I suppose you could do it all by hand but that wasn't how it was done.

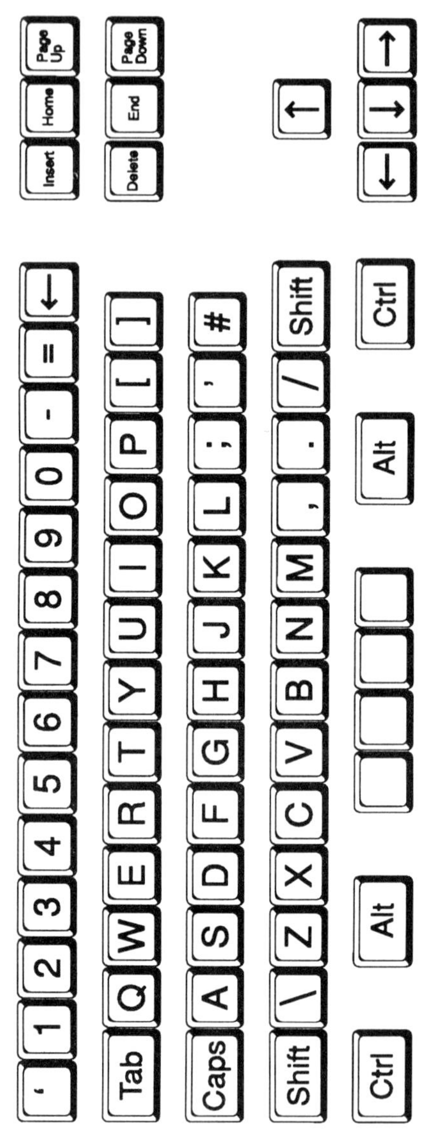

# E25 - PARAGRAPH TEXT

The text roll-up provides a quick and easy of changing text, especially when it comes to using **Paragraph Text.**

a. Start a new file, either open the **File menu** and then click on **New** or press **Alt-F N.**

b. Get the roll-up on screen. You can open the **Text menu** and click on **Text roll-up** or simply press **Ctrl-2.**

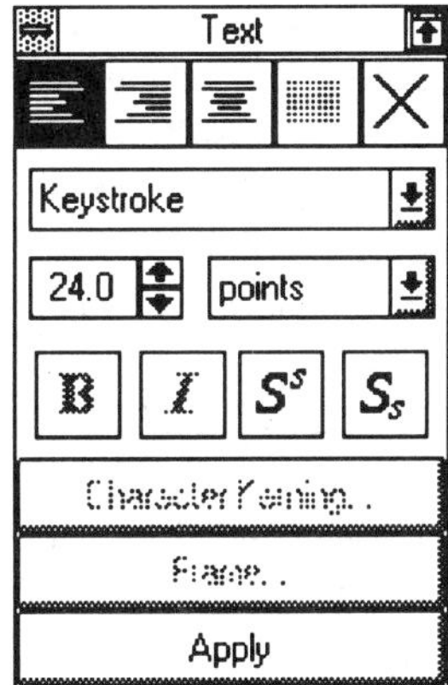


**8.08 Text roll-up**

The top line of boxes control the justification; Left, Right, Centre, Full and None. The next line gives the current typeface, below that you set the size. Under that you can set Bold, Italic, Superscript or Subscript. The button labelled Character Kerning does just that and the Frame button applies to Paragraph text.

c. Simple text first. Select the **Text tool (F8)** and write your name. Place it in the centre of the page. The text will be placed in whatever typeface you used last.

d. Switch to the **Pointer tool** - the text is automatically selected. In the text roll-up you can now select a new typeface. Click on the arrowhead at the end of the typeface line and a list box will drop down. From this you can select whatever typeface you wish. Change the size while you're at it and then click on **Apply**.

e. Unlike the Character Attributes, using the roll-up does not override the Text dialogue box. In fact the roll-up is simply a quick of using it. Change the justification by clicking on the buttons in turn. After each one you have to press **Apply** for your change to be made on screen.

f. If there is a corresponding weight then the Bold and Italic buttons will become active, otherwise they remain greyed out. These buttons are toggles so to turn a style off you have to click on the relevant button again.

g. You can also use the roll-up in conjunction with the Node Edit tool. Try selecting all the characters in your forename apart from the initial one and then clicking on **Superscript** and then **Apply**. Repeat the action to clear it.

h. Clear the screen. Select the **Text tool**. Move the cursor on to the page. Click and the drag a selection box diagonally away from where you first clicked. As you do so you will get the familiar dashed lines appearing. Release the mouse button. For the moment the size of the box is irrelevant.

i. Press a character key. It doesn't matter which one. Then switch back to the **Pointer tool**. The character will now be surrounded by what looks like a large rectangle, including the handles. It isn't though. What you have got is a **Paragraph Text** box.

j. Press **Ctrl-T** to bring up the text dialogue box. Notice that it now says Paragraph Text and not Artistic Text. Into this box you can enter up to 4,000 characters - that's roughly 600 words. A faster way though it to import text.

k. Delete whatever character you typed. (You have to have something in the paragraph text box in order to open the text dialogue box.) Click on the button labelled **Import** and a new dialogue box appears, as opposite.

l. Whether or not there are any files available to you I don't know. You can only import pure ASCII text. In the illustration above there are a couple of readme files and we're going to use one of them. (If you have no files available log into the Windows directory and load a file from there, e.g. WIN.INI.) Double click on the file you want and it will be imported.

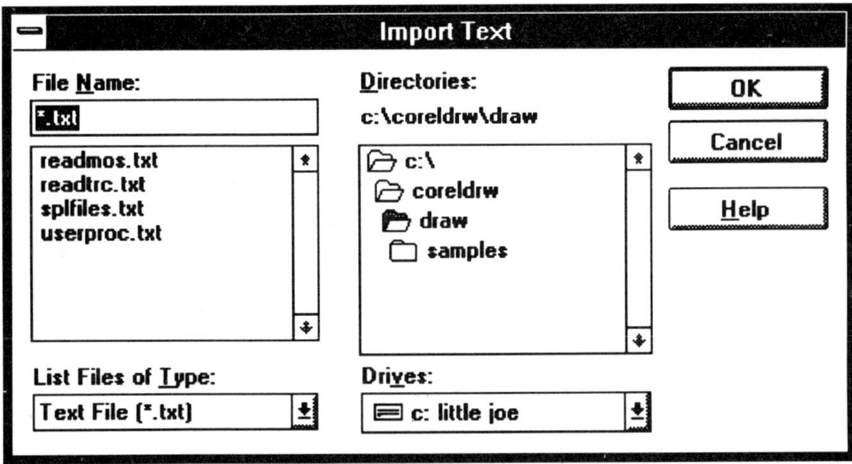


**8.09 Import dialogue box**

m. The imported text shows up in the main area of the dialogue box. Click on **OK** in the text dialogue box to close it. The paragraph text box on screen now contains the text but it's all greeked so you cannot read it. The level at which greeking occurs is controlled by the CORELDRW.INI file - see the appendices.

n. You can resize the box as if it were a rectangle just by dragging one of the handles. Stretch it so you have a horizontal rectangle. The text will be all to one side but that doesn't matter for a minute. In the Text roll-up click on **Frame** and a new dialogue box appears.

o. You use this dialogue box to set the parameters for the text within the paragraph box you have on screen. (This dialogue box in particular may be changed with the actual release of the software.) For now, just change the number of **Columns** to 2 and set the **Gutter Width** to 10. Then click on **OK**.

p. In the text roll-up you have to click on **Apply** for your changes to take effect. As soon as you do so the text will be reflowed in two neat columns, especially if you set the justification to **Full** as well.

q. As always, you can change the typeface, the size and the style. You can even mix typefaces and styles within the paragraph text by using the node edit as you did in the previous exercise. You can also move individual characters, or even complete words and phrases, around within the text box on screen. You can even colour individual letters as you would with Artistic Text.

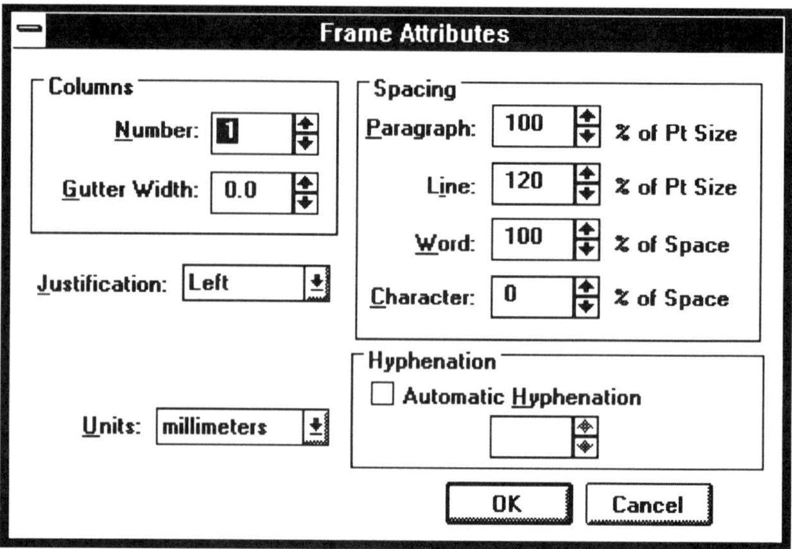


**8.10 Frame dialogue box**

There are some things you cannot do with Paragraph Text. For a start you cannot use Tabs, nor can you use Indents, as you would in a normal word processor. Of course you can create the same effect by moving the letters or words individually but it is not particularly easy to do. However, you can rotate and / or skew the paragraph text box itself and the columns will fit automatically to the new shape. Probably the most important thing you cannot do is re-shape the text box. It has to be a quadrilateral - you cannot make it circular for instance.

r. While you've got the text on screen, why not Spell Check it? You can either place the Text tool within the text or select the Pointer tool to highlight the box itself. Then open the **Text menu** and click on **Spell Check**. A dialogue box appears.

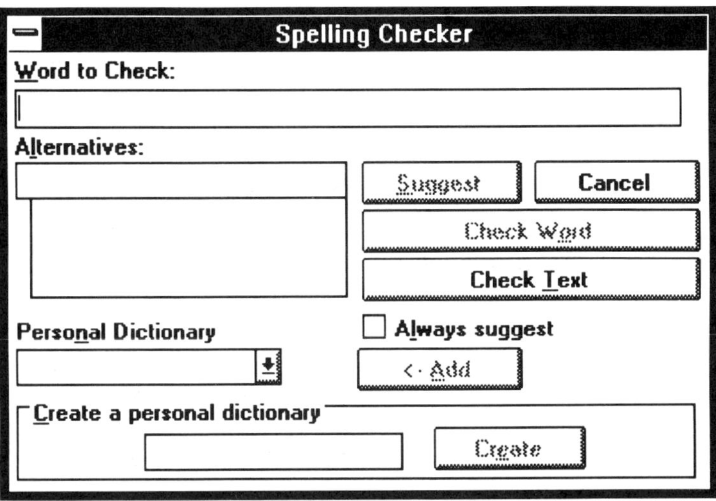


**8.11 Spell checker**

s. Move the cursor to the line at the bottom of the dialogue box that says **Create a personal dictionary**. Click the cursor in there and type a name, e.g. your own name, but remember that you can only have eight characters for it. Then click on the button labeled **Create**. The new dictionary name will appear under **Personal Dictionary**. While you're at it, click on **Always Suggest**.

t. Having set up your own dictionary you can now click on the button labelled **Check Text**. One interesting thing you will find is that the word CorelDRAW is not included in the dictionary!

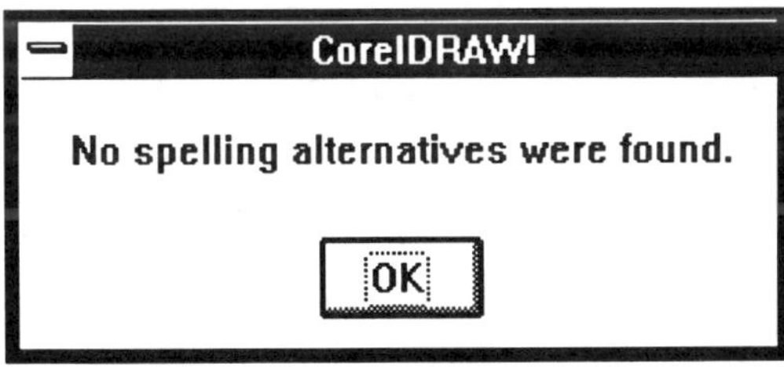


**8.12 No alternatives**

u. The worst thing about having Always Suggest turned on is that it slows down the spell checking process and you will frequently get a message box telling you that no alternatives were found. You can then either ignore the word or add it to your personal dictionary.

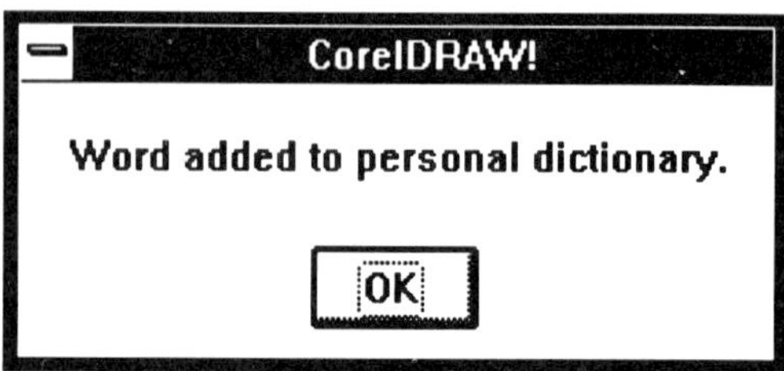


**8.13 Word added**

v. Try the **Thesaurus**. Select the Text tool and click on the paragraph text. You can then drag the cursor over any word to highlight it. Then open the **Text menu** and click on **Thesaurus**. A dialogue box appears with the selected word and the synonyms for it.

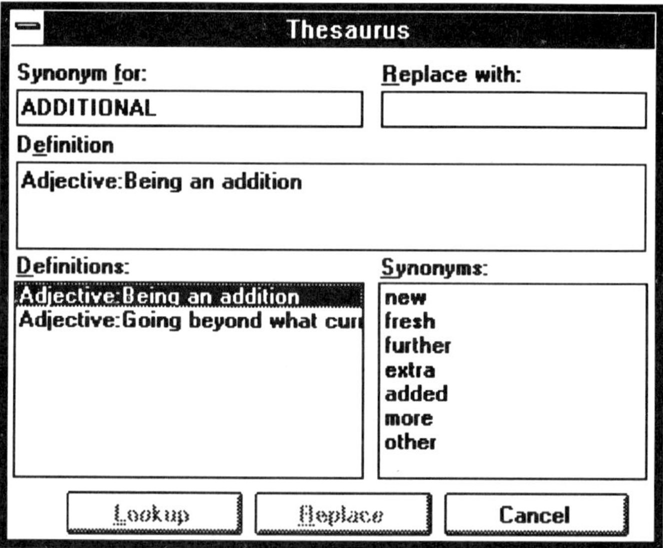


**8.14 Thesaurus**

w. Click on the word you want to use instead and then on **Replace**. The word will be replaced in the text.

A word of caution about Paragraph text. It places a large overhead on your system resources. If you think about it, you could have up to 4,000 characters - each of which has to be individually defined with their own nodes and shapes.. The result is that paragraph text can appear very slow, especially on systems that are under resourced in the first place, and the more you mix and match typefaces within it the slower it will get. The trick is to stick to a single typeface and weight within each paragraph text block and use Artistic text elsewhere, e.g. for headlines.

All text within CorelDRAW can use any fonts that you have installed on your system, be they Adobe Type 1, via ATM Control Panel, TrueType, via the Windows Control Panel, or earlier version of CorelDRAW's own WFN fonts. Because of this you have a big advantage.

Normally within Windows you cannot have more than roughly 255 fonts installed. (The actual number varies slightly according to resources but it is around that figure.) As CorelDRAW comes with 253 fonts (on the CD-ROM anyway) this is very close to the limit and it would mean that you couldn't have many more. But, CorelDRAW fonts are now supplied as both Adobe Type 1 and TrueType format. And you can have 255 fonts of either format - making a total of over 500! And if you had a lot of fonts that were previously converted to WFN format you could have another 255 of them. So theoretically you could have over 750 fonts installed on your system. (Though why you would want to is beyond me.)

However, there is, as always, a down side to this. The more fonts you have installed, of whatever format, the less resources you have available for anything else. To start with if you load 500 fonts on to your hard disk, e.g. all the CorelDRAW TrueType and ATM fonts, you're going to need around 12 Mb of disk space! And the TrueType ones take up over three quarters of that. (I've just checked to be sure.) Therefore it makes sense to install only those fonts that you actually need as the need arises. Once you're finished with them, remove them again.

People tend to go mad when they can suddenly have lots of fonts and typefaces and they mix them all up and use them simply because they are there to be used. You end up with a Printer's Pie. (That's an old phrase from the days of manual typesetting. It means that the characters from the different typefaces have all got mixed up together.) A good rule of thumb is to never have more than six fonts on a single page, preferably not more than four. Don't forget that a font means a sub-division of a typeface. Thus Times Normal, Times Italic, Times Bold and Times Bold-Italic are four different fonts even when they are all the same size.

# E26 - TEXT AND PATHS

CorelDRAW has always allowed you to fit text to a path but until now it has often been a little cumbersome. Where the text fitted depended on how you had drawn the shape, where the nodes were, etc. If you had forgotten any of that then the text wouldn't fit the way you wanted it to and you'd have to fiddle around getting it right.

No more. Fitting text to a path in CorelDRAW 3.0 is fully interactive, controlled by a roll-up, and life is very much simpler.

a. Start with a new page. Select the **Text tool** and write your name anywhere on the page. Use the text roll-up to change the typeface to Casper Open Face and the size to 48 points.

b. Draw a circle, about 100 mms in diameter. Align this to the centre of the page.

c. Select both the text and the circle and then press **Ctrl-F** or open the **Text menu** and click on **Fit Text to Path**. The roll-up will appear.

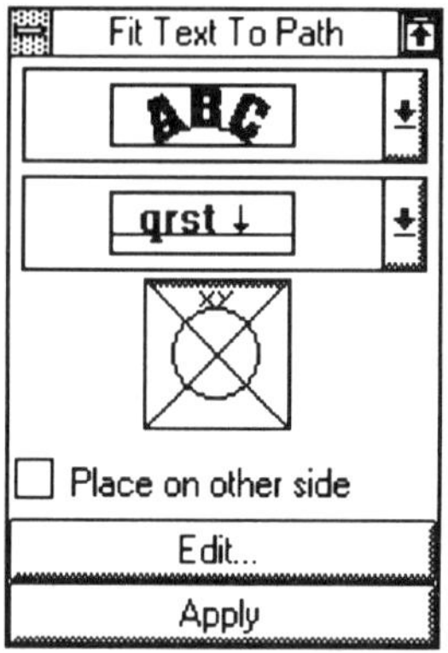


**8.15 Text to path roll-up**

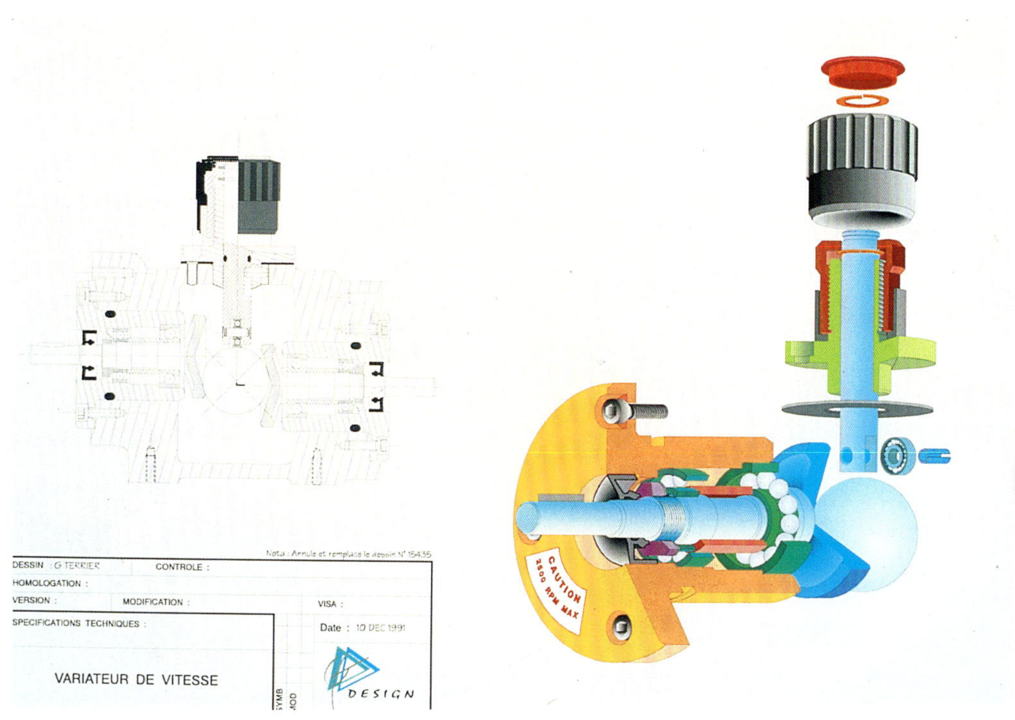


'Techdraw' by Guy Terrier (First Prize World – Technical Drawing)

'Laiva' by Matti Kaarala (First Prize World – Business, Technology and Transportation)

'Bigfish' by Gary Priester (First Prize World – Desktop Publishing)

'Venice' by Peter McCormick (First Prize World – Landmarks and Travel)

'Corel3' by Chris Purcell
(First Prize World – Logos)

'Magic' by Lea Tjeng Kian
(First Prize World – Holidays, Thematic Events and Sports)

'World' by Steven Cousins (First Prize World – Photo/bitmap)

'Lifetime' by Ceri Lines (First Prize World – Miscellaneous)

d. The roll-up is set with the defaults so just click on **Apply**. The CorelDRAW hour-glass icon will appear, even on the fastest machine, for a couple of seconds and then the text is fitted around the top of the circle.

**8.16 Text to circle with defaults**

e. Some of the letters in that text are not very legible. (I chose Casper on purpose to get this effect.) Open the text roll-up again and change the typeface to **Renfrew**. Click on **Apply**. Nothing happens. That's because text fitted to path becomes a special form of text and its attributes cannot be changed.

f. Select the text, i.e. click on it by itself, and try again. Still nothing happens. There has to be a way of changing the text. Try each of the menus you've used up to now to find a command that will allow you to get at the text. You won't find one.

g. Open the **Arrange menu** and click on **Separate**. This has the effect of severing the link between the text and the object that it is fitted to. The Status Bar will change from "**Text on a Path on Layer 1**" to saying "**2 objects selected on Layer 1**".

h. Now you can select the text by itself and change it. Change it to Renfrew 48 points. Then select the circle as well and click on **Apply** in the Fit text to Path roll-up. At least it is more legible. Save the file.

That raises a very good point about text on a path. When you fit text to a path the characters within the text string have to be adjusted to make them fit the path. But some typefaces lend themselves to this more than others. In particular any typeface that has very thin ascenders or descenders or one that is very ornate, won't lend itself very well to fitting to a path. At least not at small point sizes. They will work fine at 100 points plus but at less than that they tend to become, in varying degrees, unreadable. The moral is choose your typeface carefully when fitting text to a path.

j. The text and path are now interactive as a unit. You cannot change just the text or just the circle, although you can manually kern the text, change the colours of various characters and even change individual characters to other tyepafces using the Node Edit tool.

k. Because the text and the object are interactively linked you can use this to advantage. Select the **Node Edit tool** and click on the text. Then drag a selection box around all the nodes of the text. You can now drag the text around the circle.

   Don't do it too fast or you won't be able to see what you're doing. If you drag it slowly, you will find that you get a copy of the text string appearing in dashed blue lines. When you release the mouse button the text itself moves to the new position.

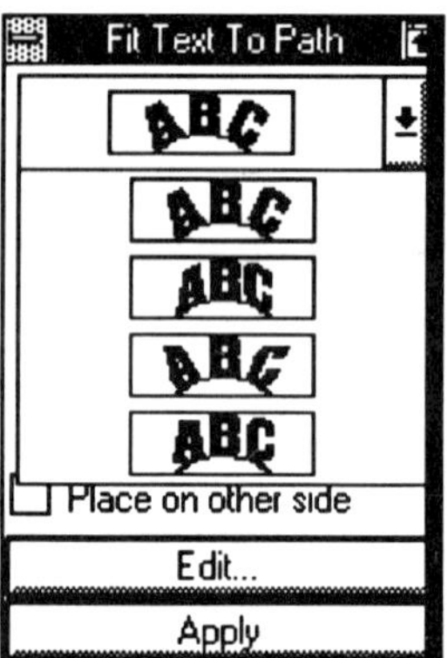


**8.17 Text orientation**

l. Put the text back where it was. The easiest way is to press **Alt-backspace,** or open the **Edit menu** and click on **Undo,** provided that you've only moved the text once. If you've made a number of movements this won't work and so you'll need to reload the file.

m. CorelDRAW provides you with four different methods of **Text Orientation** for the path. In the roll-up click on the arrowhead at the end of the ABC line.

**8.18 Text orientations applied**

The first option, top left above, is the default one. Using this the characters in the text string will be rotated as necessary in order for their baselines to fit along the path.

The second option, top right, vertically skews the characters individually so that they appear upright on the path but fitted to it.

The third option, bottom left, is similar except that it applies a horizontal skew.

The final option, bottom right in Figure 8.18, keeps all the letters upright, without any skewing being applied, but the characters fit along the path rather than around it.

n. The second set of options that the roll-up gives you are the **Distance from Path** options.

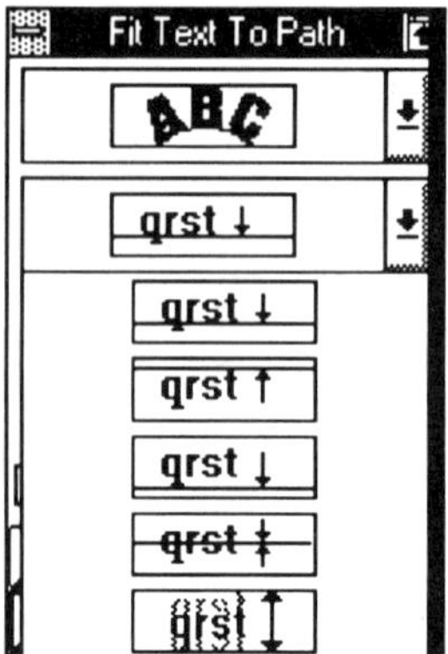


**8.19 Distance options**

The first is the default and it aligns the baselines of the text on to the path. In other words the baseline of the text in essence becomes the path.

The second option aligns the text along the top rather than the bottom. In other words if you click on this option now and then on **Apply** the text will fit inside the circle rather than outside it.

The third option aligns the baseline of the text to the path but above it. Select this option then click on **Apply**. The text appears above the circle. Now click on the text and hold down the mouse button and move it very slightly. An arrow appears with a thin circle ranging out from it. This is the new path baseline.

As you move the mouse the circle increases or decreases in diameter. Release the mouse button and the text aligns to the new baseline. The original circle stays where it was. If you try to move the baseline inside the circle then the fifth option, see below, automatically operates.

The fourth option aligns the text so that the selected path runs through the centre of the text.

The final choice is similar to choice three but you can move the baseline inside the circle as well as outside it.

o. The final option in the roll-up, as it currently is, is **Alignment**. This is different depending on whether you are using ellipses and rectangle or open paths. In this case the alignment apepars as a circle divided into four. Click on any section and then apply. The text will reflow to fit the segment you chose.

p. **Place on other side** is an sub-command of the alignment. If you turn it on then the text is placed on the other side of the path and reversed. Try it.

q. Delete the circle and text. Draw an S-shaped squiggle - a biggish one. Write the text again. Select both and the contents of the Fit text to path roll-up changes. The Alignment options are different.

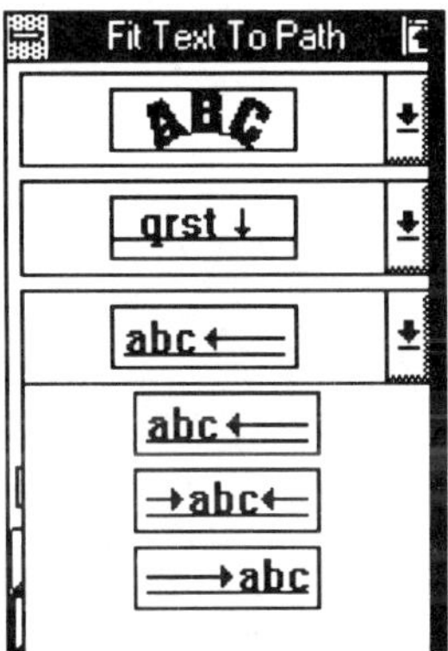


**8.20 Open path alignment**

r. You now have three sub-options. The first, the default, will align the text with the starting node of the path being aligned to. For all intents and purposes this is normally the beginning of the path.

The second option will align the text in the middle of the path.

The third option aligns the text to the last node of the path, i.e. the end of it.

There is a fourth option but it only becomes active when you move the text using the Node Edit tool. This is the interactive alignment.

Again you can use **Place on other side** to have the text appear on the other side of the line.

Note: Unlike in CorelDRAW 2.01 and earlier, text that is aligned to a path has no justification applied to it. Because the whole thing becomes interactive, justification is discarded.

With all the various combinations of four orientation, five distance settings and four alignments you have a total of 80 possible ways of aligning text to a path. This makes this command one of the most comprehensive that CorelDRAW provides. The only way to learn all the possibilities is to play with it. Some options will be effectively useless but many others will be very useful and beneficial. Play with the various options until you are familiar with them all and their use.

# Q9 - DAILY PLANET

This image was created using ellipses, circles and Fit Text to Path. Can you recreate it?

# 9 - ARRANGE MENU

The Arrange menu is concerned with the arrangement of things on screen. Most of the commands within the menu have keyboard shortcuts, all of which you should become familiar with. It will be very rare for you to find all the commands within the menu active, generally at least half of them will be greyed out because their availability depends on circumstances.

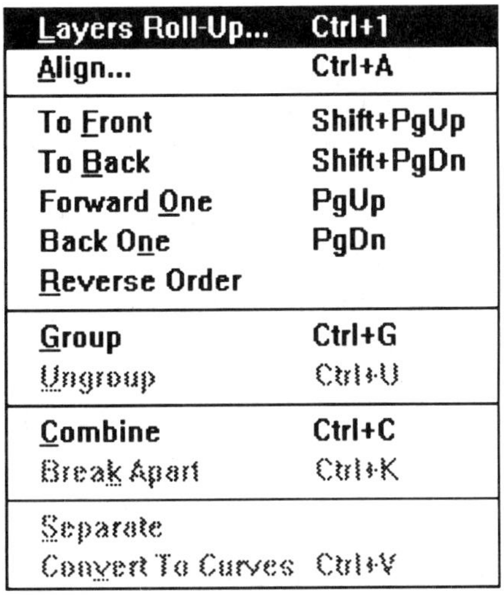

| | |
|---|---|
| Layers Roll-Up... | Ctrl+1 |
| Align... | Ctrl+A |
| To Front | Shift+PgUp |
| To Back | Shift+PgDn |
| Forward One | PgUp |
| Back One | PgDn |
| Reverse Order | |
| Group | Ctrl+G |
| Ungroup | Ctrl+U |
| Combine | Ctrl+C |
| Break Apart | Ctrl+K |
| Separate | |
| Convert To Curves | Ctrl+V |

**9.01 Arrange Menu**

**Layers Roll-up** allows you to manipulate the layers within CorelDRAW. The number of layers is unlimited, subject only to your machine resources. The keyboard shortcut is **Ctrl-1**.

**Align** you have already used a lot. It brings up the dialogue box that allows you to align objects to the page or each other. The shortcut is **Ctrl-A**.

**To Front** allows you to move an object, or selection of objects, to the top of the stack of objects on any layer. You can have any number of objects on any layer and they are effectively stacked one on top of the other. The keyboard shortcut is **Shift-PgUp**.

**To Back** is the reverse of the above. It moves objects right to the bottom of the stack. The keyboard shortcut is **Shift-PgDn**.

**Forward One** moves a selected object up one place within the stack. The keyboard shortcut is **PgUp**.

**Backward One** moves a selected object down one place within the stack. The keyboard shortcut is **PgDn**.

**Reverse Order** changes the does just that, it reverses the order of selected objects within the stack. There is no keyboard shortcut for this command.

**Group** takes selected objects and federates them into a single unit. It doesn't change any of the objects but they can then be treated as if they were a single object. The keyboard shortcut is **Ctrl-G**. You cannot Node Edit grouped objects. Grouped objects are particularly memory intensive.

**Ungroup** is the opposite of the above. It dissolves the federation as it were and gives you back the individual objects. The keyboard shortcut is **Ctrl-U**.

**Combine** takes the selected objects and turns them into a single object in the process. If a group is a federation, then combined objects are an amalgamation. It will have an effect on how the objects appear. The shortcut is **Ctrl-C**.

**Break Apart** is the opposite of Combine. It will take a combined object and split it into its component entities. This can give you odd effects. The keyboard shortcut is **Ctrl-K**.

**Separate** applies only to Blended and Extrudes objects. (Why it isn't in the Effects menu is a mystery.) It destroys the dynamic link between these objects and makes them individual objects.

**Convert to Curves** applies only to ellipses, rectangles and text. It takes these objects and turns them into curves so that they can be manipulated in the normal way by Node Edit. The keyboard shortcut is **Ctrl-V**.

# E27 - ALIGNMENT

Throughout this book so far, you have used Align to get things into the centre of the page. However, you can do other things with it such as fitting objects together.

a. Start a new file. Draw a circle, 100 mms in diameter, a square that is 50 mms to a side, an ellipse that is 100 mms on the long axis and 50 mms on the short axis. Then write the letter A in Avalon Bold 144 point. Place all these in different parts of the page.

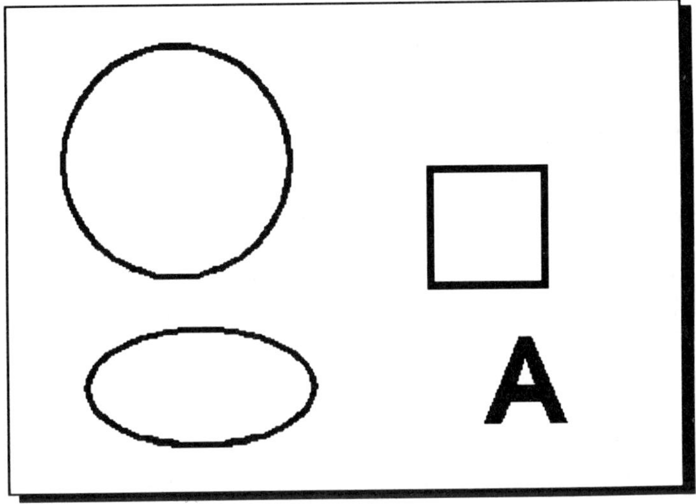


**9.02 Elements on page**

b. Select the circle and the square. Press **Ctrl-A** to bring up the Align dialogue box.

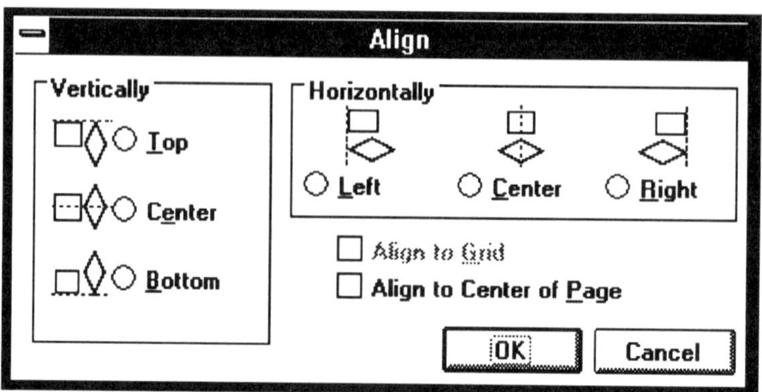


**9.03 Align dialogue box**

c. The dialogue box allows you to align selected objects in a number of different ways. You have a choice of three vertical alignments and three horizontal ones. Click on **Vertical Top** and then on **OK**.

d. One of the objects will have moved and it should be the circle. The reason is that when you use alignment the first object you select is aligned to the second one. Press **Alt-Backspace** to undo the alignment. The objects go back to their original positions.

e. Deselect the objects. Now select the square then the circle. Press **Ctrl-A** and choose **Vertical Top**. Click on **OK**. This time the square moves and the circle remains stationary.

f. Press **Alt-Backspace** again. Deselect the objects. Now select the A and the square. Press **Alt-A**. Select **Vertical Top** and **Horizontal Centre**. Click on **OK**. The A jumps into the square and aligns itself with the top centre of the square.

g. Press **Alt-Backspace** again. While the objects are still selected press **Ctrl-A** again. This time select **Vertical** and **Horizontal Centre**. Click on **OK**. This time the A moves to be centrally located within the square.

h. Now select the circle by holding down **Shift** and then clicking on it. Press **Ctrl-A**, choose **Vertical** and **Horizontal Centre** and then click on **OK**. The three objects align themselves around the centre point of the circle.

i. All three objects are still selected so press **Ctrl-A** again. Select **Vertical Bottom** and **Horizontal Right**. Click on **OK**. This time everything aligns itself to the bottom left hand corner of the bounding box used by the circle.

j. Press **Alt-Backspace** again and things move back to the previous positions. Deselect all the objects. Select the square and the A. Press **Ctrl-G** to group them together. Now select the circle again, by holding down **Shift** and clicking on it. Press **Ctrl-A** again and select **Vertical Bottom** and **Horizontal Right**. Click on **OK**.

   This time the alignment of the square and the A is not changed. Because they are grouped together the attributes of the two items are maintained so they are treated as a unit.

k. Deselect everything and then click on the A. You automatically select the entire group. Press **Ctrl-U** to ungroup them.

l. Select everything on the page. Press **Ctrl-A** and then **Align to Centre of Page**. Notice that when you do so Vertical Centre and Horizontal Centre are automatically selected. Click on **OK**. All the objects align themselves into the middle of the page.

m. Play with the possibilities. See if you can arrange things so that the bottom of the ellipse aligns with the top of the square. Or align the left hand side of the circle with the right hand side of the letter A.

You won't be able to. The reason is that what you are aligning is not so much the objects themselves as the bounding boxes that surround them. In most cases this will have exactly the same result. However, you cannot align individual sides of selected objects. So you cannot choose to align the left of one and the right of another. Both have to be either right or left.

To align things on opposite sides you physically move them, maybe using Guidelines to help the positioning. Within the Align dialogue box you actually have a choice of nine broad alignments, three vertical multiplies by three horizontal, plus the added effect of using align to page centre or align to grid. The effects of the latter are dependent on the grid frequency.

# E28 - ARRANGEMENTS

When you add elements to an image in CorelDRAW they are added like playing cards to a pile. The first object you draw goes on the bottom, the second object is next, the third follows that and so on. Eventually you end up with a stack of objects. This can happen on any Layer which is a different thing entirely. We'll come to Layers in a minute.

The difference between CorelDRAW and a pack of cards is that the objects don't have to physically be on top of each other to hold their position in the stack. It's easier to see than to explain so...

a. Start a new page. Select the **Text tool** and write **Object 1**. Then draw a red circle. Then a blue square. Then write **Object 4**. Then add a straight vertical line. You now have five objects on screen.

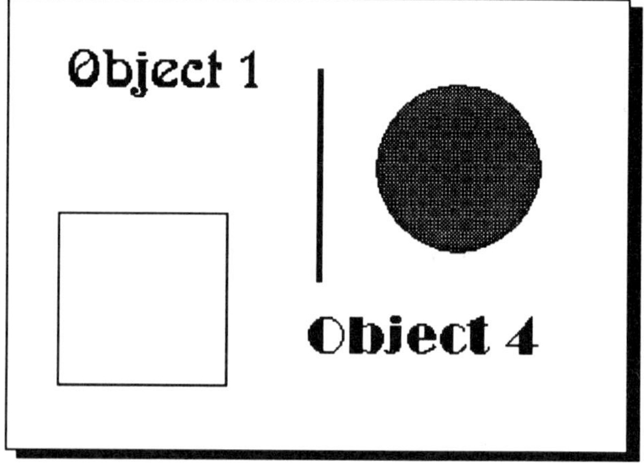


**9.04 Five objects**

b. Pick up the first lot of text and move it on top of the circle. When you release the mouse button the text disappears behind the circle. That's because the circle is higher up the stack than the text is.

c. Pick up Object 4 and move it on top of the square. This time the text lies on top of the square because it is higher up the stack.

d. Now pick up the line and place it over the circle. It lies on top of it so it's higher up the stack. But is the line higher or lower than the square? In this case you know it is because that's the way you added it. However, in the normal course of events there is no way of knowing where objects lie within the stack. You can only find out by moving them around as you've just done.

e. But suppose you wanted all the objects to be in the opposite order. That's easy to arrange. Select all the objects, open the **Arrange menu** and click on **Reverse Order**. The picture on screen instantly changes are the stack of objects is reversed. Now the line is the bottom object followed by Object 4 followed by the square followed by the circle followed by Object 1 which is now at the top of the stack.

f. Suppose you wanted to reverse the positions of the square and the circle. You can do it in two ways. Either select them both and the use **Reverse Order** again or you could move either object up or down within the stack. For example, select the square and then press **PgDn**. That moves it down one level and moves the circle up one so their order is reversed.

g. Notice that there is no noticeable difference on screen. The only way to find out whether or not you have done it right is to move the square on top of the circle. If the circle comes to the front then they have changed places, if it doesn't then they haven't.

h. The line is now at the bottom of the stack. Suppose you wanted it at the top. Select it. Now you can either press **PgUp** repeatedly until it arrives at the top or you can shortcut the process by pressing **Shift-PgUp**. Pressing **Shift-PgDn** will take it right back to the bottom again.

This exercise may seem a little frivolous but it is important that you know how to move things within the stack and, more importantly, that you realise that there is a stack there. It affects many things. For example, if you import an image now it will automatically become the top item in the stack. But if it is a multiple object image then the items within that image are also stacked.

When you import a CorelDRAW file it will actually tell you how many objects are in the image because the image is imported as a group. But...a group counts as a single item. So you could import what appears to be a file with half a dozen objects but each one could in turn be a group of a dozen objects. These will then all affect the items you originally had in your image. If you ungroup everything you could get really lost with what object is where within the stack especially if you then start moving things up and down within the stack. There is no easy answer to the dilemma. It's something you have to live with and get used to.

# E29 - GROUPS & COMBINATIONS

CorelDRAW is a memory intensive piece of software, it is also disk intensive but to a lesser degree, and as such its performance is dependent on your system resources. However, what you do with the image in front of you will have a bearing on how much memory you use for a particular piece of the image.

In certain circumstances, as with moving the letter and square in the last exercise, you will want things to move or be manipulated in their current configuration. The easiest way to do this is with groups. But creating and using groups are the most memory intensive things you can do.

Why? Essentially because you are adding another layer of complexity to the image. Take the square and letter from the last exercise. The letter itself has a number of attributes; its font, size, style, outline and fill. Then the square has the same sort of information, there is the size of it, the thickness and colour of the outline and the fill. On top of that for each element there has to be the information about any distortion, rotation, bending, enveloping and what have you. Then you group the two together. In other words you are effectively saying "I want these two pieces of image, complete with all their individual information, to be put together as a single unit and treated as such." Things are getting complex.

However, having said that groups are extremely useful. The thing to remember is not to use them as a matter of course, especially if you have only limited resources available. In the normal course of events you may want to group objects for a specific purpose but once that purpose is fulfilled, do you still need the grouping? Using Layers instead may be more beneficial. We'll come to layers in a minute.

CorelDRAW also provides you with the facility to Combine objects. This is different to making groups. When you combine objects they become a single entity that has only one set of attributes. Combinations are much simpler than groups and therefore they take up a lot less memory and resources. The interesting thing is that the combined objects don't have to be together.

a. Start a new file. Draw a circle 100 mms in diameter and position it in the centre of the page.

b. Now you want four more circles and rather than redraw each one, use the various options that CorelDRAW provides for duplicating them. Firstly, press **Ctrl-J** to open the **Preferences** dialogue box. Change the **Place Duplicate** co-ordinates to **0 Horizontal** and **50 mms Vertical.** Close the dialogue box and then press **Ctrl-D**. You get another circle appearing 50 mms above the original.

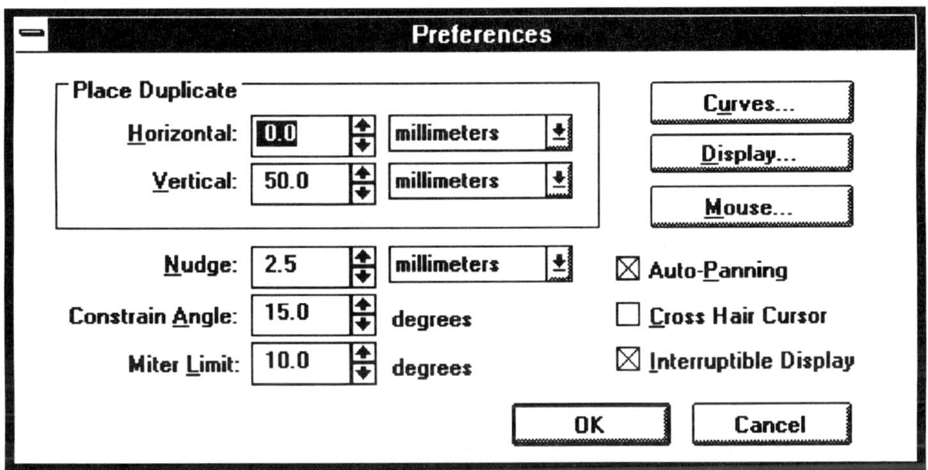


**9.05 Preferences dialogue box**

c. Select the original circle again. Press **Ctrl-L** to bring up the **Move** dialogue box. Change the Horizontal value to -50 mms and the Vertical value to 0. Click on **Leave Original**. Click on **OK** and you have a third circle 50 mms to the left of the original.

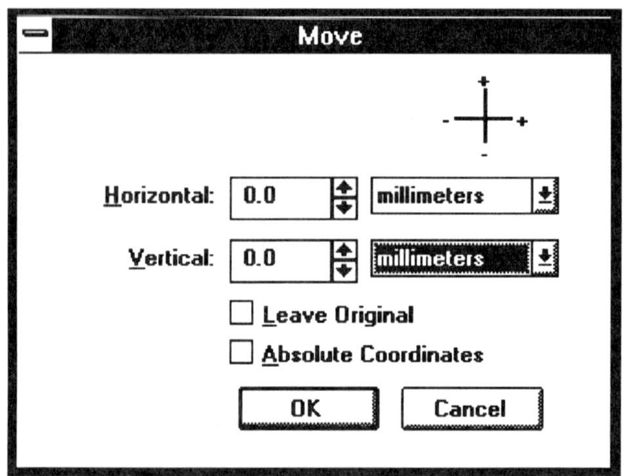


**9.06 Move dialogue box**

d. Make sure that **Snap to Grid** is turned off. If it's on it will appear on the Status Bar. You can toggle it on or off using **Ctrl-Y**. This one is tricky! Click on the original circle and then start to drag it to the right but as you begin to move it, i.e. when the dashed bounding box appears, click the right mouse button. This will duplicate the original circle and allow you to move the duplicate. Drag it 50 mms to the right - watch the Status Bar and it tells you how far you moved it.

e. Finally, select the original circle again. Press the plus key on the numeric keypad to duplicate it and then drag the circle down 50 mms. As you can see CorelDRAW provides a host of ways to duplicate and move objects. You should end up with Figure 9.07.

f. Fill each circle with a different colour, making the original one Red and filling it last. But how do you get to the original circle? It's now covered by the others in the stack. The answer is you cheat. Drag a bounding box around where you know the circle to be. Make sure you don't click on any of the other circles. If you get it right then the handles of the original circle appear. Alternatively you can press **Shift-F9** to activate the wire frame screen. You can't see colours on this but you can see outlines. Now fill the circle. Then press **Shift-F9** again to go back to the normal screen.

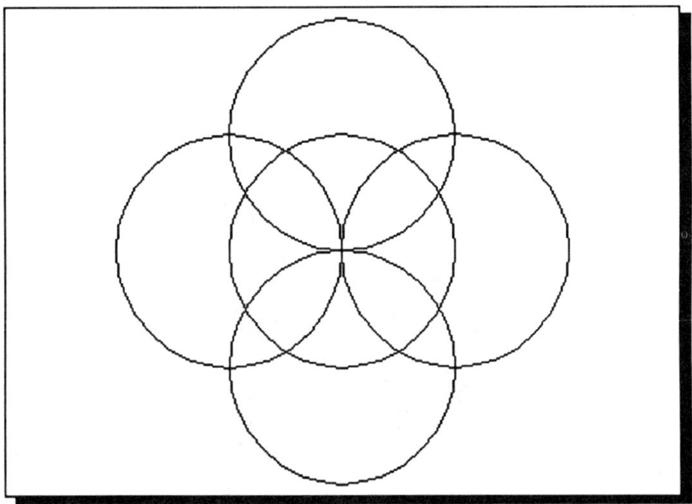

**9.07 Five circles**

g. Now drag a bounding box around all the circles and press **Ctrl-G** to group them together. The Status Bar will say "**Group of 5 objects on Layer 1**".

h. This group can now be treated as a whole, an entity unto itself. Press **Ctrl-Q** to bring up the **Stretch and Mirror** dialogue box. Put 50% into each line and then click on **OK**. The entire group is reduced to a quarter of its original size. (It's a quarter because you reduced it on two dimensions. To make the whole thing approximately half the size of the original you would need to enter a value of 71%.)

i. Press **Alt-Backspace** to undo the reduction. Select the group and then press **Ctrl-U** to ungroup it. The Status Bar now says "**5 objects selected on Layer 1**" because the five circles are selected. Whenever you ungroup a group the objects within that group remain selected until you deselect them.

j. Now press **Ctrl-C** to combine the circles. You get a pretty flower pattern. It should be Red because that was the last colour you used when you filled the circles. Remember that the white areas are not white they are holes.

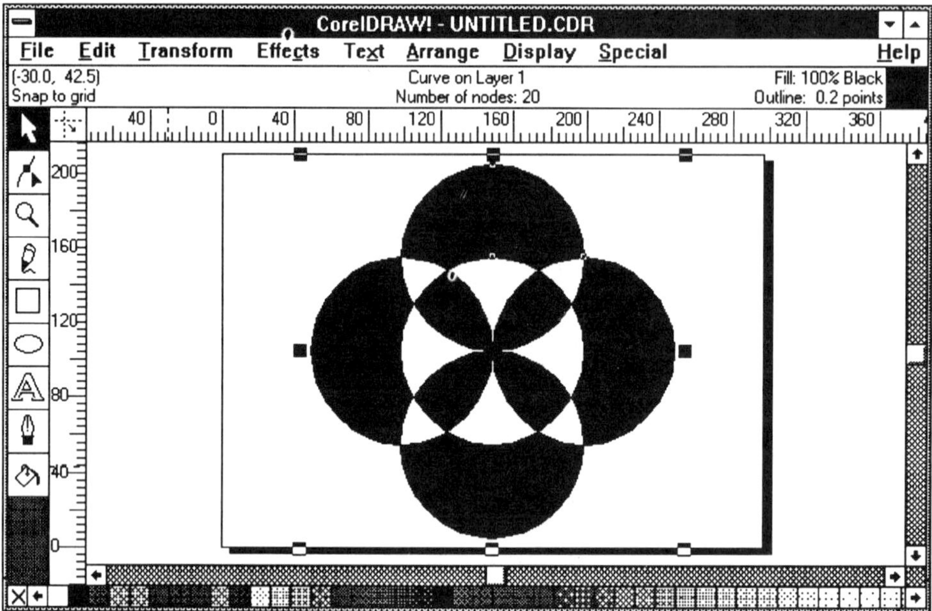


**9.08 Flower pattern**

k. Now press **Ctrl-K** to uncombine the object. You now apparently have five circles all the same colour and so you can't see the individual ones. That's the negative aspect of combinations. When you uncombine things they all end up sharing exactly the same attributes. In this case you can remedy the situation easily by simply filling all the circles with nothing, so you can see them, and then refilling them with colour.

l. One other thing to notice. Click on any individual circle. Look at the Status Bar. You no longer have a circle - you have a curve. Press **F10** to select Node Edit and you'll see that there are now four nodes around the shape instead on only one. That means that you cannot now create an arc or pie-slice from the circle because you don't have a circle.

m. There is an important point where you need to use combine and that's when you want to literally combine objects into a single shape. In this case you're going to make an arch. Clear the page. Draw a 100 mms circle and a 100 mms square. Lay the square so that it's under the circle but slightly overlapping it.

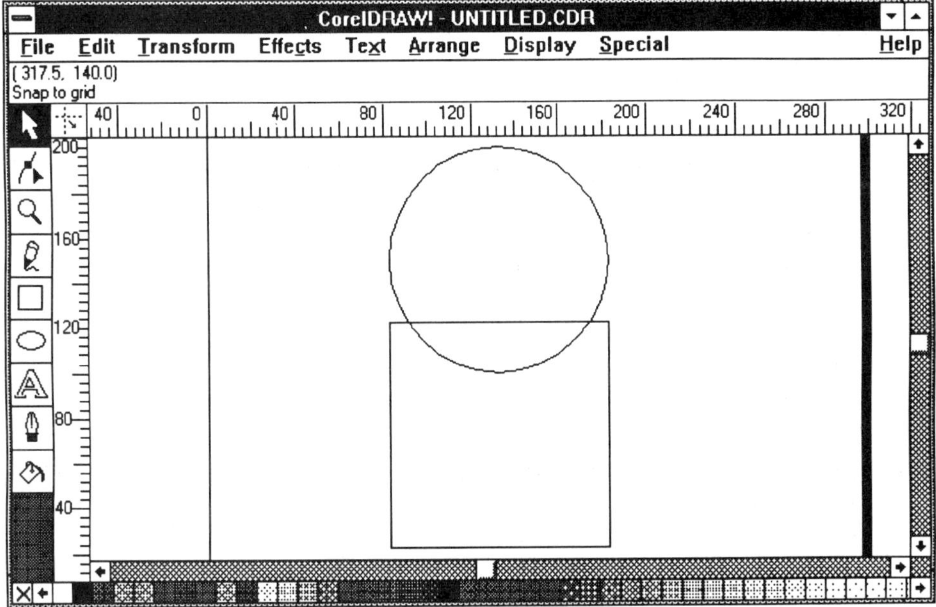


**9.09 Circle and Square**

n. Now combine the two. The Status Bar says "**Curve on Layer 1**". Switch to the **Node Edit** tool. Double click on the top line of the former square. The Node Edit button box appears. Click on **Break** and what looks like a single node is added to the line. It's actually two nodes laid one over the other.

**9.10 Node Edit button box**

o. Click on the page to deselect the nodes then drag a bounding box around the nodes that have just been added. Press **Del** to remove them. You now have an open box as it were.

p. You have to treat the circle shape slightly differently. Double click on the node at the bottom of the shape, i.e. at 6 o'clock, this selects it and bring up the button box. Click on **Break** again. You can break any line at any point, including where a node lies. Then select the two nodes again and delete them. The circle shape now becomes a half-circle.

q. Now drag one of the nodes from the square straight up, it helps if you hold down **Ctrl** as you do so, until it lies over one of the nodes on the half-circle. Do the same with the other one.

r. Drag a selection box around either pair of nodes to select them. Double click on the pair and then click on **Join** the button box. The two nodes become one. Do the same with the other pair.

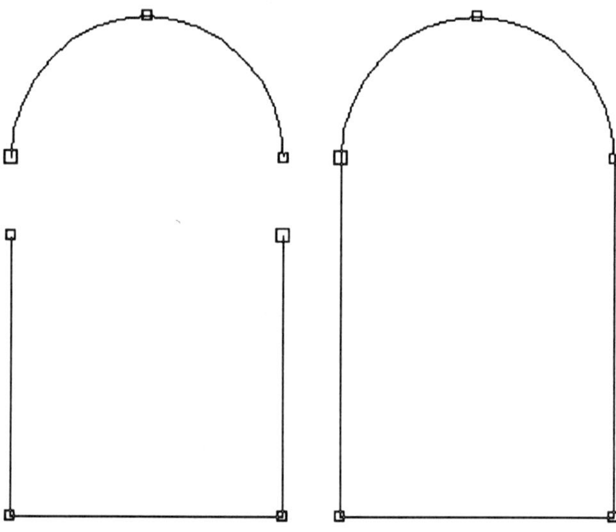

**9.11 Shape before and after**

s. That's it. You now have an arch. It contains five nodes, one each at the bottom corners of the original square, one at 12 o'clock in the original circle and two others where the two shapes join. You can now fill the resulting shape, manipulate it and use it as a normal object.

t. The arch you now have is too big for what you're going to do in the next exercise, so shrink it down. Use **Ctrl-Q** and values of **72%** for both Horizontal and Vertical. Move the arch to the left hand side of the page (this assumes you're using A4 Landscape).

u. Then press **Ctrl-L**. Use a horizontal value of 100 mms. Click on **Leave Original** and then on **OK**. You have two arches. Press **Ctrl-R** to repeat the last action and you have three.

v. The arches are actually going to be windows. So draw a large white rectangle that covers the entire page. Select it and the arches and then combine them. The arches now become holes in a white background.

**9.12 Finished arches**

w. Save the file and call it **Arches**. You'll need it for the next exercise.

# E30 - LAYERS

When I started this book I knew I was going to have to do something with the layers and I've spent the past couple of weeks trying to develop an exercise that will show them off to advantage. The trouble is that while I can design an exercise that looks great on screen it will look terrible when printed in monochrome. Equally I don't know what Clip-Art you have available, which is the classic thing to use the Layers facility with. So this exercise is very basic and simple and you'll have to play with the Layers for yourself once you've got the basic idea sorted out. What you're going to do is create a multi-layered file using Clip-Art. This exercise assumes that you have the Clip-Art that is supplied with CorelDRAW 3.0 and will use only images that should be on the floppy disk version.

The reason for having layers has to do with the complexity problems of using the stacked objects. Instead of having all the objects on a single page, you can effectively layer pages of items one on top of the other. In this way you can keep each layer relatively simple and easy to work with but you get the same effect as using multiple layered stacks.

The number of Layers you can have in CorelDRAW is limited only by the system resources you have available. At the very least you should be able to have a dozen or so layers. However, don't fall into the trap of using layers just because they are there. The circumstances when you will actually need to use the layers may be few and far between. Don't use them just because you can because they will eat into your resources and that slows everything down.

**9.13 Layers roll-up**

a. Start a new file. Press **Ctrl-1** which brings up the **Layers roll-up**. By default this contains only three layers, the bottom one contains the grid, the second one the guidelines and the top one is called Layer 1. Each layer can have an identifying name of its own. You can add layers, move them around, delete them and so on.

b. Click on the arrowhead pointing right and a menu box appears to the right of the roll-up.

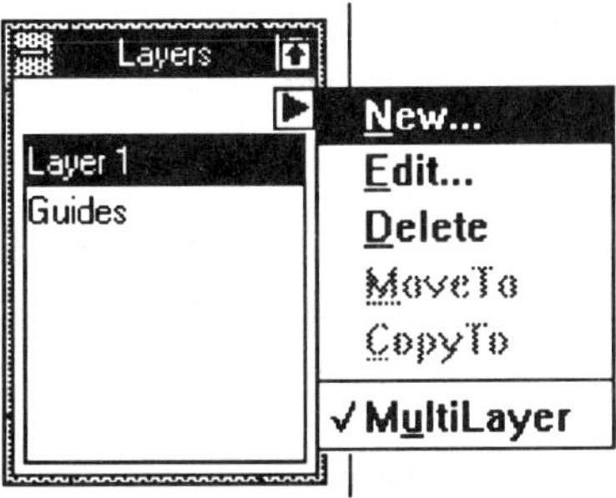


**9.14 Layers menu**

**New** creates a new layer and it brings up its own dialogue box.

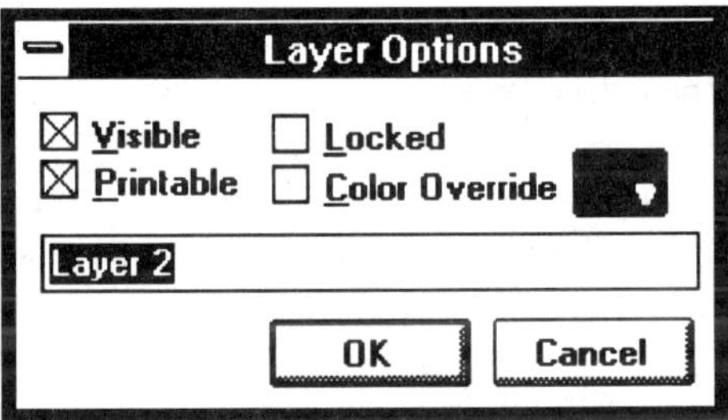


**9.15 New Layer dialogue box**

**Visible** means just that. Do you want to be able to see the contents of this layer or not? In some cases it is useful to turn certain layers off so you can work with others and then turn them back on when you're finished. It is selected by default.

**Locked** makes a layer uneditable. On any layer that is locked you cannot delete or even select objects.

**Printable** allows you to control which layers are printed. It is turned on by default. In certain circumstances you may want to print only certain layers and with this command you can do just that.

**Colour Override** changes the way things look on screen so that they appear only as wire frames in the chosen colour. It doesn't change the actual objects on the layer and they will still print correctly, if the layer is printable, but it means that you can manipulate other layers easily and simply.

The **Layer Name** is given, by default, as Layer x where x is the next layer number, in this case 2. You can change this to be anything you wish using up to 32 characters including spaces.

Another command appears if you are using the Grid or Guides layer. **Setup** brings up the normal Grid or Guidelines setup dialogue box.

**Edit** allows you to change the attributes of a layer. It brings up a dialogue box identical to the one above.

**Delete** removes a layer and its contents. Once you delete an layer the next one down becomes the active layer.

**Move To** allows you to move selected objects from one layer to another. A little arrow appears and you use this to point to the layer you want to move the objects to.

**Copy To** copies selected objects from one layer to another. It works the same way as Move above.

**MultiLayer** is a toggle that is on by default and I always turn it off. With the command turned on you can select any object off any layer and edit it - regardless of what layer you are actually working with. Turn it off and you can only edit objects on the current layer. (Which I think is more useful.)

The layers behave in the same way as the stacked objects on the normal page. That is to say that the layer at the top of the list is the top layer, the one at the end of the list is the bottom one and the ones in between occupy a position identical to their order in the list. You can change the layer order very simply. Just click and drag a layer, in the roll-up, so that it is above whatever layer you want it to be above. Release the mouse button and the layers move around to accommodate your selection.

However, you should not move the Grid or Guidelines up through the order. There is no reason why you can't but it makes more sense to keep them at the bottom as all the other layers will use these as a base.

a. Open the Layers roll-up and its menu. Click on **Edit**. Change the layer name to **Distance** but otherwise leave the defaults as they are.

b. Open the menu again and click on **New**. The name Layer 2 will be given. Change this to **Distance** then click on **OK**. You then want three more layers, called **Background, Middle Ground** and **Foreground** respectively.

c. Open the menu again and turn off **MultiLayer**. You only have to do this once because it affects all the layers. You should then have something like this:

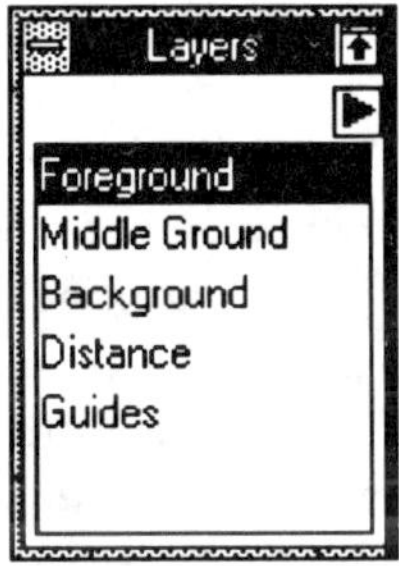


**9.16 New layers**

d. Open the Layers control box, in the top left hand corner of its Title Bar, and click on **Arrange**. That moves the roll-up out of the way. Open it up again and click on **Distance**. Images will be drawn or placed on whatever layer is currently selected in the roll-up. You're going to build up the image from the back to the front so start on **Distance**.

e. The next thing to do is import the first graphic. You must import it rather than load it or it will overwrite the current file. Open the **File menu** and click on **Import**. Find a file called **CROW.CDR** which should be in the \CLIPART\BIRD directory - assuming that the release version ships with the same clip-art as I've got. Either double click on the file or click once and then click on **OK**.

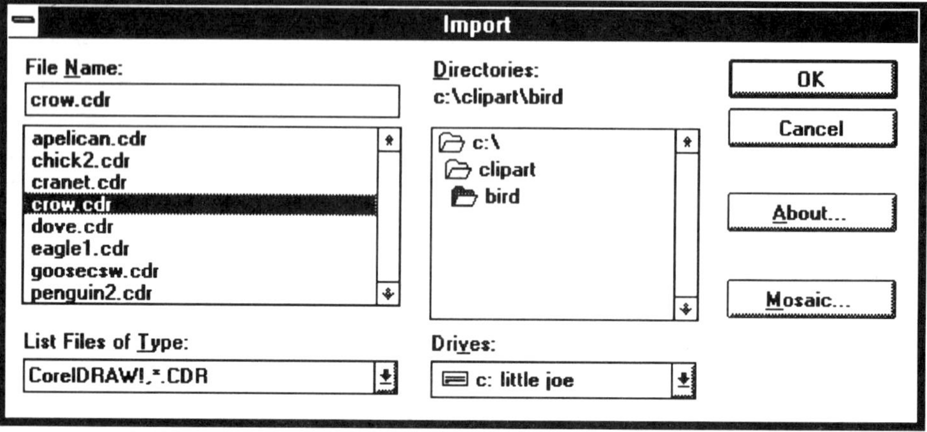


**9.17 Import dialogue box**

f. You get a huge black crow - it covers most of the page. But because it is a vector graphic you can shrink it down. However, you may find that the layer that is currently active in the roll-up is Foreground. Just click on **Distance** again. You can then reduce the crow to about 10% of its current size. Just drag one of the corner handles inwards. Duplicate the bird a couple of times, rotate one of them, and then scatter all three along the top of the page. You're going to need to be able to see them through the windows.

g. Switch to the **Middle Ground** layer and then import **Arches**. Fill this with 10% Black. With it still selected, press **Ctrl-E** to bring up the Extrude roll-up. Make the **Depth 10** and then click on **Apply**. Voila, 3-D arches.

h. Add some colour, e.g. from White to 10% Black, and then change the illumination. I made it the top left hand corner of the grid.

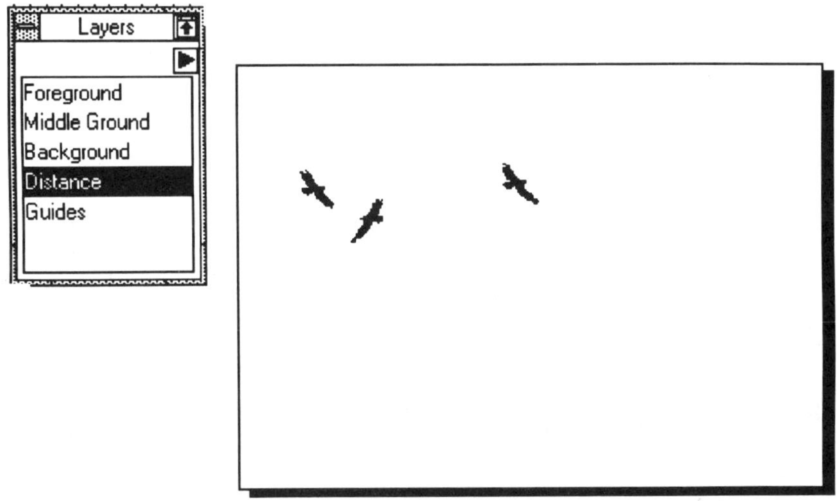


**9.18 Crows in place**

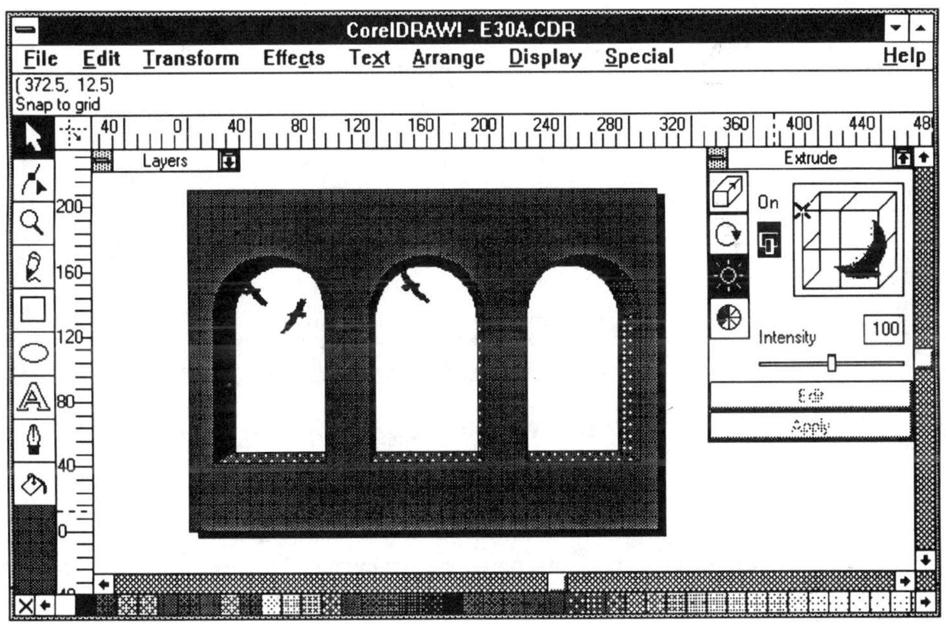


**9.19 Crows and Arches**

i. Now double click on **Middle Ground** in the roll-up. That will bring up the Layer Edit dialogue box. Click on **Colour Lock** and then on **OK**. You get the arches appearing as wire frames.

j. Let's have a funny. Switch to the **Background** layer and then import a file called **PEEK.CDR** which should be in the \CLIPART\MAN directory. The image will be placed in the middle of the page and the Status Bar says "**Group of 28 objects on Background**". You don't want the box surrounding the little figure so press **Ctrl-U** to ungroup it. Then delete the box and regroup the remaining bits using **Ctrl-G**. Then move the figure so that his fingers are just over the ledge of one of the arches.

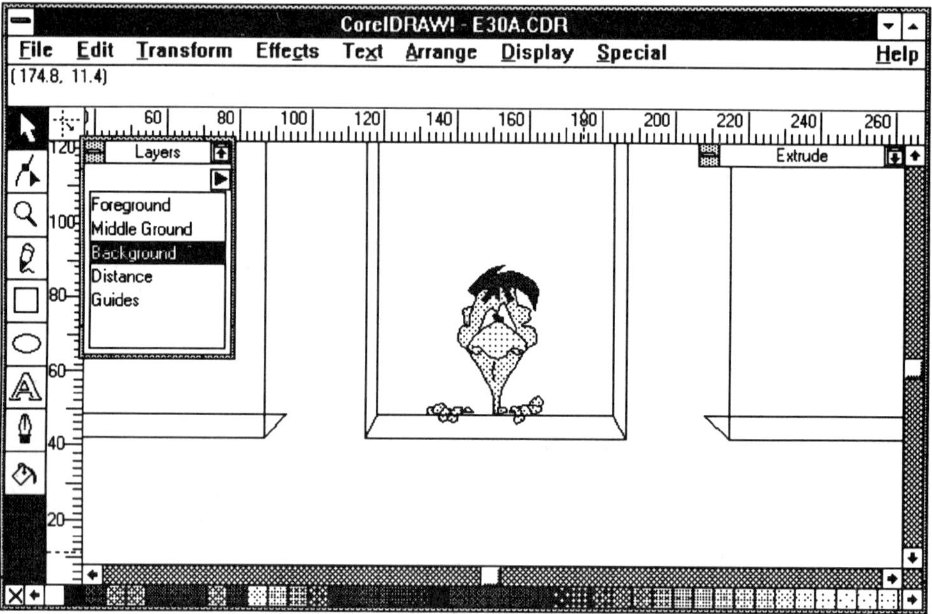


**9.20 Figure in place**

k. Find the image called **SNOWMAN.CDR** which is in the \CLIPART\MISC directory and import it - again on to the Background layer. Put it behind one of the other windows. You'll have to shrink it to fit.

l. Import the file called **CATTAILS.CDR**, reduce it slightly and place it behind the third window. Again it goes on the Background layer.

m. The distance looks a bit bare. Switch to the Distance layer and then import a file called **WITCH046.CDR** which is in the \CLIPART\MISC directory. Shrink to size and put it behind one of the windows.

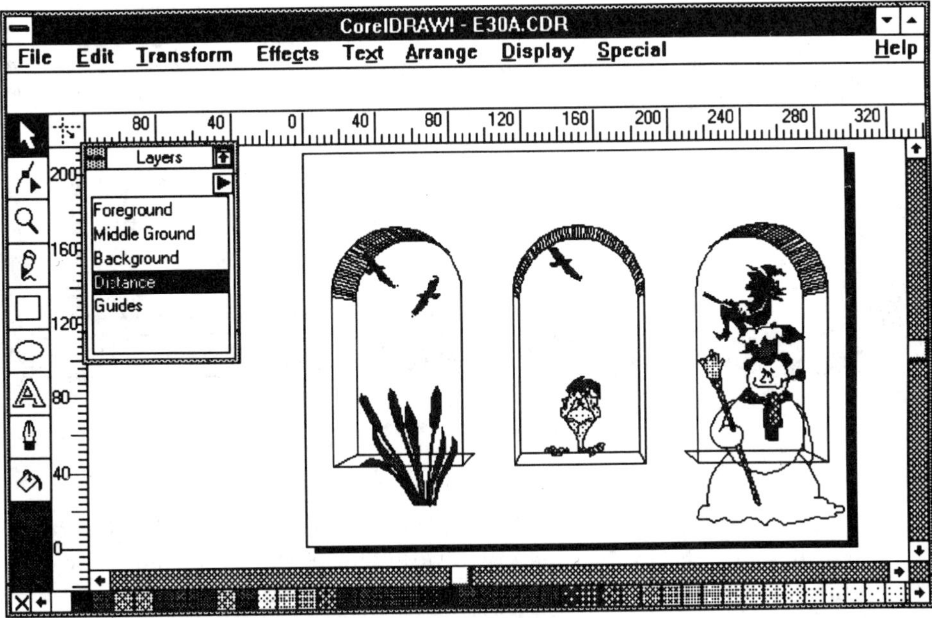


**9.21 Half way there**

n. Some clouds would be nice. The trouble is that there aren't any in the clip-art libraries. You'll just have to draw your own clouds. Add another layer called **Clouds** that will be beneath **Distance**. If you **Colour Override** the other layers you'll be able to see better. Draw a rectangle that runs along the top of the image but which you'll be able to see through the windows. Fill it with the Clouds bitmap fill. Then tile the fill to make the clouds larger. If you give the rectangle no outline, just the clouds can be seen.

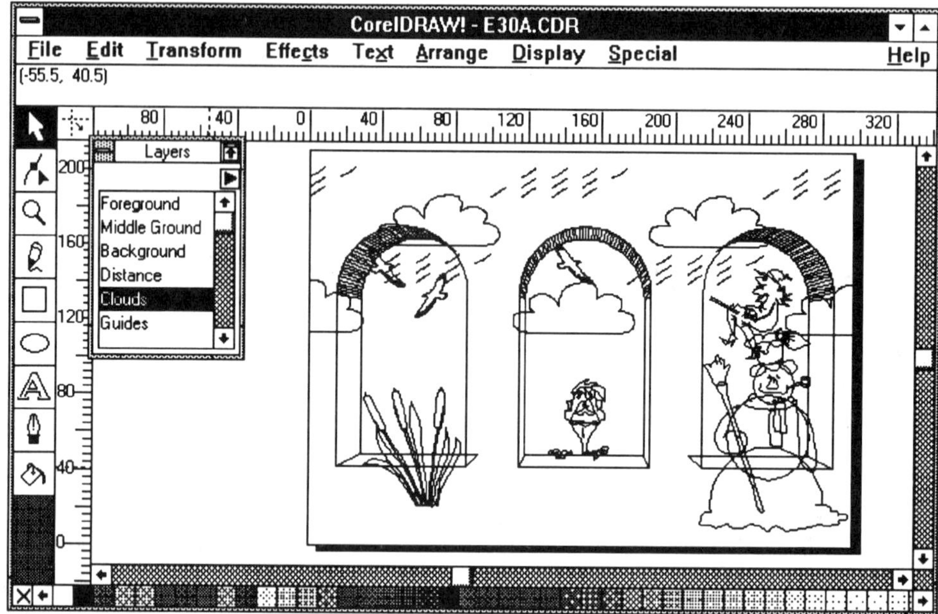


**9.22 Clouds too**

o. While you're still on the Clouds layer, import the file called **OUT_HOUS.TIF** which should be in the \DRAW\SAMPLES directory. You might want to shrink the image just a little. Then place it behind one of the windows.

p. Want to see what you've got? Edit each layer and turn off Colour Override. Save the file.

q. Now to add something to the **Foreground**. Import the file called **PENGUIN.CDR** from the \CLIPART\BIRD directory. You will definitely have to resize this because it's huge.

r. You can carry on adding whatever images you like to the various layers but I'm stopping there. The file that I've created looks like this. The middle windows looks a bit bare but otherwise it's not too bad.

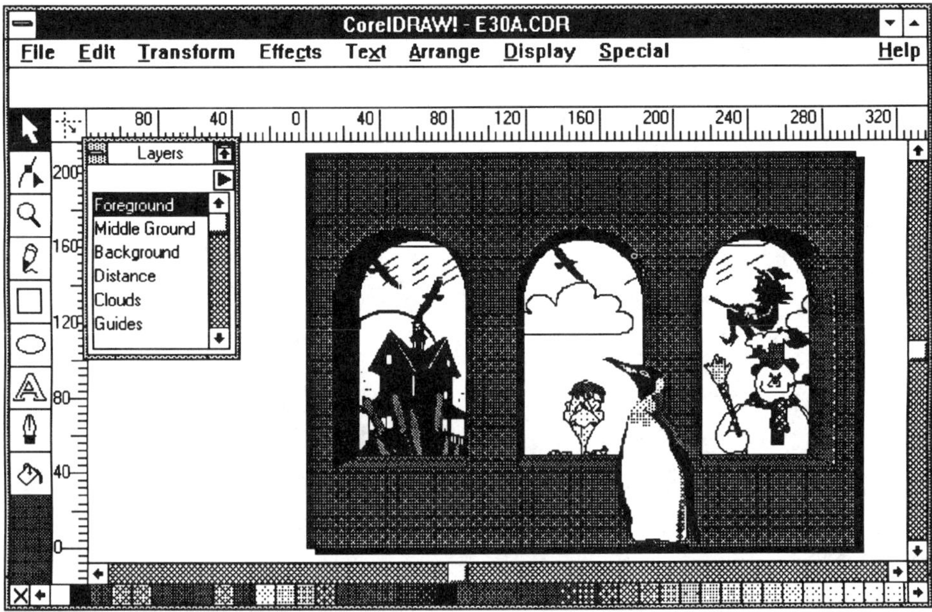


**9.23 Finished image**

s. Play with moving the layers up and down. For example, bring the Background layer to the front. If you click and drag it in the roll-up so that it lies above Foreground the entire picture changes because each layer is a separate and complete graphic.

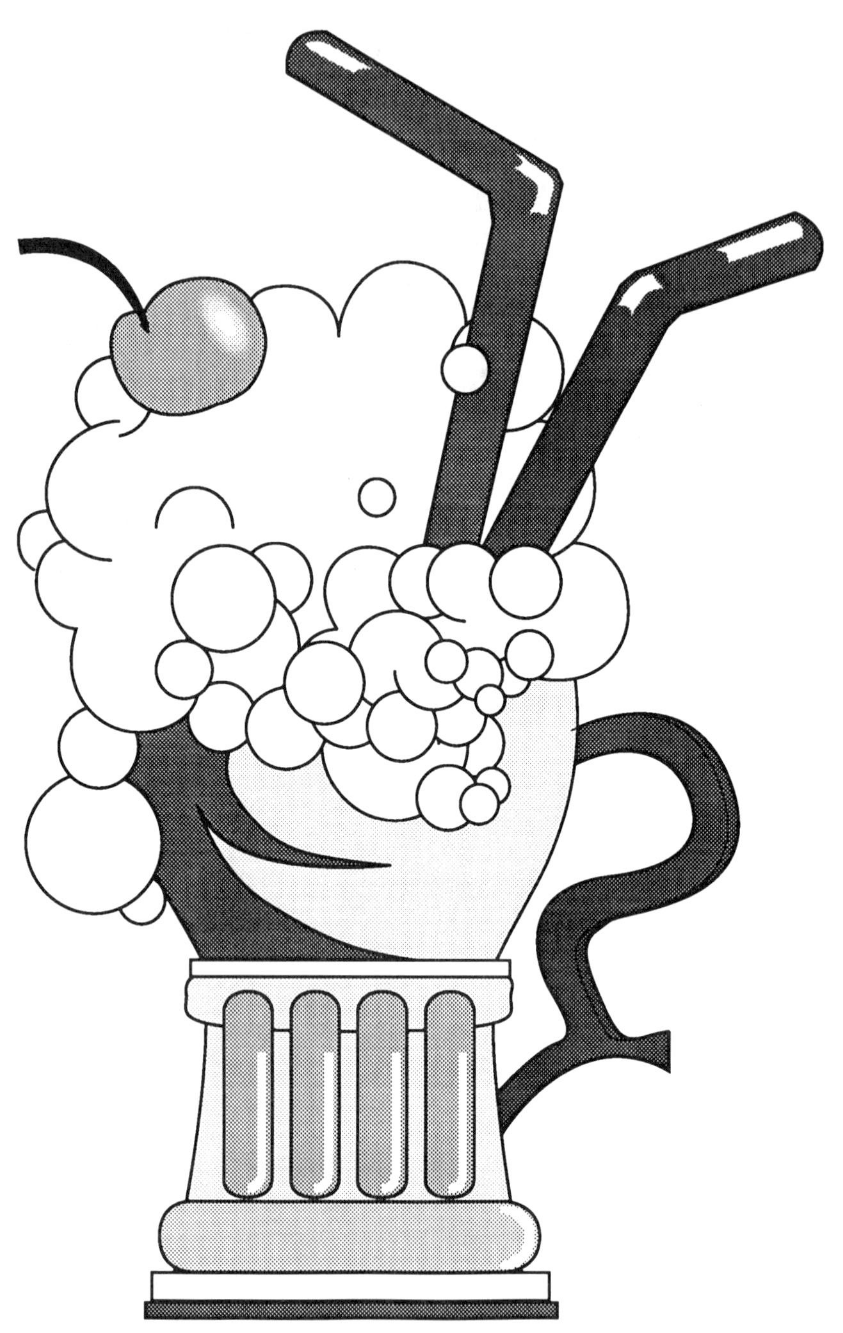

# 10 - DISPLAY MENU

The Display menu is concerned mainly with the screen and what appears on it.

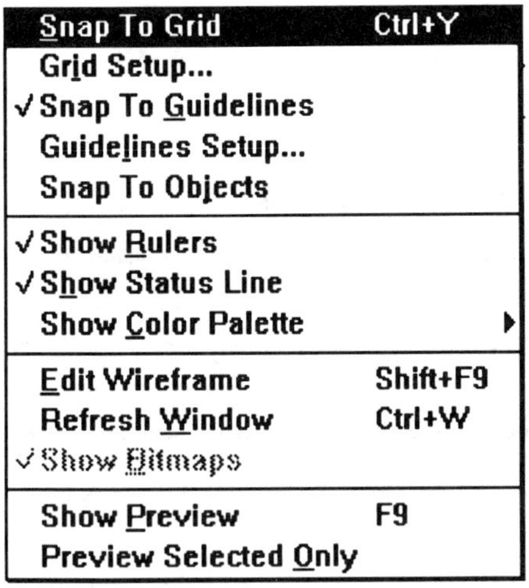

| | | |
|---|---|---|
| | Snap To Grid | Ctrl+Y |
| | Grid Setup... | |
| √ | Snap To Guidelines | |
| | Guidelines Setup... | |
| | Snap To Objects | |
| √ | Show Rulers | |
| √ | Show Status Line | |
| | Show Color Palette | ▸ |
| | Edit Wireframe | Shift+F9 |
| | Refresh Window | Ctrl+W |
| √ | Show Bitmaps | |
| | Show Preview | F9 |
| | Preview Selected Only | |

**10.01 Display Menu**

**Snap to Grid** means that your cursor does not move freely on the screen. Instead it aligns itself with the grid points that you have set up. This can be extremely useful, e.g. when you want to draw shapes of an exact size, but it can also be a nuisance if the grid frequency is incorrect. Use it judiciously and it is a boon. The keyboard shortcut is **Ctrl-Y**.

**Grid Setup** allows you to set the grid frequency via a dialogue box. It also sets the measurement system that appears on the **Rulers**. Whatever measurement system you use for the grid, e.g. millimetres or inches, will be the one used for the rulers themselves.

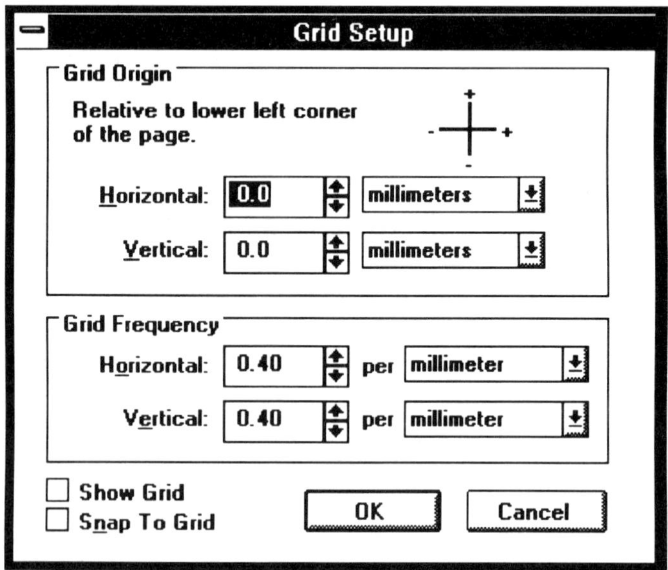


**10.02 Grid Setup dialogue box**

The dialogue box is divided into two main areas. The first is **Grid Origin** which defines where the grid starts from. By default this is always the bottom left hand corner of the page. You can change this to make the grid start wherever you wish. The values you enter into the box are relative to the normal starting point. So if you wanted the grid to start at the top left hand corner of an A4 portrait page you would enter a value of 297 mms on the vertical line.

The second main area is the **Grid Frequency**. This is the actual size of the grid but you have to be aware that you are setting the gird in terms of numbers of grid points per unit of measurement. This probably causes more confusion that anything else within CorelDRAW. In the illustration above the grid frequency is set to 0.4 per millimetre which provides a grid of 2.5 mms squares. If it was set to 1 per millimetre then it would give 1 mms squares. If you wanted a grid of 1 cm squares you would enter a value of 0.1 per mm. What you are doing is dividing the measurement system by the value. Thus 1 mm divided by 0.1 gives a value of 10 mms, which is 1 cm.

**Show Grid** causes the grid to be displayed on the screen as a series of dots. The only trouble is that no monitor is capable of showing fine enough grids. So if you set the grid as in the illustration you get little dots appearing at 20 mms intervals. (I've never seen it any finer.)

**Snap to Grid** is the same as the previous major command.

**Snap to Guidelines** is extremely useful. You can drag a guideline in from any either rule, position it where you need to and then have objects snap to the guides. This allows you to position things extremely precisely. The command takes precedence over Snap to grid once you start moving objects.

**Guidelines Setup** allows you to set the guidelines very precisely via a dialogue box.

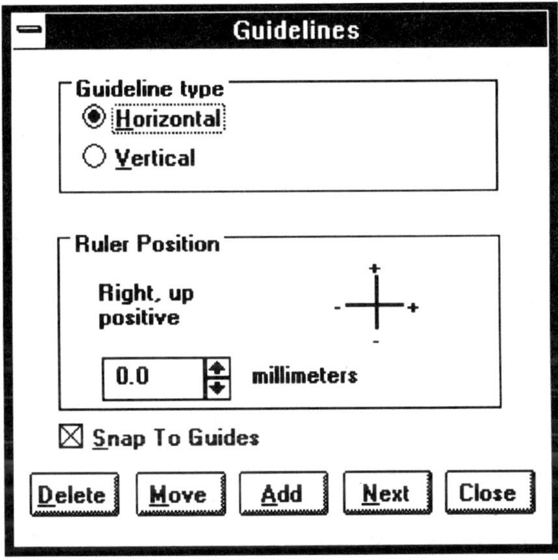


**10.03 Guidelines setup**

You may set either a **Horizontal** or **Vertical** guideline. Unfortunately you can only use a single guideline each time you open the dialogue box. If you wanted to set a dozen guides then you would have to set open and close the dialogue box a dozen times.

Guidelines are set relative to the **Ruler Position** which is based on grid position. You may enter any value you wish here.

**Delete** removes a guideline, the coordinates of which must be shown in the Ruler Position line. It's the same as if you had dragged the guide off over the rulers.

**Move** allows you to relocate guides. You select a guide, enter a new value and then click on this button to move it.

**Add** does just that. It adds the guide of whatever type you have selected at whatever position is given in the ruler position.

**Next** allows you to page through the currently set guidelines. The positions of the guides will be shown in the ruler position area.

**Close** terminates the dialogue box. Unfortunately so does clicking on any of the other buttons except Next.

**Snap to Objects** is like snap to grid or snap to guidelines but you use objects instead. See the next exercise for details.

**Show Rulers** is a toggle. Do you want the rulers displayed or not?

**Show Status Line** is also a toggle. It is so useful that I always leave it turned on. The status line tells you all kinds of information, from the position of the cursor to the size and shape of objects.

**Show Colour Palette** displays the palette along the bottom of the screen. (Personally I don't particularly want it there but because the roll-up does not have a zero fill or outline function, I have to have it so that I can use no fill or outline without having to use the tools in full.) You have a choice of **No Palette**, which turns it off, **Process Colours** which are the CMYK ones, or **Spot Colours** which are the Pantones ones.

**Edit Wireframe** gives you the same kind of display that you had in CorelDRAW 2.01 and earlier, i.e. you don't have full colour. It is fast and can be extremely useful, especially when you have developed complex illustrations. The keyboard shortcut is **Shift-F9** so you can toggle between the two displays quickly.

**Refresh Window** causes the screen to redraw completely. It is particularly useful if you use Interruptible display.

**Show Bitmaps** is a toggle. With the command turned on, bitmapped images that you have imported appear as images in full colour if that's what they are. If the command is turned off then the bitmaps appear as grey images.

**Show Preview** is a bit redundant. What it does is show you your image without the page or the actual CorelDRAW window. The shortcut is **F9**.

**Preview Selected Only** means that only those items that you have selected will appear on the preview screen.

# E31 - GRIDS AND GUIDES

So far you have used grids and guidelines only slightly. This exercise gives you a quick rundown of their use.

a. Start a new file. Make the page A4 Landscape.

b. Open the **Display menu** and make sure that **Snap to Guidelines** and **Snap to Grid** are both turned off. You may have to open the menu twice.

c. Draw a square that is exactly 100 mms to a side. Unless you can control a mouse much more precisely than I can you won't be able to. You can very close, e.g. 99.8 or 100.4, but you can't get it exact.

d. Open the **Display menu** and click on **Grid Setup**. Change the **Grid Frequency** to 0.2 per millimetre for both the Horizontal and Vertical values. Click on **OK**. Press **Ctrl-Y** to turn on the **Snap to Grid**.

e. Now go back to your square. Try to resize it to 100 mms. Again you won't be able to get the size right. The reason is that the square itself doesn't lie on the grid. Pick up the square and move it slightly. It will jump to the nearest grid points. Release the mouse button. Now resize it and you have no problem.

That's an important point. When you create anything without the grid being turned on, the object can be anywhere on the page. If you then turn on the grid the objects don't move by themselves. You have to move them slightly to make them match the gird before it effectively becomes active.

f. Drag a vertical guideline in from the left hand ruler. Place it at 40 mms. You'll find that it snaps there easily.

g. Now drag the square near the guide. It snaps to it as you get close. The grid is set to give you 5 mms squares, i.e. a frequency of 0.2 per millimetre. You know there is a grid point at 40 mms so the next one is at 45 mms. Pick up the square and move it to the right. It will snap to the next grid point. Put it back against the guideline.

h. Time to move the guide into the centre of the page. You could do this by simply dragging it to the new position but that would mean turning off the grid and then dragging the guide - because it has to be placed at 148.5 mms. But there is an easier way.

   Open the **Display menu** and click on **Guidelines Setup**. The dialogue box tells you that there is a Vertical guide at 40 mms. Change the 40 to 148.5 and then click on **Move**. The dialogue box closes and the guideline is moved to the new position.

i. Now try moving the square 10 mms to the right. You won't be able to. It will move 8.5 mms so that the right hand side of the square aligns with the guideline or it will jump beyond the guide so that the total movement is about 14 mms. The reason is that the snap to guideline is taking precedence over the snap to grid. If you turn off **Snap to Guidelines** then the grid becomes the active principle again.

j. In CorelDRAW 2.0 there was no way to lock a guide in place. CorelDRAW 3.0 fixes that problem. Press **Ctrl-1** to bring up the **Layers roll-up**. Click on the layer called **Guides** and then open the menu out and click on **Edit**. In the dialogue box click on **Locked** and then on **OK**. The guide is now fixed in place. You can no longer add guides by dragging them off the rulers nor can you use the **Guidelines Setup** dialogue box to delete, add or move guidelines. If you try to do the former a guide apparently appears but it cannot be placed.

By the way, you cannot undo a guideline addition or movement. Equally turning off MultiLayer in the Layers roll-up does not apply to guidelines.

# E32 - SNAPPING OBJECTS

**Snapping to Objects** is a yet another new feature of CorelDRAW 3.0. It works in much the same way as snap to grid or guides but it applies to objects themselves. Remember that you were unable to align two objects on opposite sides? Well using this command you can and a lot more besides.

All objects you create or import in CorelDRAW have snap to points on them, effectively they are the node points of the shape concerned with variations. The snap to points are:

Rectangles have nine points, one at each corner plus one at each mid-point of the lines plus the centre point.

Rounded cornered rectangles have points in the same positions as the nodes plus the centre point. But they don't have snap to points in the middle of the lines.

Circles and ellipses have five snap to points. One each at North, East, West and South plus the centre point.

Arcs can have between three and seven snap to points, depending on how large the arc is. There will be the normal points as above plus an extra point at each end of the arc, except where the end of the arc is one of the normal snap to points.

Pie slices will have the same number of snap to points as arcs. That is there will be the normal ellipse points plus one each at the ends of the pie slice lines. If you create a pie slice that is smaller than a single quadrant of an ellipse then the snap to points will only be on the centre points and the ends of the lines.

Open paths have snap to points at each end of the line plus one at each node on the line.

Bitmaps have five snap to points, one at each corner of the image bounding box plus the centre one. The exception is for rotated bitmaps. These have two more snap to points, at either end of the little triangle shown in the corner of the rotated bitmap.

Paragraph text has nine snap to points. One at each corner, one in the middle of each line outlining the paragraph text box plus a central one.

Artistic text also has nine points in the same way as rectangles.

Any object placed on the Guides layer can be used to snap to even if the Snap to Object command is not active. This is because anything on that layer is treated as a guide. You have to have Snap to Guidelines turned on though.

If you want to snap to a particular place on an object you can add a node at that point which then becomes a snap to point.

a. Start a new page. Again make it A4 Landscape. Notice that if you had any of the Snap to commands active before they will still be active now. Turn off all the commands except Snap to Grid.

b. Press **Ctrl-1** to bring up the Layers roll-up. Click on the **Guides** layer to make it current. Draw a 200 mms circle and align it to the centre of the page. The circle will appear with dashed lines because that's how guides are shown.

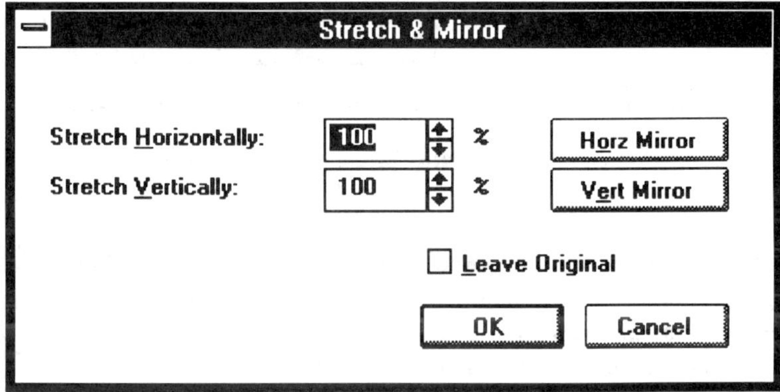


**10.04 Stretch and Mirror**

c. With the circle selected press **Ctrl-Q** to bring up the Stretch and Mirror dialogue box. Change the values to 75% in both cases, click on **Leave Original** and then on **OK**. You get a circle that is 150 mms in diameter.

d. Repeat the previous step using values of 50%, using the original circle, and then again using values of 25%. You should end up with four circles with diameters of 200, 150, 100 and 50 mms.

e. Now draw a straight horizontal line from one side of the page to the other. Hold down **Ctrl** as you do so to make sure it's straight. Align this to the centre of the page.

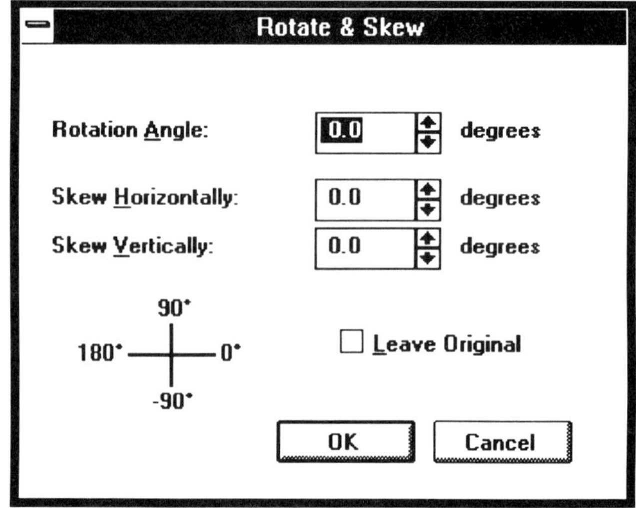


**10.05 Rotate and Skew dialogue box**

f. Press **Ctrl-N** to bring up the Rotate and Skew dialogue box. Place a value of 45 degrees on the Rotation Angle line. Click on **Leave Original** and then on **OK**. You now have a line at 45 degrees. Press **Ctrl-R** twice and you get two more. That's it finished. You now have a Polar Grid.

g. Open the **Layers menu** in the roll-up and click on **Edit**, for the Guides layer. Click on **Locked** and then on **OK**. Finally, click on **Layer 1** in the roll-up to make this the current layer.

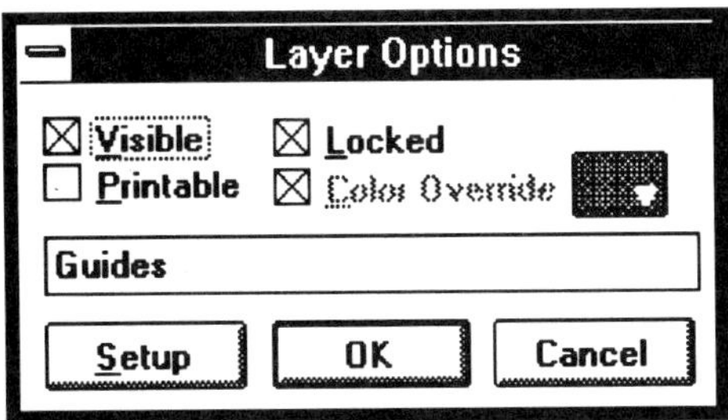


**10.06 Layers Edit dialogue box**

h. Turn on **Snap to Guidelines**. Make sure that **Snap to Grid** is turned off. Now draw a square, about 50 mms to a side. Move it around the page and watch where it snaps to. You should be able to snap the corners of the square to the intersecting lines of the circle and line guides. Duplicate the square three times and position them at the four corners of the grid.

i. Draw a circle, 50 mms in diameter. Move that around the page and watch where it snaps to. Duplicate the circle thrice. Position them.

j. Try it with an ellipse, say 50 mms by 20 mms. Duplicate the ellipse three times and place them around the grid.

k. Turn off **Snap to Object**. Now add some text, e.g. Polar Grid, and make it about 36 points. Watch what happens as you move this onto the page. It will snap to the various points of whatever object you bring it near.

l. Turn off **Snap to Guidelines** so you just have **Snap to Objects** on. Play with moving the shapes around and aligning them together. One thing you will find is that the squares and circles on Layer 1 keep trying to align to circles and lines on the Guides layer. This is because what is on the Guides layer are objects so they affect the snap to command to.

m. You should now be able to align the left hand side of one square with the right hand side of another. Play with the various snap to commands until you are happy that you understand how they work.

# 11 - Special Menu

The Special menu contains only three commands, they're really here because they don't fit anywhere else.

**Create Pattern** allows you to create full colour patterns, what used to be called Vector Fills, from any portion of an image.

**Create Arrow** allows you to create arrows that will be used at the ends of lines from any part of the current image.

**Preferences** allows you to set most of the parameters for how CorelDRAW operates. It brings up a large dialogue box.

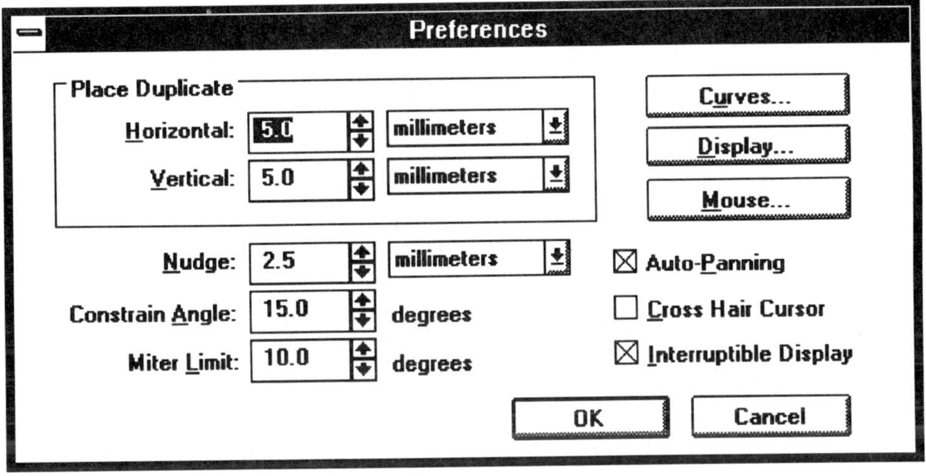


**11.01 Preferences dialogue box**

**Place Duplicate** applies to when you press **Ctrl-D** to duplicate an object or objects. The selected item will be duplicated and then moved by the amount that you specify here. By default it is set to place the duplicate a quarter of an inch up and to the right. You will find that you constantly change the value here if you do a lot of purposeful duplication otherwise you may never change the values.

**Nudge** allows you to move selected objects in small increments using the cursor keys. The increment is what you set here. You can set a nudge value as low as 0.001 inches but the dialogue box apparently says 0.00. That is because the box cannot show values to three decimal places but it will still apply. If you want to nudge an object, select it and then hit the appropriate cursor key to move it in whatever direction you need to.

**Constrain Angle** is the base angle that will be used whenever you hold down **Ctrl** while rotating an object or drawing lines. By default the angle is set to 15 degrees. This means that when you hold down **Ctrl** you can only rotate things or draw lines in multiples of 15 degrees.

**Mitre Limit** really only applies visibly if you are using thickish lines. It actually applies to all lines but you can only see the results using thick lines. What it does is cause adjoining lines to be bevelled, i.e. the point where the lines join is flat rather than pointed, if the angle of the lines is *less* than the amount set here. Why? Because, especially with thick lines, you could end up with the point produced by the lines joining extending way beyond the node point where the lines join.

**Auto-Panning** is a toggle, i.e. it's either on or off. With it turned on, which it is by default, if you move an object below the confines of the window then CorelDRAW automatically scrolls to keep the object in view. In other words the page itself moves in the opposite direction.

**Cross Hair Cursor** is also a toggle. By default it is turned off. What it does is cause the cursor to always be a cross hair instead of different shapes for different tools.

**Interruptible Display** is very useful, especially when you start producing complex images. Turn it on and then you can interrupt the redrawing process, e.g. to open a menu or move something, rather than having to wait for the redraw to finish. If you do have it on then you may need to use **Ctrl-W** to redraw the screen.

Clicking on **Curves** and a new dialogue box appears. Notice that all the values apply to Pixels, i.e. screen elements.

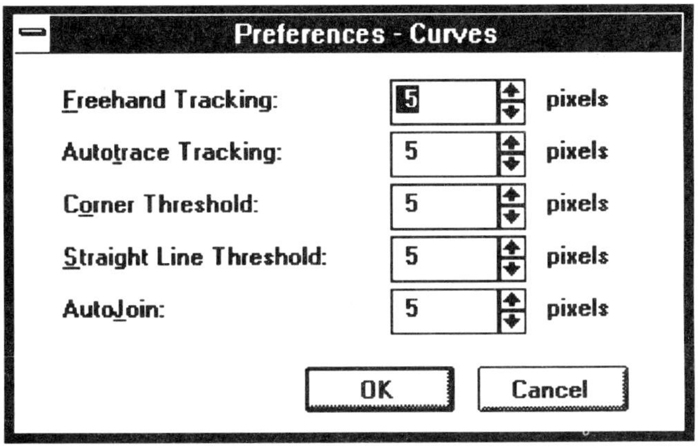

Preferences - Curves

Freehand Tracking: 5 pixels
Autotrace Tracking: 5 pixels
Corner Threshold: 5 pixels
Straight Line Threshold: 5 pixels
AutoJoin: 5 pixels

OK Cancel

**11.02 Curves dialogue box**

**Freehand Tracking** is what makes CorelDRAW track your cursor when you are drawing. With the value set low, 1, 2 or 3, then you will end up with a precise following and therefore lots of nodes on the finished line. With the value set between 6 and 10 there will be less nodes but looser lines. By default the value is five which is good compromise.

**Autotrace Tracking** is similar to the above but it applies only when you are tracing a bitmap image. Again the default is five.

**Corner Threshold** affects both freehand drawing and the autotrace. The value here changes whether CorelDRAW produces smooth or cusp nodes. The former give gentle rounding, while the latter give sharp corners. By default it is set to the compromise value of five.

**Straight Line Threshold** also applies to autotracing and freehand drawing. With a low value, 1, 2 or 3, CorelDRAW will produce curves rather than line, with a higher value it produces lines instead of curves. The default is the middle course again.

**Auto Join** is the distance apart that two lines have to be before they will automatically join to become a single line. Lines can only join at the nodes at the end of the lines, you cannot join one line to another in the middle of the second line. With a low value you need to be very precise about how far the two lines are for them to join, a high value allows you to be less definite. However, if you set the value high you can end up with lines joining when you don't necessarily want them to.

**Display** affects what happens on screen, again it uses a dialogue box.

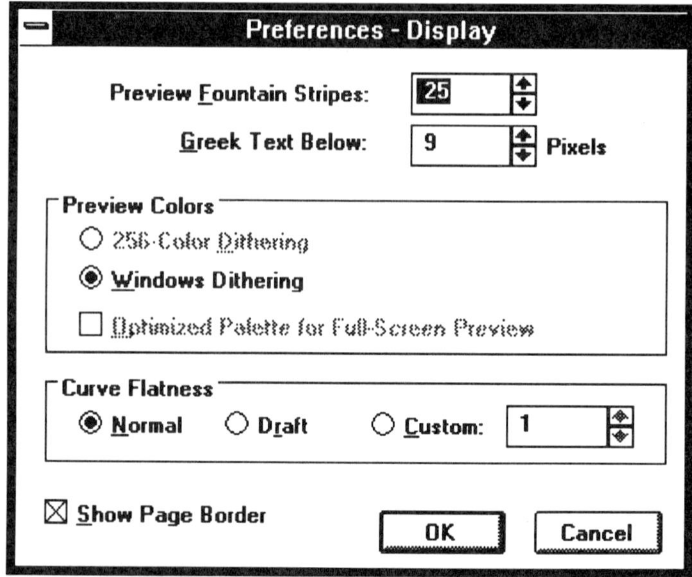


**11.03 Display dialogue box**

**Preview Fountain Stripes** is the number of stripes used for the monitor and non-PostScript printers only. It does not effect printing on PostScript printers. With a low value, e.g. about 25, you get fast drawing times but not much definition. In other words your fountain fills will appear stripey. With a high value redraw takes longer but you get few banding lines. If you set the value to its maximum, i.e. 256, then you will get hardly any banding at all but screen display and printing will be very much slower. The setting will also affect any file exported to SCODL.

**Greek Text Below** is set to 9 pixels. This is a new setting for CorelDRAW 3.0 and it applies only to Paragraph text on screen -

it makes no difference to the actual printing of text. What it does is cause paragraph text at small point sizes to be drawn as representations of characters instead of the actual characters themselves. This in turn means that the display is speeded up. The characters still appear as normal in the dialogue box. If you want to really speed up the display of paragraph text then set this value really high, like 500 or so. It will be illegible but the display speed will be very fast.

**Preview Colours** is dependent on your monitor and graphics card. You now have only two main choices, **256-Colour Dithering** or **Windows Dithering**. You can use the former automatically if your graphics card can support it, otherwise you use the latter.

**Optimised Palette for Full Screen Preview** changes the colours in use, only with 256 colours which really means a 1 Mb graphics card, so that you get 256 pure colours with no dithering. But - only if your system can do so and it will slow down your screen display something fierce.

**Curve Flatness** affects the amount of time that lines and curves take to redraw on screen or to print on non-PostScript printers. It changes the way curves are drawn. Either you get smooth even curves or you get straight line polygons. Set the flatness to Draft (which is the same as a Custom value of 10) and the circle will appear as a polygon. Custom allows you to set the value anywhere between 1, Normal, and 10, Draft. On most systems the default setting should be fine.

**Show Page Border** is a toggle. If you turn it off then you don't see the page on screen.

**Mouse** brings up a dialogue box wherein you can assign an action to the right mouse button:

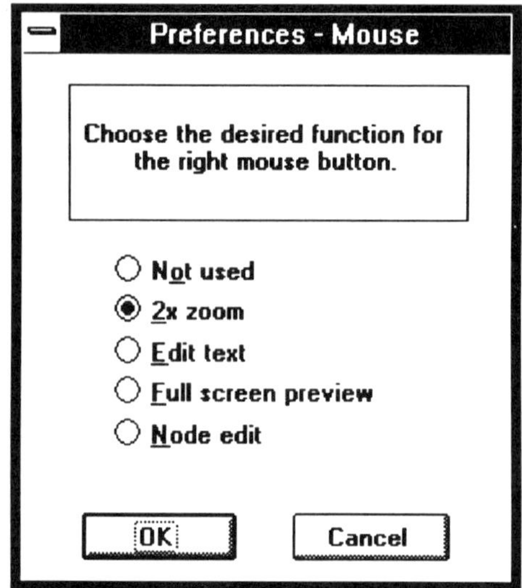


**11.04 Mouse dialogue box**

**2x Zoom** which gives you an instant way to magnify the image you are working with.

**Edit Text** brings up the text dialogue box, the equivalent of pressing **Ctrl-T**.

**Full Screen Preview** is the same as pressing **F9**. It displays your image without the surrounding window.

**Node Edit** is equivalent to pressing **F10** or activating the node edit tool by clicking on it.

# E33 - MAKE A PATTERN

In the Fill roll-up there are a number of full colour patterns that you can use. CorelDRAW allows you to take any image and assign it as a pattern.

a. Start a new page and then Import an existing image, e.g. Applea from the \CLIPART\FOOD directory. The image appears in the centre of the page.

b. Open the **Special menu** and click on **Create Pattern**. A dialogue box appears.

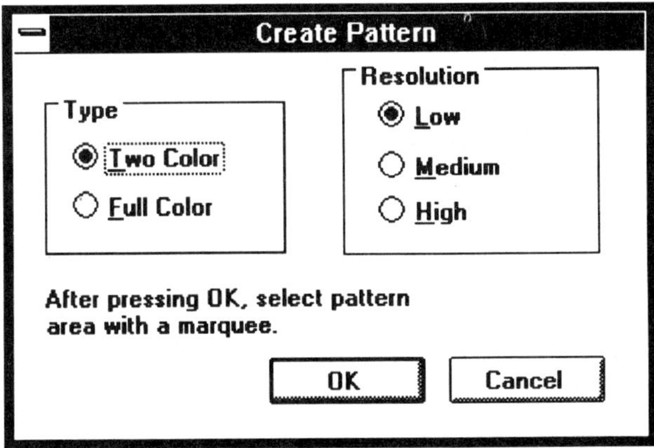


**11.05 Create pattern dialogue box**

c. As you want to create a **Full Colour** pattern click on that. The Resolution options will be greyed out. Click on **OK**.

**11.06 Creating pattern**

d. You now have a pair of bisecting lines on screen. As you move the cursor these move. Drag a bounding box from the middle of the upper left handle to the middle of the lower right handle. When you release the mouse button a message box appears.

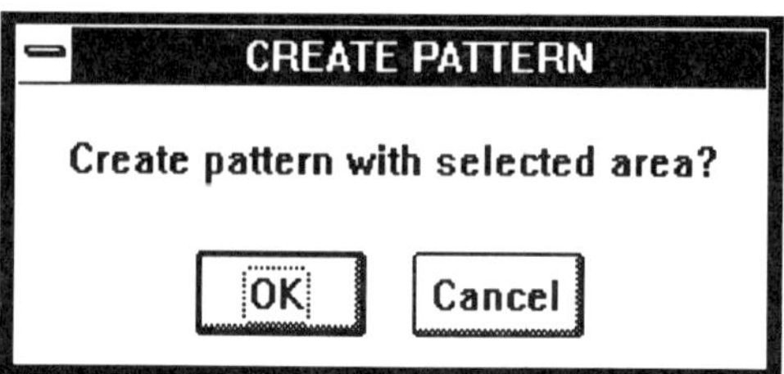


**11.07 Message box**

e. Click on **OK** and a dialogue box appears that is the same as if you were saving the file except that the extension given is .PAT. Give the file a name, e.g. Apple, and click on **OK**. That's the pattern created.

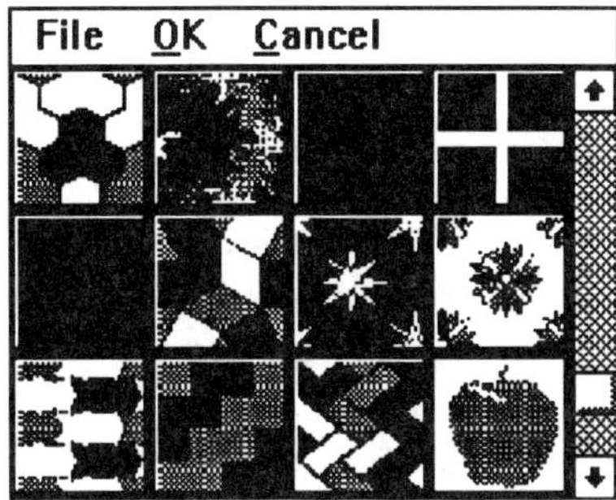


**11.08 Apple pattern added**

f. Clear the screen and draw a large rectangle. Open the **Fill roll-up** and click on the full colour fill option. Click on the large square with a diagonal line in it to bring up the list box of patterns. At the bottom should be the apple. Select this and click on **Apply**.

g. Tile the pattern up so you can see it properly and there it is.

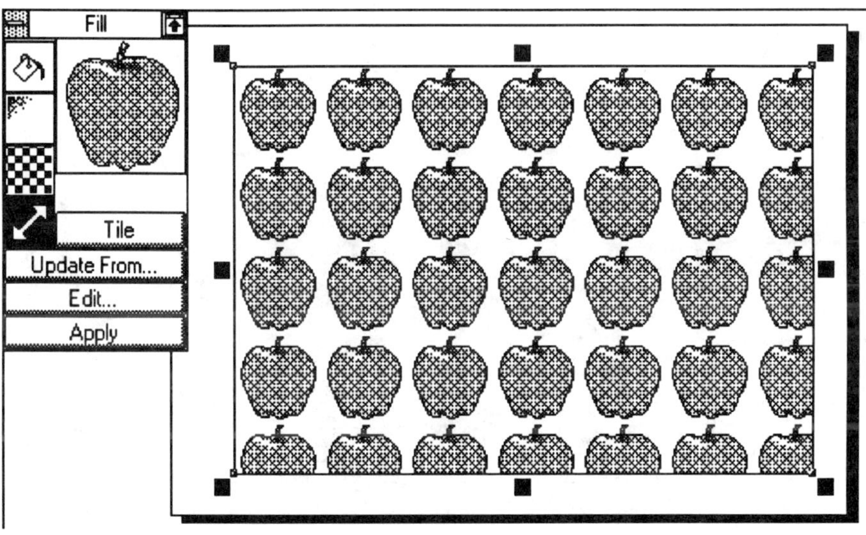


**11.09 Apple pattern**

h. Clear the screen again. Import the Witch046 image from the \CLIPART\MISC directory. (This is a single colour image so it will work well.) Align it to the centre of the page.

i. Open the **Special menu** again and click on **Create Pattern**. This time select **Two Colour**, the new name for bitmap fills, as the pattern type. You now have a choice of three Resolutions. The higher the resolution the better the pattern will print. However, it depends on what size you intend making the pattern. With small patterns the resolution won't matter too much. In this case select **High**.

j. Again you get the bisecting lines. Drag a bounding box around the shape, using the handles as a guide, and then click on **OK** in the message box. The pattern is created without any further ado.

k. Clear the screen and then draw a large rectangle again. Open the Fill roll-up and click on the checker board button. Open it out and you will find your witch in the last pattern available. Apply this to the rectangle. Tile it up and you'll be able to see it clearly.

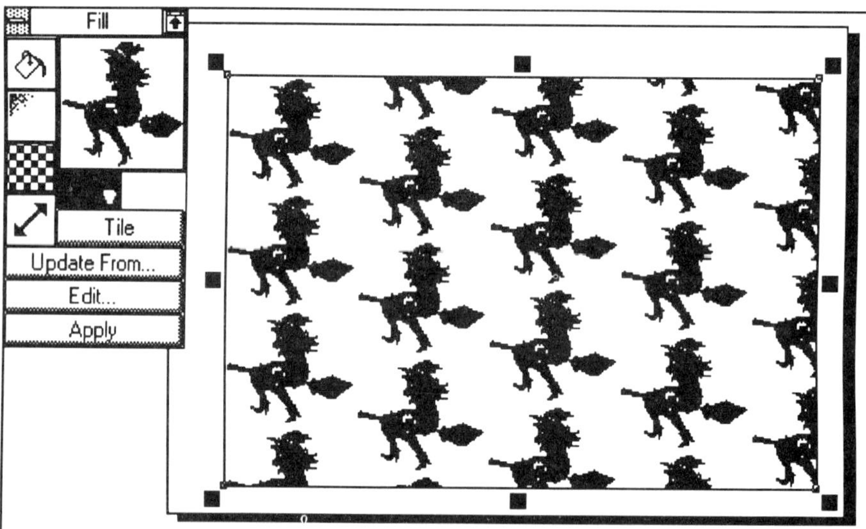


**11.10 Witch pattern**

You can create full colour patterns from bitmaps and two colour patterns from vector but it is not recommended. You can run into all kinds of funny problems doing so. We were able to do it easily with the witch image because it was a two colour image, for all that it was a vector. By all means try making two colour patterns from complex vector images but on your own head be it.

# E34 - ARROWS

We haven't used arrow much in this book for the simple reason that we've been concentrating on enclosed shapes most of the time. However, CorelDRAW allows you to use arrows at the ends of any open line.

a. Start a new page. You already know that you can use arrows with lines but you can also use them with converted ellipses and squares. Draw a 150 mms circle and align it to the centre of the page. Node edit the circle to make it into an open arc. You want to remove one quadrant of the circle.

b. Open the **Arrange menu** and click on **Convert to Curves** or simply press **Ctrl-V**. Now open the Outline roll-up and click on the left arrow button. Scroll through the arrows available until you find the airplane. Click on this. Click on the right arrow button. There's an arrow that looks like an X, click on this.

**11.11 Arrows applied**

c. Click on **Apply**. Because the line thickness is so thin you can't actually see the arrows. Increase the line thickness to about 8 points and the arrows become visible. Notice that the plane in at 3 o'clock and the X at 12 o'clock. That's because when you select the left arrow in the roll up it means the start of the line. Because I moved the node down and to the left, the start of the line is at 3 o'clock.

CorelDRAW comes complete with eighty-eight arrows pre-defined for you but you can add your own if you wish or need to up to a maximum of one hundred.

d. Clear the screen. Import the Witch again. This is a group of four objects and you cannot create arrows with groups, though you can with combined objects. So press **Ctrl-U** to ungroup the image then **Ctrl-C** to combine it. Because it is essentially a two colour image this will work well. Lots of colours don't.

e. Now open the **Special menu** and click on **Create Arrow**. A message box appears asking if you want to use the selected object to create the arrow. Click on **OK**. The CorelDRAW hourglass appears briefly as the arrow is created.

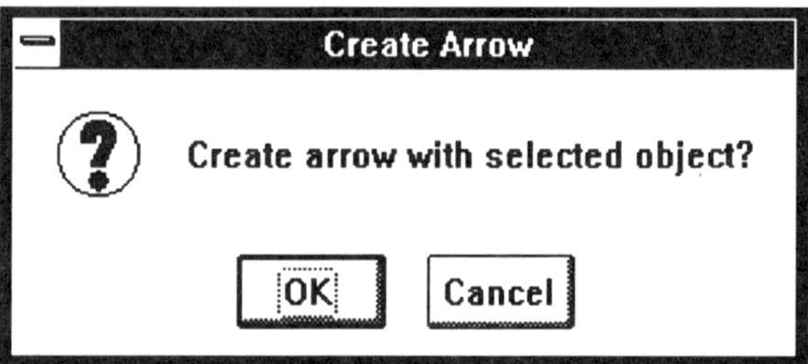


**11.12 Create arrow message box**

f. Clear the screen and then draw a line. Open the Outline roll-up and apply the witch, which will be last arrow available, to one end of the line. That's fine except that some of the detail isn't showing up. You need to edit the arrow position.

g. Click on **Edit** in the roll-up. A dialogue box apepars showing the witch as the arrow. Click on the word **Options** just below the with and a list box appears. Click on **Edit** and a new dialogue box appears. (On Page 280.)

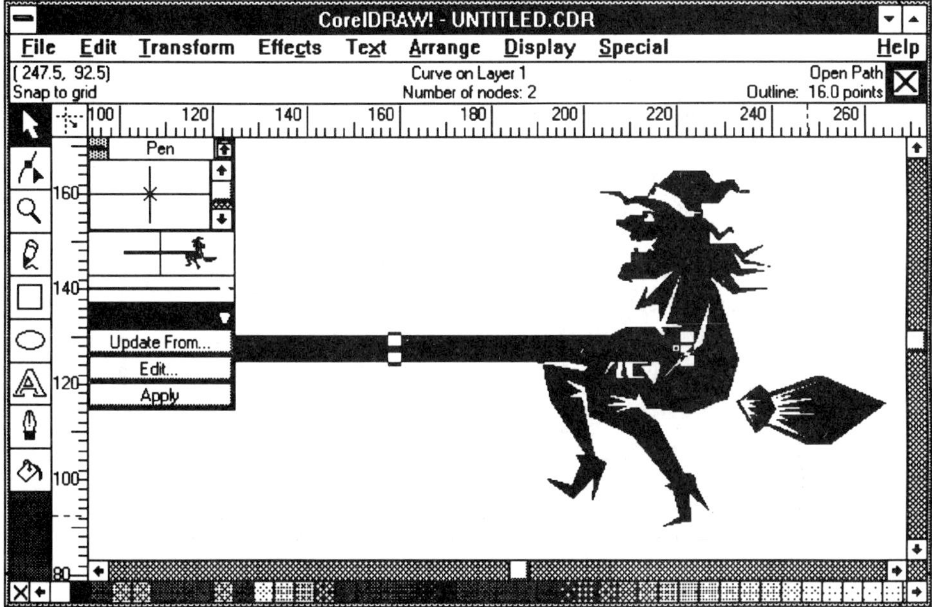


**11.13 Witch arrow**

h. The illustration is terrible but then so is the screen display on this monitor. Even on a Super VGA colour monitor is very hard to see what you're doing. You can drag the arrow image up and down, left and right very slightly. But what you really want to do is change the point where the arrow and the line intersect. That thick black line is the line that the arrow is being applied to. It has a node at the end of it and you can drag this horizontally. Drag it almost out of the frame and then click on OK.

i. Back at the Outline pen dialogue box click on **OK** again to close it and then click on **Apply** in the roll-up. Whoops, forgot the line thickness. Increase this and then click on **Apply** again. That's better, you can now see the witch and her broomstick because though the line no longer actually touches the arrow.

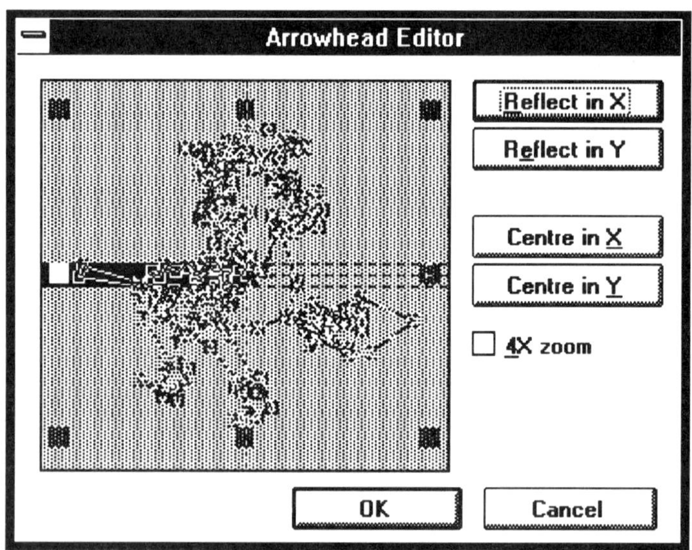


11.14 Edit arrow dialogue box

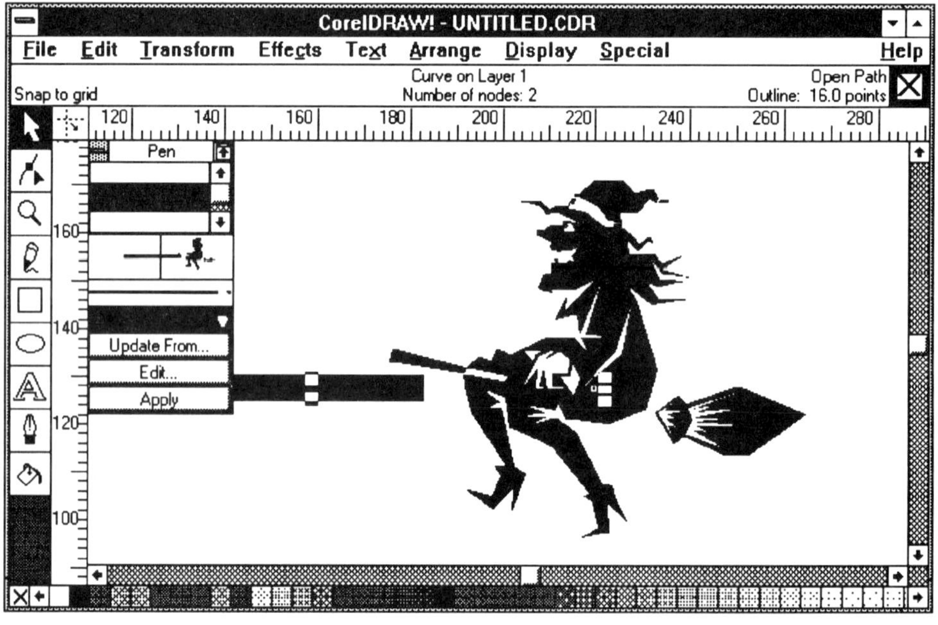


11.15 Repositioned arrow

# 12 - IN AND OUT

CorelDRAW 3.0 provides you with a huge range of import and export filters all of which fall into two categories. They are either bitmap or vector images. A bitmap is literally that - a map of bits. The bits refer to pixels and you will often hear image sizes quoted for them. For example, the Shermy bitmap which you used earlier is 453 pixels by 534 pixels. The important things to realise about bitmaps is that they are fixed resolution images. That is to say that they cannot be resized or reshaped without distorting the image itself.

To see what I mean look on the next page. The image in the top left hand corner is Shermy at his real size. It has been imported and printed exactly as it is. The larger image is the same file, duplicated, and enlarged 400%. You can see how the image becomes very jagged and coarse as a result. But then if you look at the original under a lens you'll find that it's just as jagged and rough. The little image in the bottom right hand corner of the page is the original images reduced to 25% of its size. That one doesn't look too bad and that gives you the key to using bitmaps. They tend to reduce fairly well, depending on content, but they don't enlarge at all well.

Vector graphics on the other hand don't have this problem. The second page of Shermy is the identical image but it has been converted to a vector format file using CorelTRACE. I did exactly the same thing with that. The original image is top left, then the large one is 400% and the little one is 25%. There is no loss of definition as the image gets larger. Equally there is none as it gets smaller although it looks a bit darker than the bitmap one. That's because the file is printed properly whereas the bitmap has to be squeezed to fit.

Back to the filters. CorelDRAW provides you with the following import filters:

> AI is the format used by Adobe Illustrator and it is a vector format. I haven't got any files in that format so I can't show you the effects.
>
> BMP is Windows Bitmap that appeared with Windows 3.0. I've got hundreds of them and we'll use them later.

CDR which means CorelDRAW images, i.e. vectors. You can import images from any previous version of the program though you may experience some problems with images that use text.

CGM is an old vector format. It stands for Computer Graphics Metafile and I use it a lot. The only trouble with it is that it cannot handle curves of any sort. If you create a circle and export it as CGM the shape will be turned into a multi-lined polygon because CGM can only use straight lines.

DXF files come from AutoCAD. This is another vector format and again I don't have any such files.

EPS files are the bane of CorelDRAW. There are three different EPS formats, the letters stand for Encapsulated PostScript by the way. One type is produced by CorelTRACE, the program that converts bitmaps into vectors. You can load these into CorelDRAW but I've never had much success getting them into anything else.

The second format is one of the two current standards and CorelDRAW is quite happy to accept them. These kinds of files will import quite happily into other applications, e.g. PageMaker.

The third format is the one that CorelDRAW exports. The stupid thing is that you cannot re-import an EPS file that you have exported from the program! If you export anything from CorelDRAW as EPS for Heaven's sake save the file in CDR format as well. The number of times I've forgotten to do so and have had to recreate an image from scratch you wouldn't believe!

GEM I don't know much about. I believe it is a vector format, though a limited one. For instance you can only have a limited number of colours. I haven't seen a GEM file for years.

GIF is a new filter in CorelDRAW 3.0. The letters stand for CompuServe Graphics Metafile and there are literally millions of files in this format. It is a bitmap. You will find GIF files on just about any bulletin board you care to look on. You also find them on CD-ROM disks. The files tend to be full colour, i.e. 256 colours, and photographic quality. At the last count I had about 3,000 GIF files. Unfortunately most of them can't be used in this book because they are full colour and printing them in monochrome doesn't do them justice.

PCC is one of the formats that CorelPHOTO-PAINT can export. It is a bitmap format and you can also find a number of images from various sources that use this format. They don't have to come from CorelPAINT - that's just the name of the filter.

PCT is a MAC format. You may experience problems importing files that contain text. Another problem is that many fills in PCT files are actually bitmaps and CorelDRAW doesn't handle these too well.

PCX is an old established bitmap format. As with GIF files there are millions of these. CorelDRAW says that PCX files come from CorelPAINT but they don't have to. Any paintbrush style program worth its salt will export PCX files. However, there are two versions - a compressed one and an uncompressed one - and you may have difficulties importing one of them.

You may also find that older PCX files won't import. That's because the standard for PCX constantly gets updated, at least it did until BMP files came on the scene, and older files may not conform to the same standard that CorelDRAW accepts.

PIC files come from Lotus. Files imported in this format will contain only eight greyscales and there may be problems with text as well.

PIF is another format that I know little about. I do know that such files can use transparent colours which CorelDRAW doesn't allow. Also there may be problems with text.

PLT are vectors and these don't contain any colour information, because they are intended for use with plotters, so they will not have any when you import them. Text also doesn't come across too well.

TGA is a bitmap format. There are two formats, compressed and non-compressed, but very few programs can use the former. TGA files tend to be used for photographs.

TIF is another old favourite. It is a bitmap. Some of the samples that come with CorelDRAW are in TIF format, e.g. Shermy. They have all the problems you would expect from bitmaps.

TXT means ASCII text files and you cannot have any text attributes assigned. Equally you are limited to 4,000 characters, about 600 words, and any more than this will be lost.

WMF stands for Windows Metafile. Text is the main thing that will be changed in these.

When it comes to exporting CorelDRAW gives you the following choices:

AI as for the import filter.

BMP is a bitmap and CorelDRAW exports these as compressed images. Unfortunately many applications can't use them!

CGM as for import filter. If you are using PageMaker and you want to import graphics into that then export the file from CorelDRAW in both CGM and EPS format. Use the former to place and size the image and then replace it with the EPS file. The reason is that PageMaker doesn't display EPS files too well whereas it does CGM ones.

DXF as for the import filter.

EPS files cannot be re-imported into CorelDRAW so always save the file in CDR format too.

GEM as for import.

GIF files are always compressed. I haven't had time to play with them much as yet. You can use GIF files in Autodesk Animator by the way and then use the results in CorelSHOW.

PCC as for import.

PCT as for import.

PCX files are always compressed. I've never had any problems using PCX files from CorelDRAW in any other application.

PFB files are Adobe Type 1 printer fonts. This book will not cover typeface generation and exportation.

PIF as for import.

PLT as for import.

SCD output is used in slide making machines. Again this is outside the scope of this book.

TGA export depends on the colours used. If you export a file with lots of colours you may not be able to open it in any other application.

TIF as for import filters. TIF files are always compressed.

TTF is TrueType. Again this is outside the scope of this book.

WMF as for import filters.

WPG is a Word Perfect format. Don't use fountain fills or a large number of colours, stick to 16.

The filters you use to export images should depend on the application you are going to be using the image in. Unfortunately there is no application, that I know of, that will allow you to import images directly in CorelDRAW's own format which is a great pity. The result is that you have to export the images in some format that the target application will handle. Another factor to be borne in mind is the type of printer that will be used to print the finished product. If you are going to be outputting on a PostScript printer then EPS files are definitely the best. However, there is a drawback to be aware of.

Any EPS file that is used in another application cannot normally be colour separated. So if you were to create an image in CorelDRAW that used even four colours and then you imported that image into, say, PageMaker that program could not separate the colours, even if you used the standard RGB ones that PageMaker itself uses. The fault, if that's what you want to call it, lies in the fact that the EPS file is a separate entity and PageMaker doesn't have the capability of disassembling it.

# E35 - IMPORTING

a. Start a new file. I don't know exactly what clip-art files you have available so we'll stick to using the sample files that CorelDRAW comes with. First, you're going to import a bitmap.

b. Open the **File menu** and click on **Import**. Log in to the \SAMPLES directory. You will find that there are four files available but they all have the extension of .CDR. That's because CorelDRAW assumes you will import it's own files.

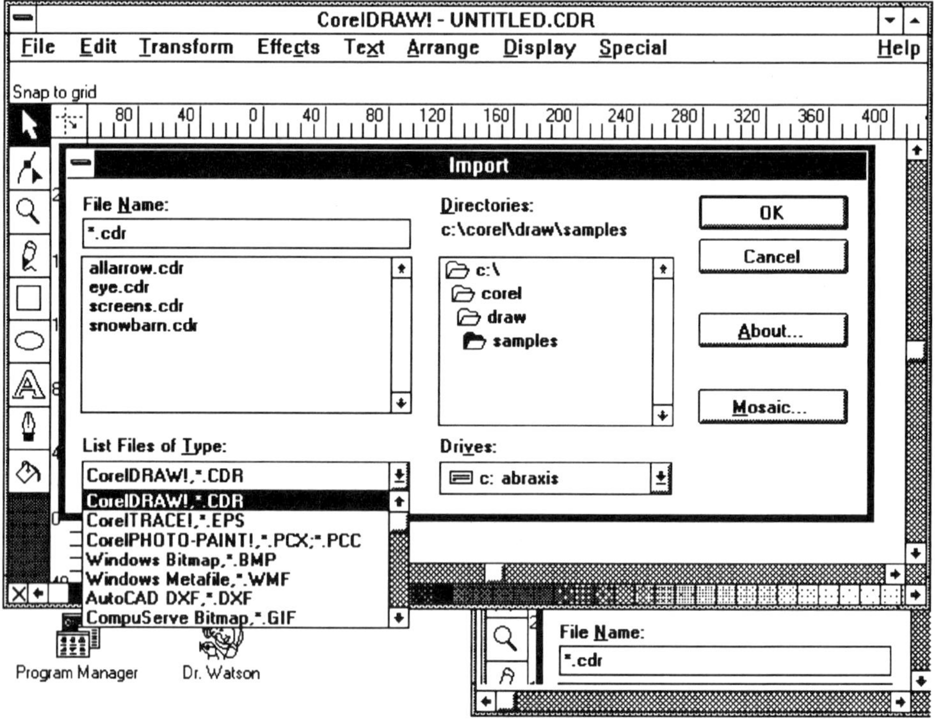


**12.01 File types list box**

c. Click on the arrowhead on **List of File Types** line and a list box drops down. Scroll through this list and find **TIFF 5.0 Bitmap, *.TIF**. Click on this and the contents of the filename box changes.

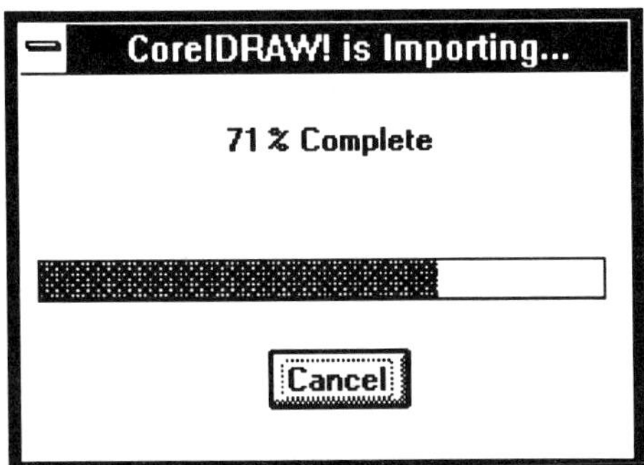


**12.02 File importing**

d. Double click on SHERMY.TIF. As the file is imported you get a message box telling you how far the importation has proceeded. (This box only appears when you are importing graphics that are in anything other than CorelDRAW format.) Shermy will then appear in the middle of the page.

e. Press **F4** to zoom in on the image. CorelDRAW will allows you to trace a bitmap and make a vector outline for it. Select the **Drawing tool**. The cursor is different to normal. It now resembles a small crosshair with a dotted line coming off to the right.

f. Move the cursor inside Shermy's face, near to the hairline, and click once. CorelDRAW begins to draw an outline. It will actually go right around the image and make a closed curve. To check press **Shift-F9**. This bring up the wire frame screen wherein bitmaps appear in grey. You can now see the outline you have just added.

g. Stay on the wire frame and trace the other portions of the image. Just move the cursor on to an element and click. The tracing is automatic. Once the entire image is done switch to the **Pointer tool**. Click on the boxed outline of the bitmap and drag it to one side. You will be left with the traced image.

h. Press **Shift-F9** to go back to the normal view and you will find that the traced image contains no colour. Fill it in with whatever colour you wish. I suggest that you group the elements together or, better yet, combine them into a single curve.

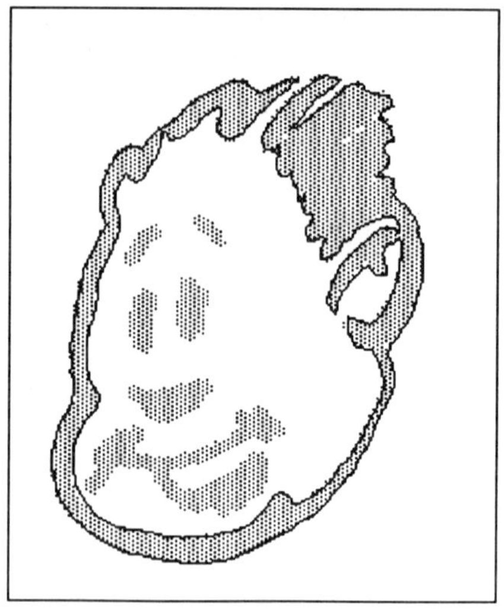

**12.03 Starting outline**

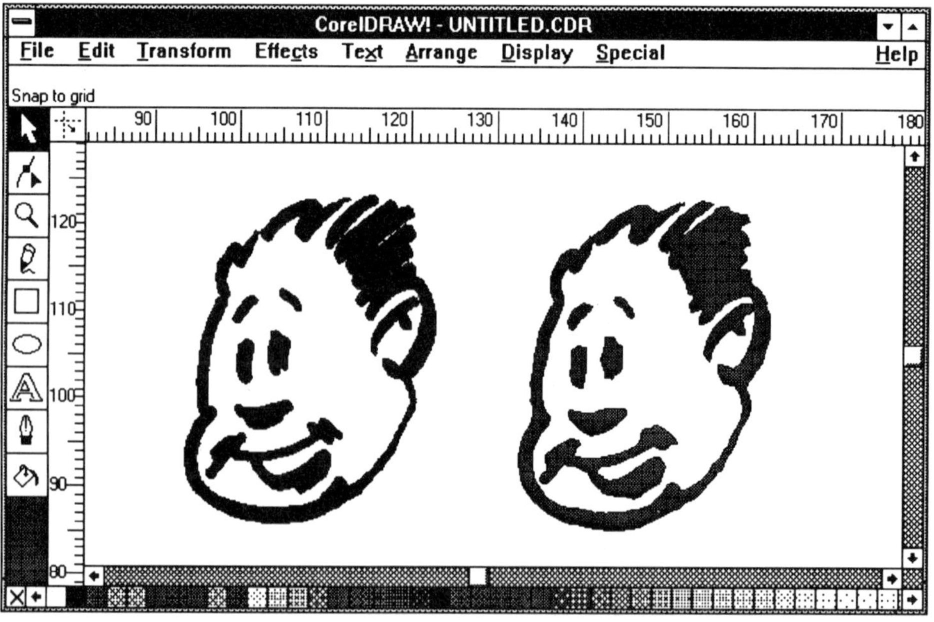


**12.04 Traced Shermy**

i. The traced image, which is now a vector, can be resized, reshaped, rotated and otherwise treated as any normal CorelDRAW image. The bitmap on the other hand only appears correctly in its normal orientation. If you rotate the bitmap, regardless of the amount you use, the image becomes a grey box with one corner of it appearing as a triangular white shape. It is only when you rotate the bitmap back to its original orientation that Shermy will reappear.

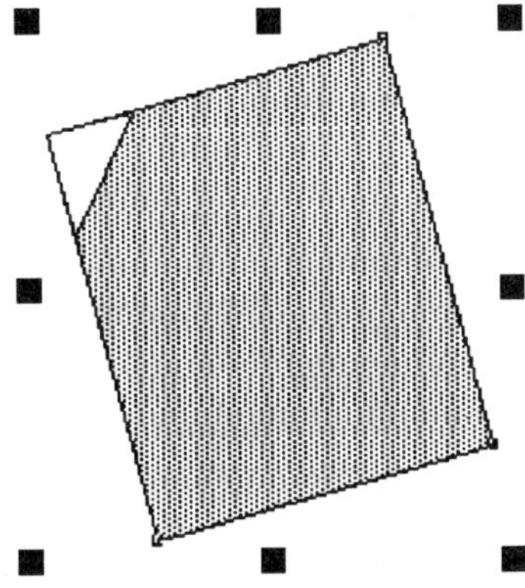

**12.05 Rotated bitmap**

j. Importing vector graphics is simpler because that's what CorelDRAW expects to use. Open the **File menu** and click on **Import** again. Change the file type to **CorelDRAW!, *.CDR** but stay in the \SAMPLES directory. Double click on SNOWBARN.CDR.

k. The image, which fills an A4 Landscape page, is imported directly without any message box appearing. However, this is a complex image - it contains a total of 171 objects most of which are fountain filled, so it may take a while to appear.

l. Try importing any other file formats you have available. You should be aware that some PCX files don't seem to import properly, especially older ones. Their aspect ratio seems to change so they come in only half the width that they should be. (This should have been fixed in the actual release version.)

# E36 - EXPORTING

Exporting files follows much the same procedure as importing with only minor exceptions.

a. Clear the page. Draw a 100 mms square and give it an 8 point outline. Press **Ctrl-N** and rotate it 45 degrees leaving the original behind. Draw an 80 mms circle and give this an 8 point outline too. Finally draw another circle, 150 mms in diameter with an 8 point outline. Align the whole lot in the centre of the page.

b. Now for the fills. Give the central circle a Radial fountain fill just using Black to White. Fill the rotated square with the first available bitmap fill. Fill the original square with Red. Finally fill the large circle with the Apple full colour fill you created earlier.

c. The images should be in the following order. Large circle at the bottom, then the Red square, then the bitmap filled square and finally the fountain filled circle on the top. Save the finished file and call it **36-1**.

**12.06 Created image**

d. What you're going to do is export the file in each of the available formats and then import it back again to see what changes have been made to it. Select all the image elements so that the handles appear around them all and the Status Bar says "**4 objects selected on Layer 1**". Open the **File menu** and click on **Export**. The dialogue box appears.

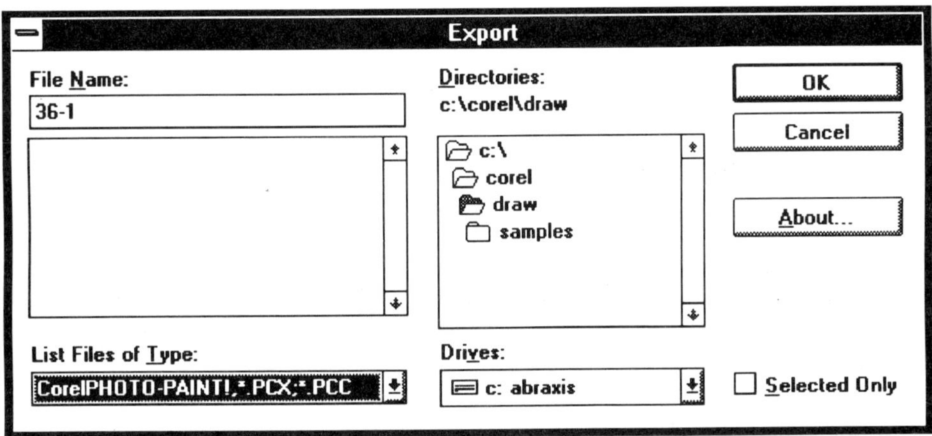


**12.07 Export dialogue box**

e. By default it shows the first possible file format which is PCX. The filename you used to save the file is given in the filename line. The one thing you have to do is click on **Selected Only**. That makes sure that only the actual image is exported rather than the whole page. Click on **OK**. Another dialogue box appears.

f. For now just accept everything as it is, notice by the way that you need 2 Mb of disk space for this file! (If you don't have that much free space then skip this.) Click on **OK**. A message box appears telling you the exportation progress and eventually vanishes.

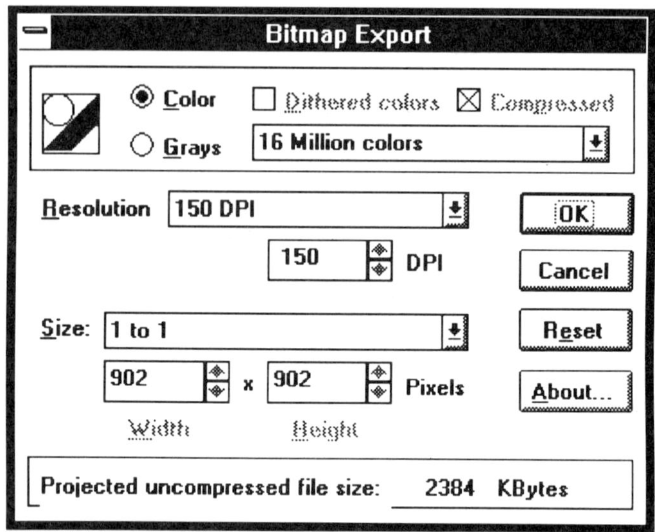


**12.08 Bitmap export dialogue box**

g. Now re-import the file you have just exported. Move the original image off to one side of the page first. Open the **File menu**, click on **Import** and then double click on **36-1.PCX**. Take a look at the image, move the original closer you can see the two easily. The PCX file colours have changed slightly, there is no difference between the bitmaps fills but the vector fill has changed. No only have the colours changed but the placement of the apple fill has moved slightly. The worst thing is the fountain fill, it has become heavily banded.

Try exporting the original in as many different formats as you wish, but don't bother with the EPS one, and then re-importing them for comparison. On the next few pages I've printed all the possible variations. (The images are actually half the size of the one you have on screen.) Each image is labelled accordingly. All the files were exported accepting the defaults as they were presented. Notice that many of the files lack patterns, in these cases a message box appeared saying "Replacing pattern with grey". Notice that the heavy banding in the fountain fill appears in each of the bitmap variations.

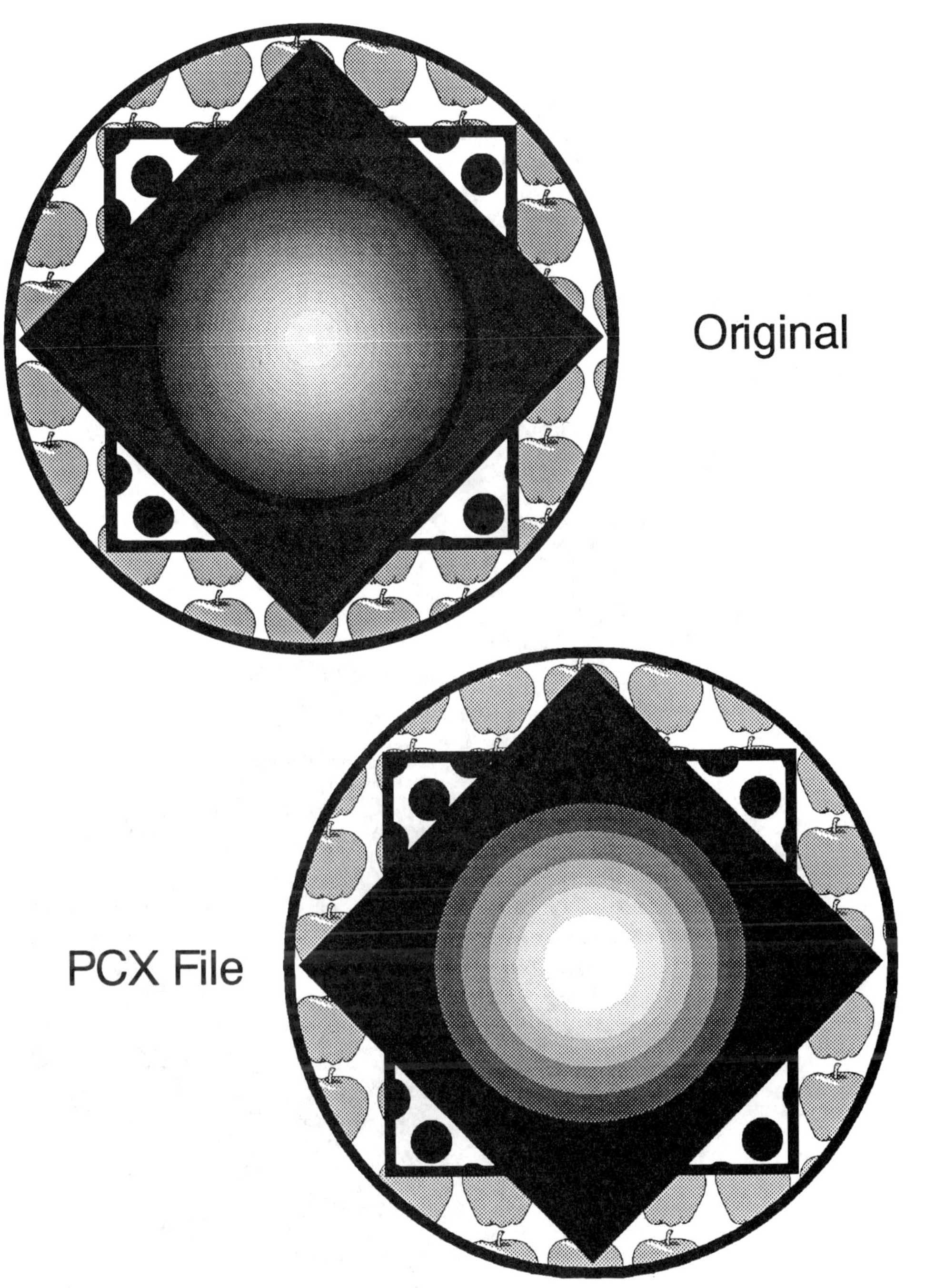
Original
PCX File

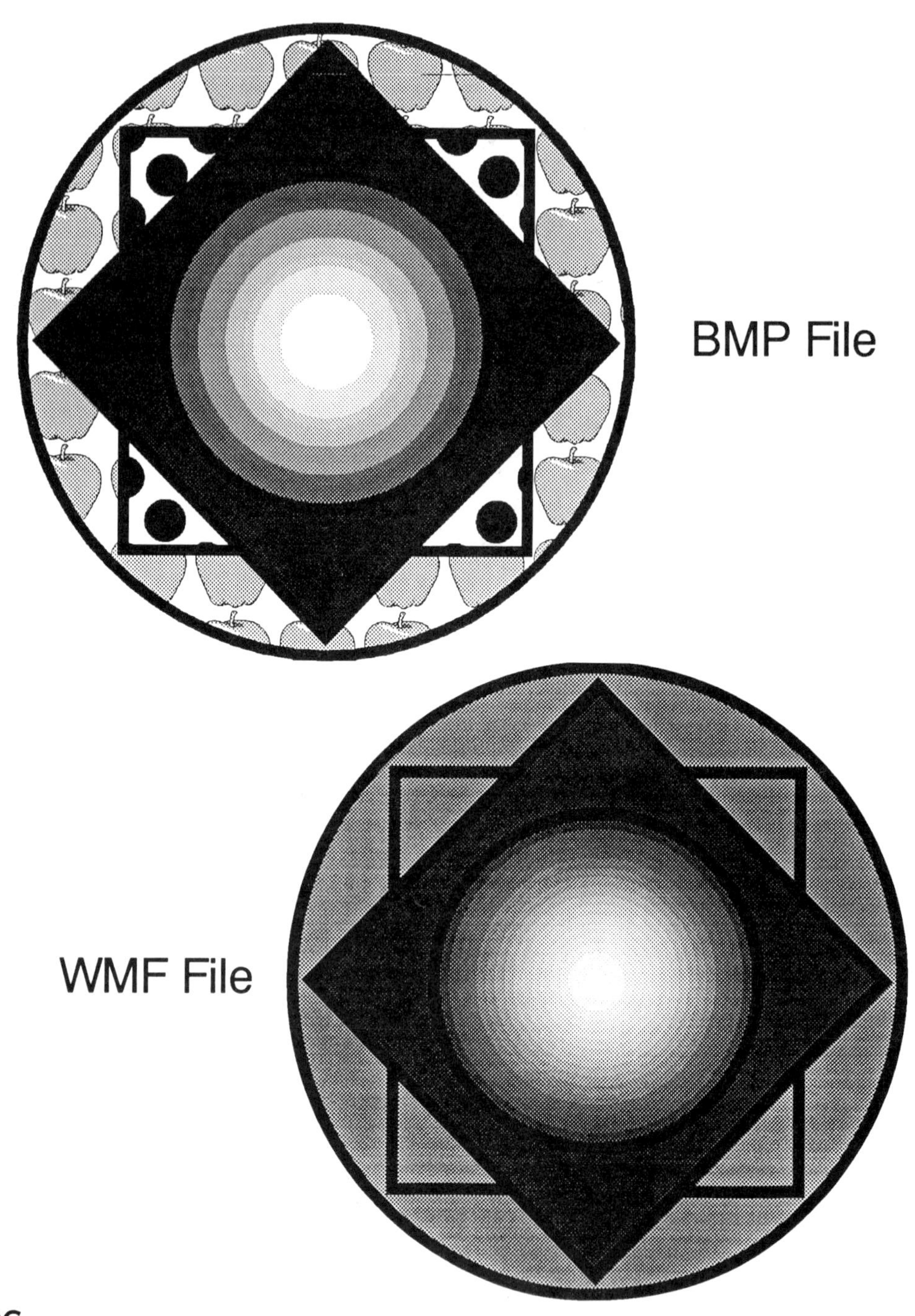
BMP File
WMF File

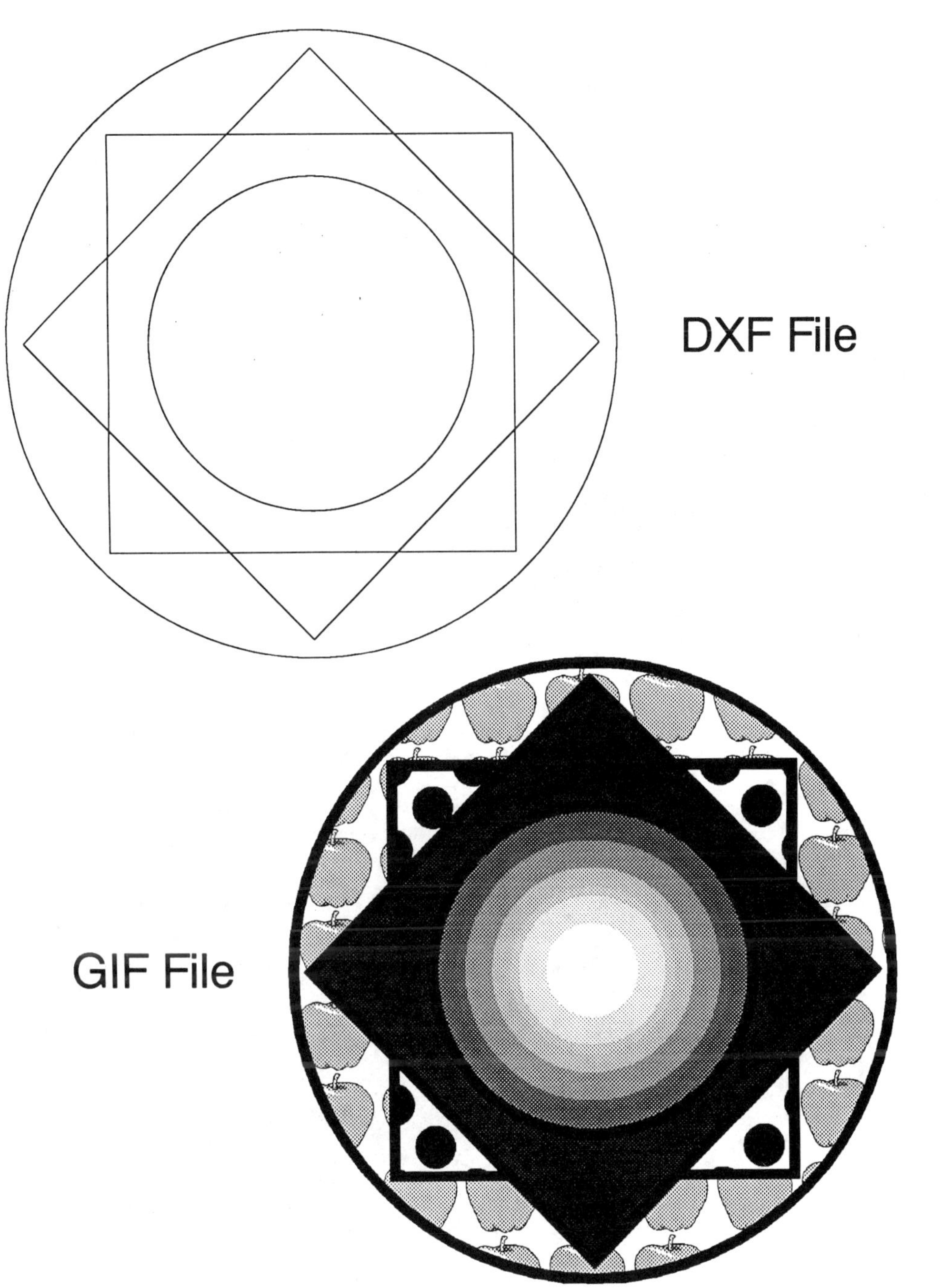
DXF File
GIF File

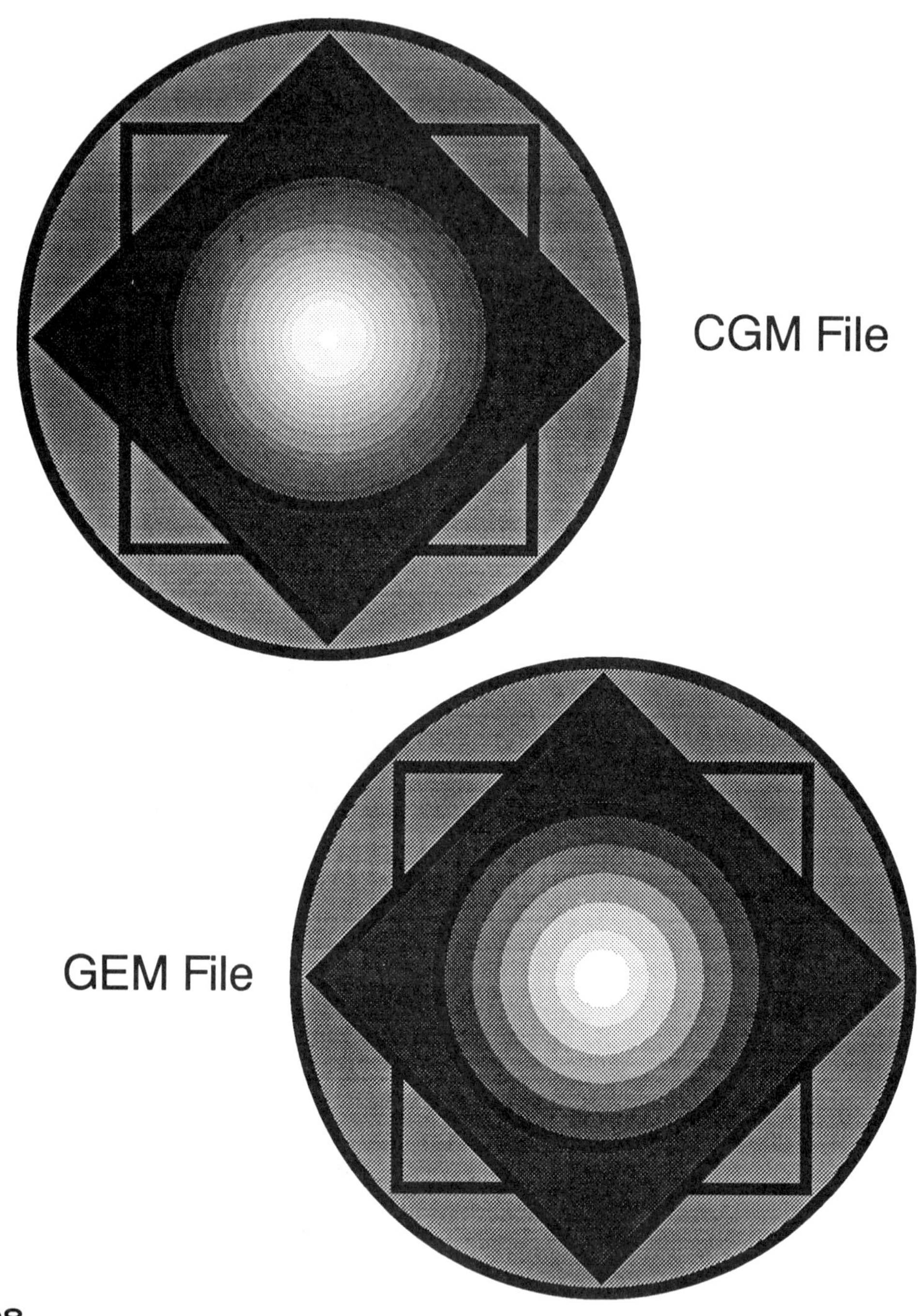
CGM File
GEM File

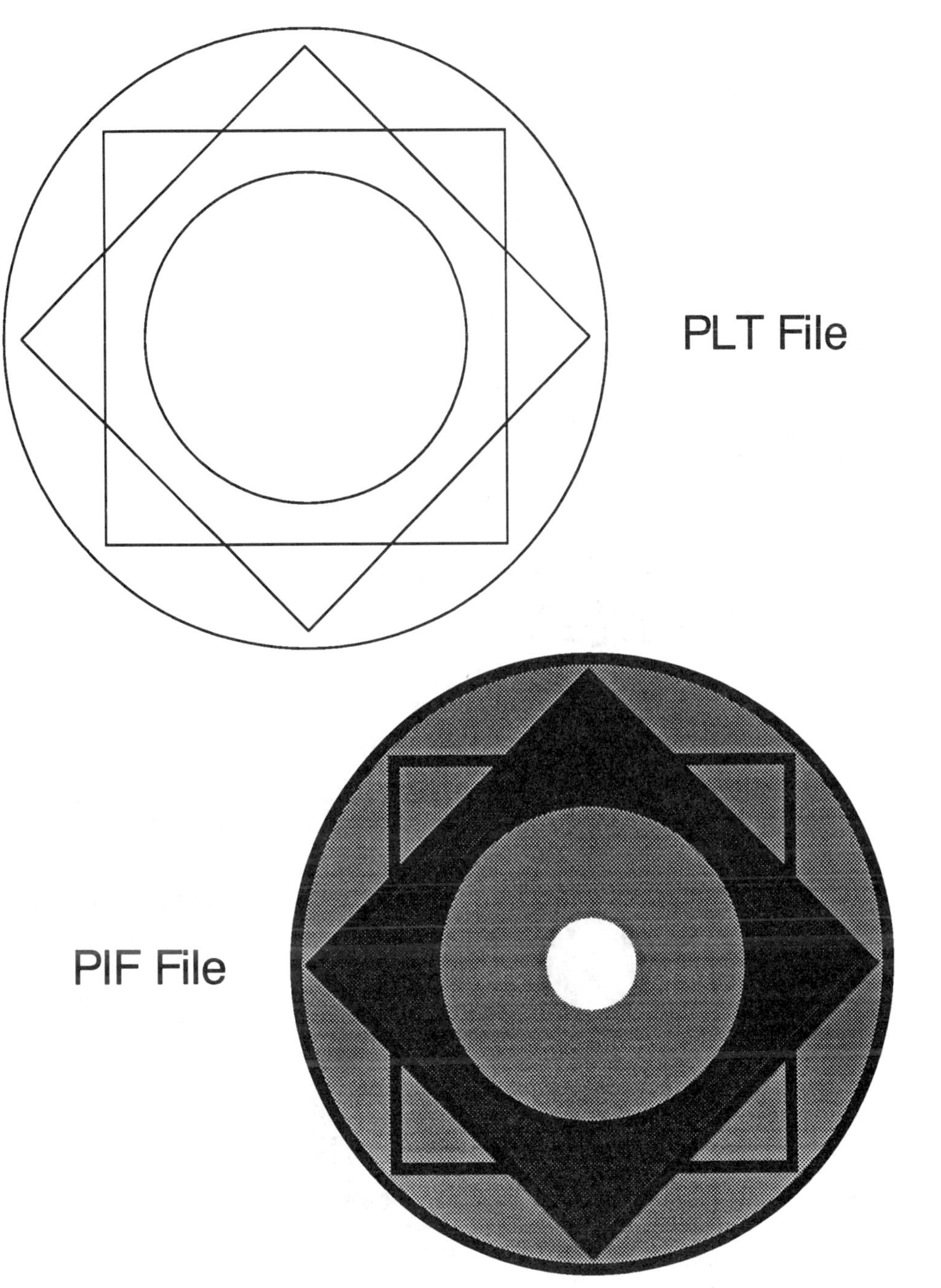
PLT File
PIF File

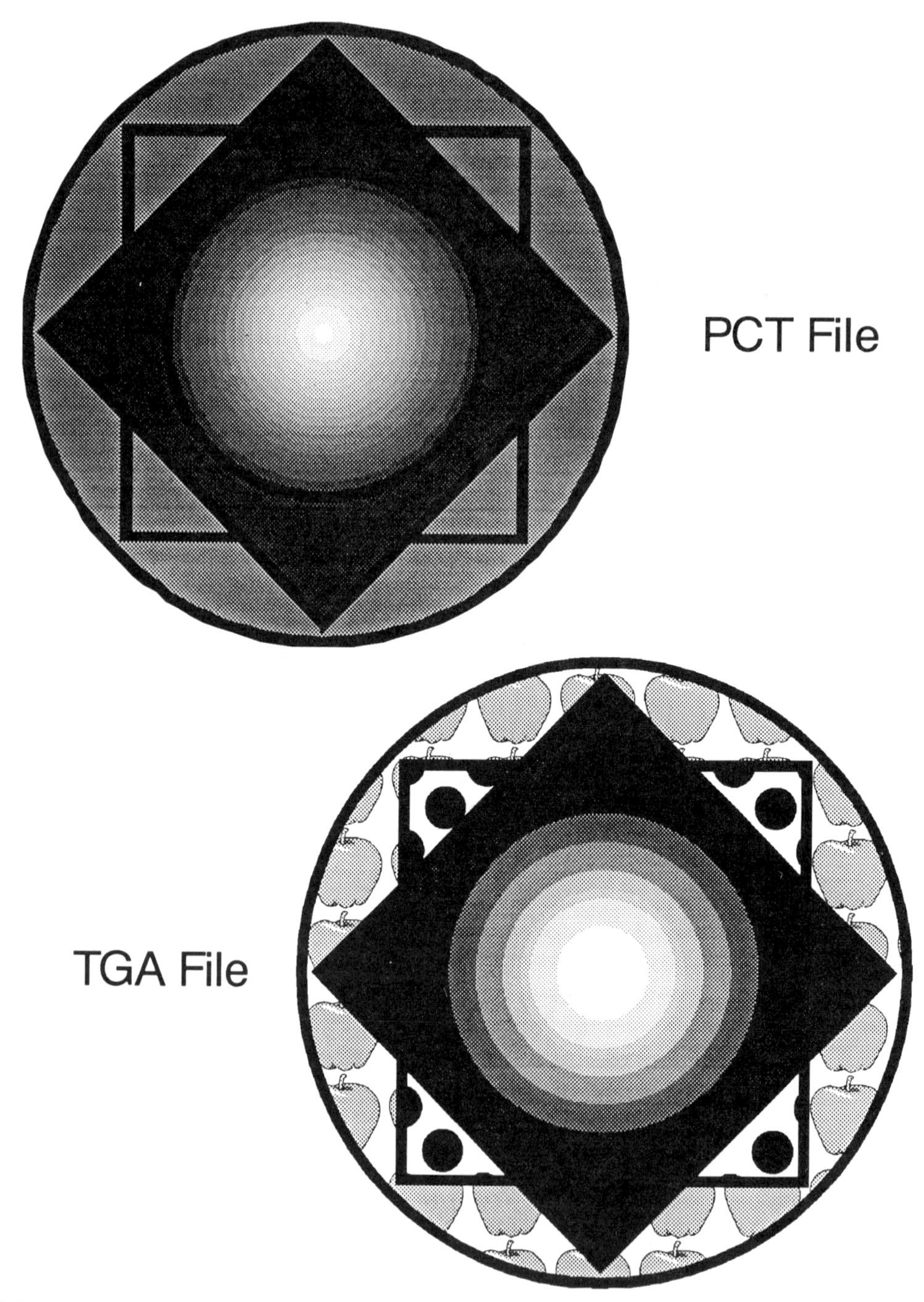
PCT File
TGA File

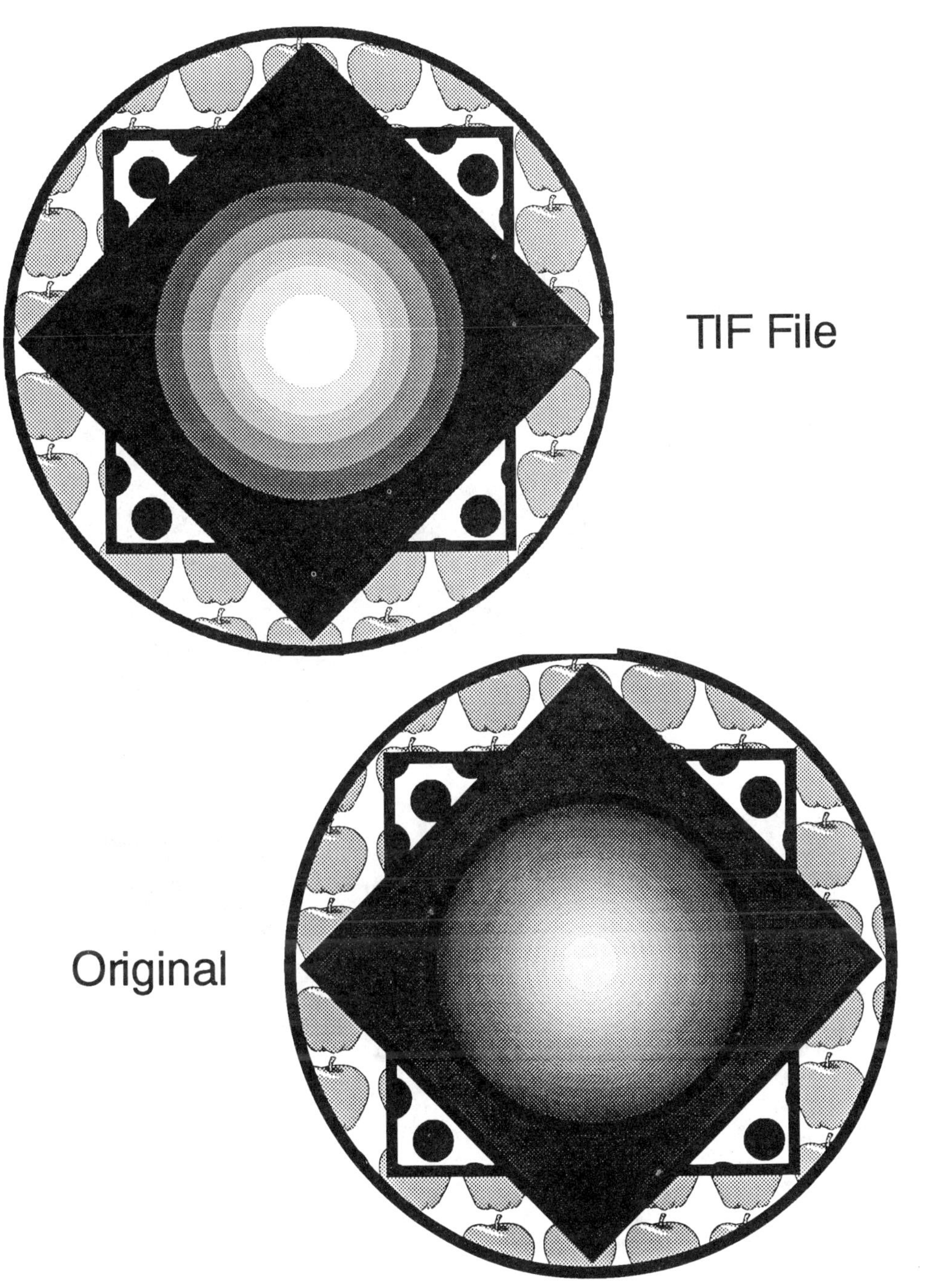
TIF File
Original

# 13 - PRINTING

The power of CorelDRAW lies in its abilities to create stunning, dynamic and/or beautiful graphics. But it is no good being able to produce all these things on screen if you cannot produce a hard copy of them and that's where the crunch comes. The kind of printer you are using will have a marked effect on your output. This chapter is devoted to the printing and the problems you are likely to experience. It is not possible to give all the problems nor all the answers - there are just too many printer types and the differences between them make too many permutations. For this reason I'm only going to concentrate on two types of printers: standard HP-compatible lasers and PostScript-compatible ones.

You can use CorelDRAW with a dot matrix printer, by the way, in fact many people do. But the quality of the output leaves a lot to be desired even on the simplest graphics. To get the best from the program you really do need a laser printer of some description and with prices tumbling it is a worth while investment.

Laser printers fall into two categories; Hewlett-Packard and it's clones and compatibles, and PostScript. The former are also called PCL (Printer Control Language) printers. It is only with a PostScript printer that you can use any of the PostScript fills in CorelDRAW. They simply will not print on anything other than a PS printer and if you try to do so you will get an error message.

One thing you will have to allow for - printing takes time, regardless of whether you are using an HP printer, in which case it will take the program a long time to send the data to the printer, or a PS one, in which case it may take a long time to actually decipher the PostScript language and so produce the hard copy. Though it has to be said that all in all a PostScript printer should be slightly faster.

Regardless of the type of printer you are using you have to allow for the memory limitation of the printer you are using. For example, if you are using a HP printer with 1 Mb of RAM then you may find that, especially when using fountain fill patterns, your graphic is cut in two. One part will appear on one page and the remainder on the next. Using the same amount of memory, and complex fountain fills, on a PostScript printer with this limited amount of memory may cause the printer to hang up. Generally speaking you should be able to produce a full A4 sized graphic on any printer that has 2 Mb of RAM or more. With only 1 Mb of printer RAM you may find that you have to limit your use of fountain fills and/or the size of the graphic you want printed. You can think of printing as the following equation:

**Size + Complexity = Time + Memory**

Increase the size or the complexity and you have to allow more time and/or more memory. A limited amount of memory means that the size and complexity of the graphic have to be reduced. Unfortunately there are no hard and fast rules about the printing and memory because there are so many parameters to the equation.

Take the series of boxes on the opposite page. These contain all the various shades of grey plus the first set of process colours available in the CorelDRAW palette, each box is a different colour. Sending this to a PostScript printer will produce a file that is 37 Kb, according to the Print Manager, and it took just under 40 seconds to print, counting from the time I pressed **Enter** in the print dialogue box. Send the same file to the printer in HP mode and the file expands to 385 Kb but still takes the same amount of time to print.

On the other hand if you fill each box with a radial fountain fill, so that each box is identical, it will take almost ten times as long to print on the PostScript printer but on an HP printer it takes only about four times as long, and most of that is in the sending not the printing! The curious thing is that in each case, colour or fountain fill, the file size remains the same - 37 Kb for the PostScript and 385 Kb for the HP.

But why should the HP be faster at doing the fountain fills? The answer to that has to do with the way that the printer operates. All printers print bitmaps, that's the first point. Regardless of the type of printer you are using the printed output is a bitmap. It's obvious if you think about it. All printers produce their images using a series of dots, the only difference is in the number of dots per inch - but they are still dots. Any image composed of dots is a bitmap. QED. But they do so in a different way. When you send a graphic to an HP printer from CorelDRAW, the program does the translation for you. It takes the image and 'scans' it line by line and it is these that it sends to the printer. As you are sending it the screen message will tell you, for example, Sending object 1 or 30 Band 20. Once the entire image has been scanned in this way and the file is completed the actual printing commences.

On a PostScript printer on the other hand what CorelDRAW sends is a program - a PostScript program. PostScript is a language, in the same vein as BASIC or COBOL or FORTRAN, and it is just as specialised as any of these computer languages. It is

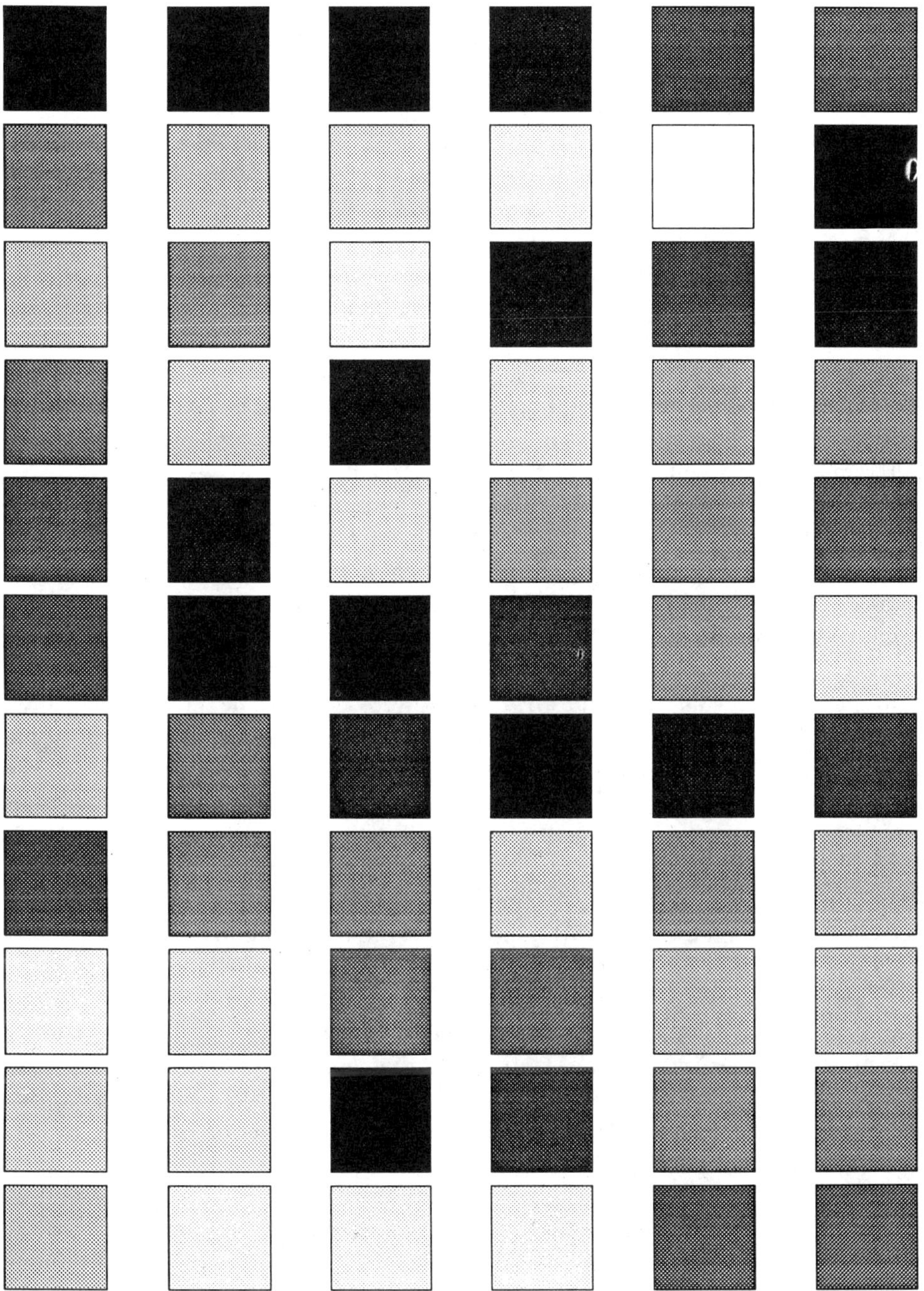

a method of coding information on a page that will make printing faster and more precise. The really important point about PostScript is that it is device independent. Thus you can create a PostScript file on any computer and output it on any PostScript printer, whether it be a 300 dpi laser or a 1200 dpi image setter. The original language was invented by two Americans, John Warnock and Charles Geschke, in 1982. At the time both were working at the Xerox Palo Research Centre and they developed PostScript in their spare time and then went on to create Adobe Systems Incorporated. The first PostScript printer was released by QMS in 1985 and today there are hundreds of PostScript printers available and at least that many again in development. (There are also some new printers called True Image printers but as yet they are very few and far between. True Image is another page description language.)

If you want to see the actual program, send a file from CorelDRAW to your printer with the PostScript printer active in the Control Panel but have the printer switched to HP mode. What you will get is the program itself not the image.

CorelDRAW is geared for use with PostScript printers and it can write the necessary program very rapidly. Once that program reaches the printer the internal chips of the printer then have to run the program, translate the result into a bitmap and then print it. With simple files, like the coloured squares, this is no problem because all it has to do is grey-scale the image but once you start using fountain fills or PostScript patterns things can take much longer. That's why, by the way, that PostScript printer need lots of memory - to store the program and the results before actually printing the graphic. It is even possible to exhaust the memory on a printer with a tiny file to such an extend that it won't actually print.

Then, just to confuse matters further, there is PostScript, PostScript-compatible and PostScript clone printers. The real, honest to goodness Adobe PostScript is found on very few printers: the majority are compatibles. But the situation is changing, these days more and more manufacturers are using real PostScript rather than a compatible version, and the price of printers continues to fall, it is in the interests of the manufacturers to use the latest version of the language that they can. Most printers will produce some kind of test or status sheet that will tell you what version of the language they are using. In general it won't make much difference, within reason, but if you try to use CorelDRAW with versions earlier than about 51.0 you may run into the occasional problem.

HP printers don't have this problem. The levels of compatibility between true HP printers and compatibles and clones it so slight as to be almost negligible, although

Hewlett-Packard have recently launched their new series of printers which have extra refinements and improvements.

These days there is little to choose from in terms of price. You can buy a PostScript-compatible printer for less than £1250 and a genuine Adobe PostScript printer for only a few hundred pounds more. Which you choose is up to you and what you want to do with it. The answer to that depends entirely on what kind of graphics you are going to produce and what they are intended for, but bear in mind that CorelDRAW was written for use with PostScript printers. If you want to use the PostScript patterns then you must have a PostScript, or compatible, printer. On the other hand if you don't want or need to use these than an HP printer will be sufficient. Of course, if you want to use full colour then that's a whole new ball game.

When it comes to colour printing the first thing you notice is the cost of the machines. You can get colour dot matrix printers for a few hundred pounds but the quality of their output is not very good and it deteriorates as the ribbon gets used up. The next step up is some form of ink-jet. These work by spraying little blobs of ink at the page. They produce very good quality images but if you use them for large blocks of colour the page will tend to buckle as it gets soaked.

Beyond that you are into the realms of Thermal Wax Transfer printing. These produce wonderful colours but they tend to be very expensive, £5,000 or more, and because they have to use special paper and ribbons the cost of consumables is very high. Typically the cost of a single A4 page from a thermal wax printer is around 70 pence or more. Thermal wax printers work by directly melting wax onto the page. The ribbon contains three, or in some cases four, page sized wax panels - in Red, Blue, Yellow and Black. The page goes in and out of the printer as many times as there are colour blocks. With each pass a single colour is laid on the sheet. Thus if you use a single Blue line all the rest of the wax on that blue panel is wasted - and it cannot be recovered.

The step beyond that is the kind of technology used in the Tektronix Phaser printers. These are superb and they produce wonderful colours. Unfortunately they are very expensive, for example the Phaser III is £11,000. However, to offset against this high capital cost the printers use ordinary paper and the consumables cost is low. I have actually seen a Phaser III print onto tissue paper! Phasers work by spraying melted wax on to the page. The surplus and/or waste gets caught in a reservoir and thus it can be reused.

The net result is that over the course of a couple of years there is very little difference between the overall costs of a thermal wax printer and a Phaser - depending on the number of prints you produce. Suppose you produce 5,000 prints a year. On a thermal wax printer these will cost you about £3,500 pounds per annum or £7,000 over the two years. Add to that the cost of the printer, £5,000, and the total cost is £12,000. Using the Phaser on the other hand the cost of the prints is around £500 a year, making a total of £1,000. Add the printer cost and you get a total of around £12,000. The difference lies in the capital cost in the first place. I will admit that I'm biased because I think the Phaser III is the best colour printer you can buy. (No, I don't own one - I can't afford it. But if I was going to buy a colour printer that's the one I'd get!)

The drawback to both the thermal wax printer and the Phaser is that the image is wax. Wax melts when it gets hot. I once ruined the drum on my laser by trying to overprint a thermal wax sheet!

Canon have just brought out a new bubble jet printer which, by all accounts, gives very good results. I haven't seen one yet so I can't comment on it but those people who have got one have said very favourable things about it.

# PCL PRINTERS

When you ask CorelDRAW to print a graphic for you when you are using a PCL printer, the following dialogue box appears. Note that this is different to the PostScript printer dialogue box. CorelDRAW 2.01 and earlier used the same dialogue box in each case but CorelDRAW 3.0 uses different dialogue boxes according to the printer in use.

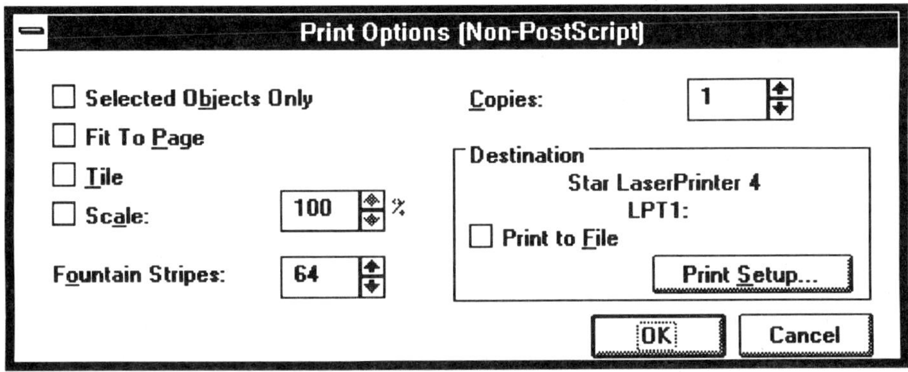


**13.01 PCL Print dialogue box**

The dialogue box gives you just five options:

**Selected Objects Only** this command is only active if you have selected an object, or a number of objects, otherwise it will be greyed out. If you click on it then only the pre-selected object(s) will be printed, otherwise it has no effect.

**Fit To Page** is an automatic rescaling facility. If you are drawing on large paper, e.g. A3, and you want to produce a proof copy onto A4 then you would select this option. The graphic will then be resized so that it automatically fits onto the paper size used in the printer, as selected in the Windows Control Panel. However, it doesn't work the other way round. If you are drawing on A4 and printing to A3 then the graphic will not be scaled upwards, it will still print as A4. In both cases the on-screen graphic is not changed, only the printed copy.

**Tile** is opposite of the above. Instead of producing a proof copy on smaller sized paper it will print the graphic at its true size but use a number of sheets of paper to do so. For example, if you have a graphic on a page that is 762 mms square, the maximum size that CorelDRAW permits, when you print it with this option checked, onto A4 paper, you will get a number of separate sheets which can then be assembled into the full sized page, each will have the normal border. You cannot do fully bled images, i.e. ones that go to the edge of the page, from CorelDRAW because the printer won't let you.

**Scale** is the complement to Fit to Page above. This allows you to produce a magnified image of a small graphic. You can use any scale in the range 10% to 1000%, i.e. print the graphic at a scale of one tenth to 10 times. If you are using a page size, on screen, that matches the printer paper size and you then scale the image to a larger size you should also check Tile, above. By default the scaling is always 100%. To scale from one A size down to another use Fit to Page instead because then the program does it automatically for you and it saves you having to work out the reduction size.

**Fountain Stripes** applies only to fountain fills, the value can range from 2 to 250. What it does is control the number of visible stripes that you can see when you print a fountain fill. Low values will produce definite visible stripes, see samples on the next pages, whereas high values produce very fine or nonexistent stripes. By default on all PCL printers the value is 64 and this will generally produce barely visible banding. Low values are not to be despised because they can be used for producing special effects. The only problem with fountain fills is that the value you use applies to all fountain fills not specific ones. Thus you cannot have one object with 10 bands, another with 30 and a third with 80. They will all be the same. Using high values for the fountain stripes will increase the time that the graphic takes to print, it does not appreciably increase the file size though.

There is no hard and fast rule about the number of stripes you should use, the default value is an average but your printer may need less or more than this value - it depends on the printer. The only way to find the optimum for your particular printer is by experimentation. The following pages show the results of changing the number of stripes. The pages were produced on my Star LaserPrinter 4 running in HP mode. The differences between 64 stripes and 250 strips are very hard to see with the naked eye, although they are there.

**Number Of Copies** allows you to produce multiple copies of the same file in a single operation. You can print any number in the range 1 to 999. When you print multiple copies the file size, as sent to the printer, remains the same as if you were only sending one copy but the information you send includes the multiplier. The advantage of that is that you are not tying up your system resources a number of times, just once.

**Print to File** writes the file to your hard disk rather than sending it to the printer. Thereafter you can print it any way you please.

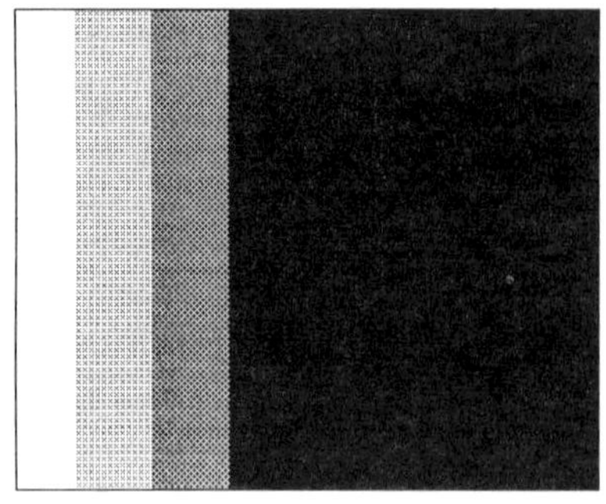

White - Black 0 Degrees

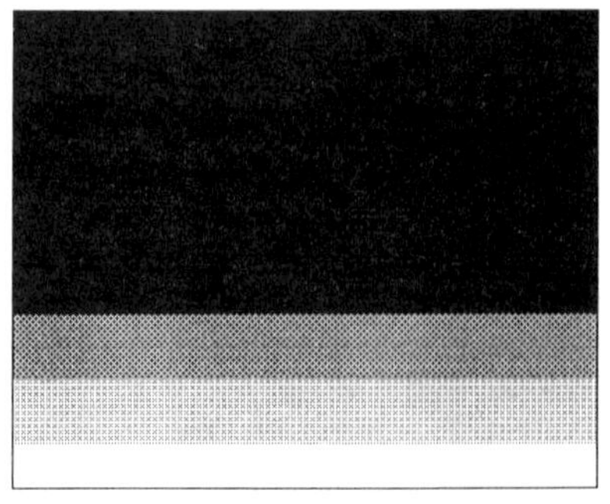

White - Black 90 Degrees

White - Black 270 Degrees

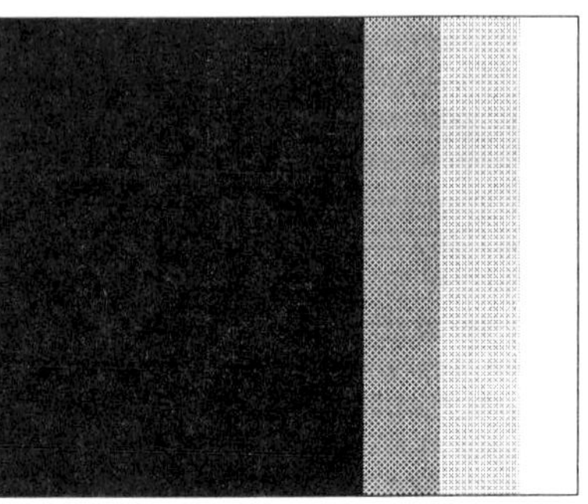

White - Black 180 Degrees

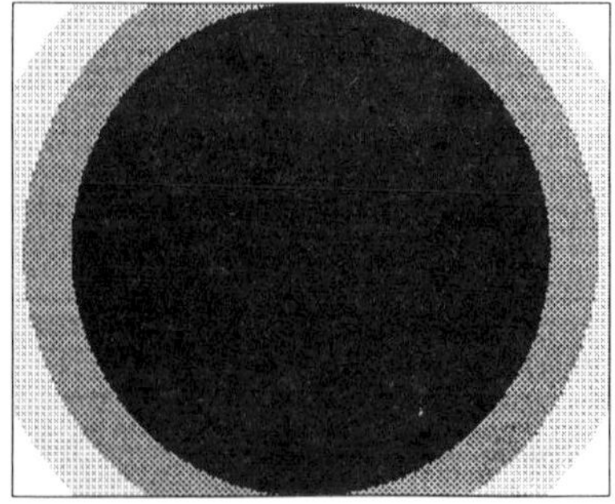

White - Black Radial

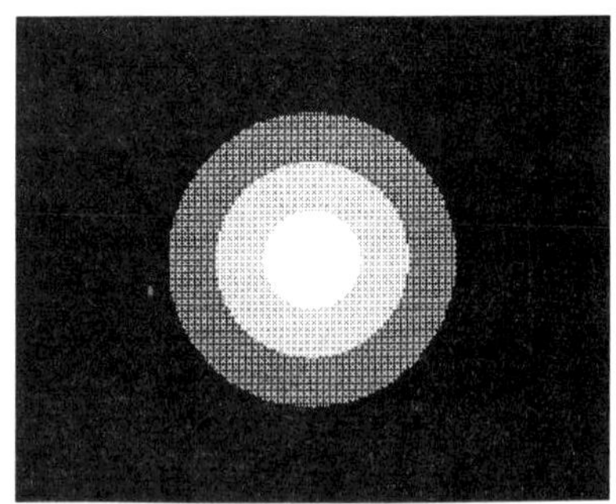

Black - White Radial

Printed with 8 Fountain Stripes on an HP compatible printer

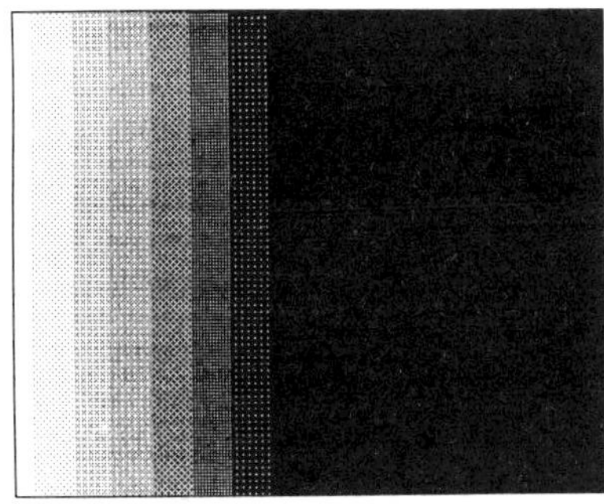

White - Black 0 Degrees

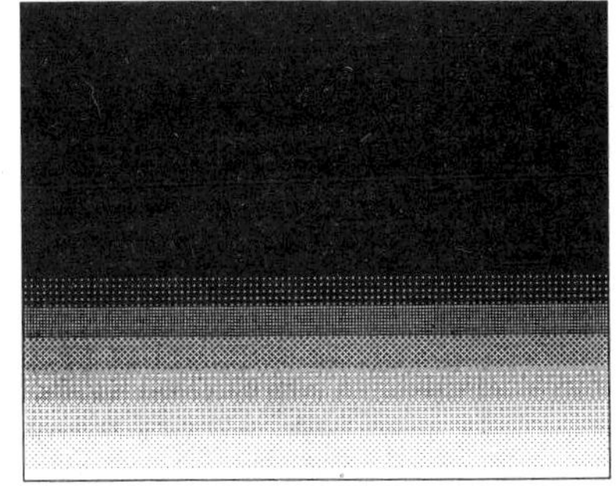

White - Black 90 Degrees

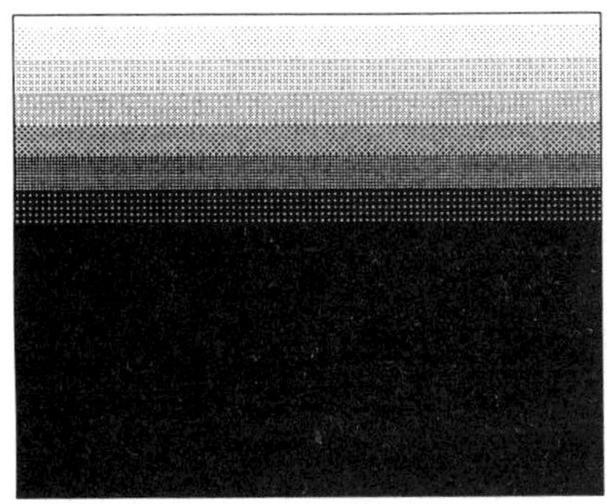

White - Black 270 Degrees

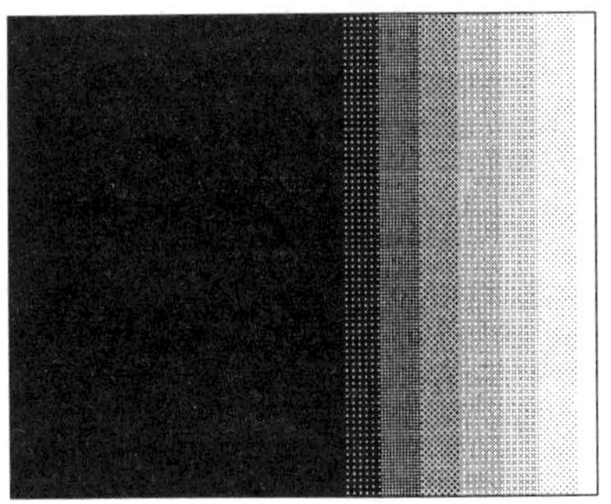

White - Black 180 Degrees

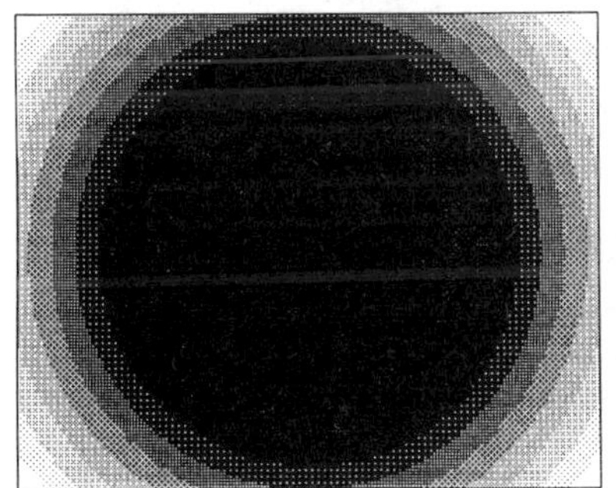

White - Black Radial

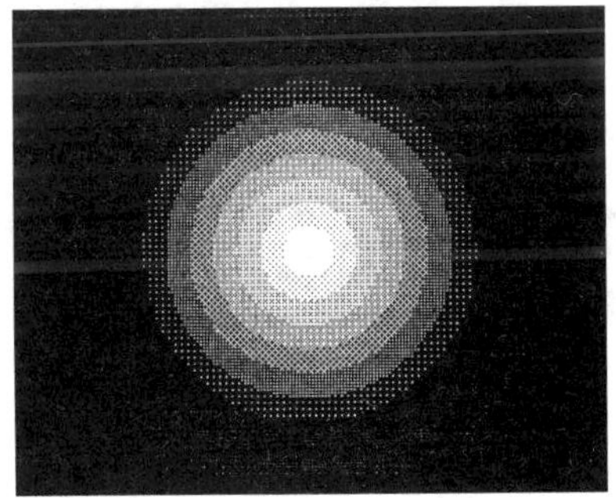

Black - White Radial

Printed with 16 Fountain Stripes on an HP compatible printer

Printed with 32 Fountain Stripes on an HP compatible printer

White - Black 0 Degrees

White - Black 90 Degrees

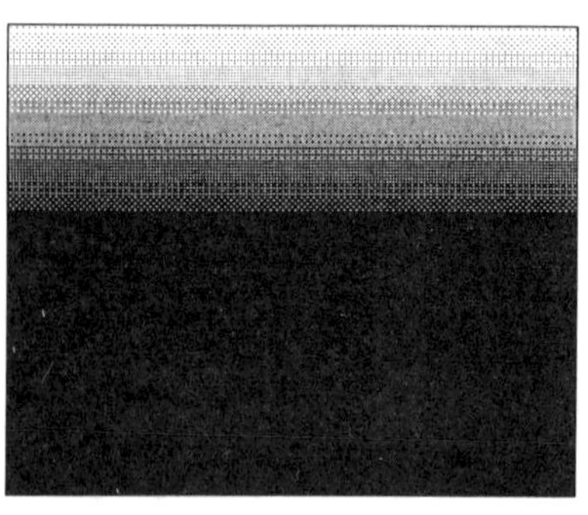

White - Black 270 Degrees

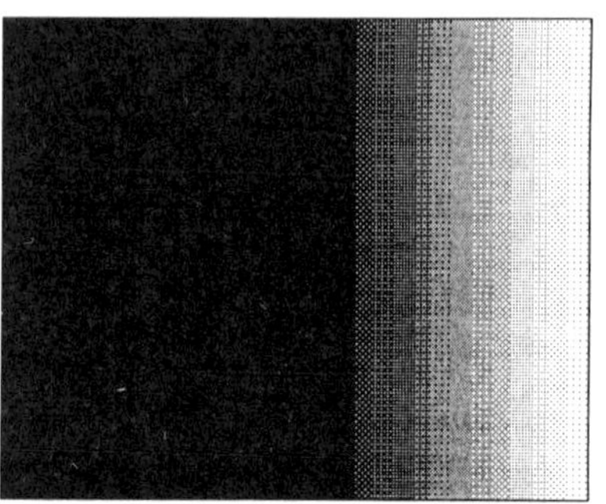

White - Black 180 Degrees

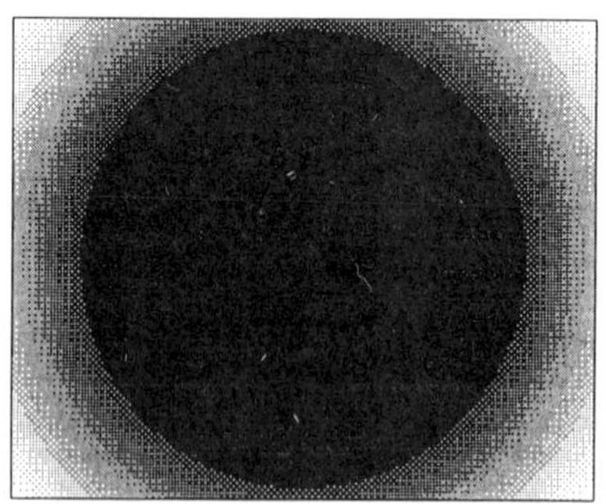

White - Black Radial

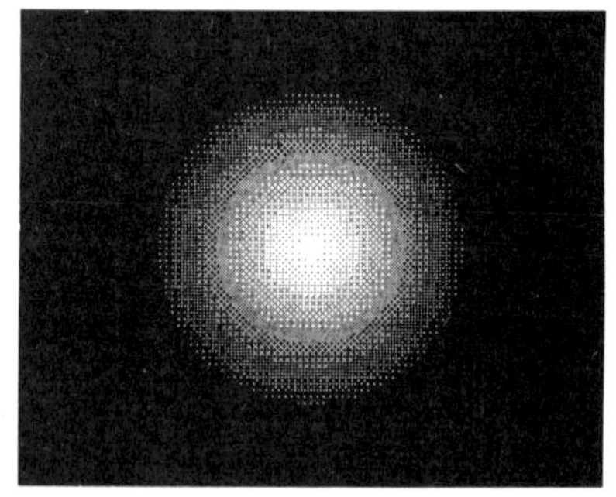

Black - White Radial

White - Black 0 Degrees

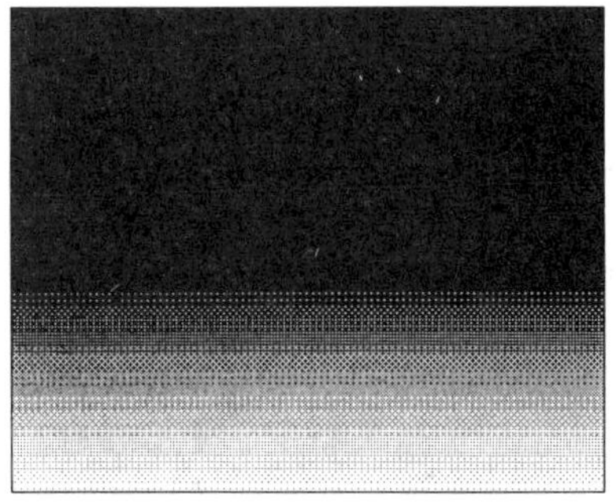

White - Black 90 Degrees

White - Black 270 Degrees

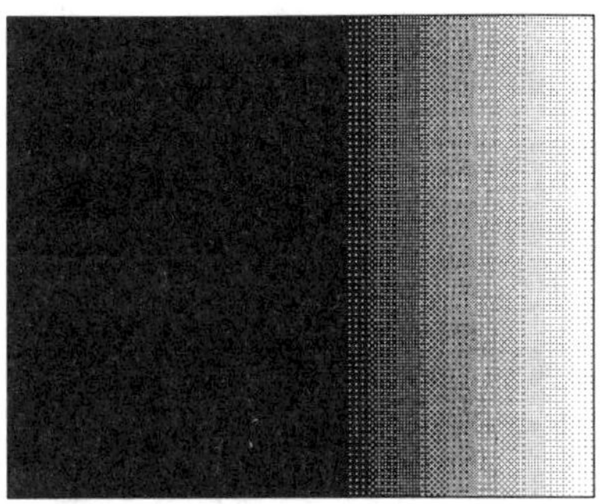

White - Black 180 Degrees

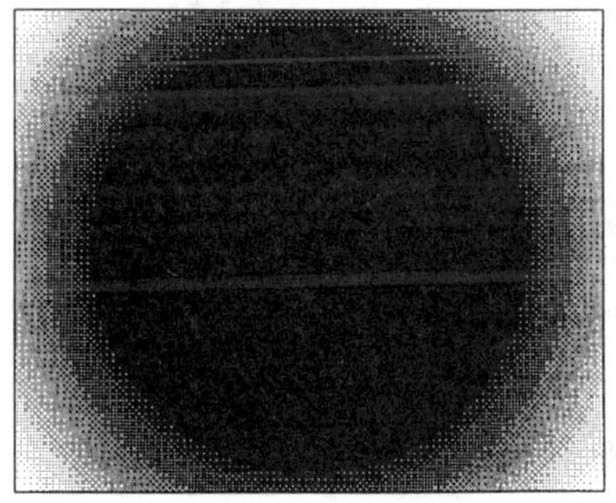

White - Black Radial

Black - White Radial

Printed with 64 Fountain Stripes on an HP compatible printer

White - Black 0 Degrees

White - Black 90 Degrees

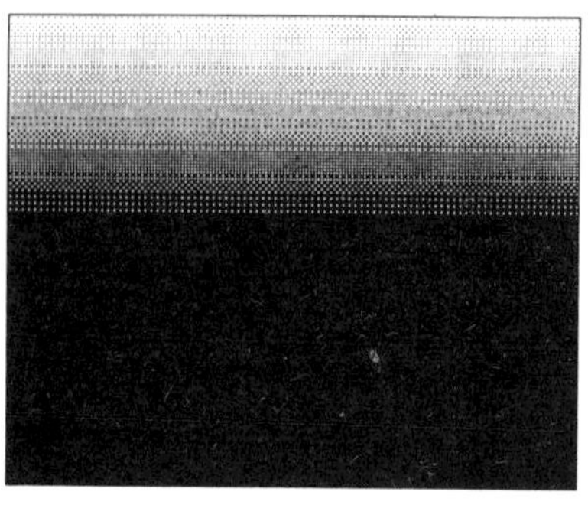

White - Black 270 Degrees

White - Black 180 Degrees

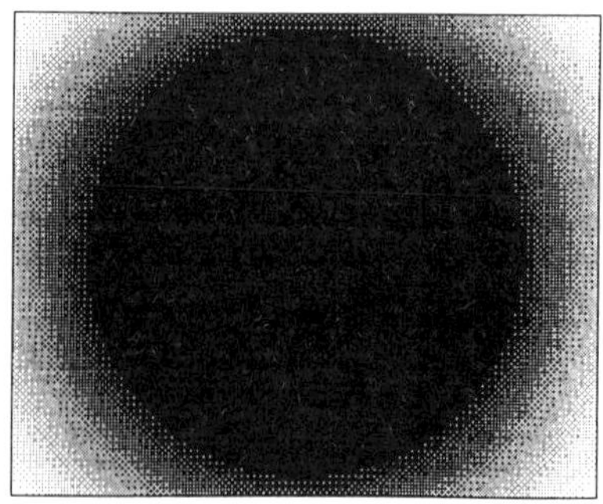

White - Black Radial

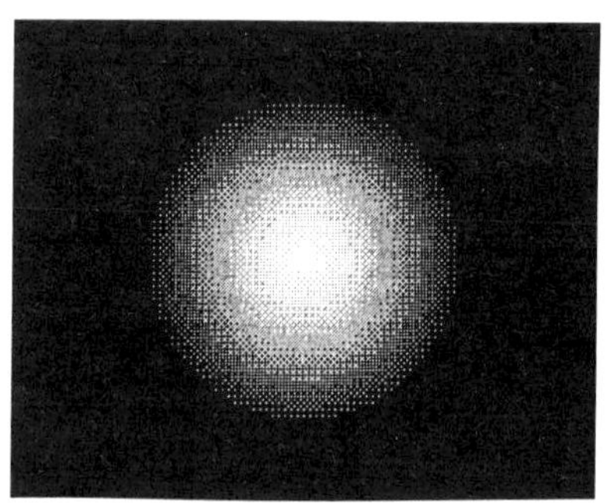

Black - White Radial

Printed with 128 Fountain Stripes on an HP compatible printer

White - Black 0 Degrees

White - Black 90 Degrees

White - Black 270 Degrees

White - Black 180 Degrees

Printed with 250 Fountain Stripes on an HP compatible printer

White - Black Radial

Black - White Radial

# POSTSCRIPT PRINTERS

When you are using a PostScript printer the dialogue box is different, it contains another range of features which are not available for PCL printers.

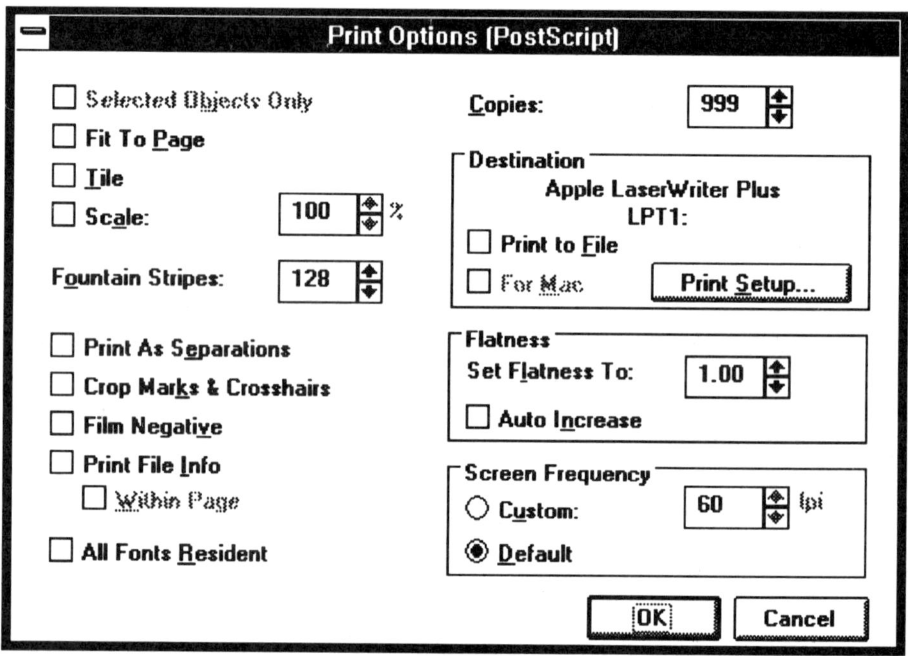


**13.02 PostScript Print dialogue box**

Certain of the options are identical to those available when using a PCL printer so we'll not cover them again. The remaining commands are PostScript specific.

**Print As Separations** allows you to print a colour graphic as a number of different images on separate sheets. Each image relates to one of the CMYK process colours. The intention is that each of these images will then be printed, by a photolithographic process, in a different colour. The different colours are then overprinted on each other to produce a full colour printed graphic. When you activate this command the three commands immediately following this one will also be activated. Click on **OK** to bring up the dialogue box.

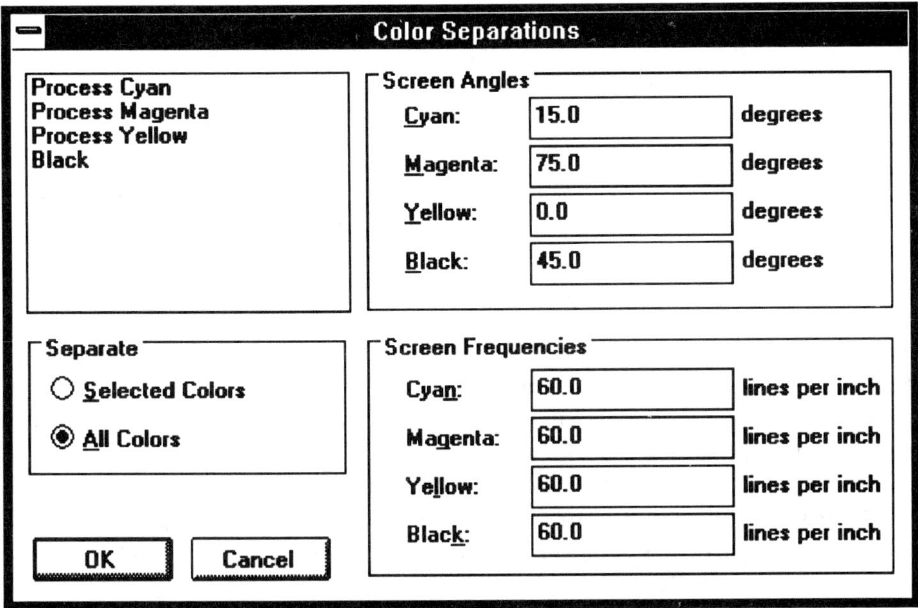


**13.03 Separation dialogue box**

This new dialogue box allows you to select which of the colours you will print, you can use this box to print a single colour if you wish rather than producing complete separations.

On the left hand side is a box which tells you which colours have been used in the graphic. You can produce a separation for all the colours or for selected ones. By default you will get all of them.

Along the bottom of the box are two options, **All Colours** and **Selected Colours**. The first of these is pre-selected. By clicking on the second you can then choose which colour separation will be printed - simply click on the colour in the list box. Clicking on a second colour will add this to the list to be printed.

The **Screen Angles** refer to the way that the different process colours will be printed. The screen frequency is the default, as shown in the main Print dialogue box, although you can change these if you wish using the arrowheads or by simply overwriting the values.

**Screen Frequencies** refer to the printers screen that will be used for the separations. The values come from the PostScript options box in the Fill dialogue box.

Clicking on **OK** will then start the actual printing process. You will get as many pages as colours you have selected and the corresponding print file, as shown in the Print Manager, will be roughly the standard file size multiplied by the number of colours.

You should be aware that printing colour separations takes time. The following pages show the colour separations for the graphic you used in the last exercise. I changed the colour of the square from red to blue and gave each shape a hairline outline, otherwise it is the same image. The whole thing took nearly ten minutes to print on my Star LaserPrinter 4 running in PostScript mode. This is a very fast printer, because it is RISC based, and so this gives you an idea of how long colour separations take to print. The first page is Cyan, the second is Magenta, the third Yellow and the fourth Black - i.e. the CMYK colours. The final page shows the graphic as it is printed normally.

**Crop Marks & Crosshairs** can be printed as part of a colour separation or as standard. These will only appear if the page you are printing onto is larger than the on-screen page size. Crop marks consist of two lines, at ninety degrees, a set of which appears at each corner of the page. The lines give the actual size of the on-screen page. Crosshairs consist of circles with crosses in them and they are used to align pages, as in colour separations, so that the pages match.

**Film Negative** produces a printout that is in negative, i.e. black appears as white and vice versa. In addition all text, either that in the graphic or any file information, is printed as mirror images. The reason for this is to allow a photo-typesetter to produce the graphic directly onto film.

**Include File Info** causes the name of the file, the colour information, the screen type and the time and date to printed. This information can be printed on a separate sheet or, if you click on **Within Page**, between the left hand crop marks, or where they would be, on the printed page. (Look on the separations and you'll see the information.) The information in this case is printed very small, about 6 point, in the standard font that the printer is set up to provide - usually Courier.

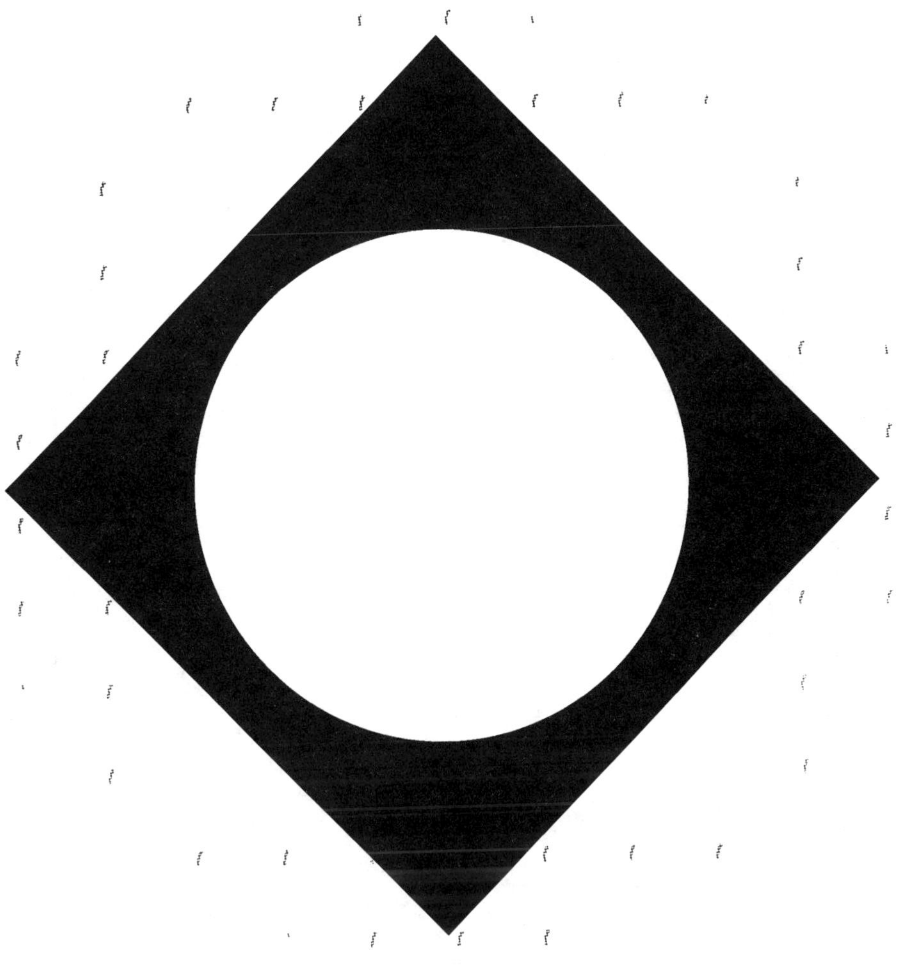
FILE:13-04.CDR COLOR: Process Cyan SCREEN: 60 lpi at 15 degrees TIME: Wed Jul 08 15:48:03 1992

FILE:13-04.CDR COLOR: Process Magenta SCREEN: 60 lpi at 75 degrees TIME: Wed Jul 08 15:48:03 1992

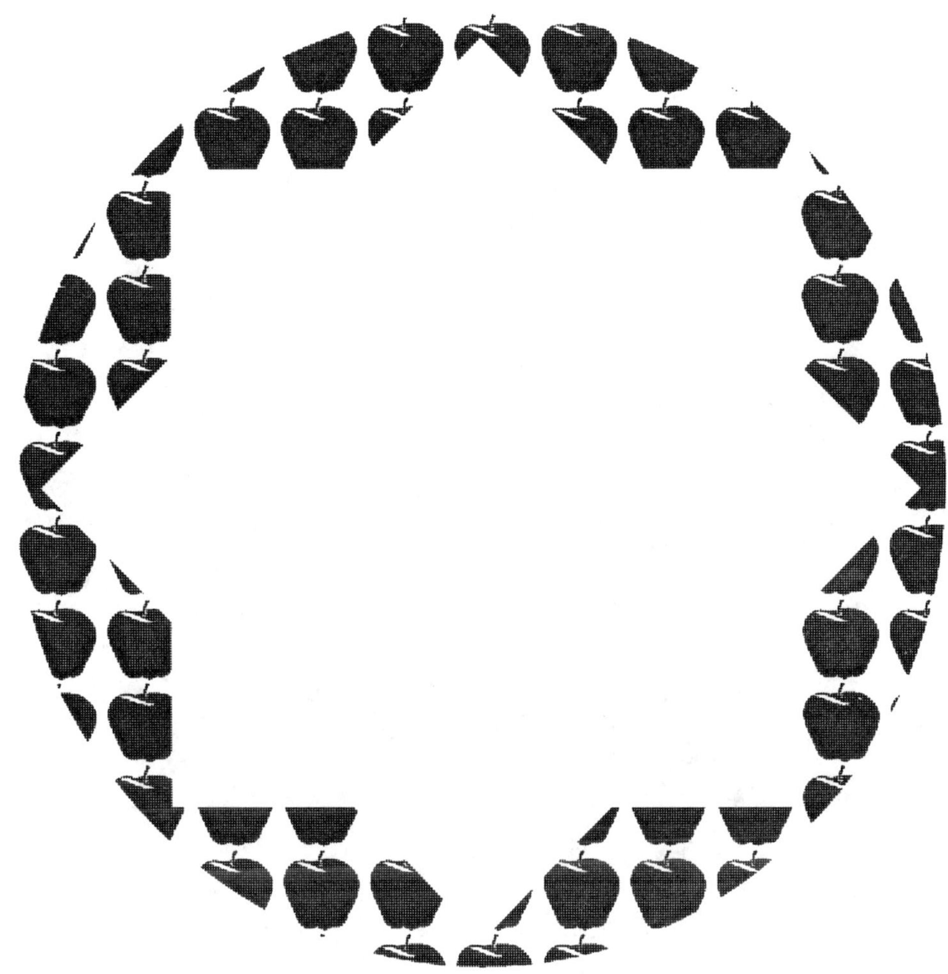

**All Fonts Resident** applies only to those graphics that will contain text - it is unnecessary to use it for other files. What it does is tell the printer that instead of using the text as it appears in the CorelDRAW file, it should instead use the fonts that are built into the printer itself. On a standard PostScript printer, including the majority of compatibles and clones, you will find the following typefaces and fonts are built in. The names in brackets refer to the corresponding CorelDRAW fonts.

**Avant Garde** (Avalon) in Normal, Bold, Italic and Bold Italic.

**Bookman** (Brooklyn) in Normal, Bold, Italic and Bold Italic.

**Courier** in Normal, Bold, Italic and Bold Italic. Courier is the default typeface on the majority of printers and therefore I never use it in any image or text file. In that way if the text does appear in courier I know something has gone wrong.

**Helvetica** (Switzerland) in Normal, Bold, Italic and Bold Italic. This typeface may be called Swiss instead.

**Helvetica Narrow** (Switzerland Narrow) in Normal, Bold, Italic and Bold Italic. Also called Swiss Compressed, Swiss Narrow or Swiss Condensed.

**New Century Schoolbook** (New Brunswick) in Normal, Bold, Italic and Bold Italic.

**Palatino** (Palm Springs) in Normal, Bold, Italic and Bold Italic. This typeface may be called Zapf Calligraphic instead.

**Symbol** (Greek/Math Symbols) in Normal and Bold. It cannot be italicised.

**Times Roman** (Toronto) in Normal, Bold, Italic and Bold Italic. May also be called Times, Dutch or Roman.

**Zapf Chancery** (Zurich Calligraphic) in Italic and Bold only. The typeface is in italics and cannot therefore be printed as Normal.

**Zapf Dingbats** (Dixieland) in Normal only. This cannot be italicised. It is possible, on some PostScript printers, to produce bold Dingbats.

By using this option when printing you will speed up the process, in direct proportion to the number of typefaces, fonts and the amount of text you have in the file. Notice that Courier has no equivalent in CorelDRAW. If you select this option and then send a file to the printer that contains typefaces and fonts that do not match then the text within that file will be printed in Courier or it may simply vanish. The command is especially useful when you are using small point sizes.

**Flatness** changes the way that curves are produced. The reason for its inclusion is to help you avoid the PostScript limitcheck error which you may run into when printing complex files. The error message, which appears on the printer and not on screen, will appear if the number of segments in any curve exceeds a specified limit, different levels of PostScript and different emulations of PostScript may all use different limits. You can use any value in the range 1 to 100 in decimal steps, i.e. you can have 5.6 or 2.3. By default the value is 1.00, i.e. normal, which will produce smooth curves. By increasing the value any curve will be produced as a series of straight lines.

**Screen Frequency** refers to the way that PostScript half-tones are printed. In order for the command to be active you must have used one of the PostScript half-tones for the Fills or Outlines.

**For Mac** is a sub-set of destination and only available if you use **Print to File**. It allows you to save the file in such a way that a bureau using Macintosh computers will be able to print the file for you. When you use this command you get the same kind of dialogue box as you do when using Save As.

On the following pages are the same sample files of fountain fills printed on my Star LaserPrinter 4 in PostScript mode.

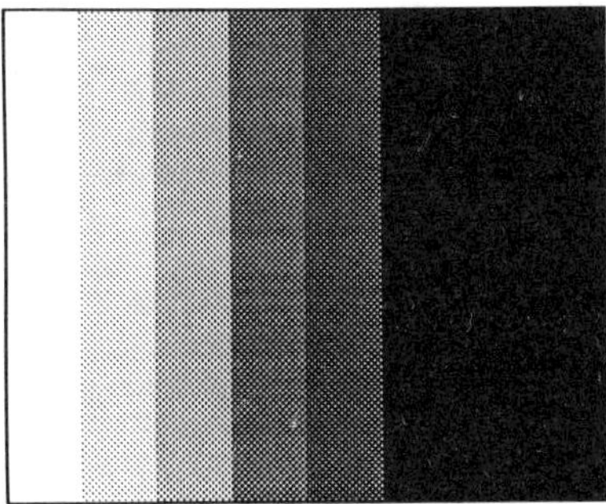

White - Black 0 Degrees

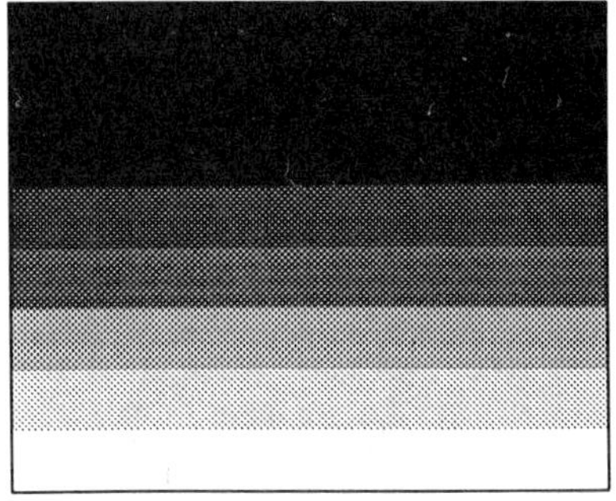

White - Black 90 Degrees

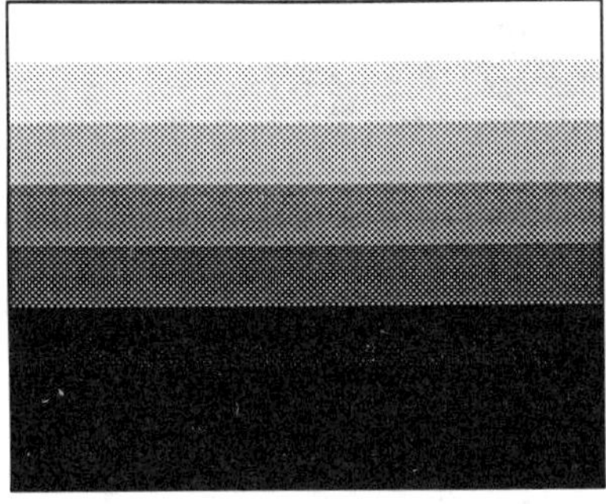

White - Black 270 Degrees

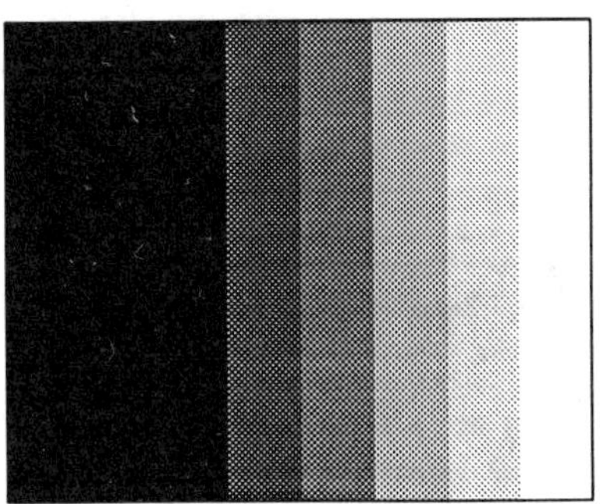

White - Black 180 Degrees

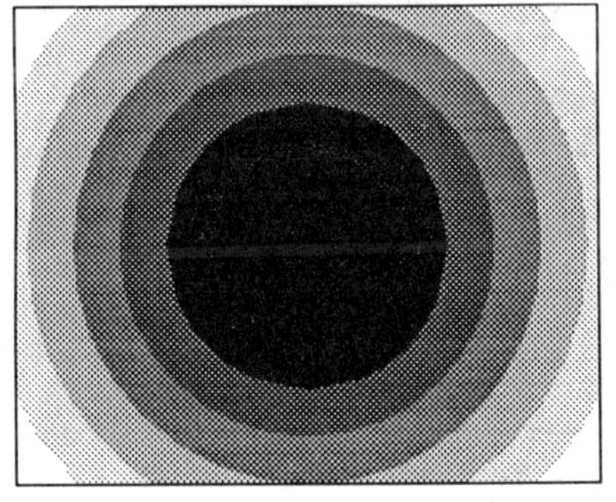

White - Black Radial

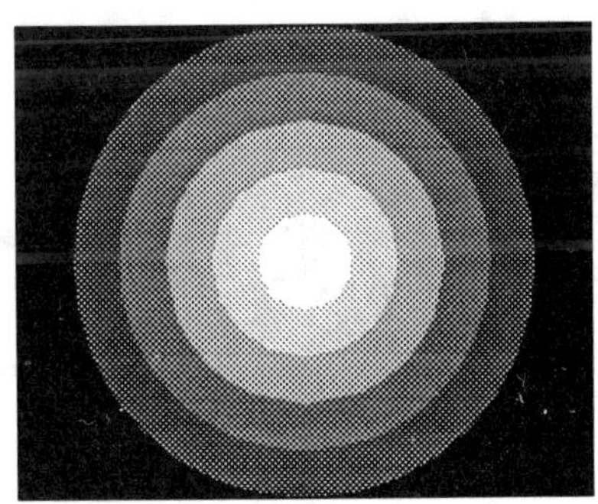

Black - White Radial

Printed with 8 Fountain Stripes on a PostScript compatible printer

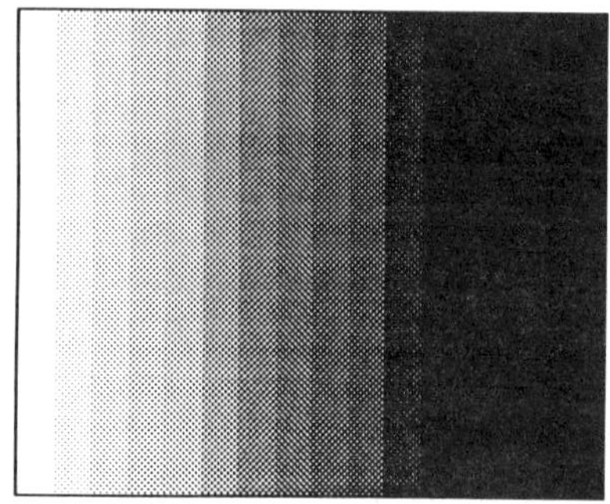

White - Black 0 Degrees

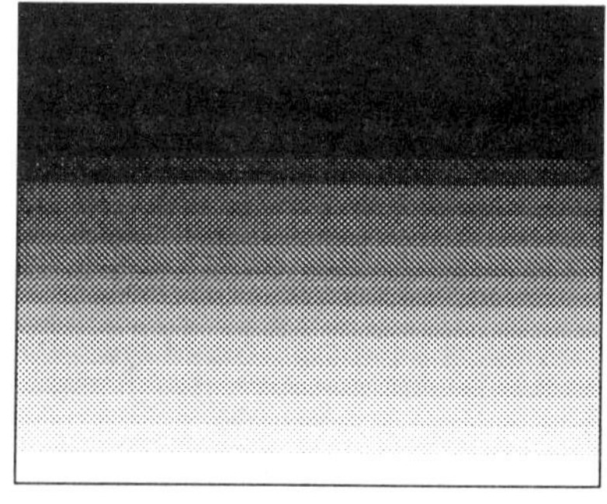

White - Black 90 Degrees

Printed with 16 Fountain Stripes on a PostScript compatible printer

White - Black 270 Degrees

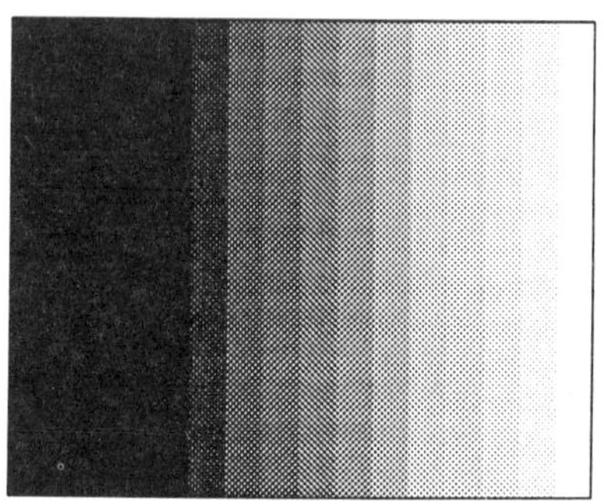

White - Black 180 Degrees

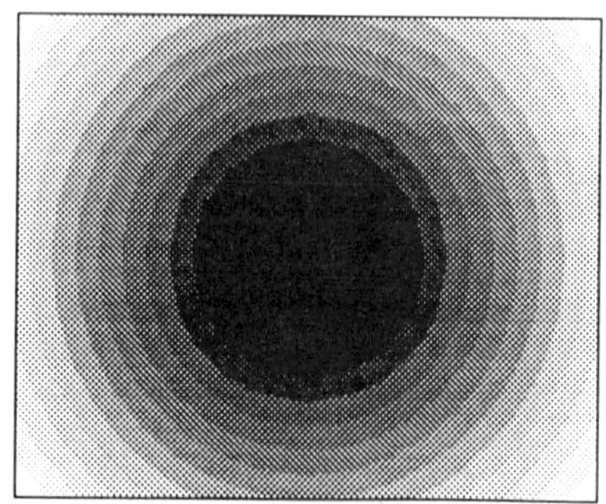

White - Black Radial

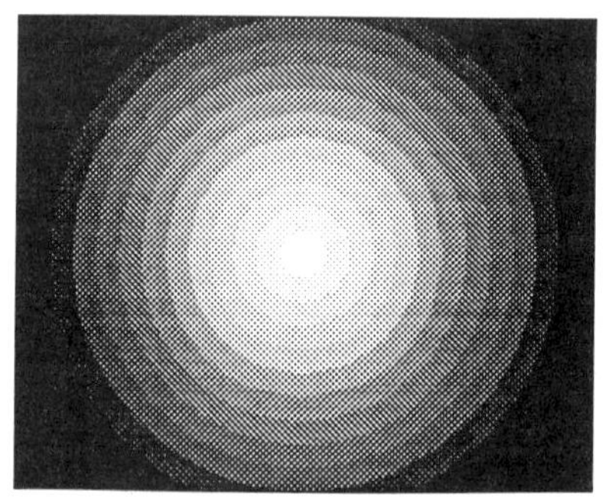

Black - White Radial

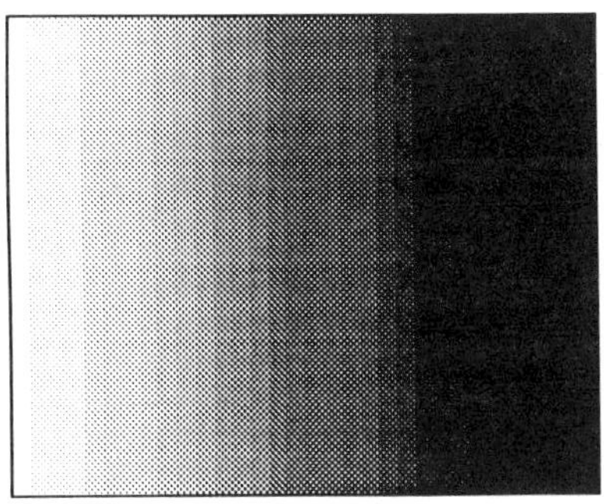

White - Black 0 Degrees

White - Black 90 Degrees

Printed with 32 Fountain Stripes on a PostScript compatible printer

White - Black 270 Degrees

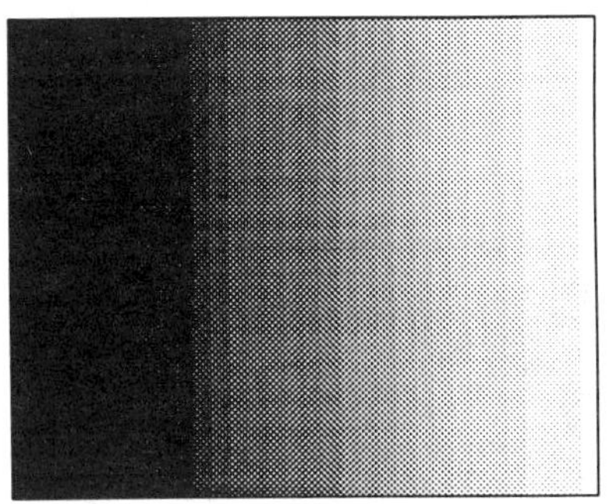

White - Black 180 Degrees

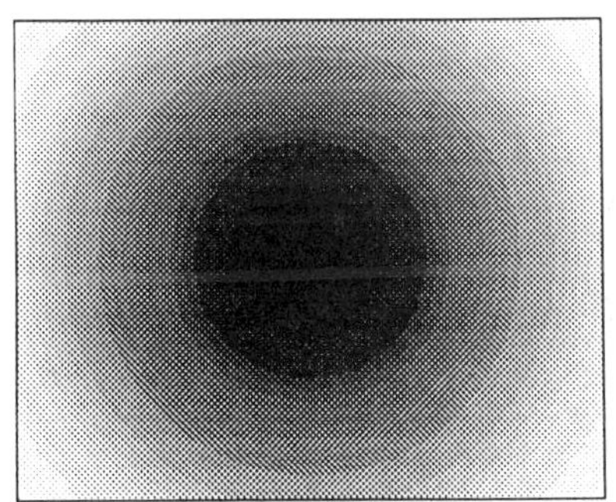

White - Black Radial

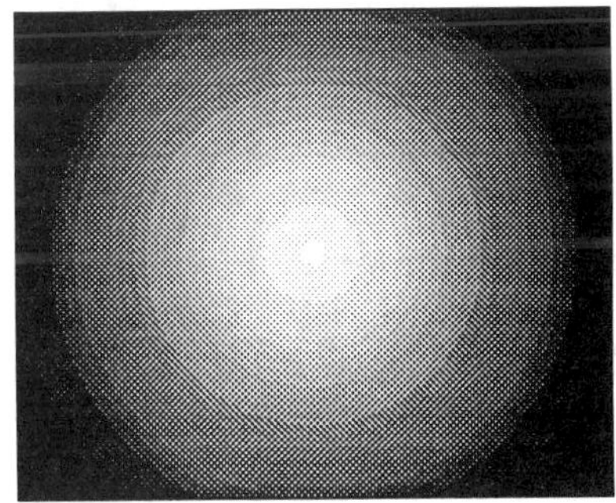

Black - White Radial

White - Black 0 Degrees

White - Black 90 Degrees

White - Black 270 Degrees

White - Black 180 Degrees

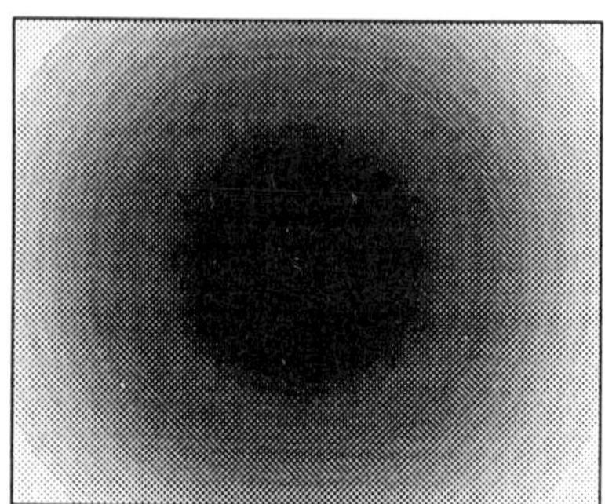

White - Black Radial

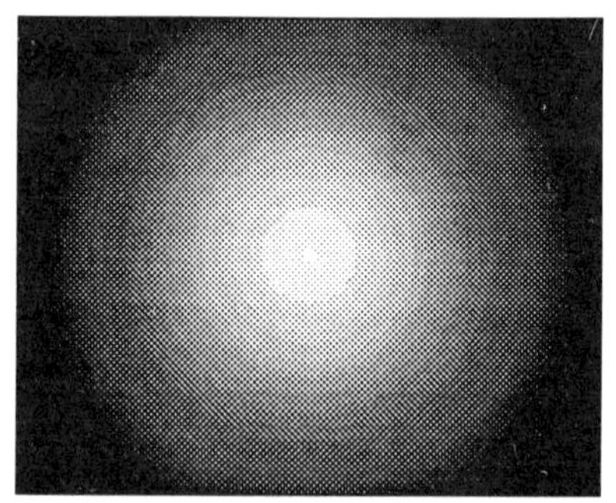

Black - White Radial

Printed with 64 Fountain Stripes on a PostScript compatible printer

White - Black 0 Degrees

White - Black 90 Degrees

White - Black 270 Degrees

White - Black 180 Degrees

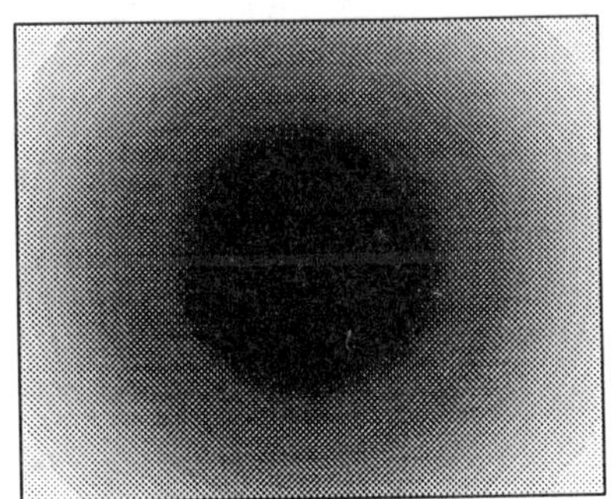

White - Black Radial

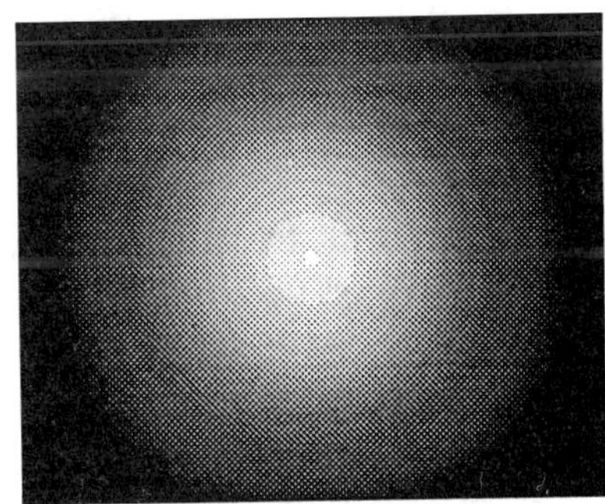

Black - White Radial

Printed with 128 Fountain Stripes on a PostScript compatible printer

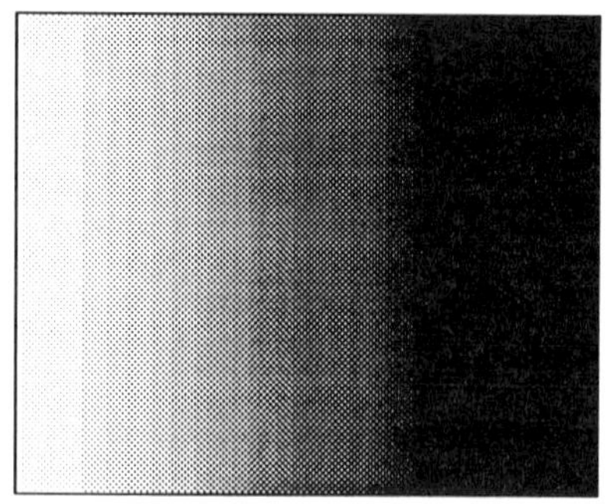

White - Black 0 Degrees

White - Black 90 Degrees

White - Black 270 Degrees

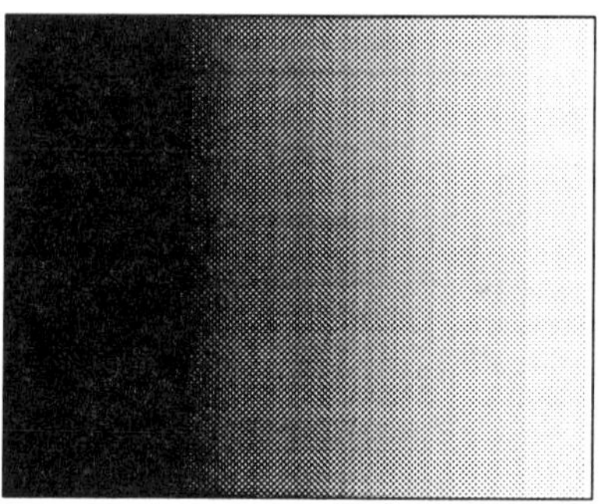

White - Black 180 Degrees

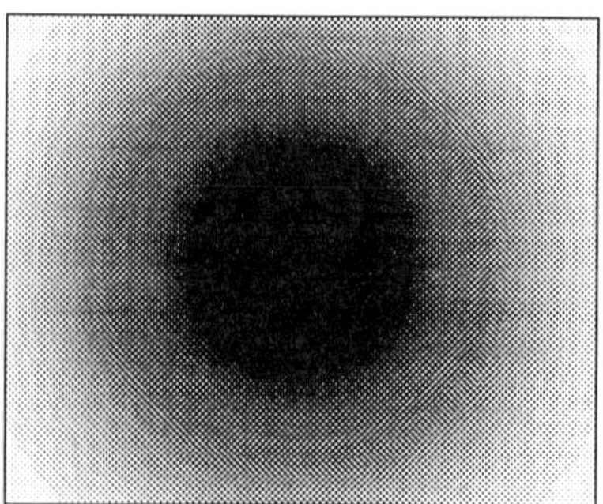

White - Black Radial

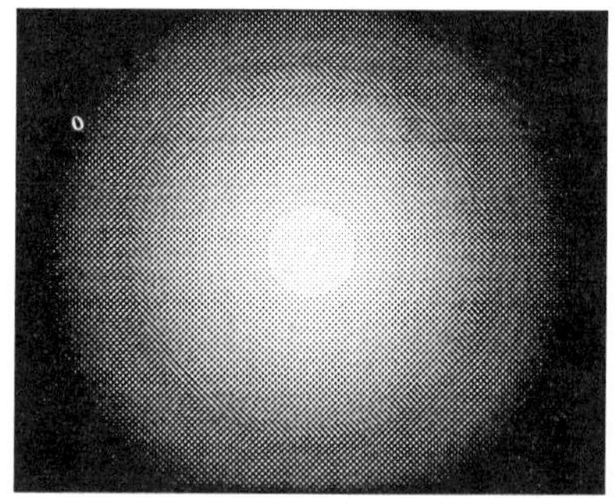

Black - White Radial

Printed with 250 Fountain Stripes on a PostScript compatible printer

# E37 - MERGE PRINTING

CorelDRAW has one other trick up its sleeve when it comes to printing. It will allow you to produce 'form graphics' in the same way that most word processors will allow form letters. In order to use this facility you have to create a file that contains the information you want to merge. The file must be in pure ASCII for the facility to work, like that produced by Windows Notepad, and it should have an extension of TXT.

So how does it work? Suppose you wanted to produce invitation to a party. The invites are to be sent to a number of different people and you want to personalise each one. There are two steps involved, one is the creation of the actual invite and the other is the creation of the merge file.

a. Start a new page. Orientate it as Landscape. Create the basic design using whatever you wish but where you want the names to appear type the word **NAME** instead. Whatever typeface, font, attributes, colours, etc. you assign to this word will be applied to the text in the ASCII file when the two are merged. Therefore you have to allow for the longest name you are going to replace even though you are only using a single word in the invite.

**13.04 Invite Stage 1**

b. Now open Windows Notepad and create the following file, though using your own names.

**1**
**\NAME**
**\Helen**
**\Lucy and Keith**
**\Monty and Melany**
**\Liz and Gordon**
**\Kevin and Frances**
**\Stephanie**

The first line, i.e. 1, contains tells CorelDRAW how many strings within the graphic will be replaced. In this case there is only 1, i.e. NAME, but you can have as many as you wish.

The second line is the name of the text string within the CorelDRAW graphic that will be replaced. You must include the backslashes with before and after this or it won't work.

Thereafter the remaining lines are the names you will use in the invite, again they must have a backslash both before and after them. You can place all the names on a single line if you wish.

c. Save the Notepad file as **INVITE.TXT** and then close the Notepad.

d. Back to CorelDRAW. Press **Alt-F M** to activate **Print Merge**. A dialogue box appears that allows you to find the INVITE.TXT file. Double click on this and then the normal Print dialogue box appears. Make whatever adjustments you want in this and then click on **OK**. The graphic will then be printed but in place of the word **NAME** you will get the actual names that are in the invite file. You will get as many copies as there are names in the list.

# 14 - PostScript

## Halftones

As has been mentioned continuously throughout this book, CorelDRAW is really geared up to use with a PostScript printer. The use of the page description language affects everything within CorelDRAW from lines and fills through to filling objects with specified PostScript patterns.

The most basic effect that CorelDRAW can produce with PostScript is that of the PostScript Halftone Screens. These can be applied to both the outline and the fill of an object - but only if you are using Spot colours, i.e. the ones based on the Pantone colours. In both the Outline and the Uniform Fill dialogue boxes there is a button labelled **PostScript**. Clicking on this will bring up the following dialogue box, provided you are using spot colours:

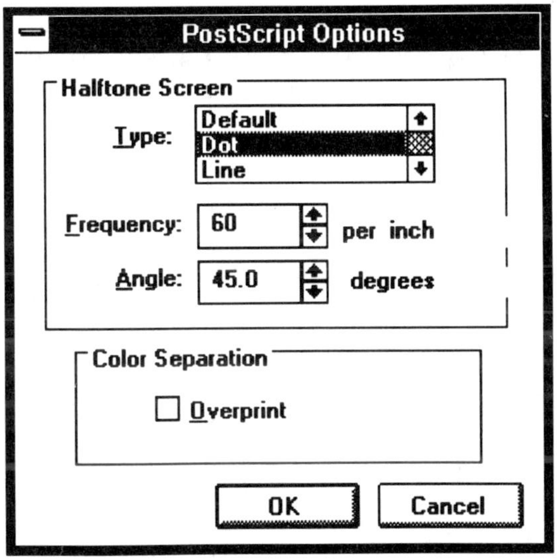

**14.01 Pantone Halftone Screen**

The list box, of which only three lines are displayed, contains the names of the eleven possible screens. The first of these is Default, i.e. that which is used by the printer itself. To select one of the others simply scroll through the list until you get to the one you want.

It is only when you select an alternative screen that the Frequency and Angle options become available: they are normally greyed out. Changing either of these can have a marked effect on your graphics but there is something that you must bear in mind. The frequency can be anything in the range 10 to 1000 and the angle can be anything from 0 to 360 degrees. A point to bear in mind is that if you are using 100% black then when you print the graphic, regardless of what frequency or angle you are using the object will be completely black. This is because the screen affects the colour within the object and black is black, grey on the other hand is a mixture of black and white and as the printing only affects the black areas you get a result.

On the following pages are examples of the halftone screens all using different frequencies. In each case the rectangle was first filled with Spot Black and then the tint was reduced to 30% before the screen frequency was changed. A word of warning: If you change from one colour type to another, e.g. Spot to process, then all frequency and angle changes will be lost. The examples are given only for the frequency range 10 to 60 because thereafter there is no real discernible difference on most standard PostScript laser printers.

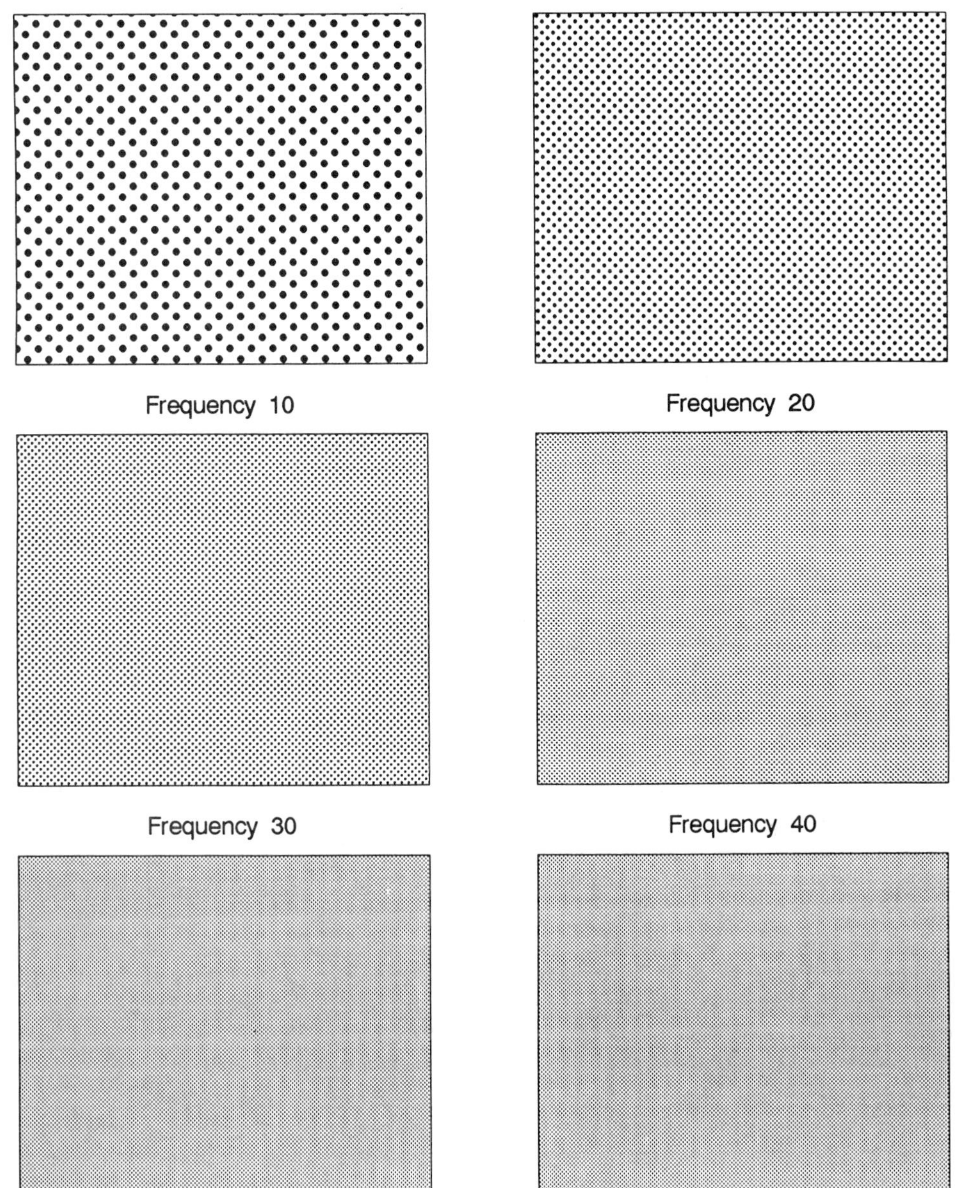
Halftone Screen : Dot
Frequency 10
Frequency 20
Frequency 30
Frequency 40
Frequency 50
Frequency 60

Halftone Screen : Line

Frequency 10

Frequency 20

Frequency 30

Frequency 40

Frequency 50

Frequency 60

Halftone Screen : Diamond

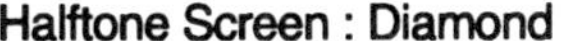

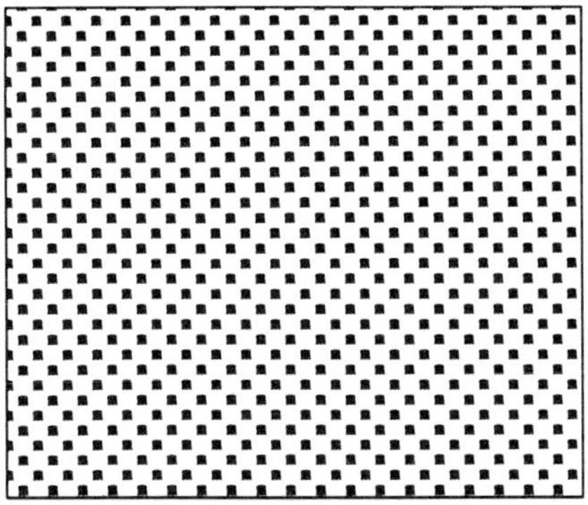

Frequency 10

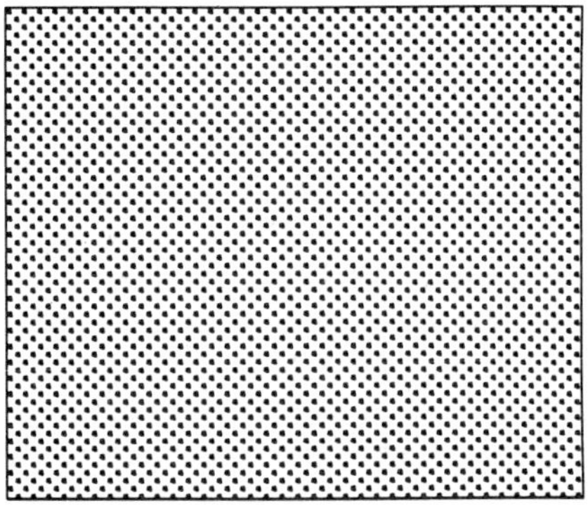

Frequency 20

Frequency 30

Frequency 40

Frequency 50

Frequency 60

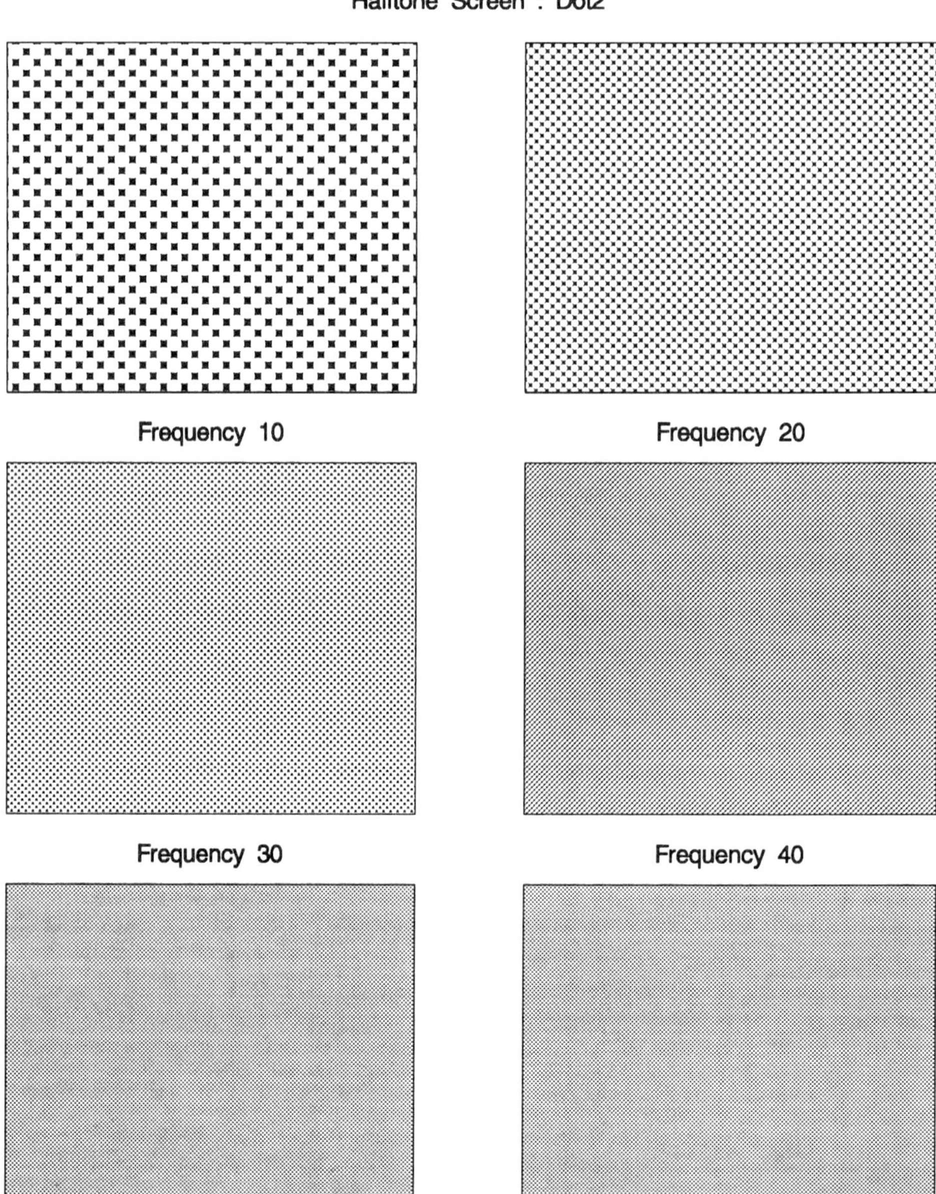
Halftone Screen : Dot2
Frequency 10
Frequency 20
Frequency 30
Frequency 40
Frequency 50
Frequency 60

Halftone Screen : Grid

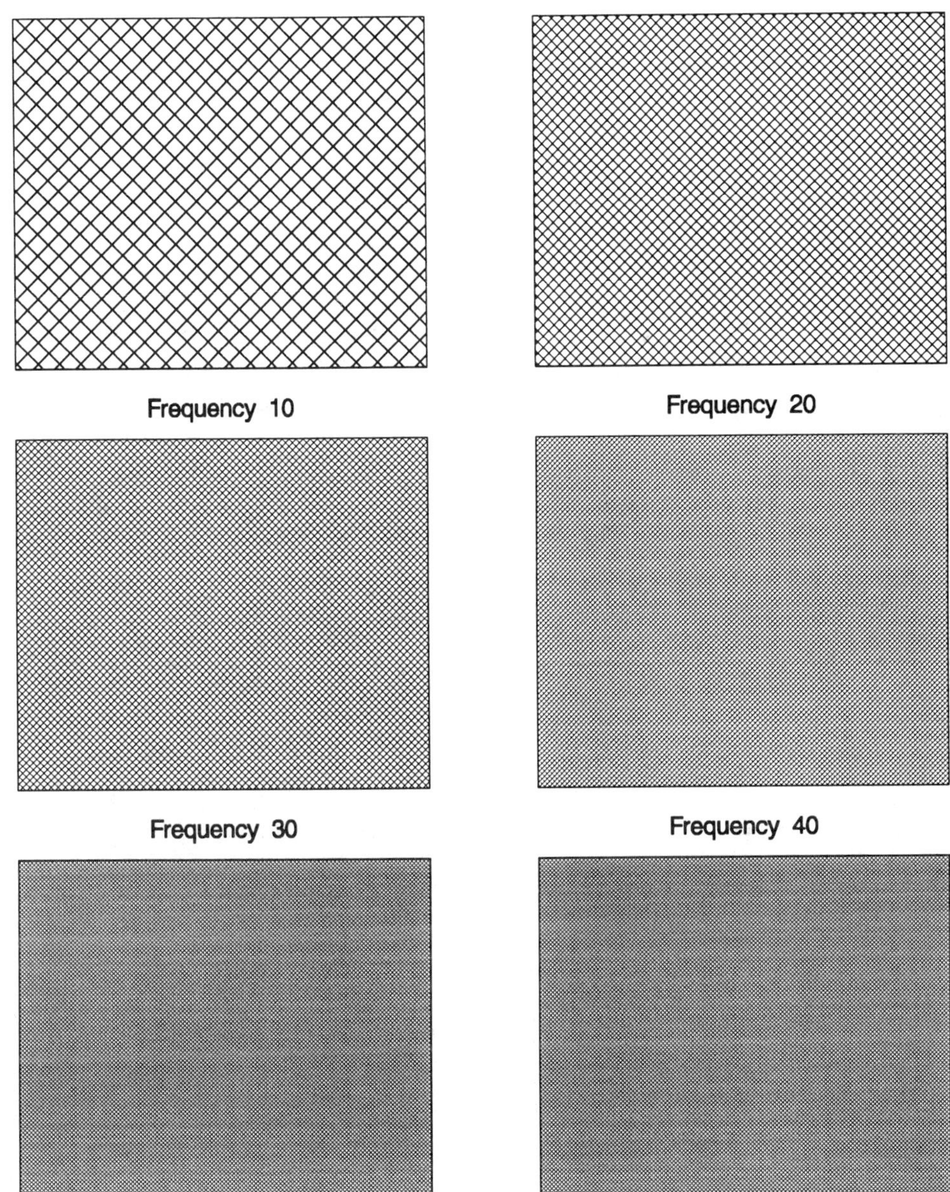


Frequency 50

Frequency 60

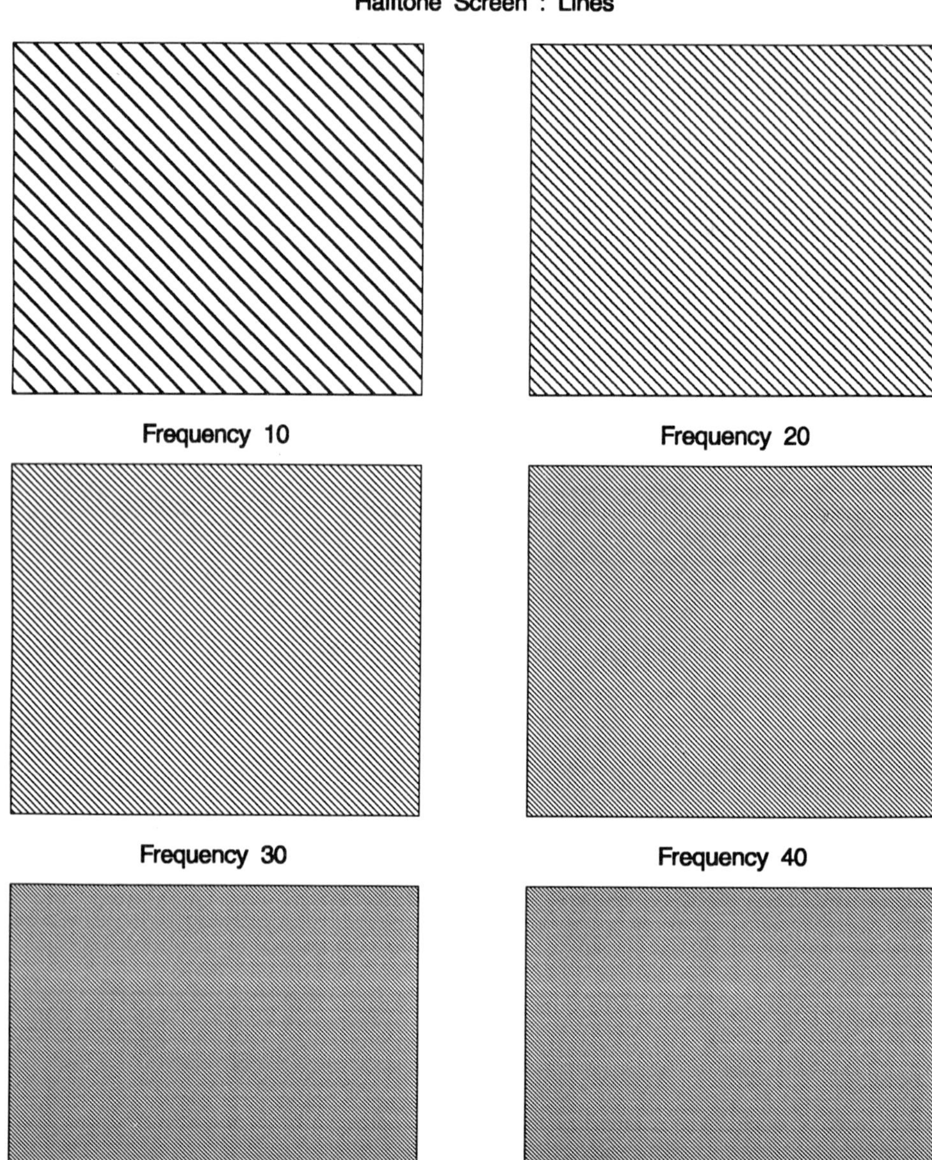
Halftone Screen : Lines
Frequency 10
Frequency 20
Frequency 30
Frequency 40
Frequency 50
Frequency 60

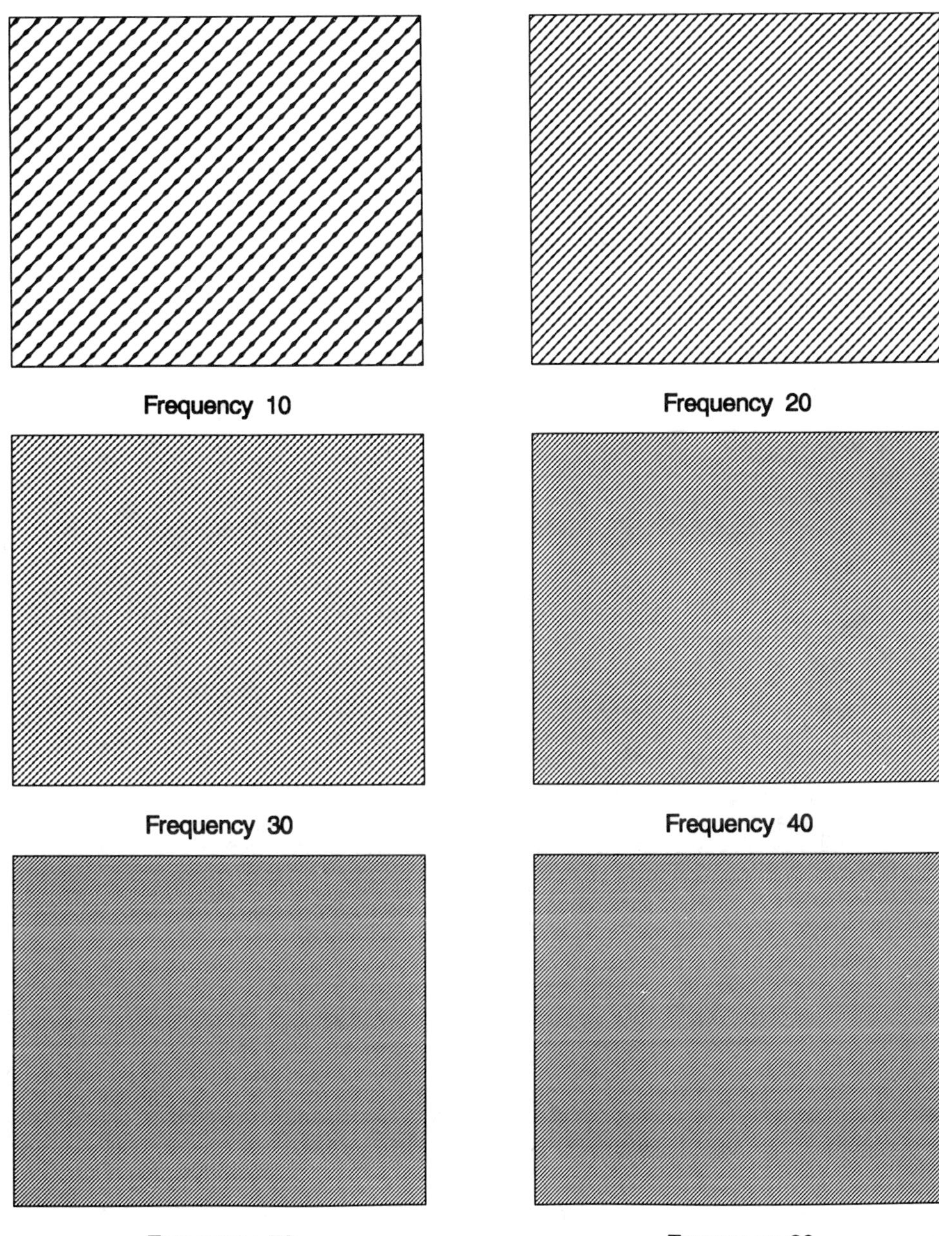
Halftone Screen : Microwaves
Frequency 10
Frequency 20
Frequency 30
Frequency 40
Frequency 50
Frequency 60

Halftone Screen : Outer Circle Black

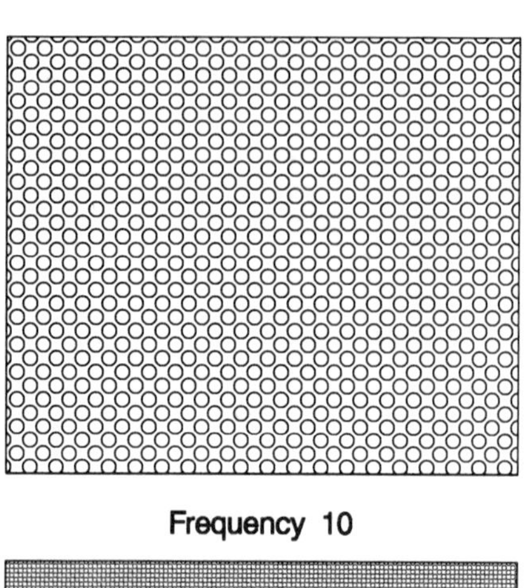

Frequency 10

Frequency 20

Frequency 30

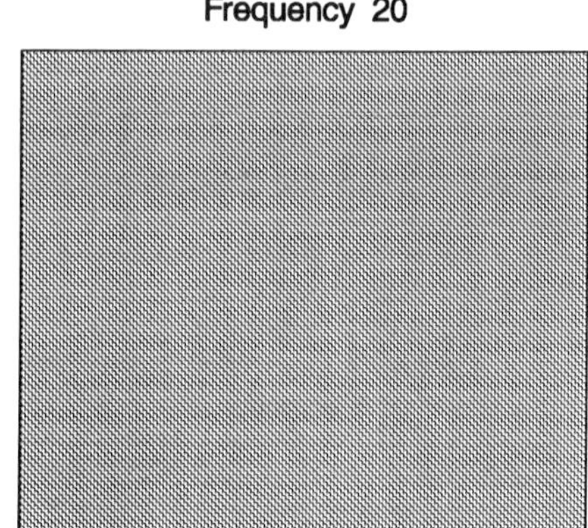

Frequency 40

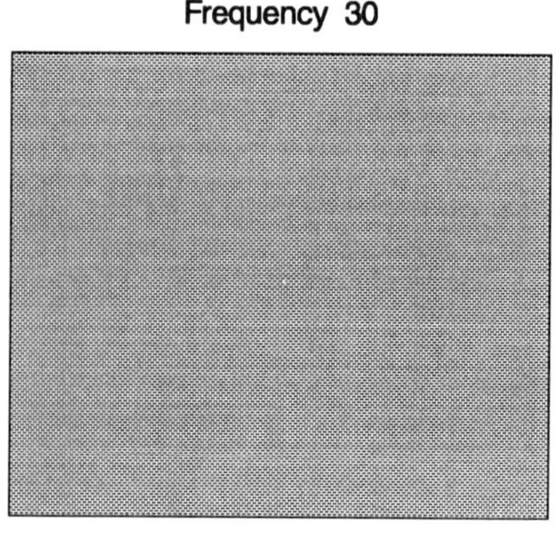

Frequency 50

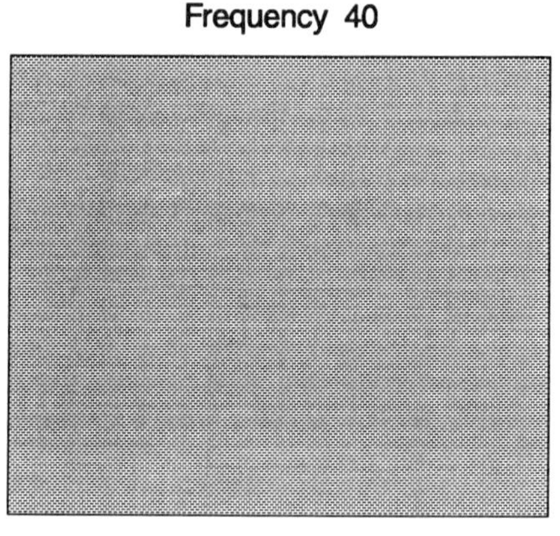

Frequency 60

Halftone Screen : Outer Circle White

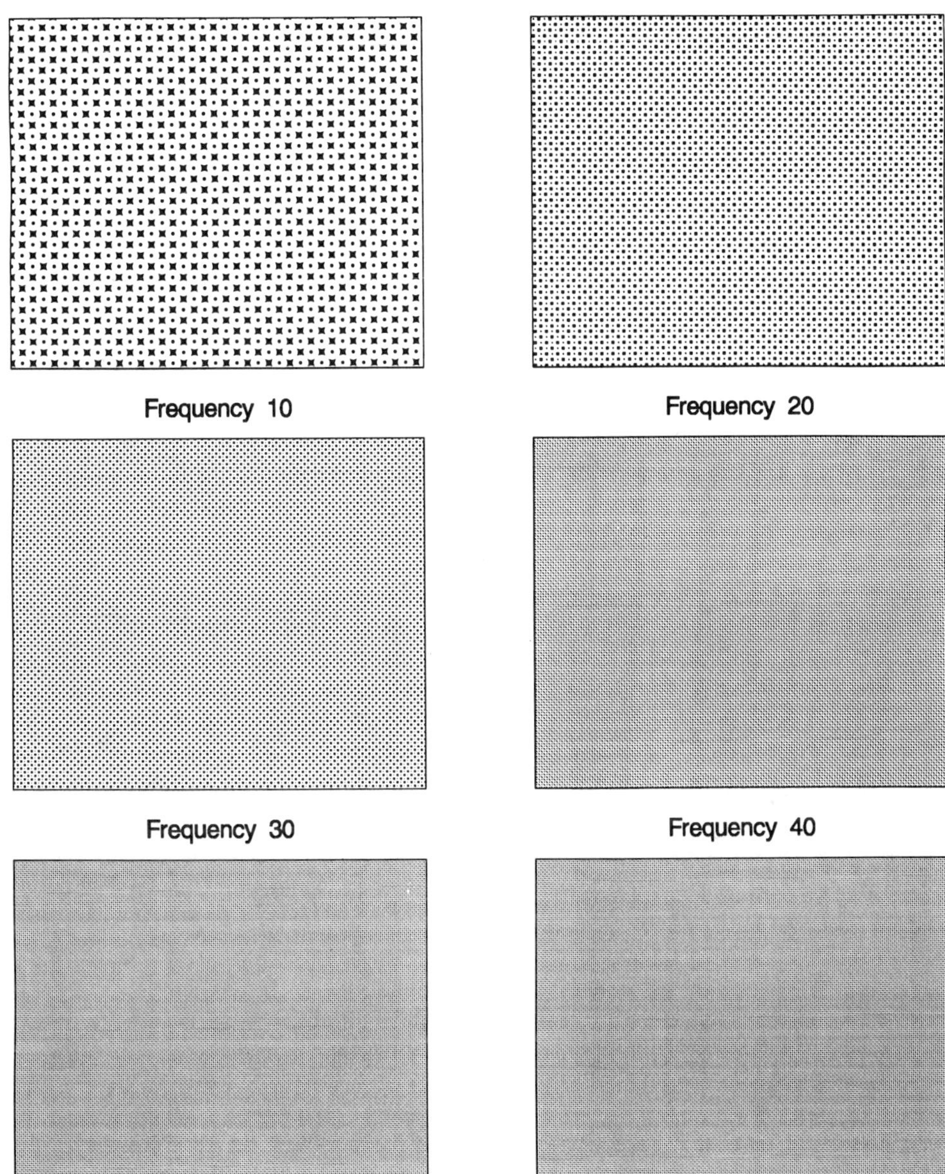

Frequency 10

Frequency 20

Frequency 30

Frequency 40

Frequency 50

Frequency 60

Halftone Screen : Star

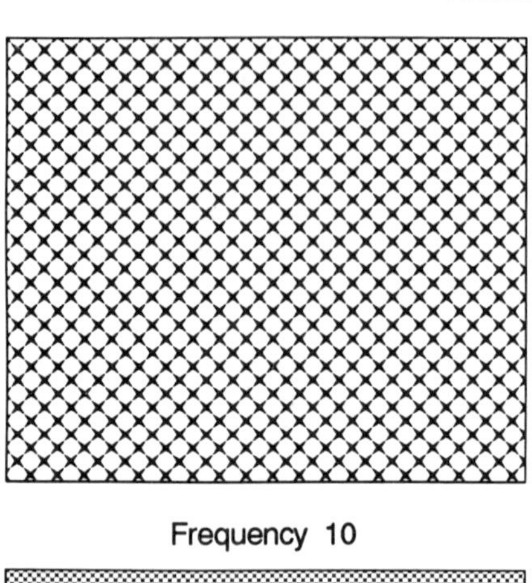

Frequency 10

Frequency 20

Frequency 30

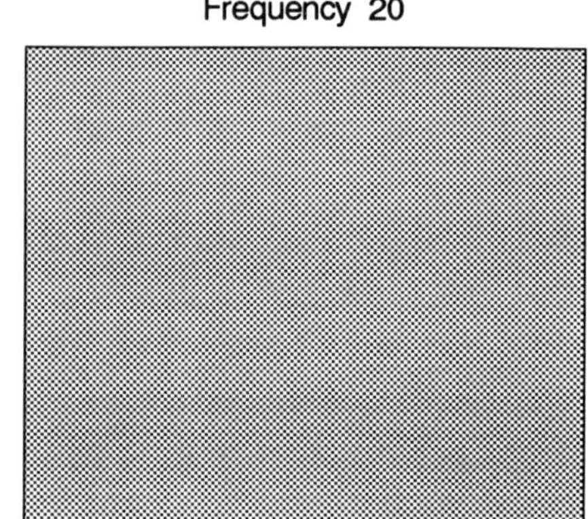

Frequency 40

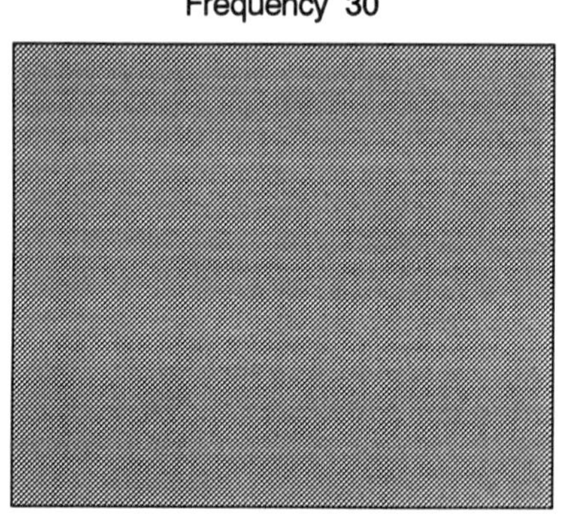

Frequency 50

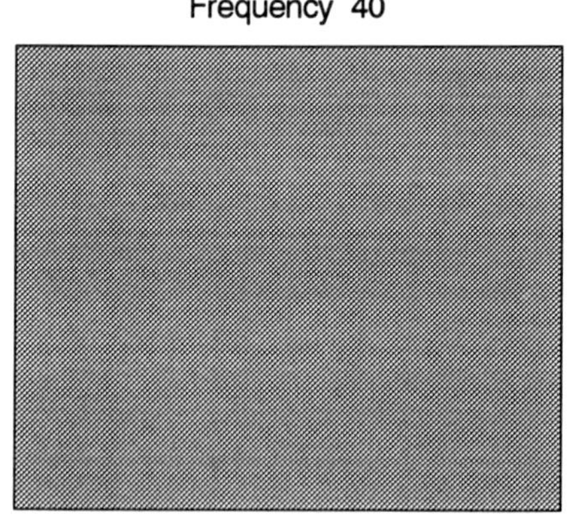

Frequency 60

# POSTSCRIPT FILLS

There is one other major thing that CorelDRAW will allow you to do with PostScript and that is to use the page description language and its program to create special fills. Fortunately the programmers at Corel Systems have already created a number of these for you and so you don't have to go out and learn PostScript before you can use them.

The PostScript Fills are found in the fill menu as the final button on the top row. When you click on the button the following dialogue box appears:

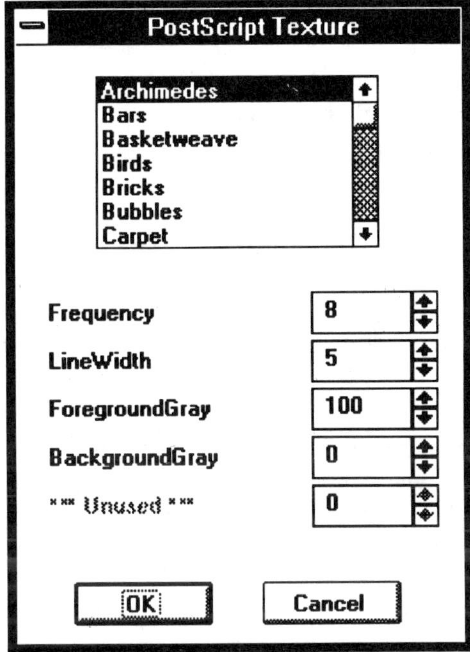


**14.02 PostScript Fill dialogue box**

The main part of the dialogue box is the list box which contains the names of the forty three patterns that are pre-programmed. The rest of the dialogue box will vary from fill type to fill type. For example, under Bars the categories are:

**Width**
**Spacing**
**Maximum Gray**
**Minimum Gray**

while under Cracks they become:

**Number**
**MaxLength**
**MinLength**
**StepLength**
**LineWidth**

I don't propose at this stage to examine each one of these in turn, I'll leave it to you to play with them and see what different effects you can produce. When you use a PostScript fill in an object, it will not be shown on the screen. Instead the object will be shown on the Preview screen as containing loads of PS's. You can only see the result when you print the file.

On the following pages are all the available fill patterns in their standard formats, i.e. without changing any of the defaults, because this book would be ten times as large as it is if I included all the possible changes. Even making a single change, e.g. changing the line width, can have a marked effect on the printed results.

I have purposely not changed the images in any way. The boxes are all the same size and they have had the different fills applied to them. In some boxes you will notice that there is a border between the fill and outline of box itself. That's the way they print on my printer. The odd thing is that the border only appears at certain sizes, make the box smaller or larger and they vanish.

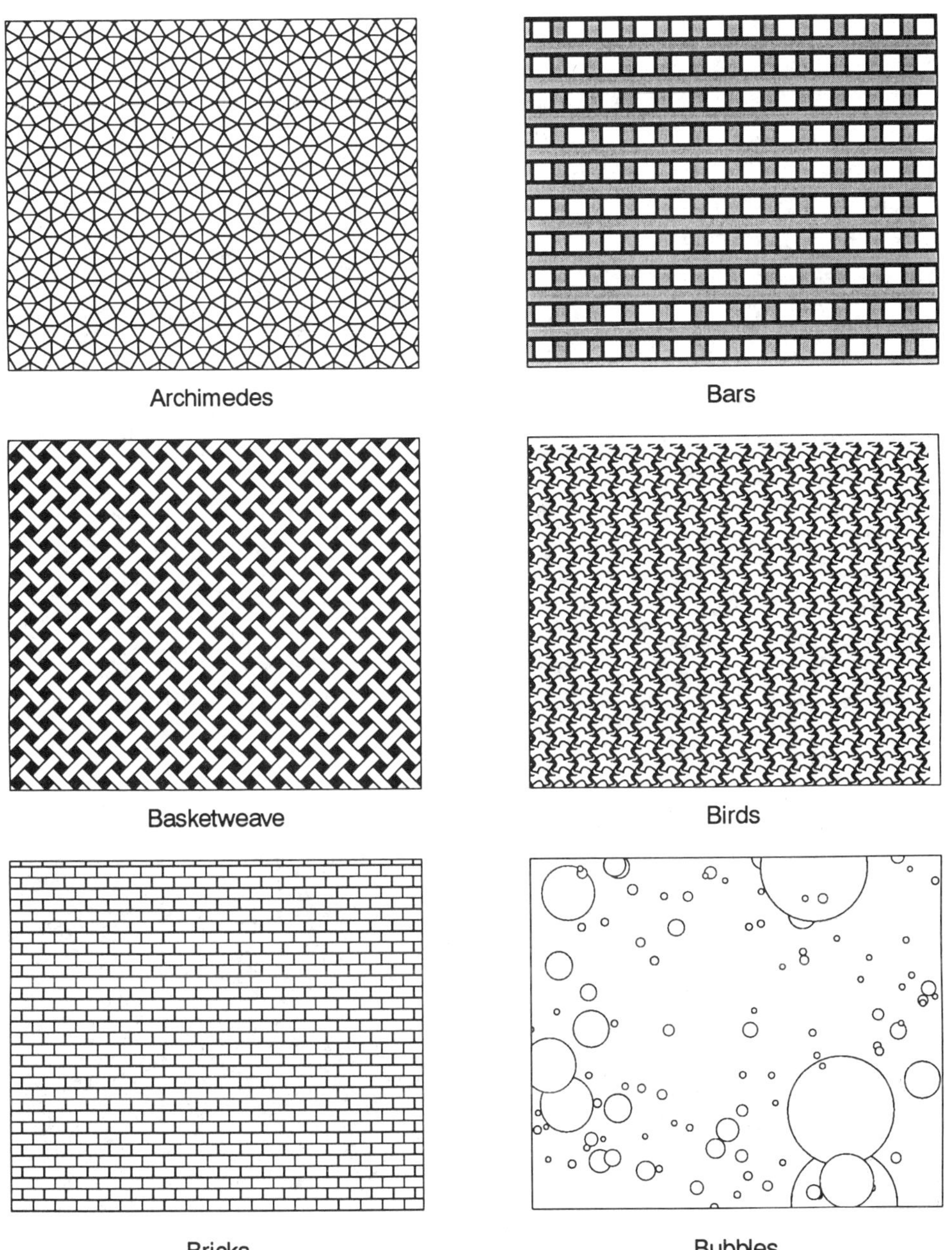

Archimedes

Bars

Basketweave

Birds

Bricks

Bubbles

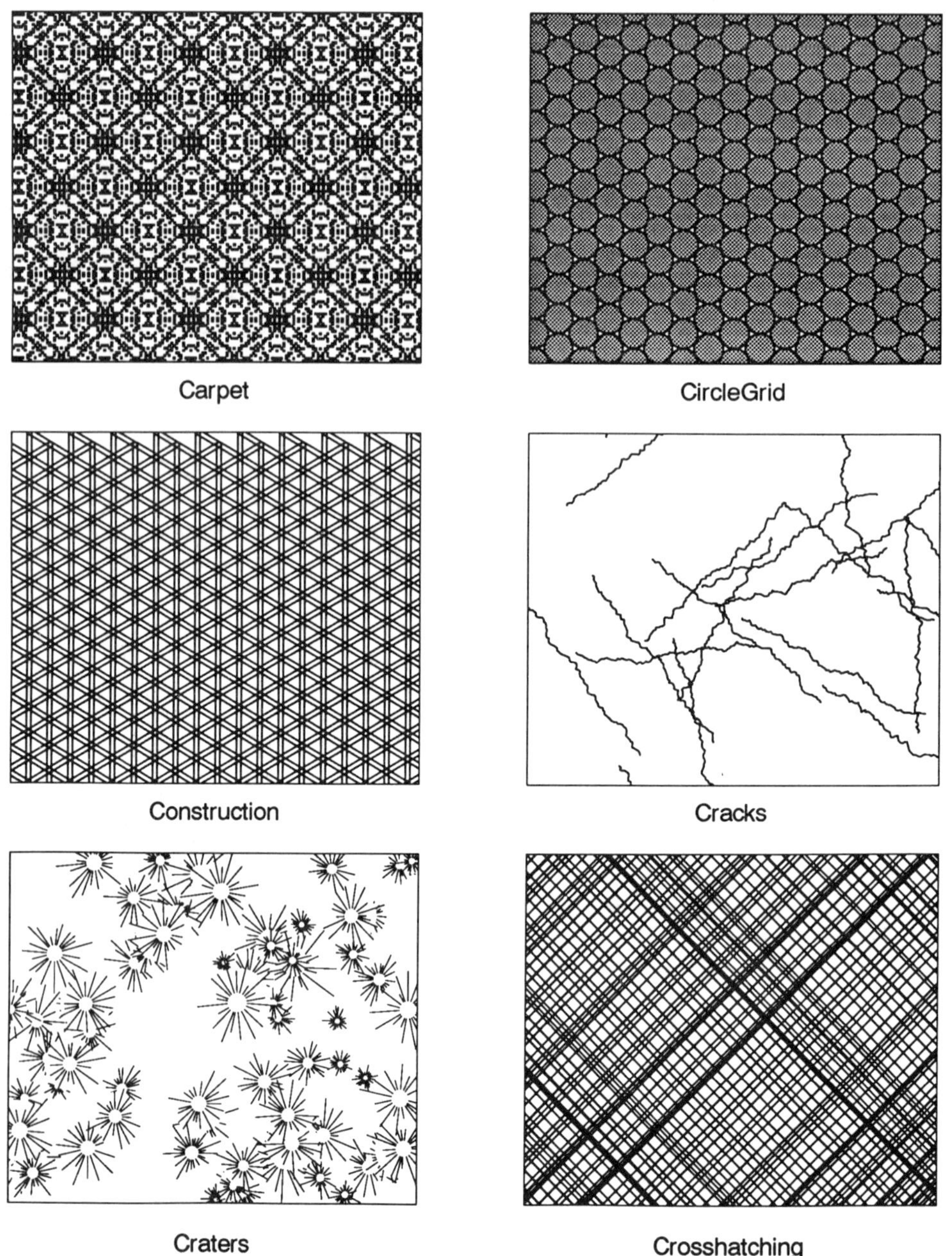

Carpet

CircleGrid

Construction

Cracks

Craters

Crosshatching

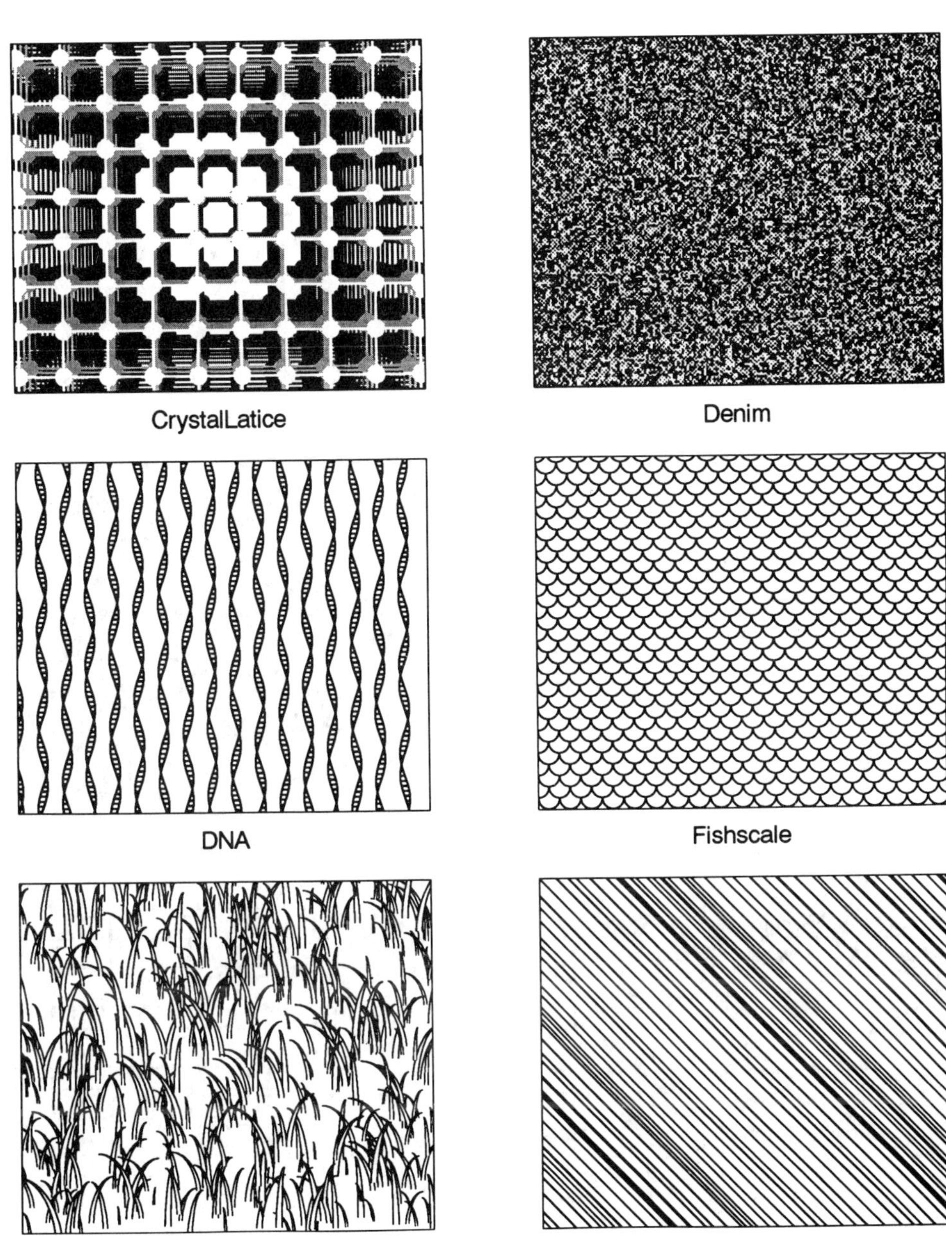

CrystalLatice

Denim

DNA

Fishscale

Grass

Hatching

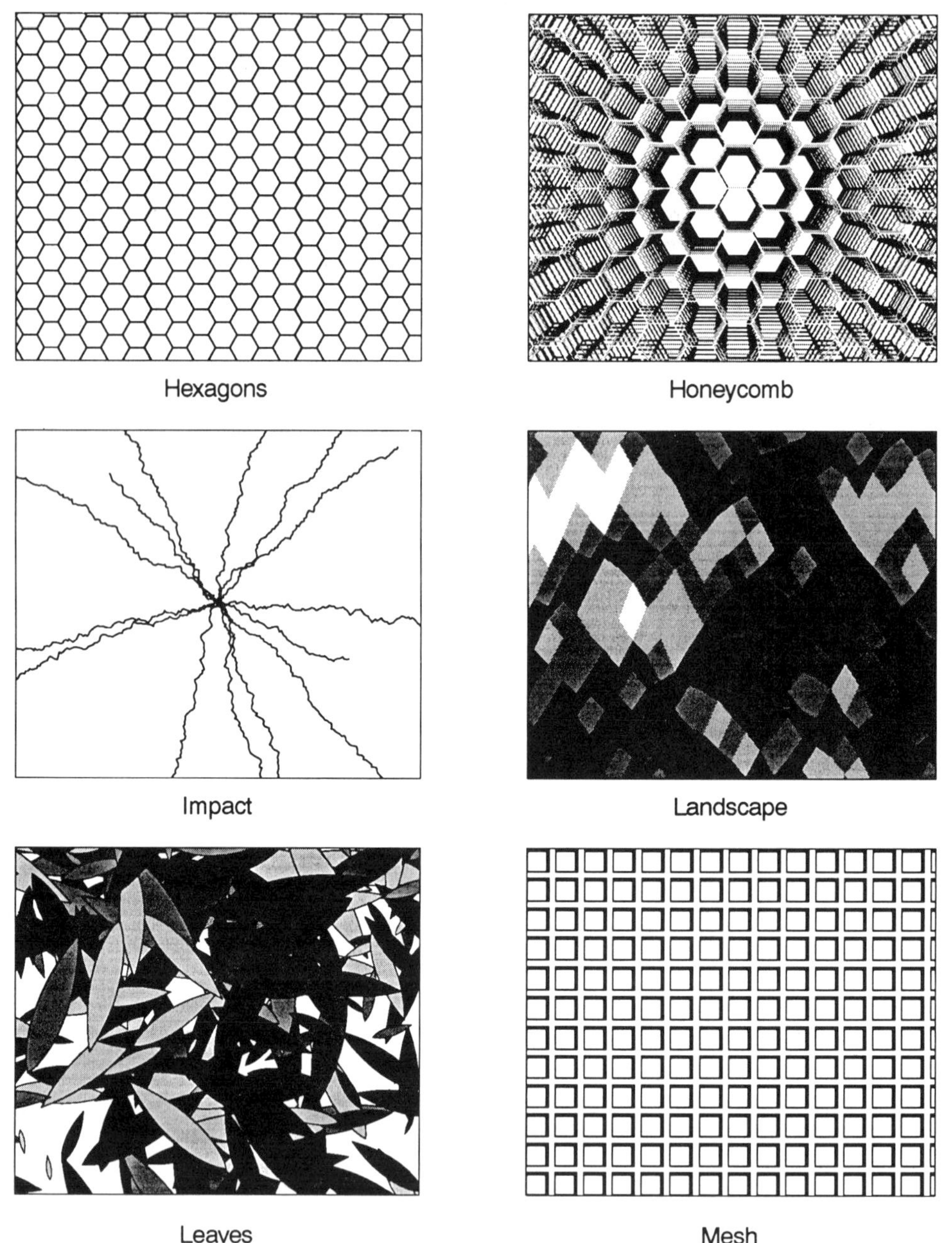

Hexagons

Honeycomb

Impact

Landscape

Leaves

Mesh

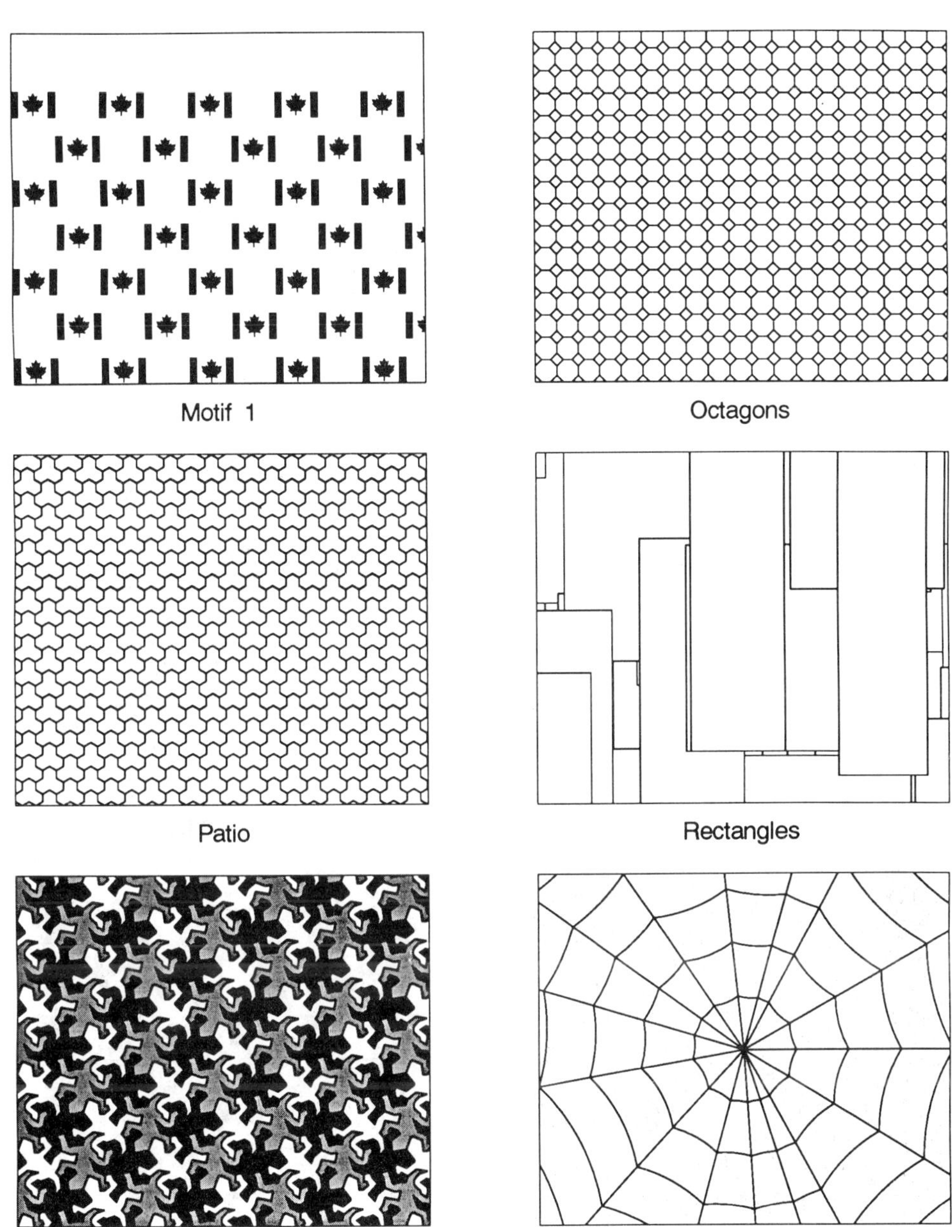

Motif 1

Octagons

Patio

Rectangles

Reptiles

SpiderWeb

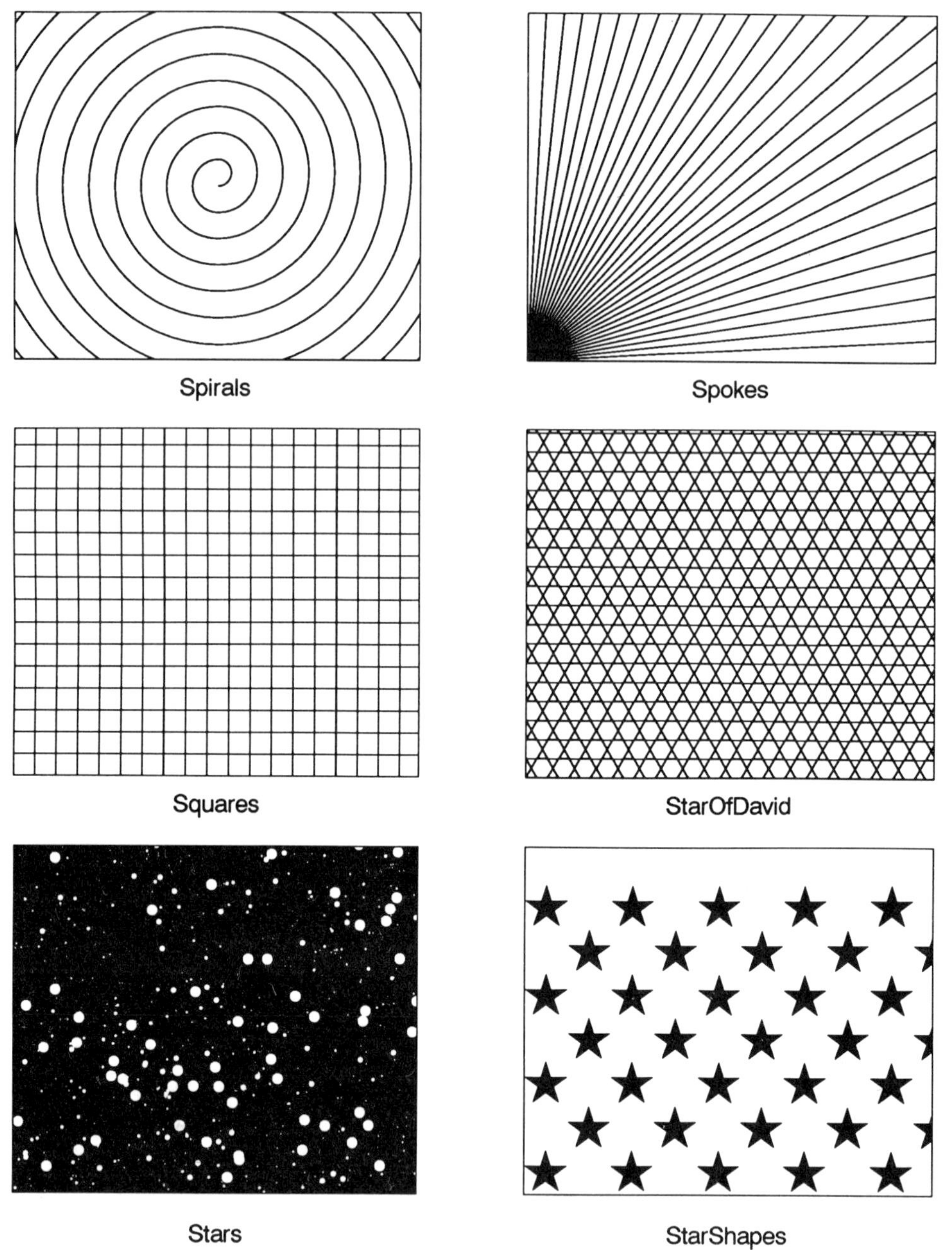

Spirals

Spokes

Squares

StarOfDavid

Stars

StarShapes

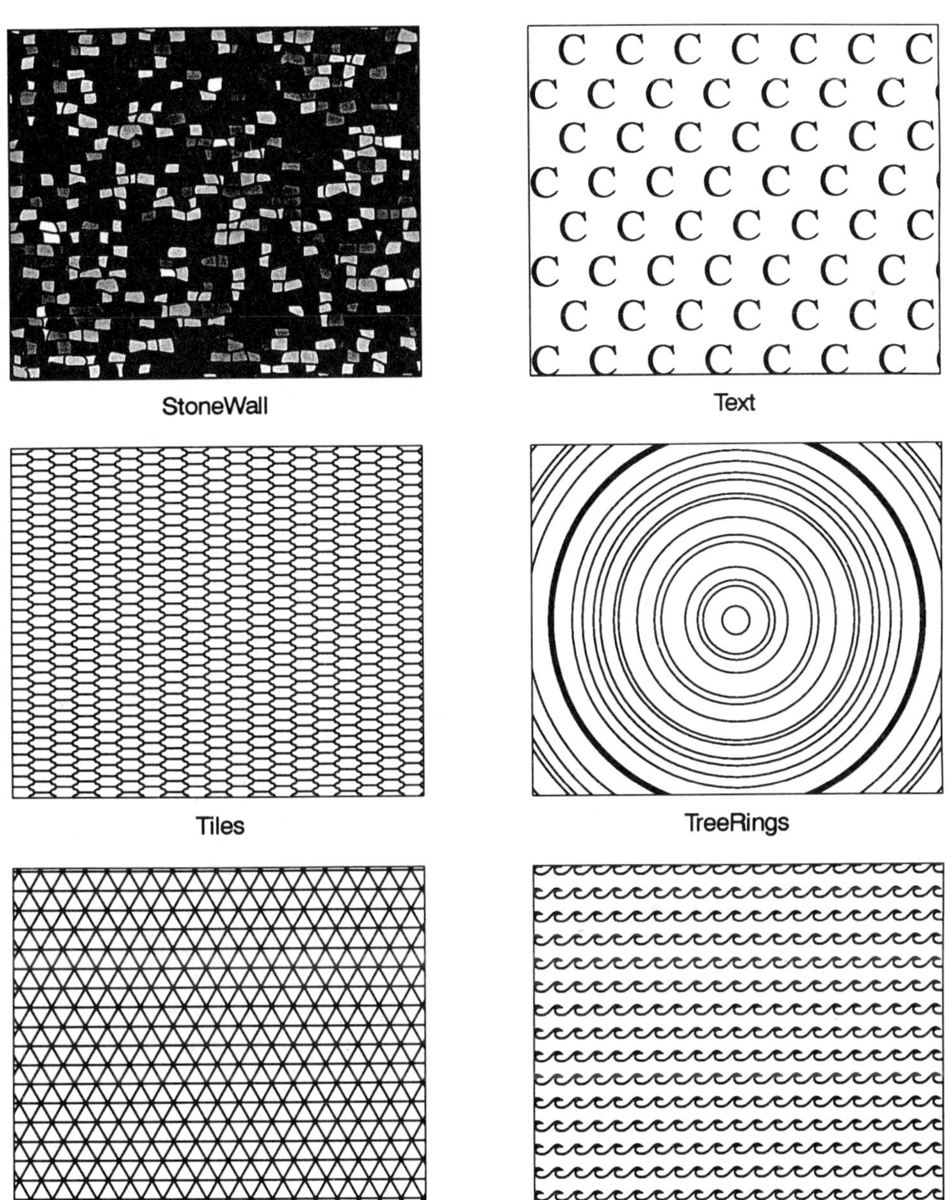

StoneWall

Text

Tiles

TreeRings

Triangle

Waves

# 15 - OLE

Object Linking and Embedding is a new feature in Windows 3.1. What it does is allow you to exchange information from one file to another, you can even have multiple files in this way. For example, you may have a sound file, a bitmapped image and a standard vector all in CorelDRAW. By using OLE you can edit or change either the sound or the bitmap directly within CorelDRAW without having to go backwards and forwards to the program that originally created them. Equally, if you make any changes to sound or bitmap outside CorelDRAW then those elements with CorelDRAW can be automatically updated without you having to do anything. Think of OLE as an automatic way of sharing and manipulating data between different programs.

At the time of writing there are very few programs that can make full use of the OLE capabilities. CorelDRAW and its associated programs are one of the first third party programs packages to do so. There are some Microsoft programs, e.g. Word for Windows and Excel, which are OLE compatible but those from third party companies are still very rare. The Corel Graphics Package is one of the first suite of programs to be fully OLE compliant.

In Windows 3.0 if you wanted to exchange information between programs you could either use the Clipboard, with Copy and Paste, or simply import the file you wanted. That was fine, after all it got the data into the application, but if you then needed to change the data for any reason you had to change it in the application that produced it and then cut, paste or import it into every other application that used it all over again. If you were only doing this occasionally then it didn't matter too much, it lost you some time but not a great deal. However, if you wanted or needed to change the data repeatedly then it became a chore and the amount of lost time escalated.

OLE changes all that. You have one set of data. You place this into as many other applications as necessary. Thereafter from any of these applications and/or the originating program you can change the data. The data in all the other applications is then updated automatically - or it can be. In other words OLE provides dynamic linking of data.

There are two ways that you can use OLE. The first is **Object Linking**. With linking you don't actually insert or copy the data as such, instead you create a dynamic link to it and the program that created it. Then at any time you can edit the data and the linkages automatically ensure that data is updated in all the files that have dynamic links to that data. You can have as many links to as many programs as you need.

For example, you might want to use the Object Linking using a graphic, e.g. a red balloon, in CorelDRAW, CorelSHOW, CorelCHART and Winword. The same image is used in each case. If you then change the colour of the balloon to yellow, the image in each of the programs that have a link to that image would automatically change, regardless of which application you change the balloon in.

The second way of using OLE is **Object Embedding**. This is similar to using the Cut and Paste options of the Clipboard but with one vital difference. The pasted data can be edited, using the program that originated it, from within the program that has the data embedded in it. This does eat into your resources so don't try doing it on a machine with less than, say, 4 Mb of RAM. Embedding actually makes a copy of the data within the program that it is pasted into, whereas Linking just makes a dynamic link. Once the data is copied there is no link to the original. Using our example again, if you embed the balloon in one of the programs and then change it in that program, the balloon is not changed in any of the others, it is only changed in the one program.

Before we go any further you need to know some terminology that is specific to OLE.

A **Client** program is one that can accept embedded or Linked files, the other type is a **Server**. CorelDRAW for example can be both a client and a server.

An **Object** is a piece of data. It can be a graphic, a document, a sound, what-have-you. It must be created in a program that has OLE capability. You can check which programs on your system have this by looking for a section called [Embedding]. This lists the programs that are OLE compliant, e.g.

```
[embedding]
SoundRec=Sound,Sound,SoundRec.exe,picture
Package=Package,Package,packager.exe,picture
PBrush=Paintbrush Picture,Paintbrush Picture,pbrush.exe,picture
```

Each line of the list gives the short program name, the name of the object, the title of the object, the actual program name (and if necessary the full path to it), and finally the type of data. It is usually called Picture - I've certainly never seen it called anything else.

A **Server** program is one that can produce data which can be linked or embedded in other programs, called Clients.

The **Source Document** is the document in which the object originates.

The **Destination Document** is the document or file to which a source document is being embedded or linked.

Within the Corel Graphics Package the programs react with OLE as follows:

CorelDRAW can be both a Client and a Server. In other words it can create images for linking or embedding or it can accept them from other sources.

CorelCHART is a Server which means it can produce files for linking or embedding but not accept them.

CorelPHOTO-PAINT does not have any OLE capabilities.

CorelSHOW is a Client program, in other words it accepts data from other OLE programs but it cannot create them.

CorelTRACE does not have any OLE capabilities.

Mosaic does not have any OLE capabilities.

# E38 - LINKING FILES

You cannot paste in linked data directly into CorelDRAW from a source application. Instead you have to open the source program, copy the data and then do it from there.

a. One of the programs on your hard disk should be Windows Paintbrush. This can act as a server program so we'll use that. Run Paintbrush and load CHESS.BMP into it. Select any part of that image and then copy it to the Windows Clipboard. Then reduce Paintbrush to an icon.

b. Now run CorelDRAW. From the **Edit menu** click on **Paste Special**. That will bring up a dialogue box.

**15.01 Paste Special dialogue box**

c. Click on **Bitmap** and then on **Paste**. The image is pasted into CorelDRAW. It is pasted just as if you had used the ordinary paste or import. Any changes you make to the original image will have no effect.

d. Delete the image. Go back to Paintbrush. Copy a part of the image to the Clipboard again. Back at CorelDRAW open the **Edit menu** and click on **Paste Special**. This time click on **Paste Link** in the dialogue box. The selected part of the image is pasted in.

e. Go back to Paintbrush. Draw a large filled circle anywhere within the area that you know the selected image came from. Back to CorelDRAW. The pasted image now contains the circle you just drew.

f. Double click on the image in CorelDRAW and Paintbrush instantly comes up with the image in it. That's the dynamic link in operation. Make a change, reduce Paintbrush to an icon and the change is already in CorelDRAW.

g. You can change the way the link operates if you wish. Open the **Edit Menu** and click on **Links**. (Notice that the preceding command now specifies where the link has come from.) A dialogue box appears.

**15.02 Pasted link object**

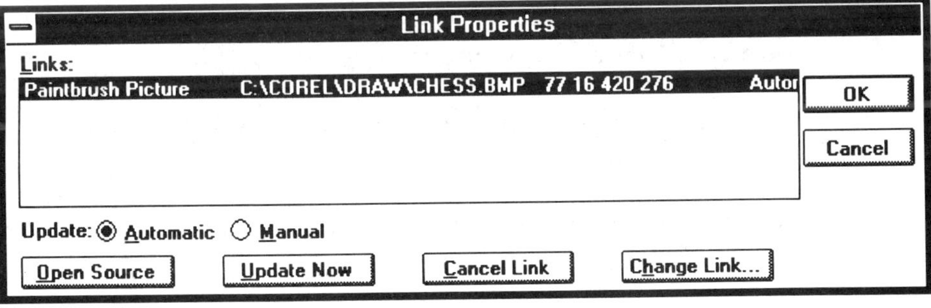


**15.03 Links dialogue box**

The dialogue box gives the information about all the links in the current CorelDRAW image, in this case there is only one. It tells you what the linked file is, a Paintbrush Picture, where the original image is stored, some numbers about the image (they are used internally and don't mean anything as such to you) and the type of link involved. It actually says Automatic but you can't see it all in this case.

The Update option is set to **Automatic** and if you change this the data line in the main area of the dialogue box changes. If you change the option to Manual then the changes you make in the original picture will not be updated in CorelDRAW for you.

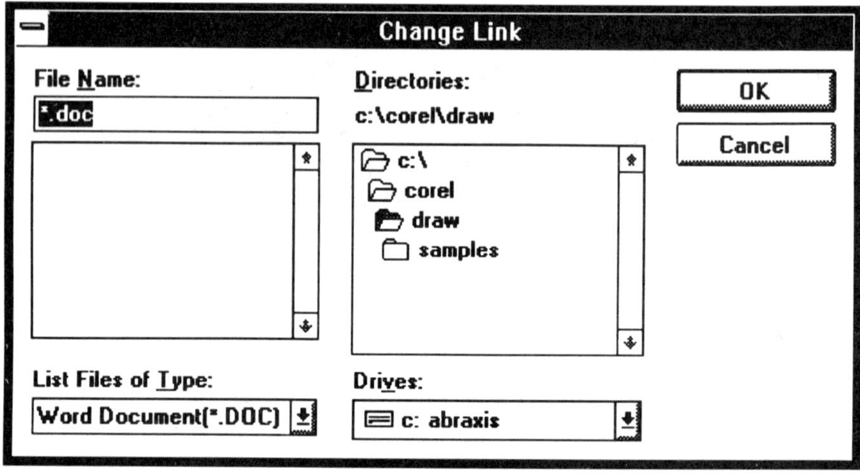


**15.04 Change Links dialogue box**

**Open Source** causes the originating program, in this case Paintbrush, to run with the source document loaded in it.

**Update Now** only applies when you have Manual links. It allows you to control when the pasted image is changed.

**Cancel Link** breaks the linkage completely so that the image becomes independent of the originating file.

**Change Link** causes another dialogue box to appear. Within this you can change the link to any other server application. You can even change the image itself using this option.

I suggest that you play with the linking options until you are familiar with the way they work. Try running Paintbrush, making changes to the image you have linked and then seeing what happens to the file in CorelDRAW.

# E39 - Embedding Files

a. Clear the page or start a new file. Open the **File menu** and click on **Insert Object**. A dialogue box appears:

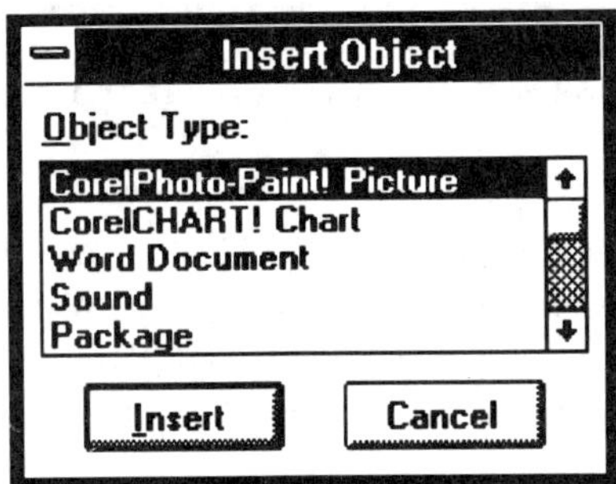


**15.05 Insert Object dialogue box**

b. The dialogue box lists all the different objects that you can embed, the list actually comes from the WIN.INI [Embedding] section. In this case you want to embed the Paintbrush Picture you used before. Find **Paintbrush Picture,** click on it and then click on **Insert**. Windows Paintbrush will run.

c. You cannot load a file into Paintbrush because that will break the link that is currently in force. However, you can use **Paste From** in the **Edit menu** to load a file. Then open the **File menu** and click on **Update**. Some applications bring a message box up at this point asking if you want to update the object but Paintbrush doesn't.

d. You can now either close Paintbrush, using **Exit & Return to UNTITLED.CDR** in the File menu, or reduce it to an icon. You will find the image is already in CorelDRAW. If you have not used Update first then a message box appears:

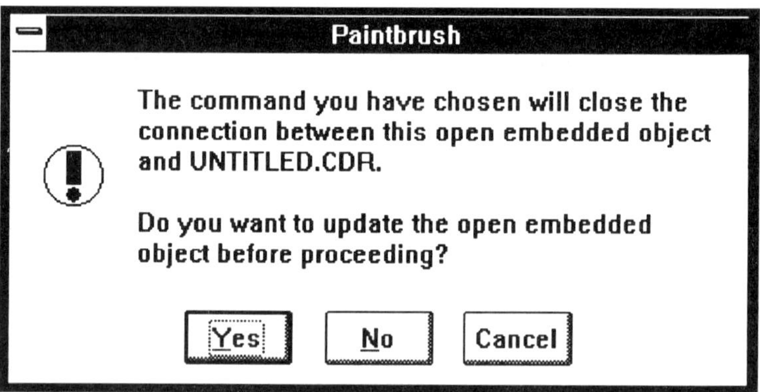


**15.06 Non-updated message box**

e. What you now have is an embedded object. You can edit it if you wish either by double clicking on it or by opening the **Edit menu** and clicking on **Edit [filename]** - provided the object is selected. Paintbrush will run in either case and any changes you make in that will be updated in CorelDRAW if you use **Update** again.

Because you have an embedded object any changes you make in the Paintbrush image without it being run from within CorelDRAW will have no effect on the bitmap in CorelDRAW. While you have just used CorelDRAW and Paintbrush in the foregoing exercises, the principles of OLE work the same way in the majority of OLE compliant programs, certainly they work the same way in the entire Corel Graphics Package.

# 16 - CorelTRACE

CorelTRACE is a nice, neat utility program that converts bitmapped images into vector format ones. It was first supplied with CorelDRAW 2.0 and it has been improved and enhanced with this new release. It is now hellaciously quick, far faster than previously. To run the program just double click on its icon.

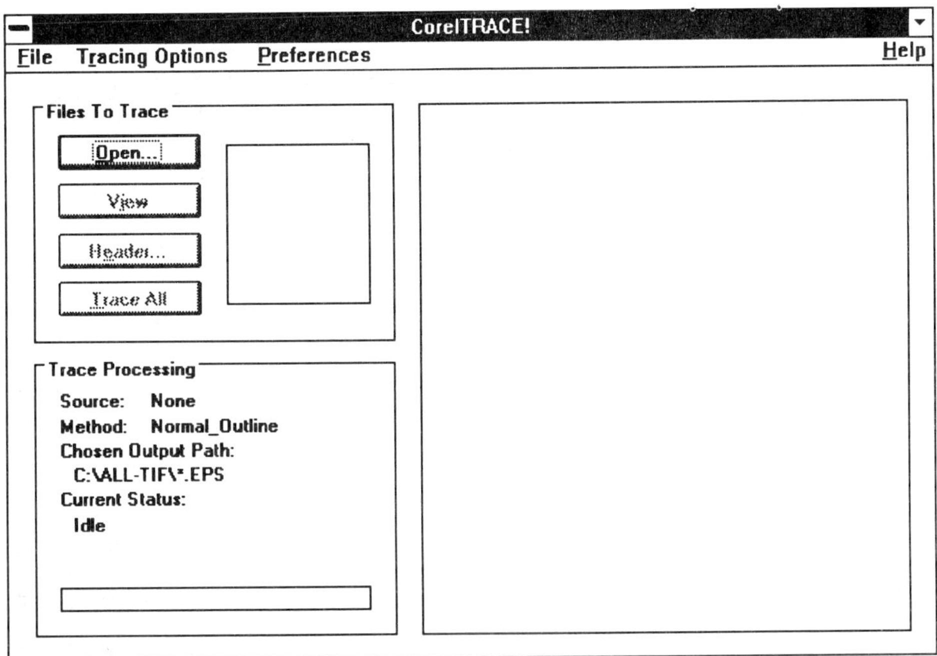


**16.01 CorelTRACE**

The window that Trace uses cannot be resized, it is a fixed resolution window, it can only be reduced to an icon.

Along the top is the **Title Bar** and beneath that the **Menu Bar**, we'll come back to the menus in a minute or three.

In the top left hand corner are four buttons and a little viewing screen. The buttons are **Open**, which allows you to load files into Trace. The filenames will be displayed in the **List Box** beside the button.

**View** allows you see the header image of the bitmap, which will be displayed in the large box on the right hand side. The viewed image isn't very good because it is displayed in grey.

**Header** brings up a dialogue box that contains a feast of information about the file you are viewing.

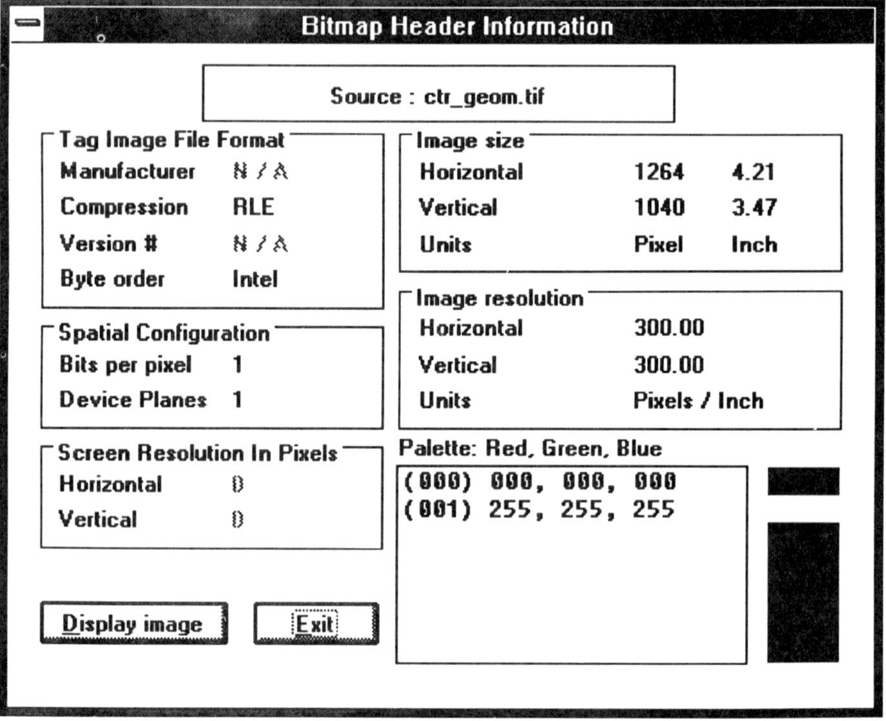


**16.02 Header information**

**Trace All** starts the tracing operation. It will trace as many files are as listed in the list box beside the buttons.

In the lower left hand corner of the window, labelled **Trace Processing**, there is a set of information about what Trace is doing or set to do.

The main area though is the huge box on the right hand side. This is the **Tracing window** and it is here that images are displayed and/or traced.

CorelTRACE provides only three menus, the first, **File**, deals with the various input/output options, the second, Tracing Options, with the way that the program treats files and the third sets the Preferences.

# E40 - TRACE AN IMAGE

For this exercise you're going to need the sample TIF files that are supplied with CorelDRAW 3.0.

a. Run CorelTRACE by double clicking on the program icon. (By the way, there are three different icons you can use for the program. Use the **Properties** command from Windows Program Manager File menu and click on **Change Icon** in the dialogue box that comes up.)

b. Click on the button labelled **Open** and a dialogue box appears.

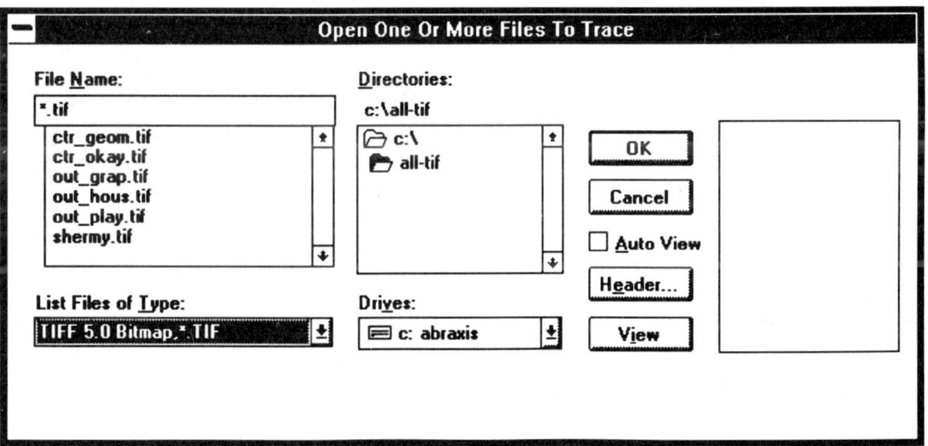


16.03 Open dialogue box

The program always defaults to looking for BMP files so you have to change it to looking for TIF files. Trace can actually trace any bitmap format file and they are all listed in the drop-down list box.

In the **Directories** box, unless you've moved the files elsewhere, you have to log on to the \CORELDRW\DRAW\SAMPLES directory. Once you do the names of all the files with TIF extensions will appear beneath **File Name**.

c. This dialogue box is slightly different to the normal one because it will allow you to select multiple files rather than just one. To select any individual file just click on it. To select more than one file, hold down **Ctrl** and click on the next file you want. To select all the files click on the first one, hold down **Shift** and then click on the last one, all the intervening files will be selected.

d. If you click on just one file you can then click on **Header** to get the information about that file. If you click on **View** then the image of the selected file appears in the little window on the right. (If you want this to happen automatically then turn on **Auto View**.)

e. Select all the sample files, there should be six of them, and then click on **OK**. The dialogue box closes and you go back to main Trace window and all the filenames are now listed.

f. Before you begin to trace the files, where do you want them to be put? Open the **File menu** and click on **Output Options** and a dialogue box appears.

The dialogue box simply allows you to designate which sub-directory of your hard disk will be used to hold the traced files. You should be aware that the files which Trace produces are EPS files but if you try to load them into any application other than CorelDRAW you will find that they have no image headers. It doesn't really matter where you put them as long as you remember where it is.

The dialogue box gives you three other options. **Always prompt** means that if you inadvertently trace the same file twice, the program will tell you that the resulting EPS file already exists.

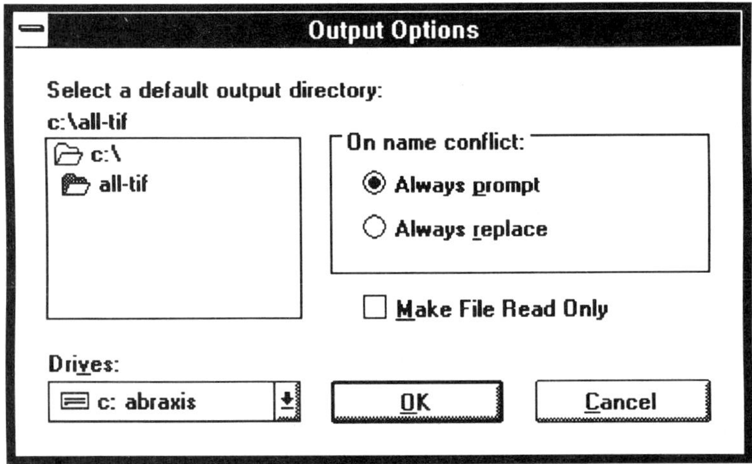


**16.04 Output options**

**Always replace** is the opposite, the file will be replaced without you being any the wiser. Personally I prefer the former just in case I have files in multiple formats but with different content. For example, I have two files SPACE.BMP and SPACE.TGA. Both are bitmaps but the images are different - I just haven't got round to renaming either of them yet. If I run either file through Trace it will produce a file called SPACE.EPS and I won't know which image it contains.

**Make File Read Only** does just that so that the file cannot be overwritten.

g. Make whatever selections you want and then click on **OK** to go back to the main window. Now click on the **Trace All** button and the program will trace the files one by one. As the files are traced the information in the bottom left hand corner of the window constantly updates and the image is traced in black in the main window on the right.

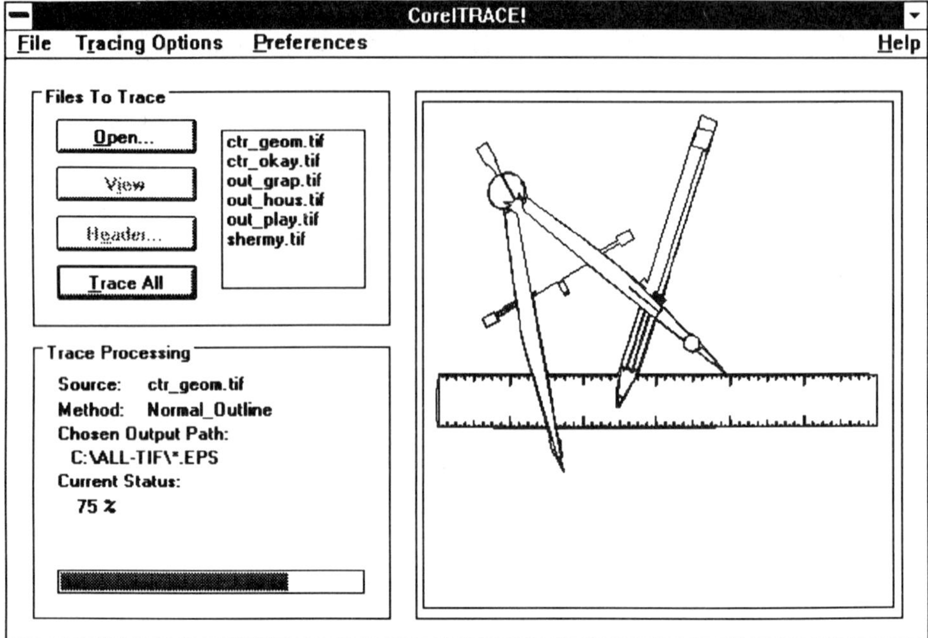


**16.05 Updating information**

h. Once the tracing is complete you will be left with the vector image of the last file traced, whether you used one or a hundred, and the data in the Trace Processing area tells you about the resulting file.

Some points about traced images. Whenever you trace a bitmap, CorelTRACE follows the separate shapes within the image to produce the curves that make up the resulting vector graphic. These curves will each contain a number of nodes. For example, Shermy produces a vector graphic will 11 Objects, i.e. curves, which contain a total of 270 nodes. That's 270 in total not per object.

Now the problem. CorelDRAW doesn't like lots of nodes and/or objects. All the files you have just traced are fine and they will load without any problems. But suppose you had a file that contained 2,000 objects and 4,000 nodes, maybe a tree in leaf for example. That may cause problems when you try to load it into CorelDRAW. I've never worked out the exact number you can get away with but if when you multiply the number of nodes by the number of objects you get a number greater than about

6,00,000 watch out. You may be better off doing the trace in chunks and then amalgamating them in CorelDRAW rather than trying to do the whole thing at once.

I just checked the previous paragraph, I write this book in real time so everything that I say or do is being done as I write it. Anyway, I have some wonderful PCX files that are scanned 18th Century woodcut images. One of these is a woodpecker and I just traced it. The trace apparently went fine, it produced 972 objects and a total of 9784 nodes. The only trouble is it locked my entire machine tight! I couldn't close CorelTRACE or even reduce it to an icon. I will admit that I have CD-Audio, Clipboard, Winword and CorelDRAW all running at the same time but I have sufficient resources to handle that. I had to press the Reset button and reboot completely! The traced image was also wrong. I loaded it into CorelDRAW and half of it is missing.

This could be simply because I am using the beta version of CorelDRAW but it is just as likely to be fault of trying to push CorelTRACE too hard. It's a shame that you can't know how many objects and/or nodes you are likely to produce before you do so. For obvious reasons though that is not possible. The moral of the story is, be careful what images you trace.

Generally speaking you can get a rough idea of which images are going to be complex ones by simply looking at them. A tree for example with lots of individual leaves may cause problems, or the Willow pattern or very large images. If the image you want to trace contains lots of separate sub-images, e.g. leaves, then the file may be too complex. Large files with little detail should be okay.

# E41 - Altered Images

In the last exercise you traced the images using the standard default characteristics that Trace provides, but you can do much more than that.

a. Open the **Tracing Options menu** and you will see that there are three commands.

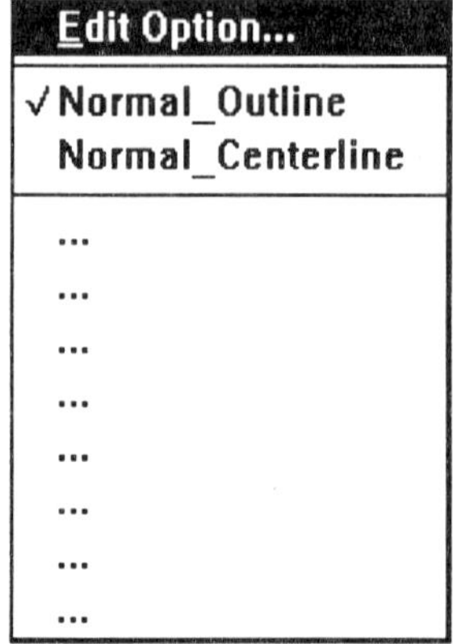


**16.06 Tracing Options**

b. Select **Normal Centreline**, the second default provided.

c. Now select Shermy again as you did before and click on **Trace All**. A message box will appear:

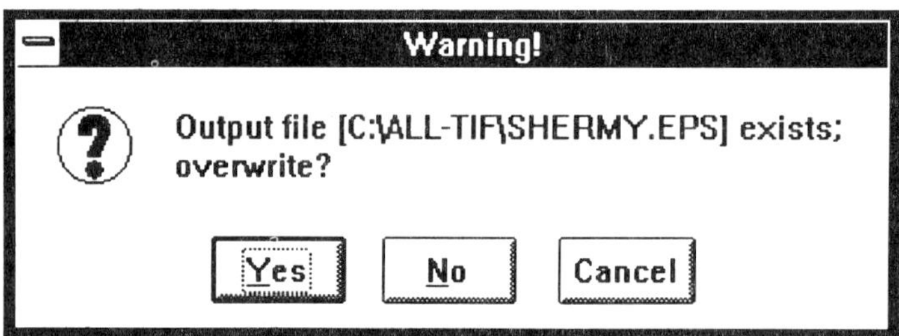


**16.07 Message box**

d. In this case you don't want to overwrite the existing image so click on **No**. A dialogue box will appear. Use this box to log on to another directory to place the new traced copy of Shermy into. You have to do it this way because you cannot rename the traced file, all you can do is place it into another directory. Click on **OK** to close the box.

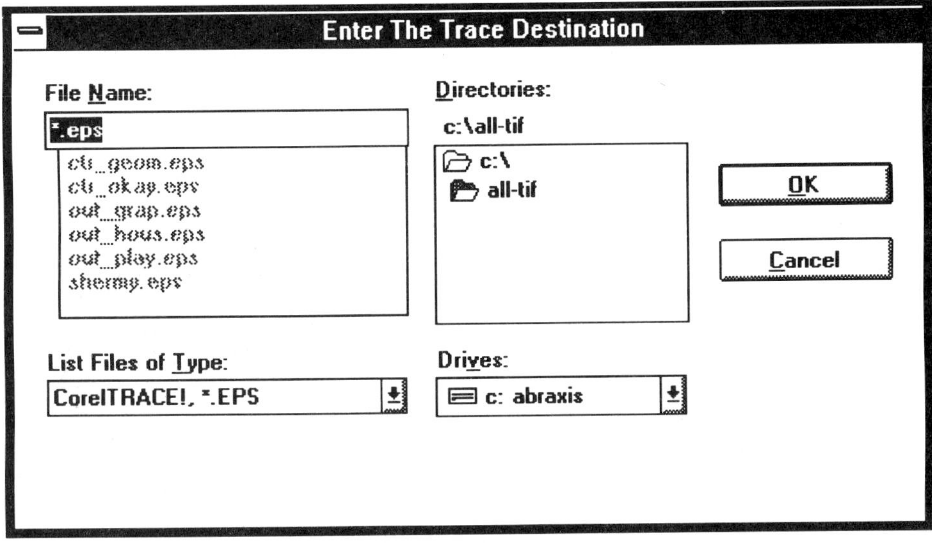


**16.08 Change target directory**

e. The tracing begins. Notice that there is no way to cancel the tracing operation once it has begun. You must let it take its course.

What you have done is change the way that Trace operates. The normal default is for the program to produce outlines. Image a circle with an wide outline. When you run this through Trace you would get two lines, one on the outside of the line and one on the inside. In other words it traces around the edges of things. The intervening gap will be filled with colour.

Using Centreline that doesn't happen. Instead the tracing line goes down the middle of all lines, in other words it produces lines not outlines. Intervening areas are not filled because they are assumed to the lines.

With some images it makes little difference, apart from creating more objects, while with others the difference is very noticeable. On the next three pages are some samples of traced files. The top image is the normal default one and the bottom one is traced with Centreline. The images have been picked on purpose to show the differences which are clearly visible. Below are the original TIF images. On the following pages Shermy has been magnified 200%.

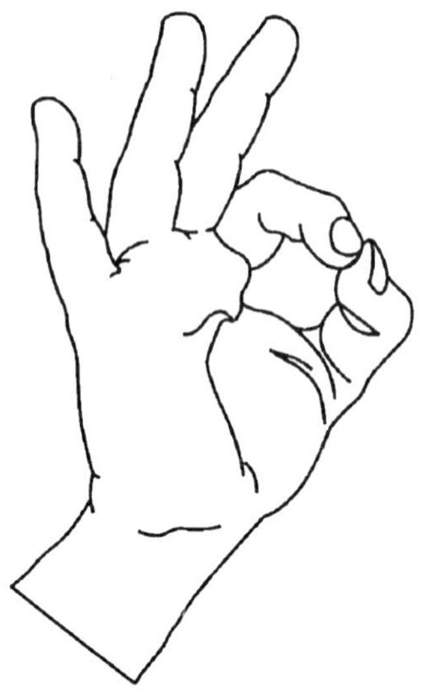

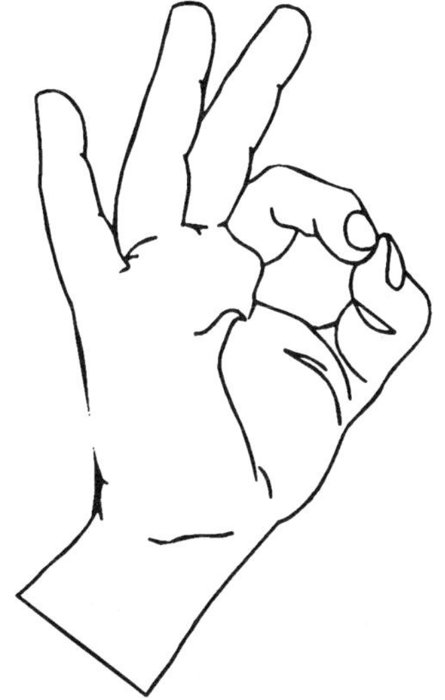

11 Objects

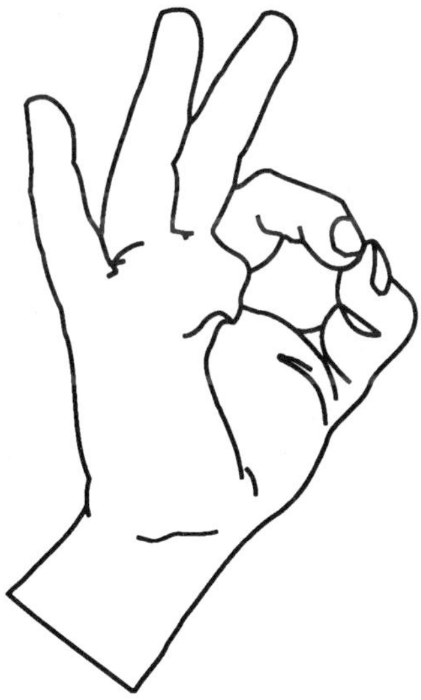

27 Objects

123 Objects

291 Objects

11 Objects

17 Objects

# E42 - CHANGING OPTIONS

CorelTRACE will allow you to change the options for tracing if you need to.

a. Open the **Tracing Options menu** and click on **Edit Option**.

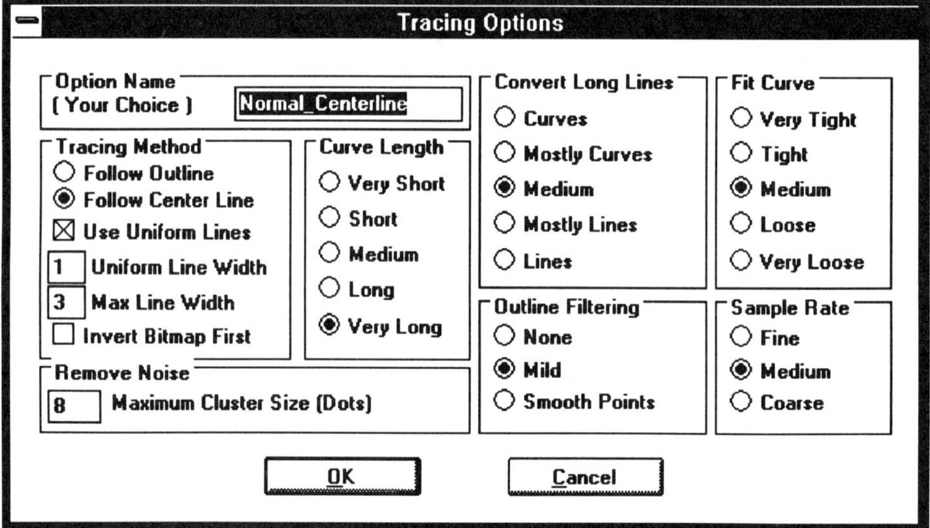


**16.09 Edit options dialogue box**

b. The first thing to do is change the name for the option. Highlight **Normal_Centreline**, click at the beginning of the words and then drag the cursor to the right, and overwrite it with a new name. That prevents you accidentally overwriting the predefined option.

c. Under **Tracing Method** you have a number of choices:

**Follow Outline** causes the program to follow the edges of the elements within the image. With a monochrome image any areas that were black with still be black when the image is traced. With colour images closest matches will be made. This method works best with images that contain lots of filled elements, like the Ghost House.

**Follow Centre Line** will cause thin objects to be traced as lines not objects. It works best for images containing lots of lines but few objects, e.g. plans or flowcharts. Images must be monochrome with black lines on a white background.

**Use Uniform Lines** is only available when using Centreline tracing. When you use this you have to assign a line thickness to use. You may specify any thickness from 1 to 99 pixels for the **Uniform Line Width**. By default it is 1. The **Max Line Width** determines what the thickest line in the traced image will be. If you set no width here then the program automatically calculates an average for you. For this reason you should not use Centreline tracing for any image that contains calligraphic effects because all you'll get are single thickness lines and the effects will be lost.

**Invert Bitmap First** does just that. White becomes black and vice versa.

**Maximum Cluster Size** under **Remove Noise** means that any element of the image being traced that contains fewer dots than what is specified here will be ignored. The range can be anything from 2 to 999 pixels. The purpose of the command is to give you a quick, rough and ready way of tidying up poor quality images.

**Curve Length** sets the line length. By default it is set to Very Long. The shorter you make the lines the more detail you will get in the final image. The negative side of that means you will get many more objects and more nodes, which means a larger file. The setting here is used in conjunction with Fit Curve and Sample Rate.

**Convert Long Lines** provides five options, with the default being Medium. What it does is control what happens to lines themselves and whether they are converted into lines or curves. The default is a compromise that should work for most images. But if you were tracing plans for example which contain mostly lines then you would use Lines. On the other hand if you were tracing text then you would use Curves. The setting here affects the type of nodes in the finished image.

**Outline Filtering** affects the smoothness of the lines created. You should only need to change this option if you are dealing with images that have been produced at low resolution, e.g. less than 150 dpi. A setting of None gives sharp edges whereas Smooth will give gently rounded ones.

**Fit Curve** and **Sample Rate** work together, in conjunction with Curve Length, to control how closely the image will be traced. The settings affect how closely the tracing follows the actual outline in the image being traced.

d. Make whatever changes you wish and then click on **OK**. The new settings will be added to the menu under the name you gave them.

e. The other thing you may want to change is the way that CorelTRACE handles colours. Open the **Preferences menu** and click on **Colour Reduction**. A dialogue box appears.

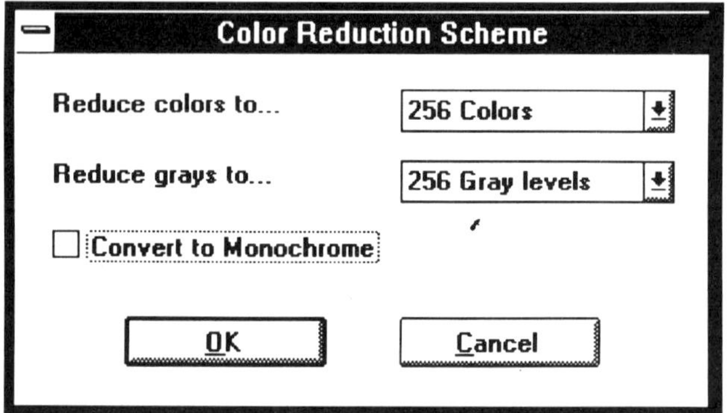


**16.10 Colour Reduction dialogue box**

f. The dialogue box allows you to control the way that colours in the original image are treated. You can set the number of colours and greys that will be used for the traced image. Again the settings here will affect the complexity of the final image. Using lots of colour and greys will create lots of objects and nodes and thus make the image larger. If you want just the overall shape of the image, i.e. you don't mind losing a little detail, then click on **Convert to Monochrome** don't use this option with full colour images. Any change you make here will apply to all images that are traced until you reset them. So if you are tracing a number of images at once the settings will apply to every image.

g. Unfortunately the only way you can see the images you trace is to import then into CorelDRAW. Use **File Import** and select **CorelTRACE, *.EPS**.

CorelTRACE is, without doubt, the best bitmap to vector conversion program that I have ever used. There are others on the market but none of them give you the degree of control and user-friendliness that Trace gives you.

For the majority of images you will find that the Normal defaults that are supplied with the program are fine and they will produce usable, useful vectors quickly and simply.

# 17 - Mosaic

Mosaic is probably the most useful and beneficial utility program that I have ever come across. What it does is allow you to view graphic images in miniature rather than having to load them into CorelDRAW. Mosaic has been around for a long time but with the release of CorelDRAW 3.0 it has been dramatically enhanced and improved. Now you can view just about any graphic file format you care to mention, with the notable exception of Windows Metafiles. You have a wide variety of choices in how these are displayed, you can select to have just one file format shown or all of them. You can even use it to create special compressed library files - and still view the files once they are compressed. I think it's wonderful and I use it most days of the week. The only thing about it that niggles me is that it won't allow you to rename files.

Mosaic is called 'a graphic files manager' and that's a very good description because that's what it actually does. It allows you see at glance all the graphics files you have on your hard disk or on the CD-ROM. You can even print catalogue style listings of your files with it, including little thumbnails of them.

## E43 - Preferences

a. Run Mosaic by double clicking on its icon. (As with Trace there are a couple of different icons you can use for the program.) The program window will appear on screen. Unlike CorelDRAW itself, you cannot automatically have Mosaic appear as a maximised window so you have to either Tile or Maximise it manually. Double click on the Windows background for the former, click on the Maximise button for the latter.

b. I've used Mosaic since I installed CorelDRAW on this machine and I now cannot remember what directory it logs on to by default, probably the \CORELDRW\DRAW one. Let's change that. Open the **File menu** and click on **Open Directory**. That will bring up a dialogue box that allows you to log on to any directory on your hard disk.

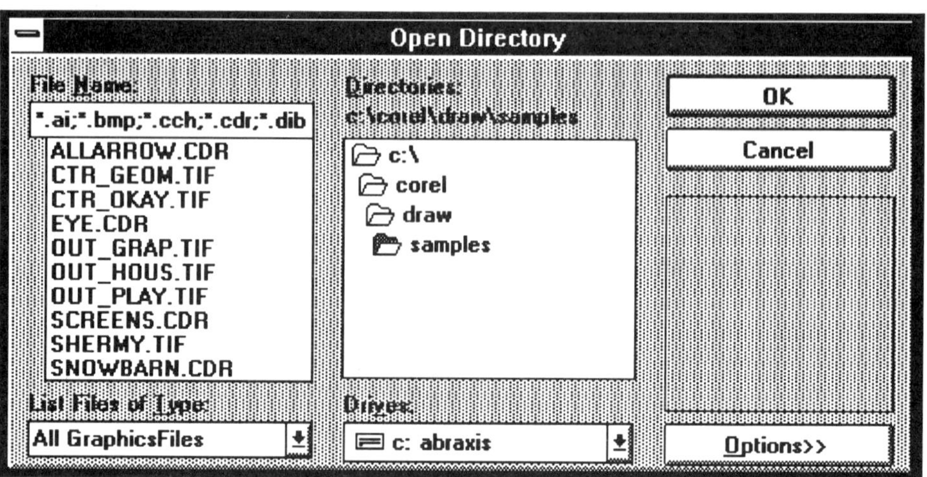


**17.01 Open Directory dialogue box**

c. Log on to the **\SAMPLES** directory and change the file types to **All graphics Files**. The filenames will appear in the list box on the left and if you click on any individual image a thumbnail of it appears in the box on the right. Click on **OK**, the dialogue box closes and Mosaic begins to display the images. Any image that is in colour will be displayed in colour.

d. By default Mosaic will display the images that size and shape. You can change this very easily. Open the **File menu** again and click on **Preferences**. (You'll have to excuse the quality of the illustration for the dialogue boxes in Mosaic I'm afraid because they all have grey backgrounds that cannot be changed.)

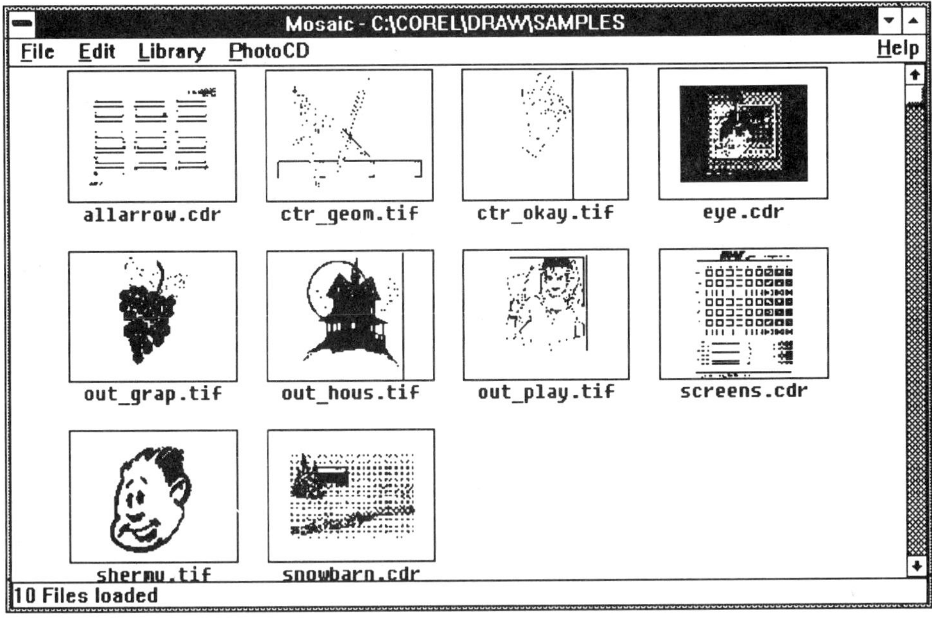


17.02 Images displayed

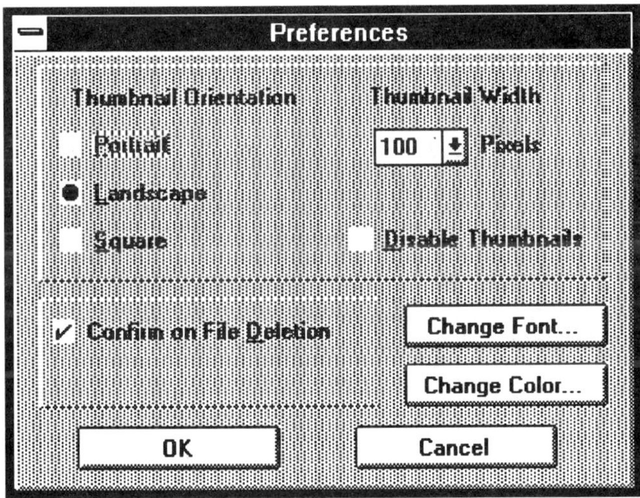


17.03 Preference dialogue box

e. Click on **Portrait** and then on **OK**. The images on screen will change to five abreast and two deep. Open the **Preferences** dialogue box again. This time click on **Square**. The images change again. Open **Preferences** again. This time click on **Disable Thumbnails** before clicking on **OK**. Mosaic now displays the data about the files, name, size, creation date and time and directory.

CorelMOSAIC

File Edit Library PhotoCD Help

| | | | | |
|---|---|---|---|---|
| allarrow.cdr | 31484 Bytes | 1992-Jun-3 | 00:00:00 | C:\COREL\DRAW\SAMPLES |
| ctr_geom.tif | 14278 Bytes | 1992-Jun-3 | 00:00:00 | C:\COREL\DRAW\SAMPLES |
| ctr_okay.tif | 9274 Bytes | 1992-Jun-3 | 00:00:00 | C:\COREL\DRAW\SAMPLES |
| eye.cdr | 31408 Bytes | 1992-Jun-3 | 00:00:00 | C:\COREL\DRAW\SAMPLES |
| out_grap.tif | 18080 Bytes | 1992-Jun-3 | 00:00:00 | C:\COREL\DRAW\SAMPLES |
| out_hous.tif | 17482 Bytes | 1992-Jun-3 | 00:00:00 | C:\COREL\DRAW\SAMPLES |
| out_play.tif | 24504 Bytes | 1992-Jun-3 | 00:00:00 | C:\COREL\DRAW\SAMPLES |
| screens.cdr | 31670 Bytes | 1992-Jun-3 | 00:00:00 | C:\COREL\DRAW\SAMPLES |
| shermy.tif | 30780 Bytes | 1992-Jun-3 | 00:00:00 | C:\COREL\DRAW\SAMPLES |
| snowbarn.cdr | 204474 Bytes | 1992-Jun-3 | 00:00:00 | C:\COREL\DRAW\SAMPLES |

**17.04 No thumbnails**

f. Play with the different thumbnail orientations. Try changing the value for **Thumbnail Width**. Different orientations have different effects when you change the width. Play with just these settings until you get a view of the images that you like. (On a standard 640 by 480 VGA monitor I find that using Landscape with a width of 75 pixels is fine. Using Super VGA at 800 by 600 resolution I use Square with a width of 100 pixels.)

g. Open the **Preferences** dialogue box yet again. This time click on **Change Font**.

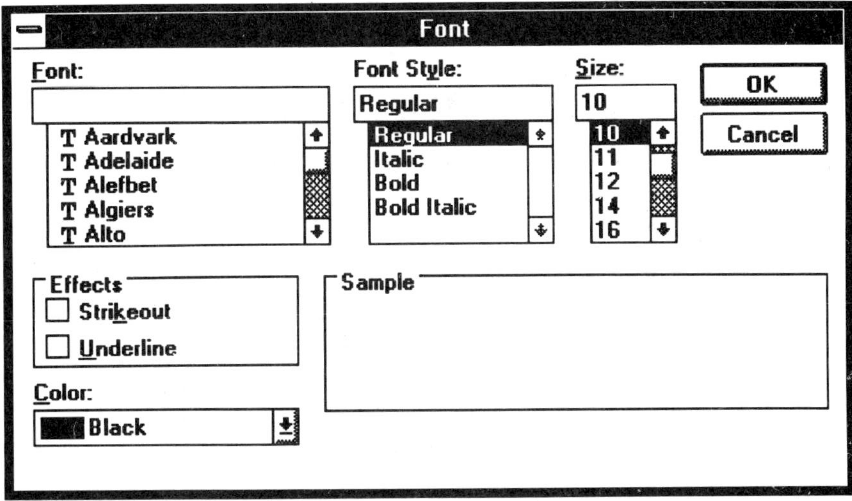


**17.05 Change Font dialogue box**

h. The dialogue box allows you to pick any font that is installed on your system, whether they be TrueType, Adobe Type 1 or system fonts. When you click on a font name it will appear in the Sample area of the dialogue box. You can also select an effect, e.g. bold or normal, for the font and a size. You can even have it appear in colour! Make whatever selection you wish and try it out.

i. Open the Preferences dialogue box one more time and click on **Change Colour**.

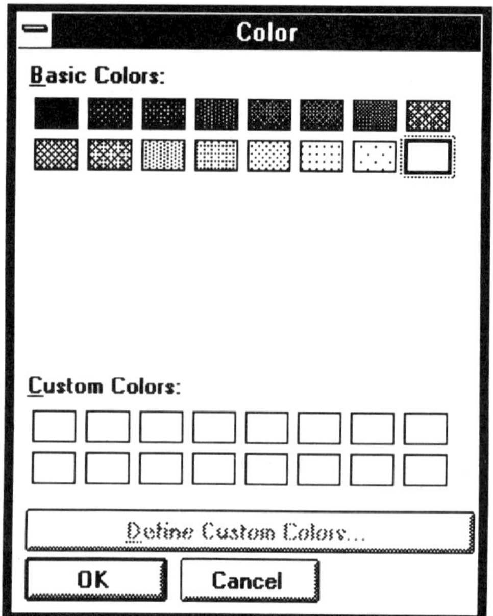


**17.06 Change Colour dialogue box**

j. The dialogue box allows you to change the background colour for the Mosaic window. (The illustration only has 16 colours in it because the monitor is running in monochrome. Normally you would get as many colours as possible.) Select whatever colour you like and then click on **OK**.

k. Back at the main dialogue box you now have a final decision to make. Do you want to prompted every time you delete a file? If not click turn off **Confirm on File Deletion**. With the command turned on, which it is by default, you will get a message box asking if you want to delete [filename] each time you press **Del**. With it turned off this doesn't happen. Make your choice and click on **OK**.

l. Set the **Page Setup** while you're at it. This doesn't mean set the page size, that's fixed by whatever size paper you have installed in your printer. It refers to the characteristics that will be used when you print from Mosaic. Open the File menu and click on the command.

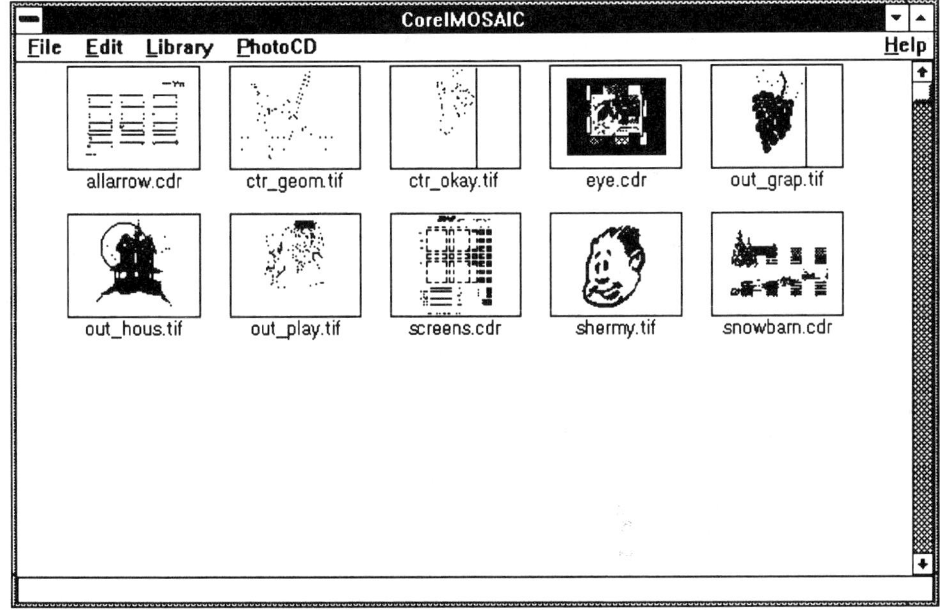


**17.07 Mosaic with new defaults**

m. The illustration above shows the defaults and these produce the Page Number followed by the directory path followed by the file type description, all printed as a header on each page. You can change the **Justification** to be Left, Centre or Right. Click on the word and a list box appears. The **File Labels** refers to the names of the files. With the settings as shown you will get the filename and extension being displayed under each thumbnail on the printed page and each thumbnail is surrounded by the fine line box.

n. Clicking on **Font** allows you to set the font to be used for printing the thumbnails. It brings up the same kind of dialogue box as you used to set the display font for Mosaic itself. You can set separate fonts for the Page Title and for the filenames. Make whatever changes you wish and then click on **OK**.

o. Clicking on **Printer Setup** in the **File menu** will display a dialogue box identical to that used in CorelDRAW itself. It allows you to select which printer you intend using to print to.

Page Setup

Current Page Settings:

Page Titles

✓ Print Title on each Page

✓ Print Directory Name

✓ Print File Type

✓ Print Page Numbers

Draw Box around Page

Title Justification

Left Justified

Font...

File Labels

✓ Print Filename

✓ Include Extension

✓ Draw Frame Around File

Number Keywords to Print

0

Font...

OK

Cancel

17.08 Page Setup dialogue box

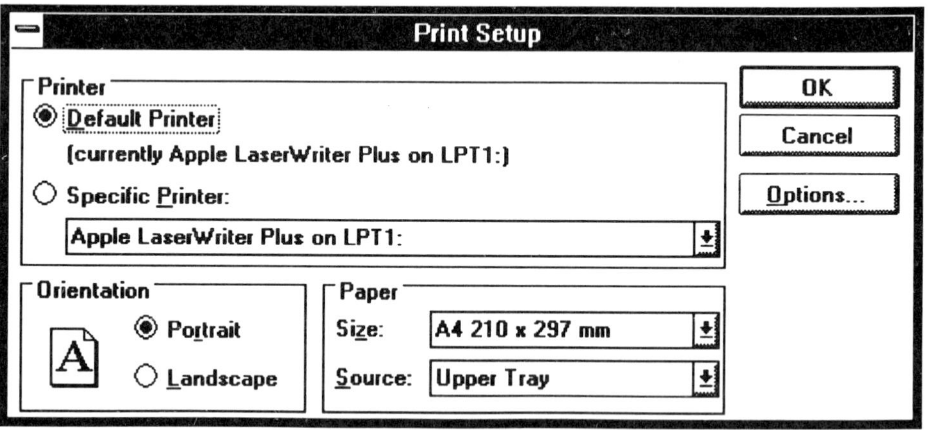


17.09 Printer Setup dialogue box

That's all the basic preferences set. When you close Mosaic it 'remembers' the settings, they are actually stored in a file called CORELMOS.INI. In fact the settings are written to this file as you make then. To be on the safe side though it is always advisable to close the any program down completely when you set preferences. Then reopen it.

# E44 - PRINTING

Mosaic will allow you to print the images in a number of different ways.

a. Make sure the printer is turned on. Open the File menu and click on **Print Thumbnails**. The thumbnails will be sent to the printer one by one and they will be printed according to however many can be fitted across the page. This will not necessarily match the screen display because it depends on how many images can be fitted across the page. Don't forget that the thumbnails are based on pixels.

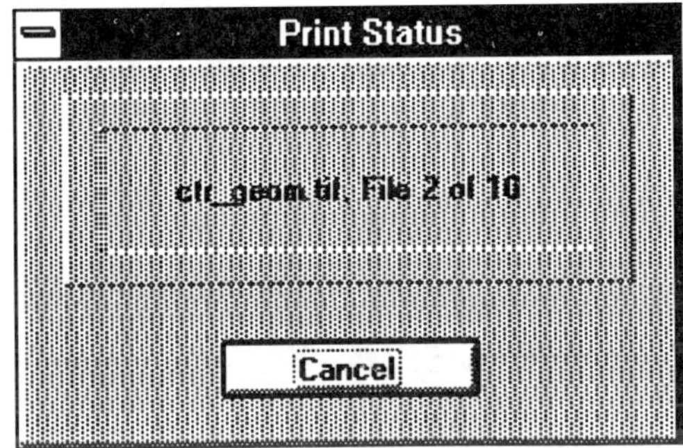


**17.10 Printing Thumbnails**

b. You can also print selected thumbnails rather than the whole lot if you wish. Select the images of the files you want to print. Click on the first, hold down Ctrl and click on the second and subsequent files. If you want to select an contiguous group of files click on the first, hold down Shift and then click on the last. All the intervening files will be selected as well. Selected files are shown by having a box around them and their titles are in inverse video.

c. When you then open the File menu you will find that the command now reads **Print Selected Thumbnails**. The thumbnails will be printed in the order that they are displayed, i.e. ascending alphabetical order, not the order that you select them in.

A note about printing in this way. Thumbnail printing takes a long time, especially if any of the files you are sending are in colour. Earlier I printed the sample files as thumbnails and it took over forty minutes for the page to appear. The reason is simple. Thumbnails contains a lot of information plus you are sending a variable amount of text. So it stands to reason that you cannot expect rapid printing in these circumstances.

The main reason for being able to print the thumbnails in this way is to allow you to produce catalogues of your files, complete with names and the images. But don't expect miracles, especially with full colour images or with very fine lines. Your printer may not be able to cope with the former and fine lines will tend to break up because you are trying to go beyond the minimum resolution of the printer.

The alternative way to print the files is to do so individually.

d. Select the files as before. Open the **File menu** and click on **Print Files** or **Print Selected Files**. CorelDRAW will automatically run and load the first selected file for you.

e. The standard CorelDRAW printing dialogue box then appears. You make whatever changes you want in this and then click on **OK** to close it. The first file is then sent to the printer.

f. The second file is then loaded or imported and it's sent - without the print dialogue box reappearing. Then the third file and so on. If you have selected files other than those with a .CDR extension then you will be prompted by a message box between each import and print.

Printing in this way is very quick, the drawback is that you only get one image per page and you can only set the print parameters once. It is an exceedingly quick way to print a multitude of files in one go.

# E45 - EDIT MENU

The Edit menu allows you to search and manipulate files. It does not provide any of the commands that you would expect from a normal Windows edit menu.

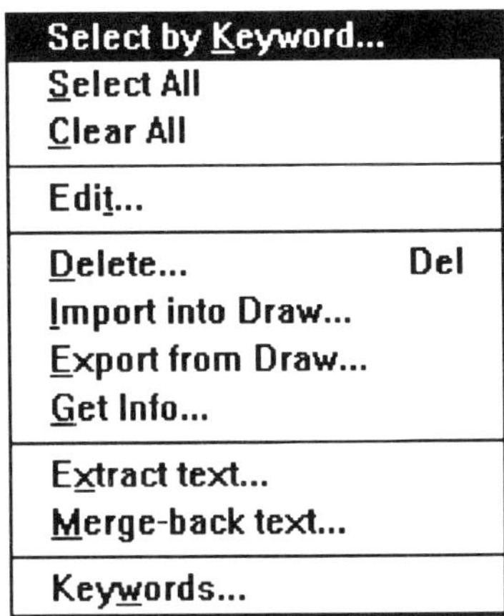


**17.11 Edit Menu**

**Select by Keyword** brings up a dialogue box from which you can search through the displayed files using the keyword facility. You obviously have to know what keywords are available for the images first.

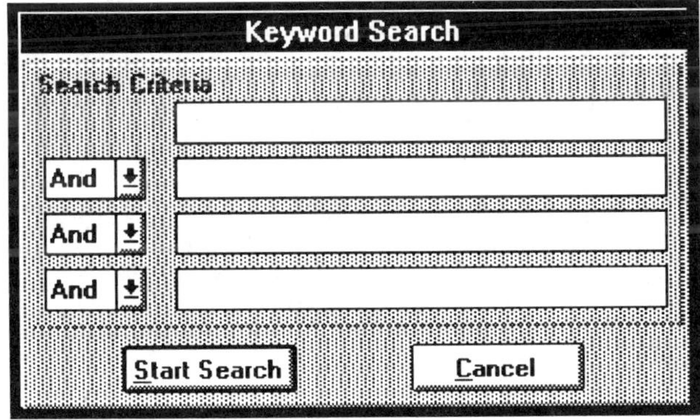


**17.12 Search by keyword**

**Select All** does just that and selects all the images in the current directory.

**Clear All** deselects everything.

**Edit** allows you to modify the image provided it has an extension of .CDR. What it does is load CorelDRAW and the open the image for you. The command is not available for files with other extensions.

**Delete** removes the selected file(s) from your hard disk.

**Import into Draw** is similar to edit but is intended for use with those images which have extensions other than .CDR. The command runs CorelDRAW and then imports the image into it for you.

**Export from Draw** seems odd at first glance but it does make sense. What the command does is run CorelDRAW, import or load the image and then activates the Export dialogue box so you can save the image in another format.

**Get Info** brings up a large dialogue box that displays a range of information about a selected image. The data will include the date and time of creation, the on-screen size, colours and actual size of the image on disk. The dialogue box also includes the keywords and notes for the selected file. You can use the command with multiple files as the dialogue box allows you to page through the information one image at a time.

**Extract Text** takes the text from a .CDR image and exports it as ASCII text for editing in something like Notepad. It only works with CorelDRAW files.

**Merge-back Text** is the opposite of the above. It places the modified text back into the image.

**Keywords** allows you to add or delete keywords that are associated with an CorelDRAW image.

# E46 - LIBRARY MENU

The Library menu provides four commands, they all deal with library files. A library is a compressed file that contains lots of graphic images. Library files were introduced with CorelDRAW 2.0 but they are not shipped with CorelDRAW 3.0. All the clip-art that is supplied with Version 3.0 is uncompressed and so there is no need for the library. You can still use the library files from version 2.0 or create your libraries using the new clip-art. However, you can only place CorelDRAW into a library, no other file formats are allowed.

a. Select all the images that have an extension of .CDR. The images will have a box around them and their titles will be shown in inverse video.

b. Open the **Library menu** and click on **Add Images to Library**. A dialogue box will appear:

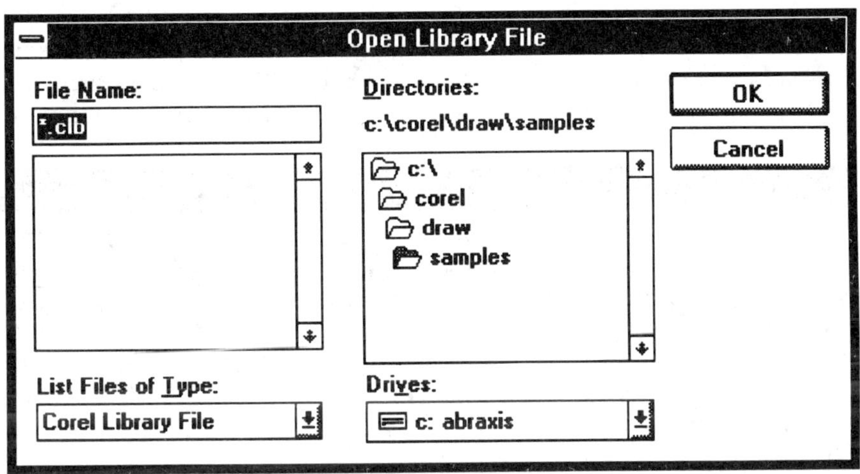


**17.13 Open Library dialogue box**

c. The program uses the same dialogue box regardless of whether you are creating a library, opening files in one or adding images to one. Overwrite *.CLB with **SAMPLES** and then click on **OK**. A message box will appear.

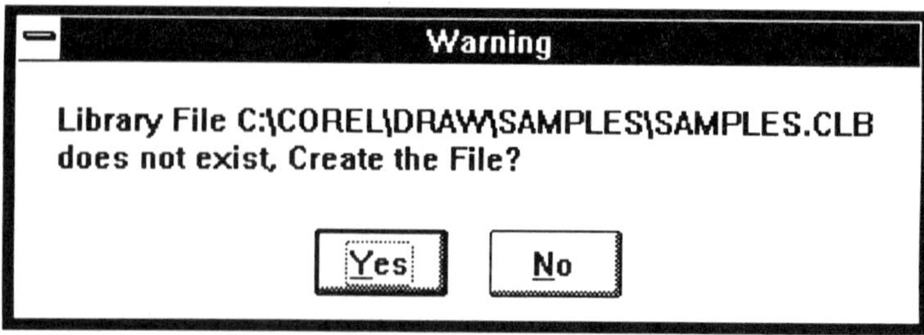


**17.14 Message box**

d. Click on **Yes** to create the library file. The program then creates the file and begins to add the selected images. It displays a progress box as it does so.

e. Check that the library is correct by opening the menu and clicking on **Open Library**. Double click on **SAMPLES.CLB** and the files will be displayed.

f. To take an image out of the library file you use the **Expand Image from Library** command. Select a file, or a number of files, and then click on the command. A dialogue box asks where you want the expanded files placed.

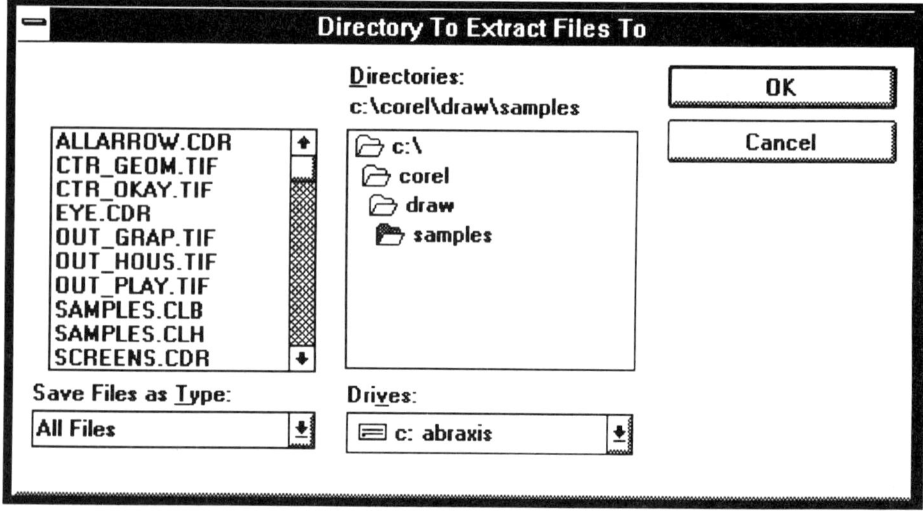


**17.15 Expanded files where?**

g. Even though you already have the files in the \SAMPLES directory you can still use this. Just click on **OK**. A message box appears telling you that the file already exists and asking if you wish to overwrite it. In this case it doesn't matter so click on **Yes**. The file will be expanded from the library file and placed into the directory for you.

h. The final Library command is **Delete Library**. Clicking on this brings up the library dialogue box. Double click in **SAMPLES.CLB**. A message box pops-up asking you to confirm the erasure. Click on **Yes** to delete the file.

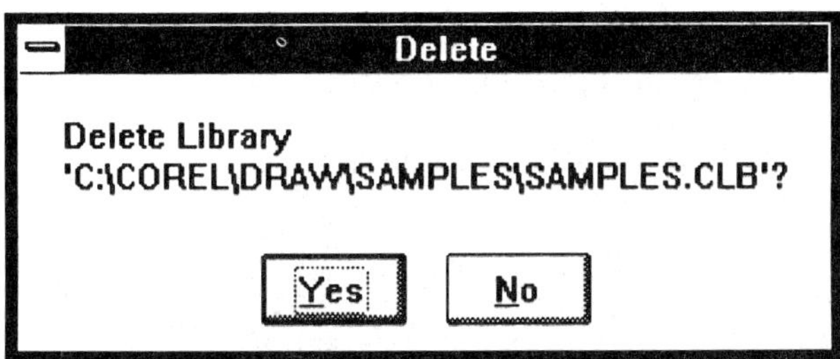


**17.16 Delete library dialogue box**

The library commands can be extremely useful as files within libraries take up much less space on your hard disk. If you have sufficient disk space there is actually no limit to the number of files you place into a library. However, as the library files get larger they can become slow to open and manipulate. Try not to put more than about 100 images into any one library.

The final menu that Mosaic contains is **PhotoCD**. At the time of writing these have not yet appearing in the U.K. - it's only just been launched in the U.S.A.

A PhotoCD is a new development, pun intended, in photographic processing created by Kodak. Instead, or maybe as well as, of having your film developed onto paper you will shortly be able to have the images placed on to a special CD-ROM. This you will be able to view in Mosaic and then incorporate the images into CorelDRAW. As you want more film developed you take the PhotoCD back to the shop and have them place the new images on it. Once the PhotoCD is full you just get another one. Sounds like a very good idea.

# 18 - CorelCHART

CorelCHART is a program that allows you to produce charts! It is the first of the three new major programs that are included with CorelDRAW 3.0. The other two are Photo-Paint and Show which are covered in Chapter 19 and 20 respectively. There is not sufficient room in this book to do justice to these three programs, each of which is independent of CorelDRAW, so in this and the next two chapters we're just going to have an overview of what the programs are and what they do.

Chart is actually produced by a company called Three D Graphics Incorporated and licensed by Corel for inclusion with the CorelDRAW 3.0 Graphics Package. The program is much more likely to used by business users than by home users.

The program and its associated files take up a lot of disk space, nearly 7.5 Mb which means Chart is the program that takes up the most space after CorelDRAW itself. So if you are unlikely to use the program you might as well have the disk space back.

But what does it do? At its simplest Chart produces charts but it's what you can then do with the charts that is interesting. CorelCHART is also an OLE server so it can produce files for use with CorelDRAW or CorelSHOW.

When you run the program for the first time you will be presented with a virtually blank screen. The window contains two menus, File and Help, an empty Status Bar and a palette along the bottom of the screen. Open the File menu and you have a choice of New, Open or Exit. Hardly the friendliest introduction. But once you begin all that changes.

a. Run the program and click on **Open** to bring up a dialogue box. Chart actually comes complete with over a hundred predesigned charts. Log into the \CHART\PIE directory and click on PIE001.CCH. Notice as you do so that the Preview screen of the dialogue box shows you a small image of what the chart is and also gives you information about it. Once you click on **OK** the file is opened and CorelCHART comes alive.

You now have six menus, plus Help, a toolbox down the left hand side and the chart is loaded into a sub-window.

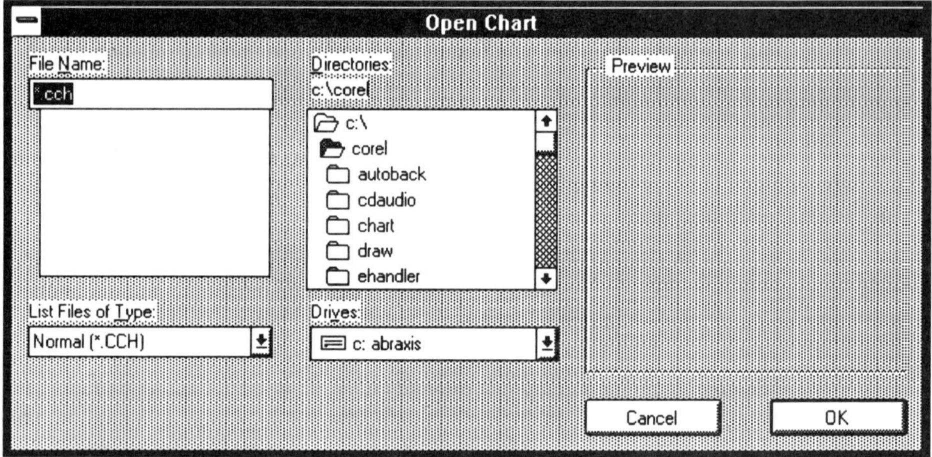


**18.01 Open dialogue box**

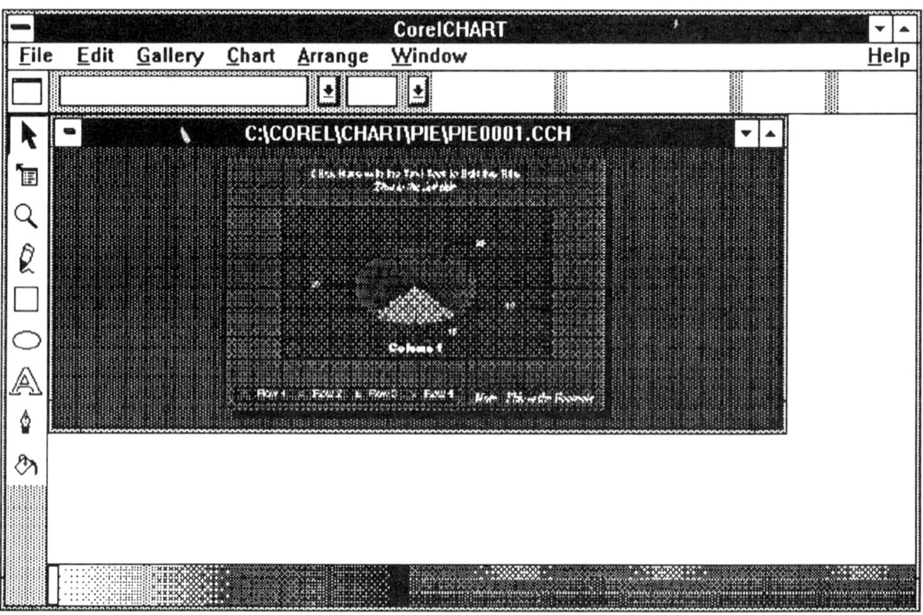


**18-02 File opened**

# THE TOOLBAR

CorelCHART provides you with nine basic tools, many of them purposely the same as in CorelDRAW.

The **Pointer tool** is used to select things as in CorelDRAW.

Next is the **Chart Element tool**. Using this you can click on any part of a chart and you get the commands and pop-up menus that apply to that area of the chart. This is extremely useful because it means you don't have to find the relevant commands within the menu, they are presented to you automatically.

The **Magnifier tool** comes next. It works slightly differently to the one in CorelDRAW. It gives you a range of magnifications, i.e. Fit, which makes the chart fit within the sub-window, and then the others are 25%, 50%, 100%, 200% and 400% - all of actual size.

The **Drawing tool** pops-out to reveal four possible pencil types. The first is Straight Line, the second is used for drawing Polygons, i.e. enclosed shapes, the third is Freehand Drawing and the final one is Arrows. With the final option you can change the type of arrows you want to use.

Next is the **Rectangle tool** which draws quadrilaterals as you would expect. You use it the same way as the tool in CorelDRAW.

The **Ellipse tool** also works the same way as in CorelDRAW.

The **Text tool** allows you to add text to the chart. It doesn't work quite the same way as in CorelDRAW, for example you cannot edit text in the same way. But once you do start using text the Ribbon Bar gives you the details of the current text. You make any changes to it from there.

Next is the **Outline tool**. Clicking on this opens out the tool in the same way as CorelDRAW does. You have a choice of line widths and colours available as you would expect.

Finally there is the **Fill tool**. Again this opens out as in CorelDRAW but the contents are slightly different. You have the usual Colour selector, a similar roll-up and a variety of fills including Vector, Bitmap and Fountain. The main difference is that you don't get shades of grey, instead you get patterns.

# DATA MANAGER

b. At the extreme left hand edge of the Ribbon is what looks like a little box with a heavy bar along the top. This is the **Data Manager** button. Click on this and you will be presented with a new sub-window.

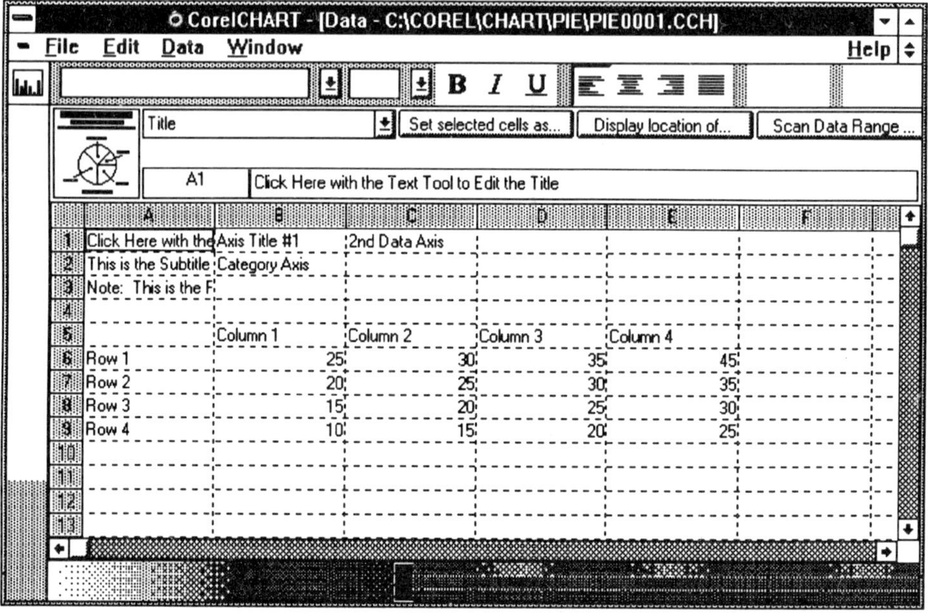


**18.03 Data Manager window**

This looks just like as spreadsheet, which is effectively what it is - in miniature. You cannot for example change the columns widths or cell heights. That's not what it is intended for. In the left hand corner you will see a representation of the pie chart you loaded.

c. Move the cursor down to cell B6 which currently says 25. The location and number will appear on the Ribbon. Change the number to 52. Change the other values in the columns as well and then go back to the chart by clicking on the **Chart button** to the left of the ribbon. The pie chart will have changed.

d. Go back to the Data Manager again. Change the figures in the second column and then go back to the Chart. There is no change. The reason is that you're using a pie chart which only allows a single set of figures.

e. Change the chart type. Open the **Gallery menu**. From here you can select different chart types. Click on any of the available chart types and a pop-out list box will appear. Click on any name in the list box but hold down the mouse button. A small representation of the chart will appear. If you move the mouse up and down the list the chart change changes as you highlight different one. If you just click on one then that's the chart type you get.

f. Click on **3D Riser** and the select **Octagons** from the list box. The entire chart changes. Go back to the **Data Manager** and change the figures in the other columns. Make them substantially larger than in the first two columns. Then go back to the Chart and see what you've got.

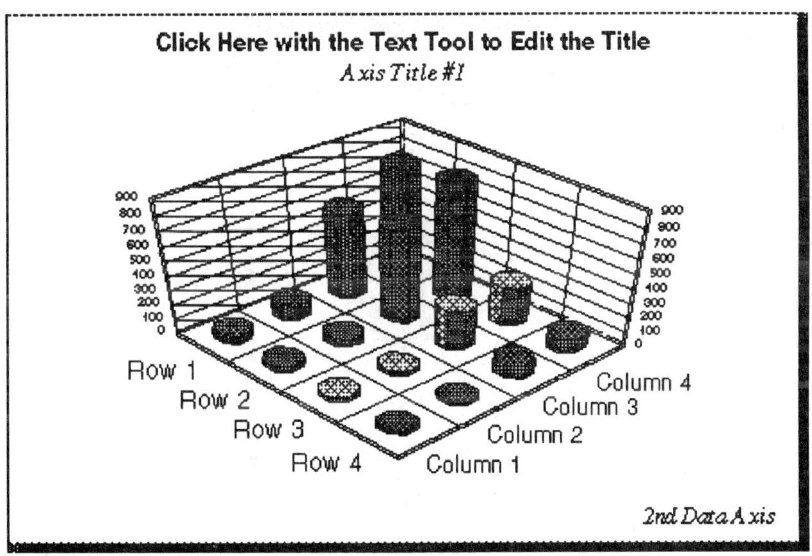


**18.04 3D Riser chart**

g. If the shapes don't look too good then change the figures again. You want the columns to be nicely stepped. The chart tells you which columns and rows are affected so you can change selected cells on the data manager very easily.

h. Now to change the colours and patterns. Select the **Pointer tool** and then select all the text and change it to Black. You have to click on each text element in turn, you can select multiples by holding down **Ctrl** as you click, and change them that way.

i. Then click on the chart background and change it to White. Change the other bits of the chart in the same way.

j. That view is a bit odd so let's change it. Open the **Chart menu** and click on **Preset Viewing Angle**. A list box appears. Click on the different angles, holding down the mouse button as you do so, and you can see the differences that the each type makes. Pick one that you like. I'm settling for Standard Angle. (What's so special about California Special?)

k. Open the **Chart menu** again and click on **Show 3D View Tool**. This is similar to the extrude rotation tool in CorelDRAW.

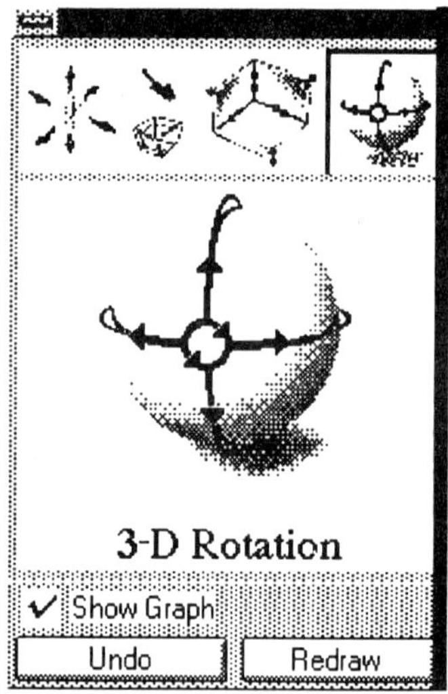


**18.05 3-D Rotation**

l. Play with this. The buttons along the top allow you to manipulate the chart by moving it, changing the perspective and panning, changing the box proportions, and rotating the whole thing. At any time if you don't like what you've done, click on **OK** and the chart will return to its original size, shape and angle.

m. Time to change the text. Go back to the **Data Manager**. Move the cursor to cell A1 and click. The contents of the cell, which provide the title for the graph, are displayed on the ribbon. Change the words to "Sample Chart Number One".

n. Change the contents of B1 to "Chapter 18". Change all occurrences of the word Row to "Period" and every occurrence of Column to "Area". In other words leave the numbers alone. Change cell C1 to "Sales for 1992". You cannot change the text style and format from within the data manager, you can only do that at the chart view. Now go back to the chart and see what you've got.

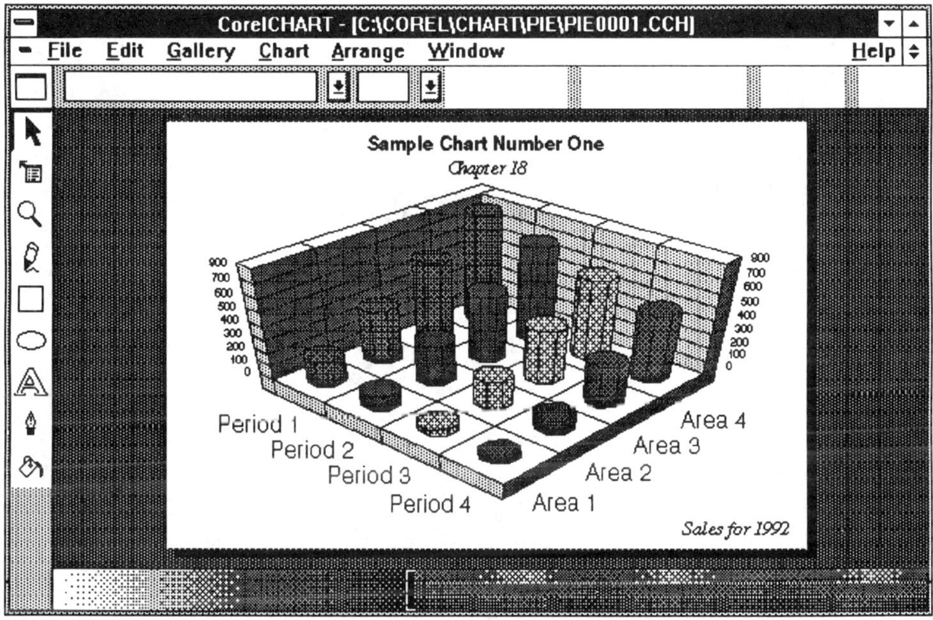


**18.06 Text content changed**

p. Let's change the actual text style on the chart. The title is a bit small considering the size of the column and row text. Select the **Pointer tool** and click on the chart title. The ribbon changes to tell you what the font characteristics are. Change the typeface to Switzerland, the size to 18 points and the justification to Left.

q. Change the sub-title text, the bit that says Chapter 18, to Zurich Calligraphic 21 point and make it right justified. Change the Period and Area text to Bahamas 10 point Normal. You can change both sets of text by clicking on one Period and one Area. Because they are all linked together any change to one changes all the rest in the series. Finally change the Sales for 1992 text to Penguin, 18 point Bold, left justified.

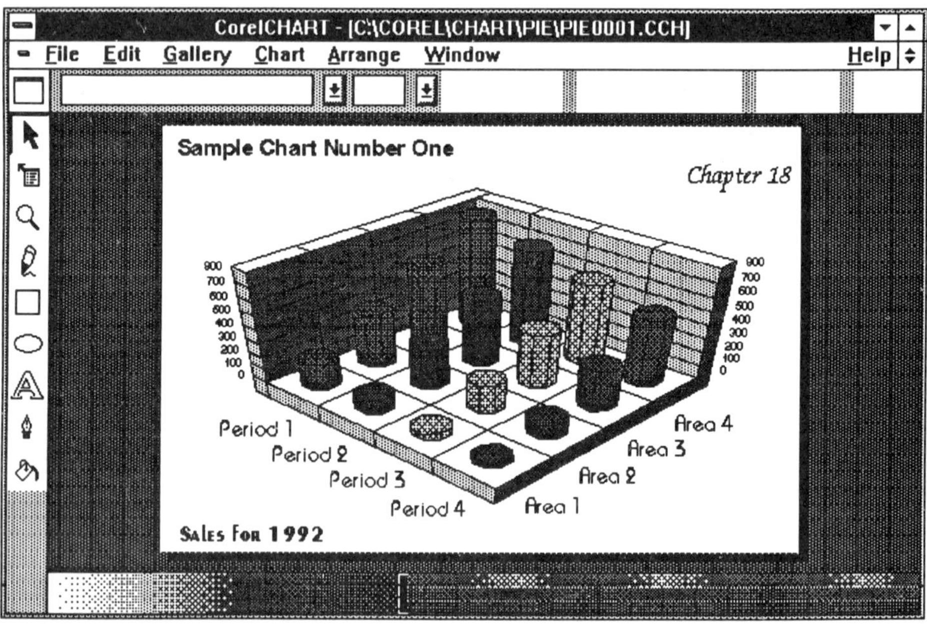


**18.07 Text attributes changed**

Play with the chart. Try changing it to different types of chart and watch what happens to the text and other attributes as you do so. Change one value drastically and watch what effect it has on the chart view. Try different rotations, colours and patterns.

r. Change the chart type to Vertical Bar, Side by Side. (You'll have to change the background and text colours again.) The contents of the **Chart menu** will also have changed. Click on **Bar Thickness** in here and then on **Major**.

s. Open the **Chart menu** again and click on **Show as Pictogram**. That converts the risers to being individual pictures. Click on any element in the first riser of the first column.

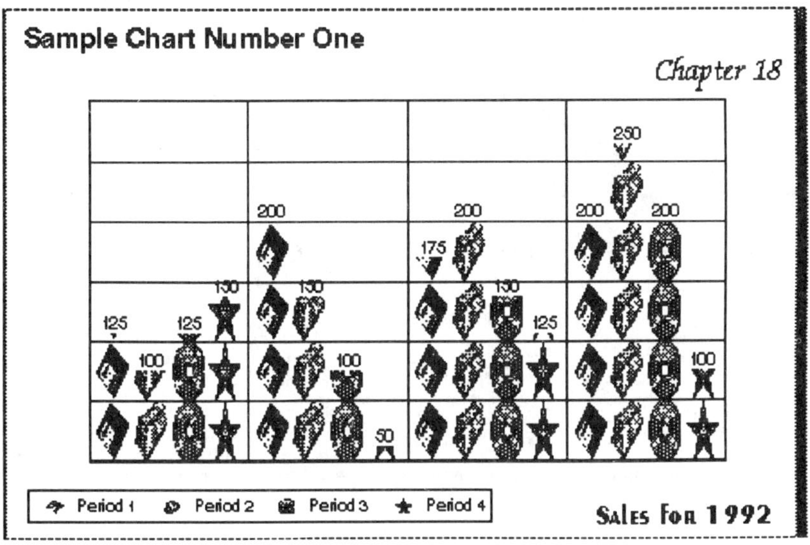


**18.08 Pictogram chart**

t. Now open the **Fill tool** and click on the **Vector fill** button, the one with the diagonal arrow. A dialogue box appears. Move up through the directory structure back to \CHART and then down to \CHART\VECTORS. Double click on DISKETTE.WMF. The chart changes as the elements of the bars become little disks. Change the other risers in the same way. The clever bit is that the pictograms are chopped as necessary in order to fit the graph.

u. You can also use bitmaps for the risers on your chart. Click on the bitmap fill button, the checkerboard one, in the box that pops out from the tool. A dialogue box appears:

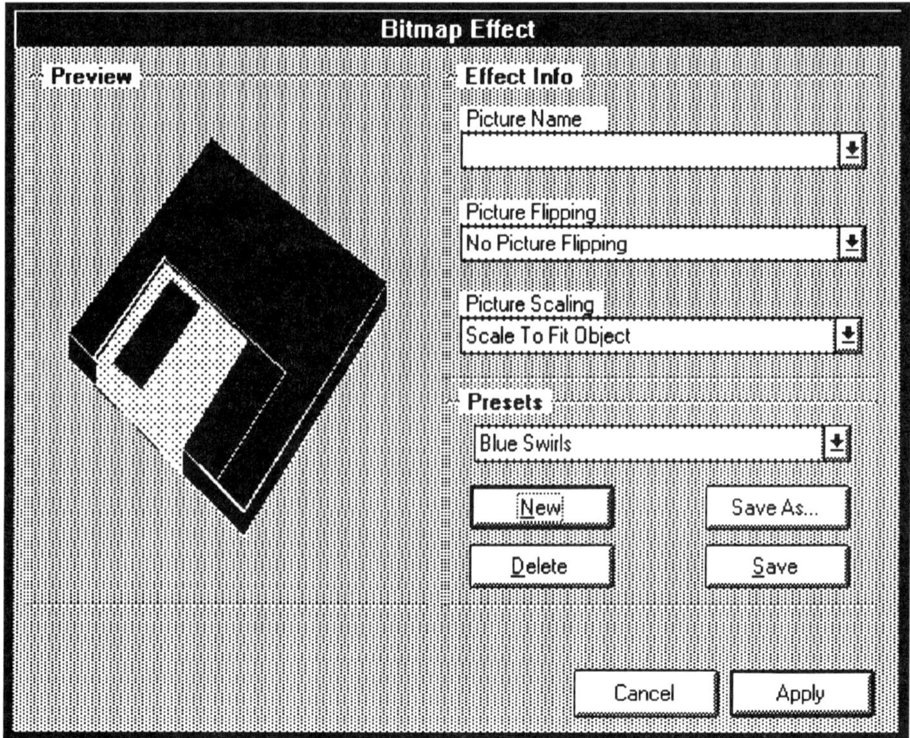


**18.09 Bitmap fill dialogue box**

You can do a lot with this dialogue box. **Picture name** will give you a range of bitmap fills as they are stored on your hard disk. All the files have an extension of .BMP.

**Picture Flipping** allows you to rotate the fill in a variety of different ways.

**Picture Scaling** affects how the picture is fitted to the image. No picture scaling means that the image is imported as it is, Scale to fit objects either expands or reduced the image and Tiled uses multiple images to fill the available space.

**Presets** are an extensive set of fountain fill effects.

w. Try out different fills. They can become quite complex due to the way that you can mix and match the various commands in the dialogue box.

# CONCLUSION

CorelCHART is certainly fun to use and the interactivity between yourself and the way that the data is presented is fantastic. For anyone who needs to use charts then this program is it, without a doubt.

Having said that though it is a bit quirky. You expect it to behave either like CorelDRAW or like Excel and it does neither, rather it sort of mixes the two together. That takes a bit of getting used to. One thing that I find strange is that you cannot use .CDR files as vector fills, you are limited to use .WMF files. There are a number of such files provided for you to use but you cannot really see them until you load them into Chart itself. .WMF files are the one format that Mosaic cannot see.

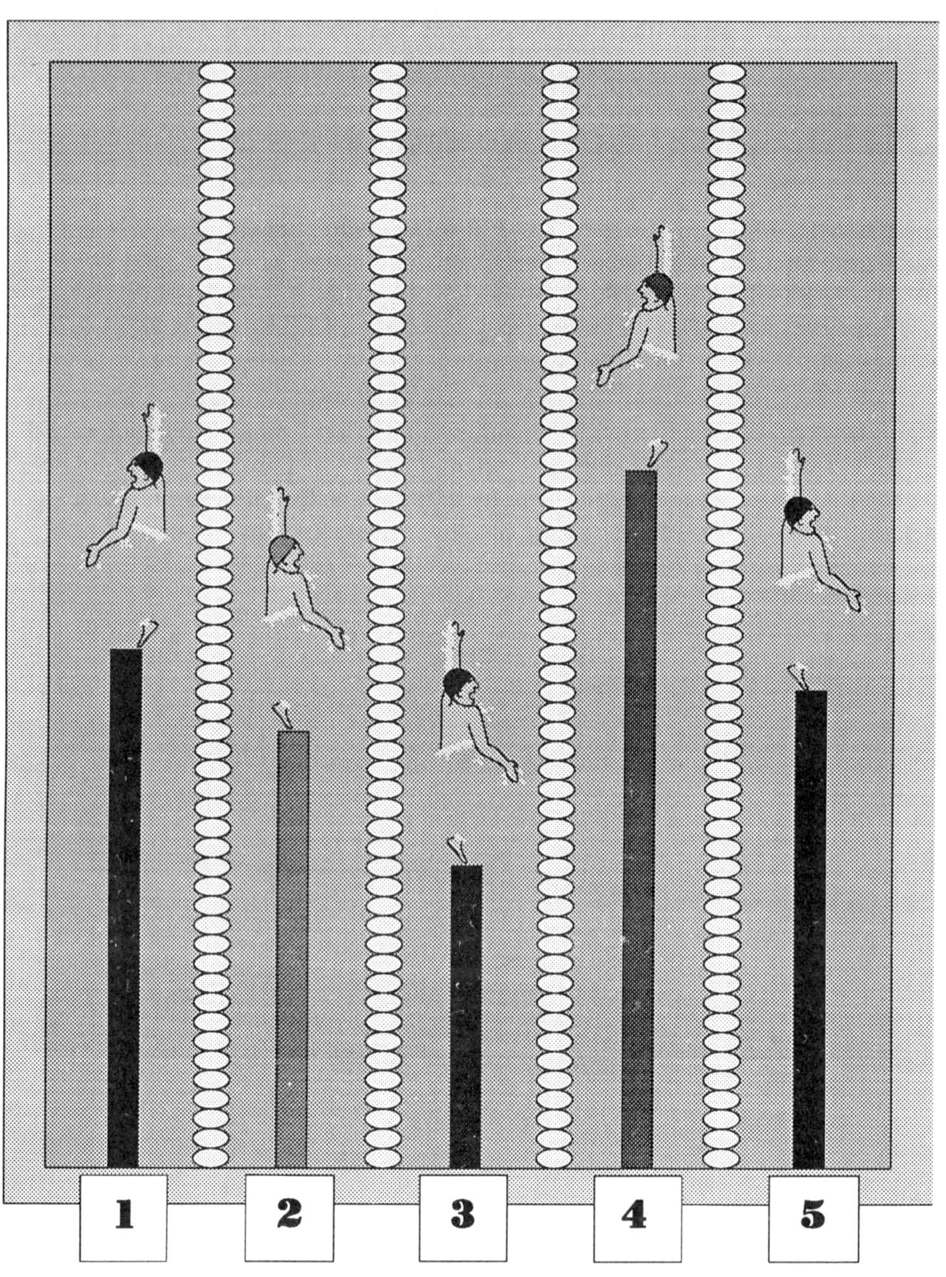
1
2
3
4
5

# 19 - CorelSHOW

CorelSHOW is, basically, a slide show presentation program in the same way that this book is a pamphlet. The program is probably the best slideshow program on the market today. What is all the more amazing is the program has been created from scratch by Corel Corporation. Whereas other slideshow programs will allow you to create static, single slide presentation, CorelSHOW will allow you to do all that but it also allows you to include full animation. You can incorporate any Autodesk Animator FLI files, known as flicks, into your presentation. To check this I made a slideshow with over 150 flicks in it and the whole thing ran perfectly. The CD-ROM comes complete with over 100 flicks for you to use while the floppy disks contain only a few.

CorelSHOW is OLE compatible and it is a client program, i.e. it will accept OLE input from other programs. With Show every slide is made up of two elements; the background, which is common to all slides, and the foreground which may be a chart from CorelCHART, a graphic from CorelDRAW, text from any word processor, and you can even include sounds if you have a sound board. With each slide you have total control over how long the slide stays on screen, the effects used to change to the next one. You can preview you slideshow on screen or you can output it to a printer.

Unfortunately there is not sufficient room here to do more than have a brief look at Show which is a pity because it is a wonderful program. (There will be another book later that covers CorelCHART, CorelSHOW and Photo-Paint in detail. That is the only way to do the three programs justice.) As with the other programs in the Corel Graphics Package, Show is a stand-alone program. You don't have to use it with CorelDRAW or any of the others, it is perfectly happy to work by itself.

When you first run the program you are given the option of opening an existing presentation, i.e. one stored on your hard disk, or starting a completely new one. Here, we're going to use an existing one for the sake of brevity.

a. Run the program by double clicking on its icon. The Show window is maximised by default. The copyright screen will appear and then a dialogue box asking what you want to do.

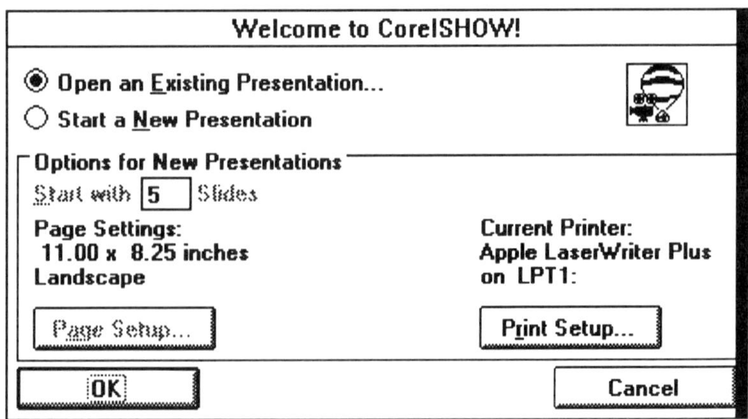


**19.01 Opening Screen**

b. Click on **OK** and the familiar load dialogue box appears. Log into the \SHOW\SAMPLES directory and find IFONLY.SHW. The slideshow will be opened in a cascaded sub-window. Click on the maximise button of this window so it fills the screen.

c. What you can see in front of you is the first slide. This presentation contains four slides, actually three slides and a flick. (It's a bit Americanised but what the heck...) You can page through the slides by clicking on the little numbers in the bottom left hand corner of the window. Each number represents a slide.

d. When you click on number 3 you may get an odd image, depending on your monitor. Don't worry - this is the flick file. Notice as you click on each number that the two clocks in the bottom right hand corner change their values. The rightmost clock gives the total run time of the slideshow. The other one gives the time from the first slide to the currently selected one.

e. To run the slideshow click on the little camera icon on the Status bar. The screen clears then the first slide opens out from the middle of the screen. It stays on view for five seconds and then the second slide appears. That stays in place for seven seconds and then the flick runs. This only lasts for 1 second and then the last slide appears.

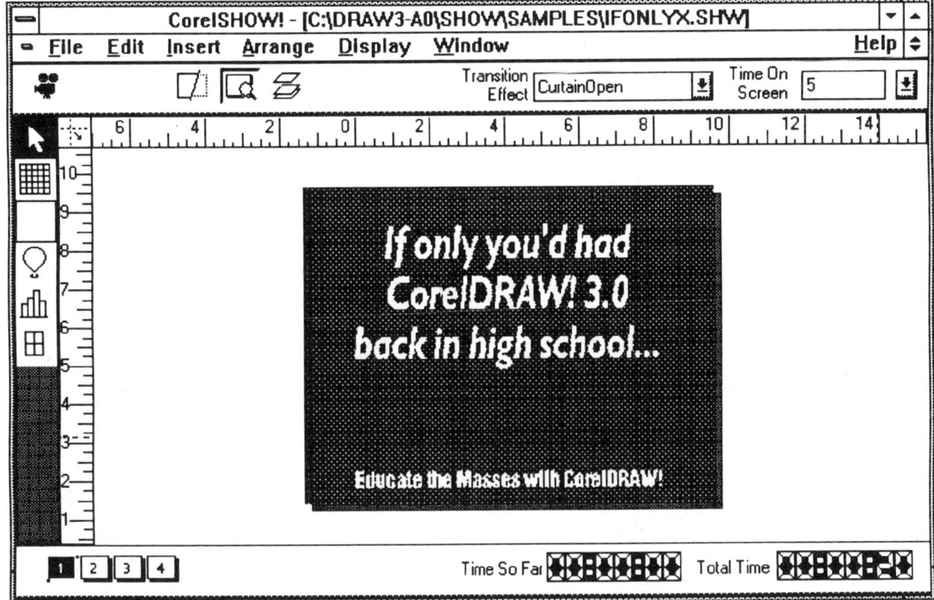


**19.02 Ifonly Loaded**

f. You can see all the slides at once if you wish. Click on the fourth icon on the Status Bar, counting the camera as the first, the one that looks like a stack of cards. This is the **Slide Sorter** and is will display the slides as thumbnails for you.

g. You can pick up any individual slide and drag it to a new position within the presentation. Equally you can delete any slide by selecting it and then pressing **Del**.

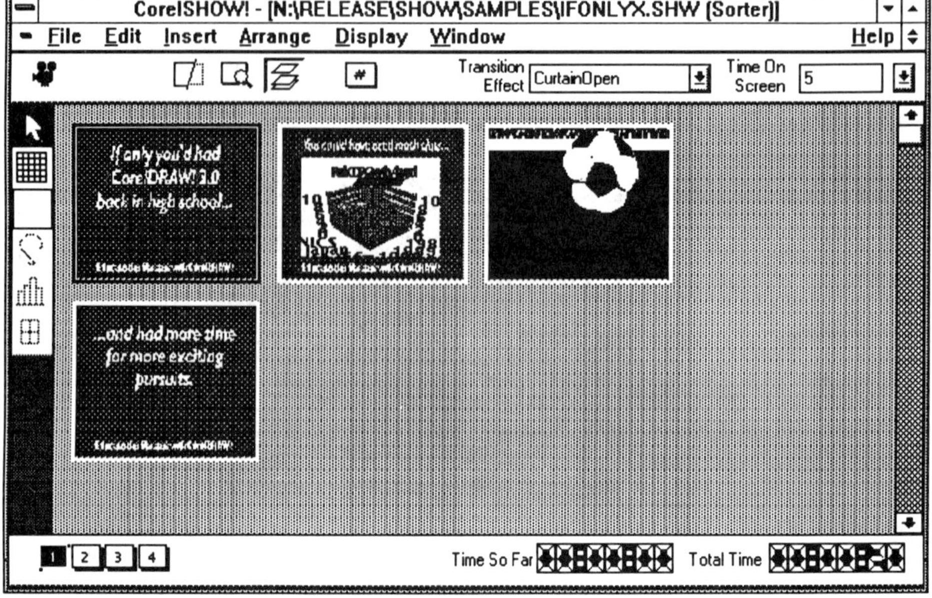


**19.03 Slide Sorter view**

h. Let's add another slide. Open the **Insert menu** and click on **New Page**. A dialogue box appears asking where you want the new page placed in the sequence. Accept the default by clicking on **OK**.

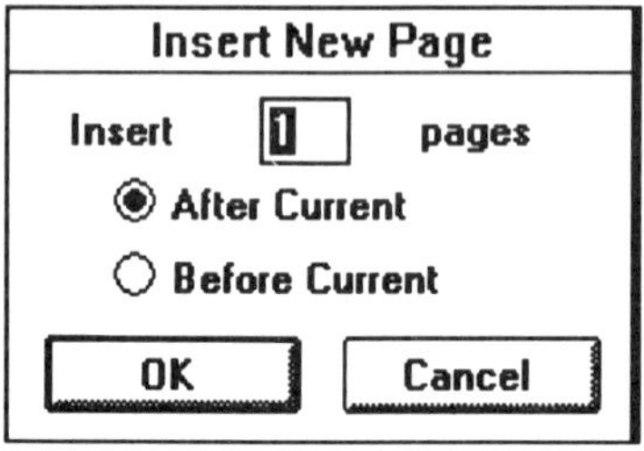


**19.04 Insert new page dialogue box**

i. The page comes in complete with the background, don't forget that all slides share the same background, and is placed after slide 1. The remaining slides get shuffled along.

j. To put something on this new slide you could paste it, use OLE or simply insert it. Here you're doing the latter. Open the **Insert menu** again and click on **Insert File**. A dialogue box appears. Double click on IFONLY5.SHW.

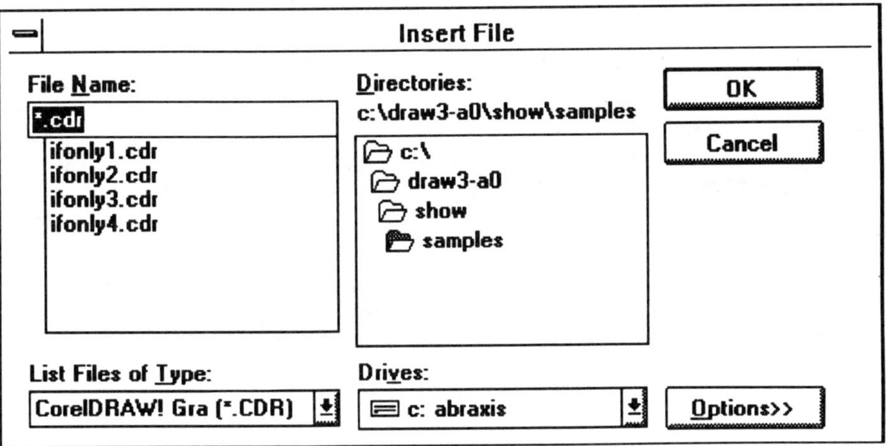


**19.05 Insert file dialogue box**

k. The cursor becomes a crosshair as the dialogue box closes. Drag a bounding box on the slide background and the file you have selected will be placed within it.

l. The words don't really fit as slide two. Go back to the **Sorter View** and move slide two to the end of the slides.

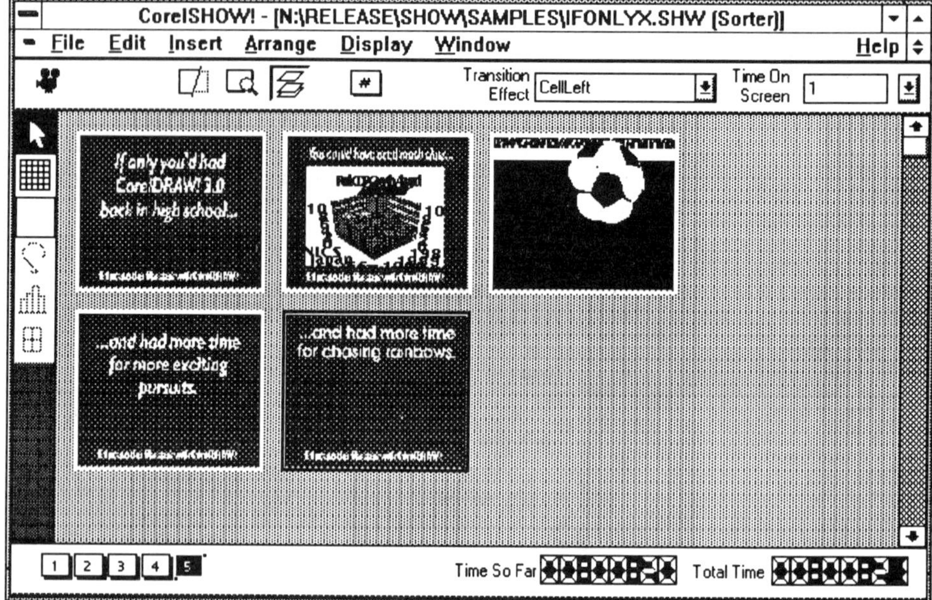


**19.06 Slides rearranged**

m. Still in the sorter view, click on the final slide to make sure it is selected. You're going to change the things that control how that slide is presented. At the right hand side of the Status bar there are two lines, the first is **Transition Effect**. CorelSHOW comes complete with 21 such effects, plus the animation one. For now select HorizBlind.

n. How long do you want the slide to be on screen? The final box on the Status Bar controls that. Set it to 5 seconds. Notice that there are only certain time ranges available to you in the list box.

o. Now run the slideshow by clicking on the camera icon. You can run a slideshow from any of the slides views that CorelSHOW allows. Try some other transition effects.

You can have lots of fun playing with the various effects. Try changing each slide to something different. As you click on each slide you will be told what effect it uses. The one you cannot change is the Animation.

# TOOLS

CorelSHOW provides you with five basic tools:

The **Pointer tool** is the same as in CorelDRAW and you use it in the same way.

The one that looks like a grid is actually the **Background Library tool**. Clicking on this brings up a dialogue box from which you can select any of the backgrounds that are stored on your disk. CorelSHOW comes complete with a number of pre-defined backgrounds, 22 on the floppy version and 138 on CD-ROM. Click on any of the available backgrounds and the current slideshow changes automatically. When you find one you like click on **Done** in the dialogue box to use it.

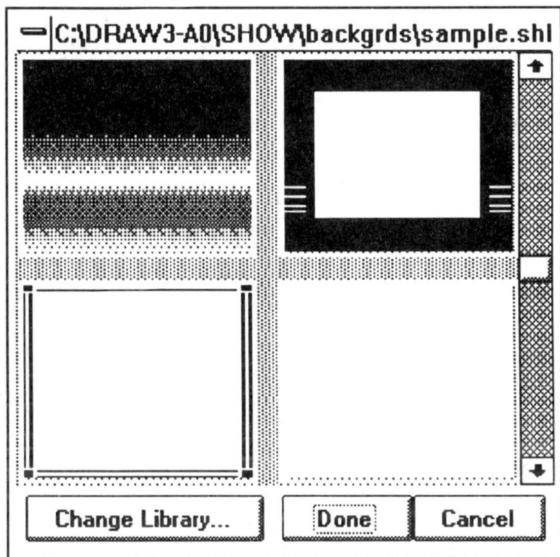


**19.07 Background library**

The third tool is the **OLE link to CorelDRAW**.

The fourth is the **OLE to CorelCHART**.

The final tool is the OLE activator for other OLE applications on your system.

# MENUS

CorelSHOW provides you with six menus, plus Help, once you have a slideshow loaded or have created a new one. The first is **File** which deals with inputting and outputting files.

**New** creates a new slideshow in a sub-window.

**Open** loads an existing presentation.

**Save** and **Save As** write the presentation to disk as normal.

**Save as Background** allows you to create your own backgrounds. You are not limited to just those samples provided.

**Close** terminates the current presentation - not the entire program.

**Print** brings up a dialogue box that allows you to print the presentation in various ways.

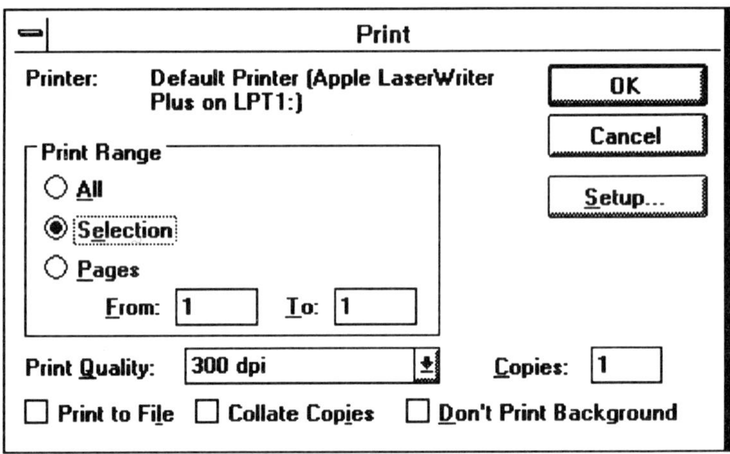


**19.08 Print dialogue box**

**Page Setup** allows you to change the page size and orientation.

**Print Setup** is used to select the relevant printer.

**Run Screen Show** is the same as clicking on the camera icon.

**Exit** terminates the program.

The **Edit menu** contains the usual Windows commands plus a couple of extra ones.

**Undo, Cut, Copy, Paste, Paste Special** and **Clear** are the normal Windows commands.

**Select All** is used to select all the objects on the current page.

**Omit Background** turns off the background for the selected slide.

**Edit Object** is the command used to edit an embedded object.

**Links** displays the linkages for the current presentation if any and their status.

The **Insert menu** places new slides or animations into the current presentation.

**New Page** adds a new slide. You have a choice of adding it before or afterwards and you can also choose to add any number of pages.

**Insert Object** embeds an object from an OLE server program.

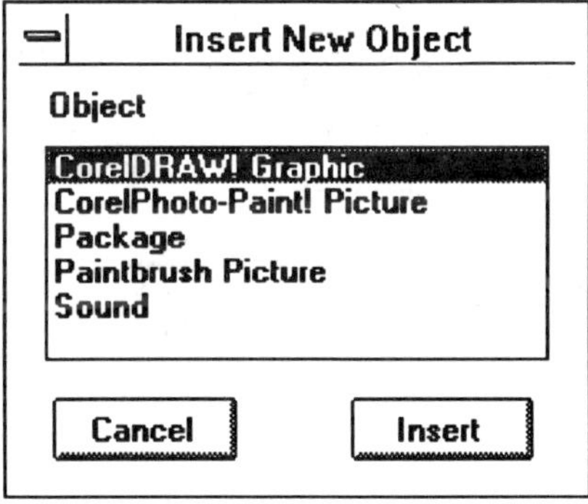


**19.09 Insert Object dialogue box**

**Insert File** adds an object and creates a link to the original for you. You can insert a graphic or a sound using this command.

**Insert Animation** allows you to place an Autodesk flick into any slide position.

The **Arrange menu** affects the arrangement of objects on individual pages.

**To Front** move the selected object(s) to the top of the stack.

**To Back** move the selected object(s) to the bottom of the stack.

**Forward One** and **Backward One** moves the selected object(s) up and down one place in the stack.

**Fit Object to Page** resizes the selected object so that it fits the page exactly.

The **Display menu** affects how the main program window is shown.

**Ruler Setup** brings up a dialogue box that allows you to set where the rulers originate, the measurement system and whether or not the rulers are shown.

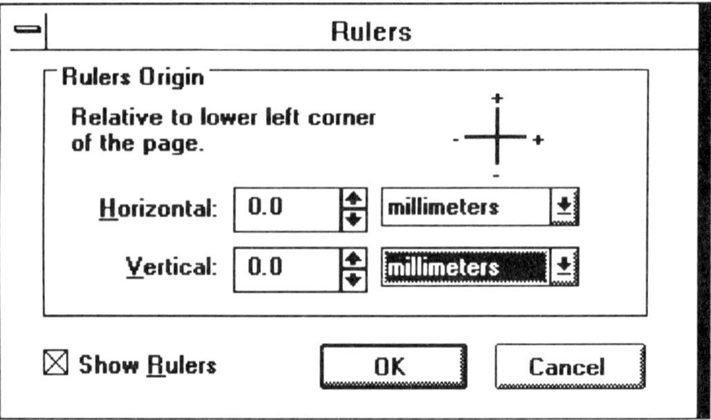


**19.10 Ruler Setup dialogue box**

**Show Rulers** is a toggle, normally on.

**Guidelines Setup** brings up the dialogue box you are familiar with from CorelDRAW. It works in the same way.

**Snap to Guidelines** is identical to the CorelDRAW command and you can use guidelines in the same way.

**Presentation Options** sets the conditions for the slideshow.

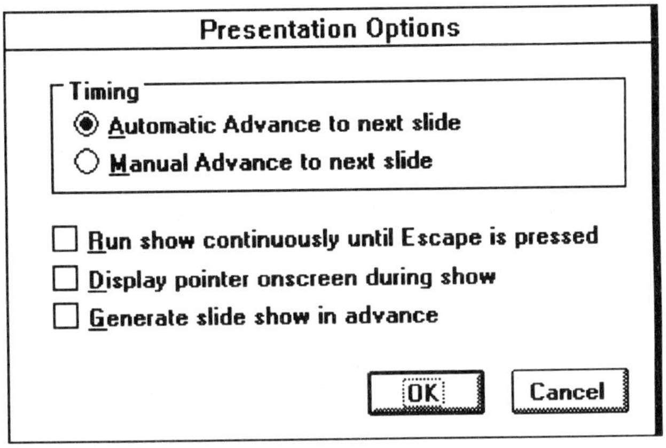

**19.11 Presentation Options dialogue box**

The **Window menu** contains the normal sub-window arrangement commands.

# SUMMARY

CorelSHOW is a wonderful program, it is easy to use, user-friendly and incorporates all the commands and effects you would expect plus a few.

Having said that though don't get carried away with it. If you are wanting to do a slideshow remember some basic rules about using slides.

1. The background should not overpower. Remember that it is going to be on screen most of the time. Don't use very bright colours. Ideally you should plan a colour scheme and then use it.

2. When using flicks don't use ones that are going to make the audience jump, unless you particularly want to make a point. A slideshow is supposed to give information, not frighten the life out of people.

3. Think about colours and how they will appear on screen especially when used with text. Dithered colours will have the effect of breaking up text and making it hard to read.

4. Be careful with typefaces. Remember that sans serif typefaces are harder to read than serifed ones but they make more impact. Don't use sans serif typefaces at small point sizes. Don't use more than four fonts on any one slide and don't use different fonts on every slide. Make a plan and use it.

5. When using sounds pick them carefully. Any sound with a heavy background beat gets very wearing very quickly. Don't use sounds that have a lot of variable intensity, e.g. a train, because it will detract from what you're saying or what is being displayed on screen.

# 20 - Photo-Paint

CorelPHOTO-PAINT is, essentially, ZSoft Corporation's PhotoFinish which Corel have licensed from its creators. The program is probably the best bitmap manipulation program you can get. It is definitely not possible to do more than have a brief look at it here, there just isn't enough room. Instead the program is covered in depth in the second book.

While CorelDRAW is superb at handling vector graphics, the tools it provides for handling bitmaps are very limited, hence the inclusion of Photo-Paint. The program provides more tools than just about any other program I know of.

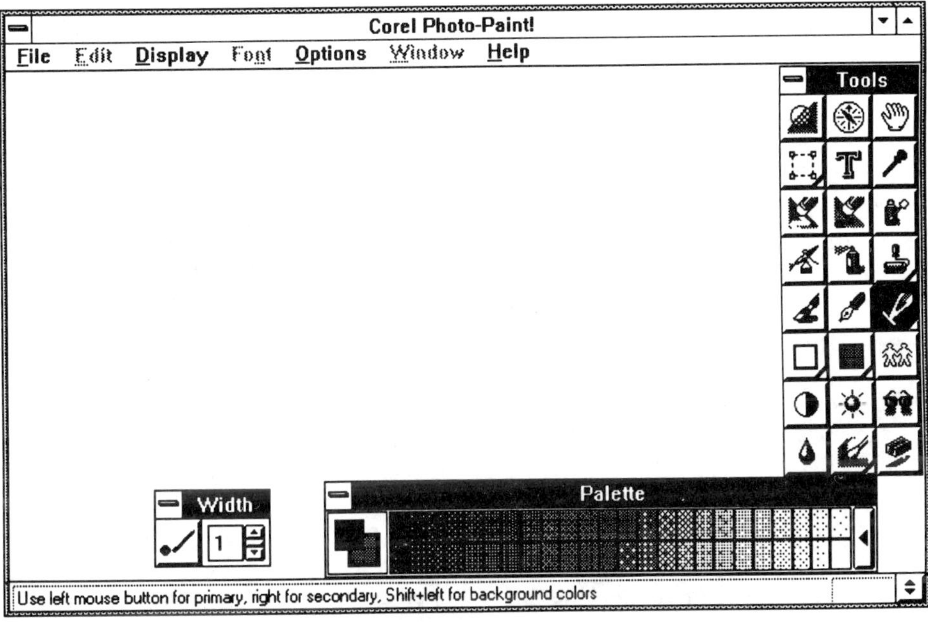


**20.01 CorelPhoto-Paint**

When you run the program you get an open window with the toolbox, palette and brush controls as sub-windows. I just wish that they'd made the toolbox into a roll-up. You can rearrange the tools if you wish.

a. Click on the toolbox **Control Box** button and then on **Layout**. You now have a choice of arrangements. If you click on **Ungroup** all the tools, all 37 of them, will be displayed. If you run the command again and then select **2 Rows** you get a long thin toolbox that will fit neatly within the window. It is only when the tools are ungrouped that you get them all.

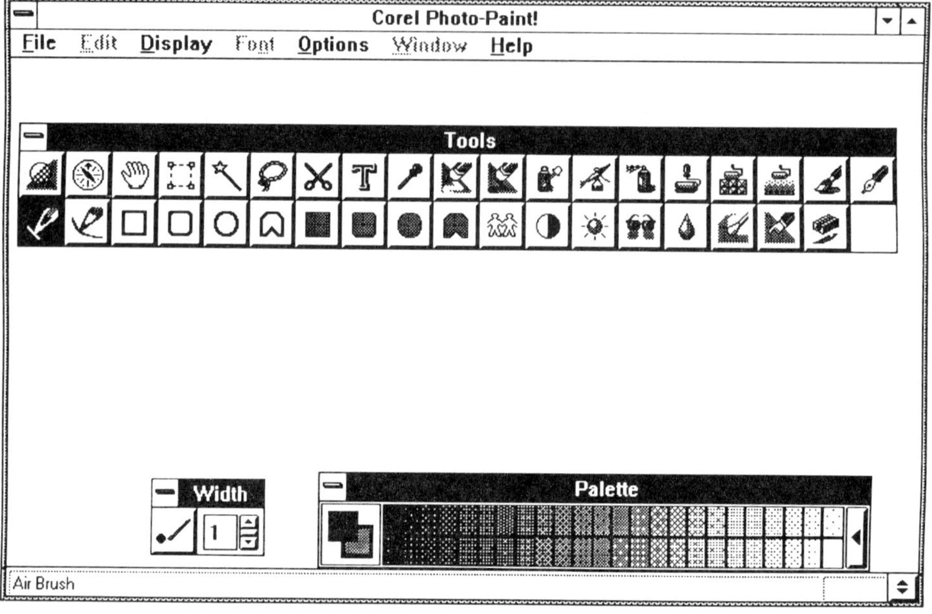


**20.02 New toolbox**

b. You can shrink the Palette to a smaller size by clicking on the arrowhead at the end of it. It works rather like a horizontal roll-up.

c. Time to load an image. Open the **File menu** and click on **Open**. The usual file input dialogue box appears. The program comes with three sample files for you, all in PCX format. Find and load BALLOON.PCX, it's in the \PHOTPNT\SAMPLES directory.

d. The image is a long thin one, so you can resize the toolbox and have everything on screen neatly.

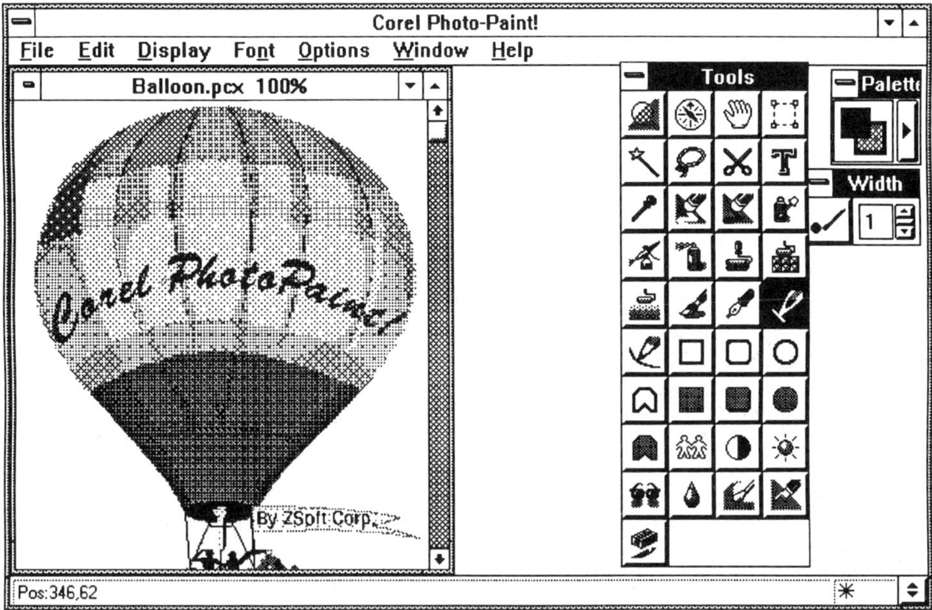


**20.03 Image in**

e. Let's blend the words into the background. Find the Smear tool. As you move the cursor over all the tools the Status Line, along the bottom of the screen, tells you what each tool is.

f. When you try to use the tool you get an error message. So let's convert the image. Open the **Edit menu** and click on **Convert To**. A pop-out list appears. Click on **24 Bit Colour**.

g. You get a new sub-window which contains the converted image, called appropriately enough **New-1.PCX**. You can now use the smear tool. But it's a bit small. Change the size of it in the Width sub-window. The size here refers to pixels, you are using bitmaps after all, and you can increase it to a maximum of 40. Once you've done so move the tool over the words on the balloon while holding down the mouse button.

h. Yuk, what a mess. Press **Alt-Backspace** to undo it. Smear it again but do it quickly. The effects generated by the smear tool are speed dependent. If you move the tool fast then you get minimum effects, if you move it very slowly then you get maximum smearing.

Play with the various tools and see what they do. At any time you can create another copy of the original balloon by converting it. You can have a maximum of eight images open at any one time.

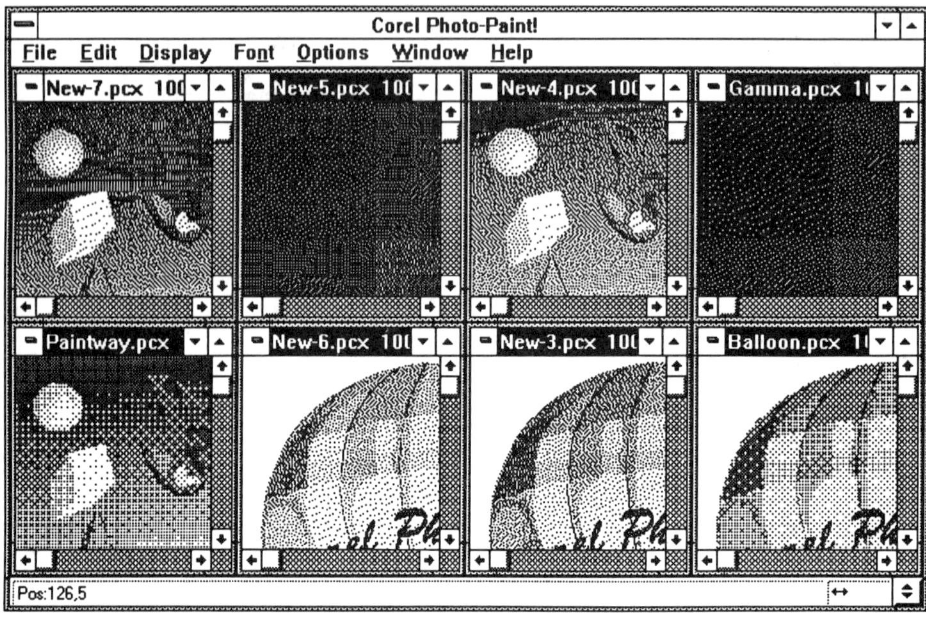


**20.04 Eight images**

# TOOLS

Here's a brief run down on all the tools available in CorelPHOTO-PAINT.

**Airbrush** gives you very fine dots. The size of the airbrushed area can be changed in the width dialogue box.

**Blend Paintbrush** allows you to smooth the transition from one colour to another. You use the tool freehand, that is by moving it around.

**Box Selection** defines a quadrilateral area of the image so it can be cut or copied.

**Brighten Paintbrush** brightens colours. Used freehand.

**Clone** is a neat little tool that allows you to copy one area of the image to elsewhere. Select the tool and click once in the centre of where you want to clone from. Then move the tool elsewhere and, holding down the left mouse button, move the cursor back and forth. You will gradually copy the image. It takes a bit of getting used to. Try using it with a large width. If you double click on the tool you get its control dialogue box.

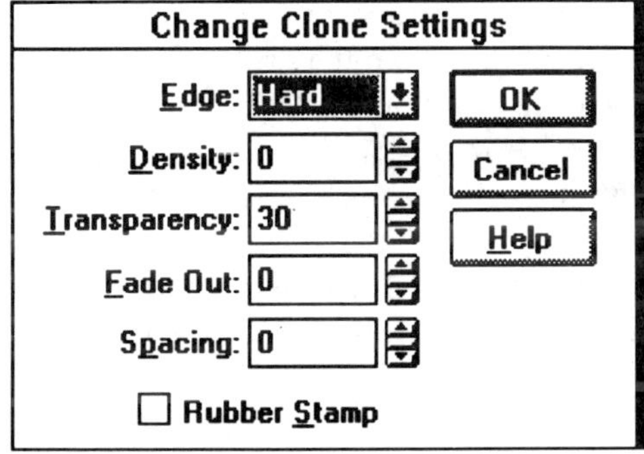


**20.05 Clone dialogue box**

**Colour Replacer** allows you to replace one colour with another. You select both colours from the palette. If you double click on the tool it automatically replaces all occurrences of the source colour with the target colour.

**Contrast Paintbrush** allows you to change the contrast of colours in freehand.

**Curve** draws freehand Bezier curves. Use the tool the same way as you would in CorelDRAW. The only difference is that you move the nodes with the tool itself.

**Erase** wipes things out!

The **Eyedropper** is a very handy tool, especially when using 256 colours. What it does is automatically select colours for you. Select the tool and then click on any area in the image. The palette automatically moves to that colour.

**Filled Box** draws filled in boxes. Use the tool as you would the rectangle tool in CorelDRAW. The outline will be in the first selected colour, the fill in the second. You can constrain the tool to produce squares by holding down **Shift** as you drag.

**Filled Box, Rounded** as above but with rounded corners.

**Filled Ellipse** as with box but draws ellipses. Hold down Shift to create circles.

**Filled Polygon** draws straight line shapes filled with the secondary colour. Select the tool and click once to anchor the starting point. Thereafter wherever you click will produce a line from the previous point to the click position. To finish the shape and fill it in double click.

The **Fountain Pen** draws freehand shapes with hard edges.

The **Hand** tool allows you to pick up an image and move it around within the open sub-window. Obviously you can only move it if it extends outside the sub-window boundary.

**Hollow Box** as with box but in outline only.

**Hollow Box, Rounded** as above with rounded corners.

**Hollow Polygon** produces straight line shapes without a fill.

**Lasso** is like the selection box but the area you are defining is freehand, i.e. a non-regular shape. You use the tool as if it was a freehand brush or pen.

**Line** draws straight lines.

**Local Undo** allows you to undo freehand areas. If you undo you cancel all actions with a given tool since you selected it. Using Local Undo you can be selective about what you undo.

The **Locator** tool displays duplicated areas in all images. Has no effect otherwise.

The **Magic Wand** selects areas with the same colours that you want to do something with, e.g. move, copy, cut, etc. Once you have defined an area you can manipulate it.

**Paint Roller** fills an enclosed area with the selected colour.

**Paint Roller, Tile Pattern** is similar to the above but it fills the enclosed area with a tiled pattern. CorelPHOTO-PAINT comes complete with a number of tile patterns you can use. Before you can use the tool you must have loaded one of these. You have to use the **Options menu** and then **Tile Pattern** to load the pattern - not load it by opening the pattern.

**Paint Roller, Gradient** is like Fountain Fill in CorelDRAW. You select a starting colour then an ending colour and you get a blending from one to the other. You can change the type of fill, there are only three choices, in the **Options menu, Gradient Type** command.

**Paintbrush** allows you to draw freehand shapes with soft edges.

**Scissors** allows you to define polygonal shapes for use with the manipulation tools or the Windows clipboard.

The **Sharpen Paintbrush** tightens up edges. Use it carefully because it can be detrimental on large areas. Stick to using it with small areas or contour lines.

**Smear Paintbrush** allows you to blend one block of colour into another, softening the dividing line between the two.

The **Smudge Paintcan** randomly mixes pixels in the selected area. The tool width can be adjusted. Use it to add texture to an image but carefully.

**Spraycan** produces random dots of a selected colour. The size of the sprayed area is controlled by the width of the tool.

The **Text** tool allows you to add text to your images. You can use any font or typeface that is installed on your system. Select the font you want to use first, from the Font menu and then click on the tool. A dialogue box appears that allows you to enter the text. Once you click on **OK** a selection appears on screen with your text in it.

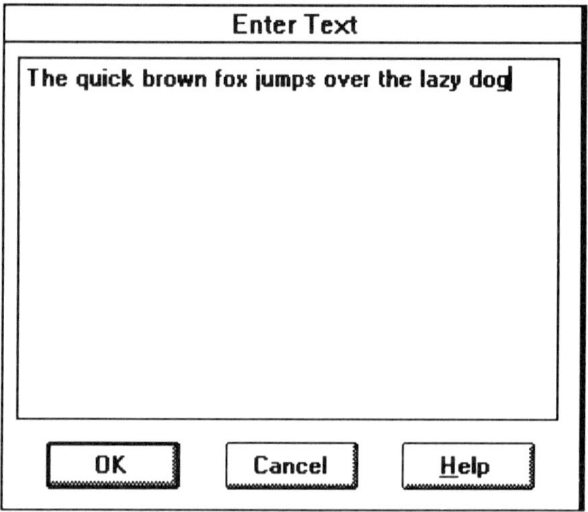


**20.06 Text dialogue box**

**Tint Paintbrush** allows you to alter colours within selected areas of the image. The colours are tinted with the selected colour to create an effect as if you were looking through coloured glass. (Computerised rose coloured spectacles?)

**Zoom** works just like the magnifier in CorelDRAW. Click on the tool and drag a bounding box around the area that you want to zoom in to.

# Menus

CorelPHOTO-PAINT provides you with six menus plus help. Here's a brief rundown of what they contain. The **File** menu is normal.

**New** starts a new image in a separate sub-window. When you run the command a dialogue box appears allowing you to specify the size and type of the image.

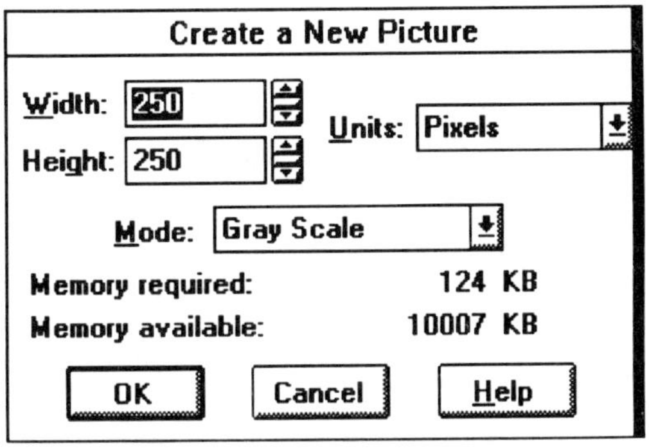

Create a New Picture
Width: 250
Height: 250
Units: Pixels
Mode: Gray Scale
Memory required: 124 KB
Memory available: 10007 KB
OK Cancel Help

**20.07 New dialogue box**

**Open** allows you to load an existing image.

**Close** terminates the current image, not the entire program.

**Save** and **Save As** work as normal with the usual dialogue boxes.

**Clear** erases everything in the current sub-window but retains the title.

**Print** produces a hard copy of your selected image. The dialogue box allows you to set various parameters.

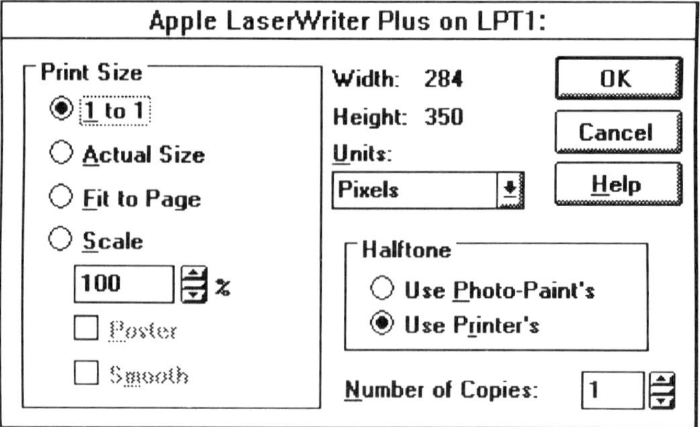


**20.08 Print dialogue box**

**Printer Setup** allows you to select a printer.

**Exit** closes the program.

The **Edit menu** contains the usual Windows commands plus a few specialised ones.

**Undo**, **Cut**, **Copy**, **Paste** and **Delete** are all standard.

**Copy To** is like using save as except that it applies to portions of an image rather than the whole. You select an area, e.g. with the scissors, and then save just that portion of the file to the disk.

**Paste From** is the reverse of the above. It allows you to paste in an entire image into the current one.

**Convert To** allows you to change the current image to a different type. You can have Black and White Line Art, Black and White Printer Halftone, Black and White Screen Halftone, 256 Colour, 24 Bit colour or Grey Scale.

**Filter** pops-out a large list box that contains twelve sub-commands. Most of them work only with 256 colours or greyscales.

**Add Noise** produces a grainy effect.

**Blend** smoothes and softens the image.

**Brightness and Contrast** lightens or darkens the images.

**Colour/Grey Map** allows you to adjust the lighting effects in the image.

**Diffuse** scatters the pixels in the selected area.

**Edge Detect** creates an outline of the image or selected areas of it.

**Emboss** is nice, it produces a bas-relief image. The command uses a dialogue box that allows you to set the way the embossing is done.

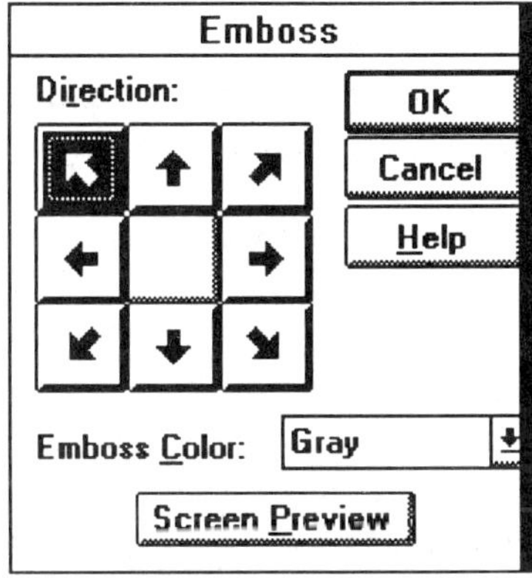


**20.09 Emboss dialogue box**

**Equalise** stretches colours. Dark areas become black, light areas become white and colours in between are sort of blended.

**Posterize** makes the image blocky, like on television when they're trying not to show someone's face.

**Motion Blur** blurs out the image to create the illusion of movement.

**Remove Spots** tidies up the image by deleting excessive blocks of pixels.

**Sharpen** enhances the detail in the image.

**Transform** allows you to flip, invert, rotate and otherwise change the image. It too uses a list box but the contents are all straightforward.

The **Display** menu controls what appears on screen.

**Zoom** allows you to magnify the current image in various degrees.

**100%** is a toggle that shows the image full size.

**Zoom to Fit** makes the image fit within the sub-window by changing the size of the sub-window to fit the image.

**Workboxes** refers to the Palette, Width and Toolbox and whether or not they are on screen. Each can be toggled on or off using **Ctrl-[initial letter]**.

**Full Screen** turns off the Title and Menu bars and maximises the remainder of the window.

**Show Screen** clears all the tools and cursor and leaves just the image.

**Optimise Display** can improve the appearance of the image on screen. It really only works if the image contains more colours than your screen can display. It only affects the display - nothing else.

The **Font** menu allows you to select fonts for use with the Text tool. It really only contains a single command, Select, which brings up a dialogue box from which you select the font you want to use. When you have selected fonts previously the menu will list the last four used.

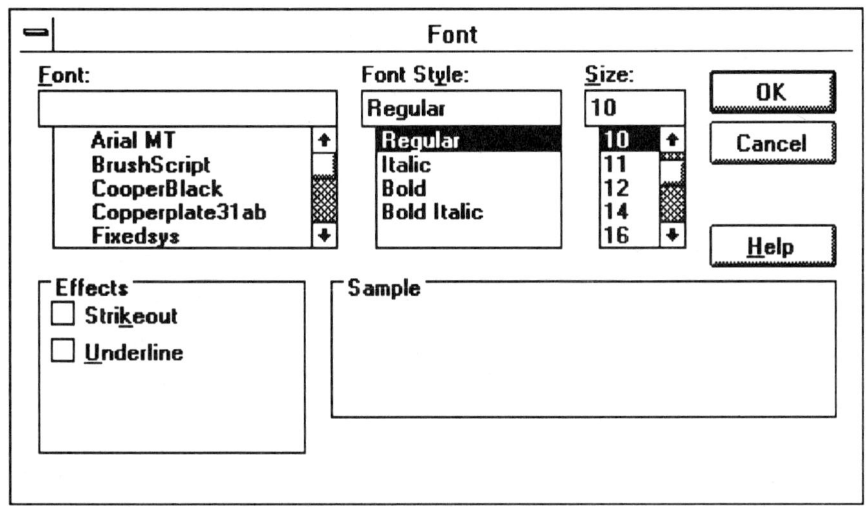


**20.10 Font select dialogue box**

The **Options** menu sets various parameters for the program and its tools.

**Brush Style** allows you to select a brush shape.

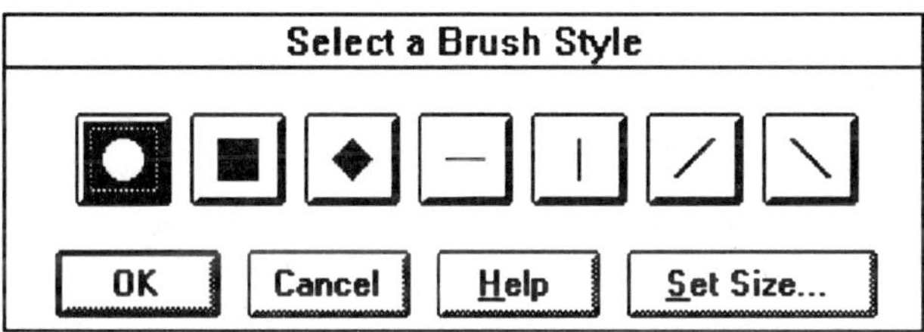


**20.11 Brush Styles**

**Colour Tolerance** is used to specify a range of colours for use with the roller, colour replacer and Magic Wand tools.

**Gradient Type** sets the gradient fill.

**Palette** allows you to select the kind of palette you will use.

**Preferences** sets the basic parameters for the program operation.

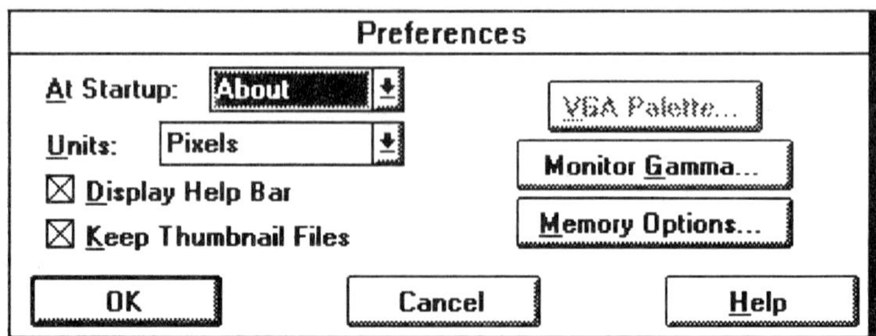


**20.12 Preferences dialogue box**

**Soft Brush Settings** applies only to soft tools, Paintbrush, Airbrush, Smear and Clone. It changes the way they operate and can only be used with 256 colours and greyscales.

**Tile Pattern** allows you to load an image for use with the Tile Roller.

The final menu, **Window**, controls the display of sub-windows. The only extra command is **Duplicate** which makes a duplicate of the current image.

# SUMMARY

CorelPHOTO-PAINT is a full blown program in its own right which has been licensed from ZSoft Corporation by Corel. It is, without doubt, one of the best bitmap editing programs on the market. It combines ease of use with a huge range of tools and effects that will make using bitmaps much easier.

# Appendices

# A - WINDOWS 3.1

CorelDRAW 3.0 is designed to work best using Windows 3.1, e.g. it has full OLE capabilities. You can use the program with Windows 3.0 but you will get better results using the later version. Arguably CorelDRAW 3.0 is the first major software release to be fully Windows 3.1 compatible - and that includes those programs from Microsoft themselves.

Here's an interesting little snippet about Windows 3.1 for you.

a. Run any of Windows own associated applications, e.g. Notepad, Write or Control Panel.

b. Open the **Help** menu and click on **About**. A message box will appear. In the top left hand corner of the box will be a little icon of the program you are running.

c. Hold down **Shift** and **Ctrl** and then double click on the icon. Nothing will happen - yet.

d. Click on **OK** to close the message box. Click on **Help About** again to bring up the message box. Hold **Shift-Ctrl** and double click on the little icon again. This time you will get a little Microsoft flag, fluttering in the breeze, and a message.

e. Click on **OK** to close the message box again. Then open it a third time. Repeat the **Shift-Ctrl** double click. This time you get a little cartoon character and a scrolling list of the people responsible for the Windows 3.1 programs.

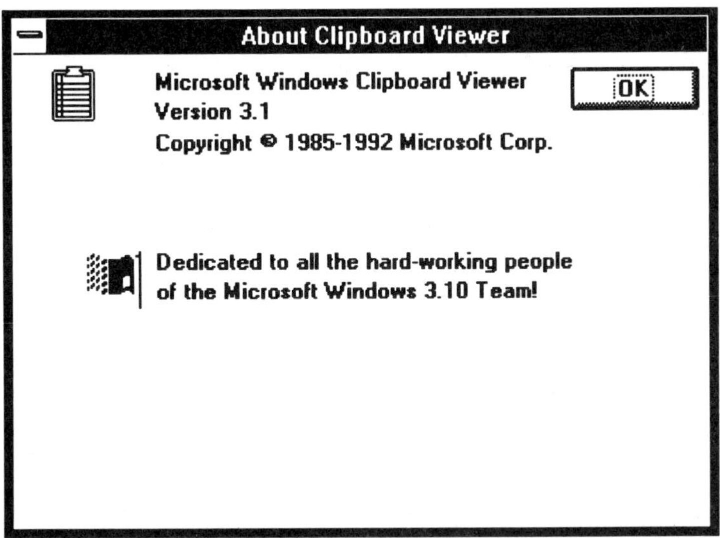


**A.01 Character cartoon**

There are actually four possible cartoon figures and one of them will appear at random:

One is intended to be Bill Silverberg, the Windows Product Manager. He wears glasses and is bearded.

Another is a teddy bear dressed in a suit. I haven't been able to find out who this is supposed to represent.

There is also a cartoon of Bill Gates.

The final figure is a balding guy whose name is Steve Ballmer - he's Microsoft's co-president.

# B - CORELDRW.INI

In this appendix we're going to look in a reasonable amount of detail at the contents of the CORELDRW.INI file. You will find this in the directory that contains the program files and it can be loaded into any text editor, e.g. Windows Notepad.

A word of warning. If you intend making any changes directly to this file then you must make a backup copy of it first.

The first section of the file is concerned with the main configuration of the program.

**[CDrawConfig]**
**Applic=C:\COREL\DRAW**
**ConfigDir=C:\COREL\DRAW**
**FontsDir=C:\COREL\FONTS**
**CorelFiltersDir=C:\COREL\FILTERS**
**AutoBackupDir=C:\COREL\AUTOBACK**

The first few lines are largely self-explanatory. Where is the program located? Where are the fonts? And so on.

**AutoBackupMins=10**

This line is the time interval, which range from 0 to 99 minutes, between automatic saves. By default is set to 10 minutes but you can change it, safely, to anything you wish. If you set it to zero then you turn the facility off. Any file created by the auto backup will be deleted whenever you do a proper save using Save, Save As or use the New command. Backups are placed into the Autobackup sub-directory and they have an extension of .ABK - not .BAK. If you don't specify a separate directory for the backups, in the previous line, then they will be placed into whatever directory contains the CORELDRW.INI file. If the program should crash, for any reason, you can get back to the last backup by simply renaming the .ABK file to a .CDR one.

**BigPalette=0**
**BigToolbox=0**

These two lines are intended for sue by anyone using a high resolution monitor, e.g. 1024 by 728. At such a resolution the toolbox and palette can be minute. By turning these settings on, i.e. changing the values to 1, the palette and toolbox are magnified fourfold.

**CalligraphicClipboard=1**

This allows you to send images with calligraphic effects, e.g. a pen angle, to the Windows Clipboard. If you change the value to zero then the effect is turned off, this produces smaller clipboard files but loses calligraphic effects. The setting can also affect certain of the vector format export filters.

**ClipboardFountains=0**

Allows you to export fountain fills to the Clipboard. By default it is turned off, i.e. has a value of 0. If you turn it on you should be aware that it places a heavy strain on your system resources. An alternative is to export the image as an EPS file and then import that into whatever application you would have pasted the clipboard content to. EPS format files retain all the information about fountain fills and calligraphic lines.

**CMYKPalette=CORELDRW.PAL**

The name of the current palette. This entry is updated whenever you close CorelDRAW.

**DefaultFont=Avalon,1,24**

Self-explanatory really. The font name, its effect and size in points. The font name must be one of those as it appears before the equals sign in the [PSResidentFonts] section, see below. The effects must be one of the following: 1 - Normal, 2 - Bold, 4 - Italic or 8 - Bold-Italic. The maximum point size is 1440 which gives 20" letters!

**ExportTextAsCurves=1**

Some programs will overwrite a CorelDRAW font with their own fonts when you import an image that has been exported from CorelDRAW. This can lead to problems, hence this setting. With it turned on, i.e. the value is 1, which it is by default then any text exported is not sent as text but as graphical images. This prevents any overwriting by the importing program. It is not necessary to convert text to curves within the CorelDRAW image first - the process is automatic.

**FontRasterizer=1**

Toggles the font rasterizer on or off. By default it is on. What it does is improve the quality of printed text at small point size, i.e. below about 6 points. If you never use such small text you could turn it off, otherwise leave it on.

**INKPalette=CORELDRW.IPL**

The name of the current ink palette! As with the palette this is updated whenever you close CorelDRAW.

**MakeBackupWhenSave=1**

With this turned on, which it is by default, you automatically make a backup of your files with the second and every subsequent save. The first time the file is written to disk as normal. The second time, the first file is renamed to [filename].BAK and then the file is written to disk as [filename].CDR. Each subsequent save then continues the process. You can only have a single backup copy though.

**MaximizeCDraw=0**

Makes CorelDRAW appear in a maximised window or not. By default this setting is turned off, i.e. has a value of zero, so that CorelDRAW appears in a tiled window.

**OLEServerEmulateMDI=1**

This has to do with the Object Linking and Embedding features of Windows 3.1. What it does is specify that for the purposes of registration CorelDRAW will register itself as a server during a single session of use. Normally all Windows 3.1 applications would open a new copy of the program every time you it needed to register. In other words in this area CorelDRAW breaks the Windows dictates. Essentially it means that you can edit a linked or embedded object in the current CorelDRAW program rather than having to open a second or subsequent copy to it. (I can see OLE causing more technical support problems that anything else!)

**PSBitmapFontLimit=8**

This applies only if you are printing text to a PostScript printer. The range is 0 to 250 with a default of 8. The object is to prevent the printer running out of memory and thus producing an error message when you are printing lots of text, especially at small sizes. I just leave it alone because it works fine with my printer.

**PSComplexityThreshold=3000**

When you print complex images you get a message box telling you that the program is sending item x of x. At some point you may find an additional message saying **(Complex Object)**. It means just that. You can stop the message occurring, and speed up printing, by increasing the value here. By default it is set to 3000 which refers to the number of nodes on a single path. You can increase it all the way to 30,000, or decrease it to 20.

Mind you, I suggest you don't. If the message keeps occurring then try increasing the value slowly, say in increments of 500. You should find that at a particular value everything is okay. Bear in mind that if you increase it too far you may lose definition. The only answer is to play with the setting I'm afraid. Low values may resolve any problem using fountain, bitmap or full colour fills.

The value should apply only to PostScript printers. However, if you are using an Inkjet you may find that you get better images by adjusting this value. Don't ask me why - I don't know - but it does work.

**ShowObjectsWhenMoving=0**

Does just that. By default it is turned off, to turn it on change the value to 1. With it turned off, as you move things you only see a bounding box. This makes moving somewhat faster. If you turn the setting on then you will see the actual object but it can slow down any move operation.

**TextOnClpMetafile=0**

Specifies that any text which is cut or copied to the Windows clipboard should be text and not curves. With a value of 0 the text is text, with a value of 1 it is curves.

**WarnBadOrientation=1**

CorelDRAW can automatically turn the paper around in the Control Panel if it needs to. In other words you no longer need to make sure that you have the paper orientation correct because the program does it for you. This is great - until you come to use another program that doesn't turn the paper back again. But that's not CorelDRAW's fault.

However, you can have a warning message about this is you want. By default the value is 1 to produce the message, turn it to 0 to turn it off. If it is on then whenever you try to print something that is oriented "wrongly", e.g. you use landscape instead of portrait, you will get an error message. From there you have a three choices of how to proceed.

**3DLook=1**

Affects many of the buttons and dialogue boxes. By default it is on. Change the value to 0 to turn it off. If it is off then you can use the Windows Control Panel colours for the dialogue boxes instead of that awful grey!

**SpellLanguage=English**
**SpellDict=IENM9150.DAT**
**HyphenateDict=HECRP301.DAT**
**ThesaurusDict=COM_THES.DIS**

The last four lines in this section can be treated as one. They simply give the filenames of the various dictionaries that CorelDRAW uses. Don't change them manually.

**[CorelDrivers]**
**MGXPS=1**
**PSCRIPT=1**

Turns various drivers on or off. You should not need to change these manually.

**[Mosaic]**
**Applic=C:\COREL\DRAW\mosaic3.exe**

Specifies the location of the Mosaic program file.

**[CDrawImportFilters]**
**CDR=IMPCDR,"CorelDRAW!",*.CDR**
**...**
**TXT=IMPTXT,"Text",*.TXT**

This section gives the names of file extensions, the filter that will be used to handle them, the name that appears in the import dialogue box and the actual extension names that are valid for that filter. You are unlikely ever to need to change them manually.

**[CDrawExportFilters]**
**PCX2=EXPPCX.DLL,"CorelPHOTO-PAINT! Bitmap",*.PCX;*.PCC**
**...**
**TTF=EXPTTF.DLL,"TrueType Font",*.TTF**

As with the import filters, each line gives the file type, the filter to be used, the name as it appears in the dialogue box and the actual file extension.

**[CorelAIExport]**
**V88Header=aihead.dat**
**V3Header=ai3head.dat**
**V3Footer=ai3foot.dat**

Information about the Adobe Illustrator filter. Don't change these.

**[CorelDXFExport]**
**Header=dxfhead.dat**

DXF export filter information. Do not modify these settings.

**[300dpi]**

**...**

**[3386dpi]**

I've left out the lines from each of the above sections. The sections apply to doing colour separation on various devices. The values are sets of screen angles and frequencies which have been preset for certain output devices. The object is to prevent the appearance of moiré patterns. You should never need to change the values in the lines manually.

**[CorelDrwFonts]**
**Aardvark=2 aardvark.wfn**
**...**
**ZurichCalligraphic=4 zurich.wfn**

Lists the old WFN fonts that CorelDRAW used to use. If you want to still use them in version 3.0 you must copy them on to your hard disk. The name before the equals sign is the name that appears in the text dialogue box, the number after the equals sign is the total weights available and the final name is the actual font name. Really these are no longer needed because they have been superseded by the TrueType and Adobe Type 1 fonts that accompany the new release. The names are preceded by an semi-colon, so they are inactive. If you want to use a particular font just delete this.

**[CORELDRWSymbols]**
**Animals=animals.wfn**
**...**
**Weather=weather.wfn**

The list of symbol library names and their associated files. The name before the equals sign is what appears in the dialogue box, the name after the sign is the actual filename. You should not need to change these.

**[PSResidentFonts]**
**Aardvark-Bold=Aachen-Bold 0**
**...**
**ZurichCalligraphic-Italic=ZapfChancery-MediumItalic 3**

The list of fonts available in CorelDRAW and their equivalent PostScript names. Don't change any of these settings.

**[CORELDRW20FontMap]**
**aardvark.wfn=Aardvark 0,606,0,0**
**...**
**zurich.wfn=ZurichCalligraphic 0,0,472,0**

This section of the file matches the fonts from the previous versions, i.e. 2.0 and 2.01, with the fonts in this new release. Its purpose is to allow you to load a file that was created in an earlier version of CorelDRAW without losing textual information. Do not change the contents of this section.

# C - QUIZ ANSWERS

## Q1 - RECTANGLES AND CIRCLES

a. Draw a rectangle that is 150 mms by 125 mms.

b. Draw a single circle with a diameter of 25 mm.

c. Use Align to align the circle to the top left hand corner of the rectangle.

d. Select the circle.

e. Duplicate it using the plus key on the numeric keypad. Move it straight down 25 mms.

f. Repeat step e until you have a line of circles down the left hand side of the rectangle.

g. Select all the circles. Duplicate them and align them to the right hand side of the rectangle.

h. Select one of the corner circles. Duplicate it and move it along the top of the rectangle. Repeat until you have a complete line.

i. Repeat previous step using one of the bottom circles.

j. Select the rectangle and all circles. Combine them using **Ctrl-C** and then fill with black.

k. Duplicate the finished shape and resize it to fit within the blank space in the centre of the shape.

l. Duplicate the resized shape and resize it again to fit within the centre again. That's it.

## Q2 - DIAMOND SQUARES

a. Draw a square, as it happens it was 100 mms to a side.

b. Duplicate it and then rotate it left 15 degrees - hold down **Ctrl** as you rotate.

c. Repeat step b four times.

d. Select all the squares, combine them using **Ctrl-C** and then fill with black.

e. Duplicate the first shape and resize it to fit within the original.

## Q3 - SYMBOLIC

a. This image contains mainly images from the symbol library, imported and resized.

b. The text was added and speech balloon was sized to fit around it.

## Q4 - TRIGON

a. This one is slightly odd. The top triangle is a square that has been converted to an arrowhead shape.

b. The remainder is simply a series of lines that were combined and then overlaid on the top shape.

c. The whole was then combined and fountain filled.

Don't ask me why this works - it shouldn't because the lines are open ended - it just does. I found it entirely by accident.

### Q5 - SPHEREVILLE

a. This was done to show how you can create complex illustrations using simple shapes. The central circle was drawn first. It was then duplicated and resized six times to make the series of middle circles. These were then duplicated and rotated to fit between the others.

b. The connecting lines are actually just rectangles that were laid in and then sent behind the circles.

The original image was in full colour, but it took me about six hours to get all the angles (especially those of the fountain fills in the connectors) right, but it actually looks better in monochrome. Even having the connector tubes blank works well. It has to be admitted that the printout of this image is not very good - it looks much better on screen.

### Q6 - VALENTINE

a. Draw a circle. Use the Straight Line envelope edit and drag the central top down while holding **Ctrl**. That gives the heart shape.

b. Add the text. In this case the typeface is Arabia. Place it over the heart and use the Single Curve envelope option to bend it fractionally.

c. Draw a rectangle. Use the Two Curves envelope to shape it into a ribbon. Duplicate this, mirror it and align it to the first ribbon. Place the duplicate ribbon behind the heart.

d. Add the final words. Use the Two curve envelope to fit them to the front ribbon.

e. Fill the ribbons with a linear fountain fill and the heart with a radial one.

## Q7 - SANDGLASS

a. The ellipses are simply that. A large outer one and a smaller inner one, which is 10% of the original. The two were blended with 20 steps. Originally the ellipses were filled with a radial fountain fill but that always appears circular and that wasn't what I wanted. (There is no way to make an elliptical radial fill unfortunately.)

b. The words "Time and Tide" and "for no man" has been envelope edited, using Single Arc envelopes on all sides, to make them appear rounder. Both text strings are outlined and filled with white.

c. The word "wait" has been enveloped edited to squeeze the sides in but rounded top and bottom. (It doesn't show up too well unfortunately.)

d. "Time and Tide" was blended to "wait" with 20 steps. Then "wait" was blended to "for no man" with 20 steps.

e. The pillars on either side are simply ellipses, a smaller one in the centre, blended from the top to the middle and then the middle to the bottom with 20 steps. I did the left hand one and then duplicated it and moved it to the right.

The finished image is only one part of a more complex graphic that I was doing about time and age. You could try using it as the basis of something else yourself.

## Q8 - KEYBOARD

This is a bit of a cheat because it was done using the Keystroke typeface that is only available on the CD-ROM version. While it is possible to do the exercise by drawing all the keys, adding the letters and then aligning them all it would take ages. But this is how it was done.

a. In Keystrokes all the standard characters are the lower case ones, e.g. [A] is lower case "a" and so on. So they are easy to do. To get the extra characters you have to use the Upper case letters. For example, J is the Caps key. (If you use the Windows Character Map you'll be able to see them all.)

b. The hardest part was aligning the cursor keys. You do that by moving the characters individually. If you use guidelines it is relatively easy.

c. There isn't a character for a long Spacebar so I put in four blank keys (the letter A). You could try creating a spacebar of your own by drawing it.

d. Add the Function Keys too. You will find that you have characters for F1 to F10, the others you will have to create.

### Q9 - The Daily Planet

This is not as easy as it looks.

a. Draw the circle for the planet. Draw an ellipse for the first ring and then duplicate it.

b. You have to Node Edit each ellipse so that one will be in front of the circle and the other will be behind. You have to do this because otherwise the ellipse will be completely in front of the planet - you cannot have the circle slotted into the ellipse.

c. Now write the words, twice. I used Helvetica 48 point. Fit one lot of text to one arced ellipse, and the second string to the second ellipse. Both use vertically skewed orientation.

d. You will find that you can't get one lot of text to align the right way round. You have to mirror one of the ellipses because where the main node of the ellipse is affects how the text runs.

e. From there on, everything else is embellishments. The planet figure is one of the Symbols from Space. The extra rings are simply additional distorted ellipses.

# D - SPACE SAVING

One question that gets asked a lot is "How can I reduce the amount of space that CorelDRAW, and its associated programs, takes up on the hard disk?" The answer to that depends on the type of system you have and the kind of work you are going to be doing with the entire package.

The CorelDRAW Graphics Package takes up nearly 34 Mb of disk space as it is installed from the floppy disks, assuming that you are using Windows 3.1. This is how that breaks down:

If you install all the fonts, including the Symbols, then these will take up over 13.5 Mb of space. The TrueType fonts account for over 12.5 Mb of that and the symbols use just under 1 Mb.

CorelDRAW itself, in its entirety takes up 5.6 Mb of space.

CorelCHART takes just over 7.5 Mb of space.

CorelSHOW requires just a smidgen over 3 Mb.

Photo-Paint takes up just under 1.3 Mb.

Trace and Mosaic together take up less than 1 Mb.

The remaining files, bits and pieces take up just over 1.5 Mb.

The quickest and easiest way to save space is to not use the TrueType fonts. They take up far and away the most amount of space. However, if you are using the floppy disk version of the program then you have little choice because that's the way the fonts come to you. If you have the CD-ROM version then you have a choice because you can use Adobe Type 1 fonts instead which take up less than 2 Mb of space.

The arguments for and against using TrueType continues to rage. There are those who argue that TrueType gives better definitions, which for the screen is true, but then others point out that they will be downloaded as Adobe Type 1 fonts unless you have a True Image printer so why bother. I admit that I am of the latter persuasion.

TrueType fonts take up a lot of room on your hard disk and they reduce your Windows Systems Resources by anything up to eight or nine per cent. I prefer to use the Adobe Type 1 Fonts which take up a fraction of the room and make little difference to your available resources. But then I have a CD-ROM drive and so I have the choice. Many people won't have.

You can by the way use the old fonts that came with earlier versions of CorelDRAW if you wish - just modify the CORLEDRW.INI file as explained previously. You have to copy the fonts to the CorelDRAW directory but that's easy enough to do.

The next thing to do is limit the amount of sample files and clip-art that CorelDRAW installs. In fact if you don't load any of the sample files you can save nearly 4 Mb.

You then come down to not using some of the programs themselves, or at least not having them installed permanently. If you are unlikely to want to use charts or slide shows then don't bother installing Chart and Show. Together they occupy nearly 10.5 Mb of space.

So if you left off the TrueType fonts, CorelCHART and CorelSHOW and all the sample files then you would reduce the amount of space required from nearly 34 Mb to just over 6 Mb. But that will leave you with a very basic CorelDRAW system.

In the end it's all a matter of choice. What choice do you have? If you are using floppies then you don't have the option of using Adobe Type 1 fonts in place of TrueType. What programs do you want? Do you need charting facilities or slide shows or photo-retouching?

The installation procedure for 3.0 is very good because it will let you pick and choose which elements to install. Take your time and use it to advantage.

# INDEX

## SYMBOLS



## A

# B

# C

# D

# E

# F

## G

## H



## I



## L

# M

## N

## O



## P

# R

## S

# T